SOCIAL AND LEGAL NORMS

Social and Legal Norms

Towards a Socio-legal Understanding of Normativity

Edited by
MATTHIAS BAIER
Lund University, Sweden

Routledge
Taylor & Francis Group
LONDON AND NEW YORK

First published 2013 by Ashgate Publishing

2 Park Square, Milton Park, Abingdon, Oxfordshire OX14 4RN
52 Vanderbilt Avenue, New York, NY 10017

Routledge is an imprint of the Taylor & Francis Group, an informa business

First issued in paperback 2020

British Library Cataloguing in Publication Data
A catalogue record for this book is available from the British Library

The Library of Congress has cataloged the printed edition as follows:
Social and legal norms : towards a socio-legal understanding of normativity / by
Matthias Baier.
pages cm
Includes bibliographical references and index.
ISBN 978-1-4094-5343-7 (hardback)
1. Sociological jurisprudence. 2. Social norms--Philosophy. 3. Law--Philosophy.
4. Normativity (Ethics) I. Baier, Matthias, 1962- editor of compilation.

K376.S577 2013
340'.115--dc23

2013011510

ISBN 978-1-4094-5343-7 (hbk)
ISBN 978-0-367-60122-5 (pbk)

Contents

List of Figures and Tables

Figures

Tables

Notes on Contributors

Johanna Alkan Olsson holds a PhD from Linköping University, Sweden. Her research interests lie within the area of law and policy making and implementation, focusing on the use of information and communication technologies (ICT) as a facilitating tool. She is a member of the Cybernorms research group, which specializes in the interaction between people, technology and regulations, mainly in the areas of environment, agriculture and development. Recent publications focus on the Swedish implementation of the European Water Framework Directive.

Karsten Åström, LLD, MA, is professor in sociology of law and is also member of the board of the Renato Treves international PhD programme in law and society. His main areas of research are theories and methods in sociology of law, social welfare politics and implementation of welfare legislation, legal means for social and ecological sustainability, law enforcement professionals, expert knowledge in legal processes, and decision-making in courts.

Matthias Baier, LLM, PhD, is senior lecturer in sociology of law at the department of Sociology of Law, Lund University. He is currently head of department. His main interests concerns general sociology of law, citizens' participation in legal decision-making, law in the public sphere and environmental regulation.

Reza Banakar, PhD, is the Professor of Sociology of Law, Lund University. Previously he was Professor of Socio-Legal Studies at the University of Westminster, London and the senior Research Fellow at the Centre for Socio-Legal Studies in Oxford. He has also taught at the International Institute for the Sociology of Law in Oñati, Spain. Among his publications are *Merging Law and Sociology: Beyond the Dichotomies in Socio-Legal Research* (Berlin/Wisconsin: Gald + Wilch, 2003), *Theory and Method in Socio-Legal Research* co-edited with Max Travers (Oxford: Hart, 2005) and *Rights Discourse: Law and Justice in Late Modern Society* (Aldershot: Ashgate, 2010). His research interests and teaching are in comparative law and jurisprudence.

Karl Dahlstrand, LLM, PhD, is working as acting lecturer at the department of Sociology of Law, Lund University and as visiting lecturer at law schools in Gothenburg and Stockholm. His doctoral thesis (2012) deals with the conditions for compensation and estimations for non-pecuniary loss among victims of crime. The title of the thesis is *Violation and Satisfaction. A Sociology of Law Study of Non-Pecuniary Damages to Victim of Crime.*

Eva Friis, LLM, PhD. Senior lecturer in Sociology of Law. Friis' research focuses on social welfare, particularly in the field of social work with vulnerable children and families, in which she, among others, has made a study of social investigations into criminally abused children within the family. Friis is also studying questions related to immigration and labour, and has recently completed an evaluation study of a labour market project for long-term unemployed immigrant women in Rosengård, Malmö.

Susanna Johansson, PhD in Sociology of Law, Lund University and currently holds a post-doctoral position in social work. Her main research interest is in general sociology of law, tensions between criminal and welfare law, organizational institutional theory and theories of power, as well as comparative and critical methods in social science. Her PhD thesis from 2011, *Law, power and institutional change. A critical analysis of public agencies' collaboration in Barnahus*, analyses inter-organizational collaboration processes and institutional change from a critical perspective.

Marcin de Kaminski is a PhD candidate in Sociology of Law, Lund University. He has a clear focus on Internet-related research and is a part of the Cybernorms research group. The focus of de Kaminski's research is mainly on the relation of legal rules and social norms in an online context, more specifically the formation of inter-group norms in net-based communities and the norm-creating processes that appear in the wake of the changing information technology.

Stefan Larsson, LLM, SM, Licentiate in Technology in Spatial Planning, and PhD in Sociology of Law from Lund University, with his 2011 thesis, *Metaphors and Norms – Understanding Copyright Law in a Digital Society*. He currently holds a post-doctoral position and has written a number of publications on metaphor theory in relation to law and norms, but also what the Internet means in terms of social and legal change (for example, in relation to copyright, file sharing and online anonymity). He is a member and co-founder of the Cybernorms research group, participates in and contributes to projects on open data as well as on cyber security, an education program on Social Innovation in a Digital Context, and a project on Swedish wind power regulation. In 2012, he received the Podgógecki Prize for 'emerging socio-legal scholars' awarded by the Research Committee of Sociology of Law (RCSL) of the International Sociological Association.

Ulf Leo, PhD, is a senior lecturer at the department of Sociology of Law, Lund University. His research and teaching are related to leadership, democracy, children's rights and sustainable development. He has been a teacher and a school principal in the basic school system for 25 years. He is currently working in an international training programme, 'Child Rights, Classroom and School Management', and in the Swedish national principal training programme.

Lars Persson, PhD in Sociology of Law, is currently working as a municipal development leader in education. His main interests are school development, leadership and governing, and education for sustainable development, especially democracy issues. The engagement in educational practice, together with connections to social and educational sciences, makes questions like learning organizations, theory-practice applications and action research a natural part of his work.

Lucas P. Konzen, from Brazil, is a PhD in Sociology of Law of the Renato Treves International PhD in Law and Society, at the University of Milan, Italy, and Lund University, Sweden. Between 2011 and 2012, he was a Swedish Institute scholarship holder at the department of Sociology of Law, Lund University. He is particularly interested in the socio-legal field of Critical Legal Geography, and is focusing his doctoral dissertation on studying public space regulation in tourist cities. He is a member of the Research Committee on Sociology of Law (RCSL/ ISA) and Law & Society Association (LSA).

Kari Rönkkö is Associate Professor in Software Engineering, with an emphasis on cooperative and human aspects, at Blekinge Institute of Technology in Sweden, and is currently also a guest researcher at Lund University. He has eight years of action research experience together with industrial actors concerning usability framework that lead to a *de facto* standard. He is Product Development Officer in an IT company. Dr Rönkkö's research has centred on communication and human aspects of software development, flexible research approaches, usability evaluation and user experience. Current research topics are code as law, how norms influence software design, social media, social innovation, and value-based design.

Eva Schömer is a senior lecturer in Sociology of Law. She has an LLM at the Faculty of Law, Lund University, and a PhD in business law, specializing in sociology of law, labour law and gender. She served as a recorder at a district court and worked at as investigation secretary at the Swedish government at some commissions of inquiries. Schömer's research has focused on equality and gender equality from an intersectional perspective during the last 10 years. One main point in this research is that, while equality is a value-laden term, which stresses similarities between people, it masks differences between people, and that fear (conscious choice) when it comes to not seeing 'the others' leads to a kind of covert racism, which flourishes because nobody makes an effort to reject it.

Måns Svensson is PhD in Sociology of Law at Lund University, head of the Research Team Cybernorms (www.cybernormer.se), and head of the department of Work Environment and Leadership (WEAL) at Lund University. He is member of the board of the Swedish National Association for Work Life Research. In his thesis (2008), Svensson develops a theory and method tied to the concept of norms in sociology of law. Since then, he has written a number of articles where he continues to investigate the relationship between social norms and legal rules in society.

Rustamjon Urinboyev (from Uzbekistan) is a PhD in Sociology of Law at the department of Sociology of Law, Lund University. His main research interests focus on law and social norms, welfare structures, rule of law and corruption, public administration, and social rights. Rustamjon obtained his LLB degree in 2007 at the University of World Economy and Diplomacy in Tashkent, Uzbekistan. In 2007, Rustamjon received a full scholarship from the Maastricht Graduate School of Governance, Maastricht University (Netherlands) to study MS in Public Policy and Human Development.

Ana Maria Vargas Falla is a PhD candidate in the Renato Treves international PhD programme in Law and Society, and is writing her dissertation in the area of legal empowerment of the poor for informal workers. This program is organized by a consortium of universities, including the University of Milan as the central base and Lund University, which hosts Ana Maria as visiting researcher. Ana Maria is from Colombia, where she studied her bachelor in Law, and she has a Master in Development Studies from Lund University. Ana Maria's research is focused in the fields of good governance, legal empowerment, and development.

Per Wickenberg, Professor in Sociology of Law, Visiting Professor at Inner Mongolia Normal University, and Chifeng University, China. He studies education as an arena of norms and has a focus on implementation of Environmental Education, Education for Sustainable Development and Child Rights in Education. He has recently published *Accessing water through rights-based approach: problems and prospects regarding children* (2012, with Nandita Singh); *The unknown but well-known wells in Holma. Public participation and norms in the City Tunnel Project in Malmö* (2011); *Progressive Development of Environmental Education in Sweden and Denmark* (2010, with Sören Breiting); and *Taking Child Rights Seriously* (2009, ed.).

Preface

In the early 1990s, Håkan Hydén, Professor in Sociology of Law at Lund University since 1988, began to take an interest in the concept of norms as a key perspective on understanding socio-legal problems. The main motive at the time was the emergence of sustainable development as a scientific field. A field of research founded in a normative claim about change must focus on the question of how change comes about, Hydén argued. Equipped with a focus on norms, sociology of law would be well-suited to this kind of science. Can law, as we know it, manage this kind of change? Or is change dependent on other normative structures? These were questions that Hydén posed. In the years thereafter, more scholars at the department of Sociology of Law in Lund have engaged in the development of the concept of norms in different ways, realizing its potential for other areas and for other scientific problems. More than 10 doctoral theses in Sociology of Law, since the end of the 1990s, have found inspiration in Hydén's elaboration of the norm perspective and have also contributed further in developing this theory.

This book serves several purposes: it offers a collection of studies of the relations between social and legal norms that are held together by a common perspective on norms; it is also a contribution to the debate about how normativity comes about, and thus fills a space between Philosophy or Legal Theory and Sociology; and it aims to provide a link between earlier and ongoing research, while posing theoretical challenges for future study.

We would like to thank Håkan Hydén not only for his inspiration, but also for the research environment that has emerged during his time as a professor of Sociology of Law in Lund.

Matthias Baier
21 August, 2013

Chapter 1
Introduction

Matthias Baier

Back to norms[1]

Norms are an essential part of the social structure and thus always of interest for the social sciences. Few aspects of social life are conceivable without relating to norms in one way or another. Norms are an essential part of the lifeworld, and so they integrate society in a very basic sense. Since norms also proscribe behaviour, norms are ordering social life and in this way norms can also be understood as coercive. By reducing complexity, norms also coordinate actions and contribute to an effective organisation of society. Norms of the legal system have similar functions but are also strongly connected to the political structure; law communicates politics (Hydén, 1978). Societal norms permeate almost all parts of society and are essential for what we call 'society'.[2]

Since societal norms are pivotal for society, relations between social and legal norms ought to be fundamental to the scientific study of law in society, be it in the study of law and society, sociology of law, socio-legal studies, criminology, anthropology of law, or any other scientific study of the normative aspect of society. As will be elaborated by Karl Dahlstrand (in Chapter 6), this argument could also be valid for the more internal and theoretical studies of law. Accordingly, it is easy to see that the study of law in society actually has taken norms as one point of departure. Several of the sociological classics have explicitly devoted their studies to a normative understanding of society. Émile Durkheim is a prominent example. He used law to understand changes in society and developed theories understanding normative integration. His

1 This formulation is directly borrowed from Göran Therborn's article 'Back to Norms! on the Scope and Dynamics of Norms and Normative Action', *Current Sociology* 2002 50:863. This book can, in a sense, be considered to be a response to this invitation.

2 In this book, 'norms' are used as the overall category, sometimes with the prefix 'societal' as an additional clarification. The terms 'legal norms' and 'legal rules' are used to distinguish the category of institutionalized norms that are intended to regulate society. The term 'social norms' is used as a comprehensive category for other kinds of norms. Following Måns Svensson's theoretical definition of norms in this book, also elaborated on in Chapter 4, it should become clear that the basic structure of all norms is the same (referred to as the essence of norms); at the same time, particular norms can have distinctive features (referred to as the accidence of norms). The differentiation between social and legal norms is thus made for analytical reasons.

theories concerning norms, morals and collective conscience are still of great importance in understanding the social world. Several other classics discussed norms from a more or less explicit socio-legal perspective. This intense interest probably has historical explanations. At the time, it seemed natural for many social scientists to devote at least some effort to the nature of different normative systems and the relations between them. William Graham Sumner's *Folkways* is one example, but also sociologists like Georg Simmel and Ferdinand Tönnies took an interest in these issues. Mathieu Deflem has read Tönnies from a socio-legal perspective and points out that Tönnies differentiated societal norms into three subcategories: order, law and morality. In Tönnies' Gemeinschaft und Gesellschaft law, order and morality express themselves differently (Deflem, 2008), and these two concepts can therefore be viewed as two normative structures. Last but not least, Eugen Ehrlich and his work on the forms and relations between different norm systems must be mentioned (Ehrlich, 2002; Hertogh, 2009).

The interest among early sociologists must, however, be understood in the light of the status of the legal system in the nineteenth century. By and large, it was different from the modern legal system we know today. Even though nineteenth-century law was, to a high degree, professionally organized, the development of the law and other subsystems has thereafter been characterized as a further functional differentiation. Today we can describe this situation as a technocratic rationalization of the law. The functional differentiation of modern legal systems, along with increased legal autonomy, has in some sense diminished the interest in relations between different normative systems. Instead, the relations between the legal system and the political system have become of great importance. Still, several other scholars have taken an interest in a norms perspective during the twentieth century. Roger Cotterrell has written about the social basis of law, more generally in his text books (1992), but also displayed in his interest in Durkheim (Cotterrell, 1999 and 2010).

A modernisation of society with further differentiation of the legal system during the twentieth century does not make it less interesting to study the relations between legal and social norms. On the contrary, there are several reasons to revitalize the study of relations between the formal legal system and other normative systems. Beginning with the assumption that legislation today is the dominant producer of legal norms, where does this leave social norms as a basis for the production of legal norms? Are folkways, mores, conventions, morals and so on of no relevance, either for the production of law or for the application of law? For instance, we find lay judges or jurors in many criminal matters, but other areas of law are often administered by professional judges or other technocrats. Kaarlo Tuori (2002) argues that law is more than the mere application of legislation. Law is also a legal culture expressing important principles and a deep paradigmatic structure, and both have relations with the surface (that is, legislation). This broader understanding of law, of course, raises questions of the relations between these parts of law and social structures in society.

From this perspective, the question for contemporary law is whether the political system itself can constitute the sole social basis for law, even for highly politicized areas of law like welfare legislation? Many studies point to the fact that there are problems in the application of the law resulting from a poor connection to, or incomplete understanding of, the social norms relevant to the field. This book offers such examples. We see these problems following the materialization of law, like in welfare law, but there are other examples. Today we see examples of de-regulation and re-regulation, with the purpose of better connecting the law and its application to the social sphere. Alternative dispute resolution is one such example. But also aspects of so-called reflexive law and other self-regulatory mechanisms can be viewed as attempts to reconnect to the social structures.

A similar problem is the fact that modern law and other subsystems of society, according to Jürgen Habermas, have tendencies to colonize the lifeworld. This means that communication in the lifeworld takes place by means of money and power, for instance. In the case of law, this means that social conflicts are increasingly referred to and thematized in terms of law. For example, in Sweden, conflicts among children at school tend to be resolved by means of law. Here we do not see juridification in terms of legal norms replacing social norms, but rather as a new way of communicating about certain problems. Insofar as the legal-administrative system responds to such problems, we can expect different kinds of perturbations in the social system. Again, we now see attempts to solve this problem by efforts to set limits for the law or by devising new quasi-social mechanisms for solving these kinds of conflict.

In his theory of communicative action, Jürgen Habermas (1987) has argued that law can be seen either as an institution or as a medium. As an institution, law is part of the lifeworld; as a medium, law operates instrumentally. This is one way of understanding the problem of law's decoupling from the social world. Habermas has later argued (1996) that law is always part of the lifeworld. The mere instrumental aspects of law must be complemented with a more moral dimension, he says. From this follows that law can always be normatively grounded, even for those areas of law that are merely technical. This means that normative structures of the lifeworld are always relevant in the application of law. In Sweden, recent trends in public trust in the law and the courts clearly indicate this. The last decades have shown a decrease in public trust, and the courts are now trying to improve public trust by means of procedural techniques, perhaps aiming at more moral legitimation. One political response to this problem has been to set up the Commission on trust in the courts (SOU, 2008: 106).

Consequently, there are complex relations between law, politics and the lifeworld constituting several kinds of problems. These problems are even more complicated, given the increased diversity of values and complexity of cultures in present-day society. Whatever label we prefer, globalization and increased migration are two developments that point to what is often labelled a multi-cultural society. Given this development, law faces enormous challenges in integrating society. A parallel development can also be described in terms of an erosion of (legal) norms (Frommel, 1996). Motivating this trend are the many observations of a law failing to achieve its goals, a decrease in obedience to law, and even mobilization against law. Even agents of the state follow the law to a lesser degree, and at the logical conclusion of this trend lies the death of *homo legalicus*.

Michel Foucault offers quite another perspective. If the discussion so far has taken law and its functions in the modern society for granted, Foucault puts much more emphasis on other normative structures than law. Biopolitics, discipline and governmentality are concepts that, at first glance, seem to give another view of the relations between social and legal norms. What is of interest to Foucault are the new mechanisms that attempt to discipline the human body and regulate the population. Foucault described strategies to replace criminalization with positive regulation of, for instance, hygiene, sexuality or health, by techniques such as ordering and normalization. This has even led to claims that Foucault's view can be described as an 'expulsion of law from modernity' (Hunt, 1992: 2). This categorical interpretation of Foucault's view on law, however, needs an explanation. According to Foucault, biopower as a new mode of governance replaces the juridical mode of governance. The juridical mode is connected to sovereignty and characterized by force, seizure, repression and other methods where law exerts negative power.

The strong focus on governance through normalisation procedures, of course, puts an emphasis on norms. This notion of norms differs somewhat from classical conceptions. Discipline operates through norms, that is 'standards that the subject of a discipline comes to internalize or manifest in behaviour, for example standards of tidiness, punctuality, respectfulness etc' (Hunt and Wickham, 1994: 49). Foucault's 'norm' can then be understood rather as the principle of generalisation, a way for a group to measure conduct and make it normal in the sense of statistics. See also Francois Ewald's (1990) discussion of how insurance can be subsumed under the concept of norms. The fact that Foucault focused on the structural aspects of normativity, however, does not make him less interesting when understanding the relations between legal and social norms. Nikolas Rose and Mariana Valverde argue rather more convincingly that there is a 'co-existence, hybridization and mutual inter-dependence of law and norm' (1998: 542).

The purpose of making these sketchy references to Habermas and Foucault is merely to provide examples showing that social norms are part of many contemporary important theories of society; and it thus becomes clear that the relations between legal and social norms are as relevant as ever to the study of law in society. It has also been argued that a basic societal concept like norms might actually serve as an integrating concept, especially when studying law in society (Hydén, 2011). There are also other arguments for developing the norm perspective. One argument concerns the contemporary problems of society, referring to, for example, the body, integrity and internet technologies that need to be viewed in a perspective including social norms. What is significant for these new areas of life is a strong focus on the social aspect, often in combination with technological advancements. What actually is a body? What actually are a 'man' and a 'woman', given the technical possibilities of today? What is called the technological imperative can itself be viewed as a norm in Foucault's sense, but it also produces a vast set of norms on a more concrete, action-oriented level. It is, for example, clear that social life on the internet produces or changes many social norms that are far ahead of legal development. Here we also see a strong connection between the social and the personal; and, in many areas today, norms seem to be important for shaping our identity. Law is also challenged in the area of, for example, copyright law when social norms about file sharing contradict legal norms of copyright. The problem is highly relevant, at least in Sweden, where a large portion of the population is file sharing (see Chapter 18).

Another argument for studying law and social norms is the fact that globalization, increased mobility, migration and similar trends further undermine the idea of a shared consensus about values in society. We might easily arrive at a consensus on values such as life, health, well-being, security or social recognition. But other values are less evident for a majority, and modern society is increasingly described as a society where people hold different sets of values. Freedom, autonomy, self-realisation, democracy, authority, duty, self-control, material welfare or sexual equality are examples of values held differently, according to political and cultural settings (Baurman et al., 2010). And, if norms are seen as instruments for the realization of certain values, changes in the value structure result in changes in the norm structure. What these changes will look like is not clear. Does an increased value plurality lead to a corresponding norm plurality – and, if so, what effects will this have on law? Can law continue to exist as a coherent system of legal norms, or are other normative systems better suited to respond to these challenges? We certainly need to understand law as one of several parts of societal norms. Perhaps we need to address societal norms in a post-modern sense and ask the question, What constitutes a post-modern normativity?

The field of law and social norms

There are a growing number of studies into the field of what might be labelled as 'law and social norms', and some examples will be provided here. As mentioned earlier, the definition of the concept of norms has direct relevance for how the research field should be described. Assuming that there is something like law and that social norms do exist, there are several concepts with an underlying claim to normativity outside the legal system that are still not labelled as norms. There are also concepts with an ambition to transgress, or even challenge, the division of societal norms into law and social norms, on the one hand, and other kinds of non-legal norms on the other. One early example is Eugene Ehrlich's concept of living law (Ehrlich, 2002).

Hanne Petersen uses the term 'informal law' to describe normative practices in a workplace that are not law, but still normative (Petersen, 1996). She also uses the concept of 'home knitted law' (ibid.). A fourth example is 'indigenous law' (Galanter, 1981). All discussions of law and social norms pre-suppose that these two concepts can be defined – something that some research contests. As mentioned earlier, for analytical reasons we believe that law and social norms can be separated, but that they are both part of the overall concept of societal norms. Our ambition is – as in many sociology of law studies – to understand not just the relations between the two as separate normative systems, but also their similarities, their interdependence, and how they might merge into one normative practice.

Having made this remark, there are several contributions in what we label the field of law and social norms.[3] This is not surprising, since one key question in sociology of law is how social order is upheld in the absence of law or despite the law. This is an even more central question in anthropology of law. For this reason, one might expect more contributions devoted to law and social norms. Nevertheless, this field has of late been largely occupied by scholars of law and economics. Robert Ellickson's study of disputes among farmers in Shasta County (1991) is perhaps the first of this kind. Later, this perspective has grown rapidly and now includes several entries.[4] Common among most of these scholars is a rational choice model of human behaviour entailing a methodological individualism, assuming that each individual is rational and is motivated by its self-interest (Ellickson, 2001). For a critique of what has been labelled the new behavioural law and economics, see Rostain (2000) and Scott (2000). In criminology, Meares and Kahan (2000) offer an example of the law and social norms perspective.

Mathieu Deflem (2008) explicitly takes a norm perspective in accounting for the field of Sociology of Law. Deflem devotes the chapter called 'Law and culture: the balance of values through norms' to this issue, but in fact the norm perspective permeates most of the book. Many aspects of social life can easily be connected to, or reduced to, norms and normative issues. This is even more true of socio-legal concepts, such as general prevention, compliance with the law, sanctions or legal cultures. Early work worth mentioning is Stewart Macaulay (1963), showing that social norms complement or even replace legal norms in contract relations. Another important contribution is Sally Falk Moore's notion of semi-autonomous fields, which is an example of the in-betweens of law and social norms (Moore, 1973). More recent examples are Joseph Sander's work on law, norms and lay tribunals (2006) or Dorothy Thornton's study of compliance with environmental regulation (2009).

3 There are, of course, contributions within other fields like Sociology, Political Science and Social History: Bicchieri et al. (1997); Hechter and Opp (2001); Bicchieri (2006); Ernst (2006); Wiener (2008).

4 For a good overview, see McAdams (1997); Posner (2000); Hetcher (2004); Drobak (2006). There have also been several symposiums: 'The legal construction on norms' (2000) 86 *Virginia Law Review* 1577; 'Social norms, social meaning and the economic analysis of law' (1998) 27 *Journal of Legal Studies* 537; 'Law, economics and norms' (1996) 144 *University of Pennsylvania Law Review* 1643.

For some time, the department of Sociology of Law at Lund University has taken an interest in the concept of norms. Several dissertations have more or less used the concept of norms as a tool to understand society. In the field of environmental regulation, there is Appelstrand (2007), Baier (2003), Bergman (2009) and Gillberg (1999). In the field of schools and education, there is Hallerström (2006), Leo (2010), Persson (2010) and Wickenberg (1999). There is also Larsson (2011) concerning language, Olsson (2003) concerning rights, and Svensson (2008) dealing with compliance. Last but not least, Håkan Hydén's seminal work, translated as *Normscience* (2002), must be mentioned.

Outline of the book

The overall purpose of this book is to revitalize a genuine normative understanding of society. This ambitious endeavour is realized through mapping and analysing normative focal points resulting from concrete normative instances in which law and social norms are active. Much simplified, we can say that many of the contributions intend to unfold the normative set-up pertaining to each case. Many of the contributions are adaptations of dissertations, and so they can be treated as case studies working with different empirical methods, in different empirical fields, dealing with different legal forms of regulation and applying different theoretical points of departure. As a result, they do not make up a planned series of studies, nor are they part of a coherent research program. On the other hand, they make up a rich blend of different areas, problems and legal operations. Most of the examples are from Sweden, but there are also international cases provided by Rustam Urinboyev and Måns Svensson when studying corruption in Uzbekistan (see Chapter 16), by Ana Maria Vargas Falla's example of legal empowerment in Colombia (see Chapter 14) and Lucas P. Konzen's example of street vending in Mexico (see Chapter 9).

The book starts with some more theoretical, reflective chapters. The purpose of Part I is to narrow down the scope of the book and to provide the reader with the necessary questions, terminology and definitions. In Chapter 2, Reza Banakar discusses law's normativity. By asking if legal sociology can account for the normativity of law, we hereby set the direction of the book: what is the normativity of law? The answer to this question lies in the many cases provided for in the book, all of which have taken as a point of departure the two normative lenses of law and social norms. In this way, we might also contribute to the discussion of which questions it is possible to address within law and sociology respectively.[5] The argument is that, when departing in an abductive manner from concrete cases, it is clear that social and legal norms are, in many cases, jointly normative.

Måns Svensson elaborates (in Chapter 3) on a definition of norms in general, that accordingly extends over social and legal norms. In this book, the ambition

5 See preferably Cotterrell (1998) and Nelken (1998).

of this definition is again to overcome the demarcation between social and legal norms. Svensson's definition is, at the same time, succinct as well as flexible. In Chapter 4, Matthias Baier builds on this point of departure, and elaborates on a strategy for how to study the field of social and legal norms. The strategy considers four aspects of normativity: social norms, legal norms, social practice and legal practice. These four aspects, in turn, open up several normative relations that can work as a common language for understanding, sorting and conducting empirical studies in the field of social and legal studies. The first Part finishes with Karsten Åström's discussion (in Chapter 5) of parallel norm creating processes, which can be seen as an elaboration of the previous chapter. By this chapter, we have an idea of how certain cases and certain areas of law will be looked upon.

The second Part gives room for perspectives on norms by connecting them to legal theory, language, institutions and space. Chapters 6, 7 and 8 all argue in different ways for a broad understanding of norms and even a dismantling of the barriers that often separate social and legal norms. Karl Dahlstrand also argues for a break-up of the internal and the external view on law, but does so by starting in legal theory. He analyses H.L.A. Hart's concept of the meta-norm, by applying it, in relation to compensation for non-financial damages, to victims of crime. Susanna Johansson elaborates on the concept of norms by comparing it to the concept of institution. It is argued that there are similarities and differences between the two, and that this knowledge is of importance when understanding the normative character of norms. Stefan Larsson's contribution can be seen as an addition to, or comment on, this strategy when introducing metaphors as a possible bearer of normativity. Metaphors can thus be seen as (unintended) strategies to exert normative influence by simply describing something. Larsson's point is that metaphors are used both within law and in social norms. Finally in that Part, Lucas Konzen (in Chapter 9) connects norms with space, using legal geography as a theoretical tool. Social and legal norms are connected to space in certain ways, he concludes.

The two following parts contain contributions that are based on empirical studies. They offer results based on either a direct application of the norm perspective or an interpretation of previous results based on this perspective. Part III takes an actor perspective. In Chapter 10, Eva Friis describes how social workers are mandated to mediate between social and legal norms in order to solve social problems. In doing so, social workers have to simultaneously adopt two quite different models for how to address social problems. Other professions can be found within the school. Lars Persson shows (in Chapter 11) that many professionals today work in very complex normative environments. For teachers, the situation is so complex and the obligations so diffuse that meta-norms have emerged as a reaction to the situation. The meta-norms can be viewed as a result of negotiation between social and legal norms. Ulf Leo continues the investigation of the school in Chapter 12, and offers an insight into the problems that principals have when transforming the law that regulates the schools into professional norms. Of importance is the complex context, but also the fact that the profession itself is not very integrated.

In Chapter 13, Per Wickenberg deals with education in different settings. The main focus lies in the role that 'souls of fire' have as catalysts of change. This capacity as change agent goes beyond profession, status and similar qualifications, but is very important to achieve real change in organisations. Both social and legal norms depend on these 'souls of fire' in order to be effective, Wickenberg shows.

The last Part addresses structural aspects, and Chapter 14 begins with Ana Maria Vargas Falla's investigation of legal reform aimed at development for displaced persons in Colombia. Her conclusion is that, paradoxically, social norms supersede legal reform that is intended to improve the situation for displaced persons. The reason why legal reform fails is not just about certain thresholds in the labour market. Eva Schömer comes to a similar conclusion in Chapter 15 when studying the Swedish labour market. A new legal strategy, with the ambition to change the social structure of the labour market, has been introduced; but, analysing the situation with the concept of intersectionality, it is clear that the social norms still stand strong. In Chapter 16, Rustam Urinboyev and Måns Svensson carry out an empirical analysis of the underlying normative structure that actually makes corruption possible. Different social norms (including authority and cronyism) tend to reinforce each other in ways that actually leave the formal legal system behind. Chapter 17 deals with the uncertainty and unpredictability of law. Investigating planning procedures, Stefan Larsson points to the fact that, as well as having to struggle with contradicting factors like social norms, law has to struggle with itself. Finally in that Part, Marcin de Kaminski, Måns Svensson, Stefan Larsson, Johanna Alkan Olsson and Kari Rönkkö provide (in Chapter 18) a summary and overview of studies dealing with the differences between legal norms coming from an industrial age and social norms emerging in a digital age.

The book ends with a chapter that aims to answer the question of how normativity comes about. This is not done by providing a clear-cut answer, but rather by taking the previous contributions as an empirical and theoretical foundation from which a future direction can be discerned. It is proposed that socio-legal normativity is expressed through four aspects of normativity: social norms, legal norms, social practice and legal practice. It is also proposed that normativity might be the result of norms, but also that norms are the result of normativity.

References

Appelstrand, M. 2007. *Miljömålet i skogsbruket: styrning och frivillighet.* Diss. Lund: Lunds universitet.

Baier, M. 2003. *Norm och rättsregel: en undersökning av tunnelbygget genom Hallandsåsen.* Diss. Lund: Lunds universitet.

Baurman M. et al. 2010. 'Introduction', in *Norms and values. The role of social norms as instruments of values realisation.* Edited by Baurman M. et al. Nomos: Baden-Baden.

Bergman, A.-K. 2009. *Law in progress?: a contextual study of norm-generating processes: the example of GMES*. Diss. Lund: Lunds universitet.

Bicchieri, C. (ed.) 1997. *The dynamics of norms*. Cambridge: Cambridge University Press.

Bicchieri, C. 2006. *The grammar of society: the nature and dynamics of social norms*. New York: Cambridge University Press.

Blegvad, B.-M. 1982. 'Interaction between indigenous and official norms: examples of norm generation in the consume field in Denmark', *Zeitschrift für Rechtssoziologie* 3, 43–58.

Cotterrell, R. 1989. 'Why must legal ideas be interpreted sociologically?', *Journal of law and society*, 25(2), 171–92.

Cotterrell, Roger 1992. *The Sociology of Law: An Introduction*. 2. rev. ed. London: Butterworth.

Cotterrell, R. 1999. *Émile Durkheim: law in a moral domain*. Edinburgh: Edinburgh University Press.

Cotterrell, R. (ed.) 2010. *Émile Durkheim: Justice, Morality and Politics*. Farnham: Ashgate.

Deflem, M. 2008. *Sociology of Law: Visions of a Scholarly Tradition*. Cambridge: Cambridge University Press.

Drobak, J.N. (ed.) 2006. *Norms and the Law*. Cambridge: Cambridge University Press.

Ehrlich, E. 2002[1936]. *Fundamental principles of the sociology of law*. [New ed.] New Brunswick: Transaction Publishers.

Ellickson, R. 2001. 'The Evolution of social norms: a perspective from the legal academy', in *Social norms*, edited by Michael Hechter and Karl-Dieter Opp. New York: Russell Sage Foundation.

Ellickson, R.C. 1991. *Order without law: how neighbours settle disputes*. Cambridge, Mass.: Harvard University Press.

Ernst, W. (ed.) 2006. *Histories of the normal and the abnormal: social and cultural histories of norms and normativity*. New York: Routledge.

Ewald, F. 1990. Norms, discipline and the law. *Representations* 30(138–61).

Frommel, M. (ed.) 1996. *Normenerosion*. Baden-Baden: Nomos-Verl.-Ges.

Galanter, M. 1981. 'Justice in many rooms: courts, private ordering, and indigenous law', *Journal of legal pluralism* 19, 1–47.

Gillberg, M. 1999. *From green image to green practice: normative action and self-regulation*. Diss. Lund: Lunds universitet.

Habermas, J. 1987. *The theory of communicative action. Vol. 2, Lifeworld and system: a critique of functionalist reason*. Cambridge: Polity.

Habermas, J. 1996. *Between facts and norms: contributions to a discourse theory of law and democracy*. Cambridge, Mass.: MIT Press.

Hallerström, H. 2006. *Rektorers normer i ledarskapet för skolutveckling*. Diss. Lund: Lunds universitet.

Hechter, M. and Opp, K.-D. (ed.) 2001. *Social norms*. New York: Russell Sage Foundation.

Hertogh, M.L.M. (ed.) 2009. *Living law: reconsidering Eugen Ehrlich*. Oxford: Hart.

Hetcher, S.A. 2004. *Norms in a wired world*. Cambridge: Cambridge University Press.

Hunt, A. and Wickham, G. 1994. *Foucault and law: towards a sociology of law as governance*. London: Pluto Press.

Hunt, A. 1992. 'Foucault's expulsion of law: Toward a retrieval', *Law and social inquiry* 17(1), 1–38.

Hydén, H. 1978. *Rättens samhälleliga funktioner*. Diss. Lund: Lunds universitet.

Hydén, H. 2011. 'Nine reasons for norms', in *Understanding Law in Society. Developments in Socio-legal Studies*, edited by Knut Papendorf, Stefan Machura and Kristian Andenaes. Hamburg: LIT Verlag.

Larsson, S. 2011. *Metaphors and norms: understanding copyright law in a digital society*. Diss. Lund: Lunds universitet.

Leo, U. 2010. *Rektorer bör och rektorer gör: en rättssociologisk studie om att identifiera, analysera och förstå professionella normer*. Diss. Lund: Lunds universitet.

Macaulay, S. 1963. 'Non-contractual relations in business: a preliminary study', *American Sociological Review*, 28(1), 55–67.

McAdams, R. 1997. 'The origin, development, and regulation of norms', *Michigan Law Review*, 96(2), 338–433.

Meares, T. and Kahan, D. 1998. 'Law and order in the inner city', *Law and Society Review*, 32(4) 805–38.

Moore, S.F. 1973. 'Law and Social Change: the Semi-Autonomous Social Field as an Appropriate Subject of Study', *Law and Society Review*, 7(4) 719–46.

Nelken, D. 1998. 'Blinding insights? The limits of a reflexive sociology of law', *Journal of Law and Society*, 25(2), 407–26.

Olsson, P. 2003. *Legal ideals and normative realities: a case study of children's rights and child labor activity in Paraguay*. Diss. Lund: Lunds universitet.

Persson, L. 2010. *Pedagogerna och demokratin: en rättssociologisk studie av pedagogers arbete med demokratiutveckling i förskola och skola*. Diss. Lund: Lunds universitet.

Petersen, H. 1996. *Home knitted law: norms and values in gendered rule-making*. Aldershot: Dartmouth.

Posner, E.A. 2000. *Law and social norms*. Cambridge, Mass.: Harvard University Press.

Rose, N. and Valverde, M. (1998). 'Governed by law?', *Social and Legal Studies*, 7(4), 541–51.

Rostain, T. 2000. 'Educating *homo economicus*: cautionary notes on the new behavioural law and economics movement', *Law and Society Review* 34(4), 973–1006.

Sanders, J. 2006. 'Law, norms and lay tribunals', in *Law and Sociology*, edited by Freeman, M.D.A. Oxford University Press.

Scott, R.E. 2000. 'The limits of behavioural theories of law and social norms', *Virginia Law Review* 86(8), 1603–47.

SOU 2008. *Ökat förtroende för domstolarna : strategier och förslag.* Statens offentliga utredningar 2008: 106. Stockholm: Fritzes.

Svensson, M. 2008. *Sociala normer och regelefterlevnad: trafiksäkerhetsfrågor ur ett rättssociologiskt perspektiv*. Diss. Lund: Lunds universitet.

Svensson, M. and Larsson, S. 2009. *Social Norms and Intellectual Property. Online Norms and the European Legal Development.* Research Report in Sociology of Law, Lund University.

Thornton, D. 2009. 'When Social Norms and Pressures are not Enough: Environmental Performance in the Trucking Industry', *Law and Society Review* 43(2), 405–36.

Tuori, Kaarlo 2002. *Critical Legal Positivism*. Aldershot: Ashgate.

Wickenberg, P. 1999. *Normstödjande strukturer: miljötematiken börjar slå rot i skolan.* Diss. Lund: Lunds universitet.

Wiener, A. 2008. *The invisible constitution of politics: contested norms and international encounters*. Cambridge: Cambridge University Press.

PART I
Norms and Normativity

Chapter 2
Can Legal Sociology Account for the Normativity of Law?

Reza Banakar

This chapter challenges the assumption that legal sociology should apply itself to the external or factual properties of the law and leave the internal and normative aspects of legal phenomena to doctrinal scholars and moral philosophers. It argues that legal sociology explores the normative contexts of the law and other social systems but, being restricted by its 'scientific' mode of expression, it describes and analyses them in sociological rather than moral terms. Legal sociology is, and should be seen as, a different language game from moral and legal philosophy, and its treatment of normativity should be understood on its own terms. The assertion that legal sociology should limit its scope of analysis to the study of the empirical aspects of law, and leave the study of law's normative dimensions to other branches of legal studies, is itself a normative supposition and part of the competing discourses which constitute the field of legal research. These discourses aim at demarcating the disciplinary boundaries between various epistemic approaches to the study of law and creating disciplinary identities rather than exploring the methodological scope of socio-legal research.

Introduction[1]

Professor Håkan Hydén maintains that norms should be the subject matter of legal sociology, but he also explains that the study of norms should proceed in a non-normative and scientific manner, because 'the science of norms is not … the same as normative science … [It is] empirical and normatively unprejudiced in its ambition' (Hydén, 2011: 131). The idea that legal sociology should treat norms as the platform from which to explore the relationship between law and society is motivated by the assumption that norms are the fundamental constitutive parts of action systems (Hydén, 2002: 114) and, as such, they 'govern human

1 This paper was delivered at the conference on *The Normative Anatomy of Society* arranged by the Institute for the Sociology of Law at Lund University in April 2012 and is dedicated to Professor Mauro Zamboni, whose normative arguments on the disciplinary limits of legal sociology prompted this paper in the first place. See Zamboni, 2006 and 2007.

behaviour' (Hydén, 2011: 140) while bridging the paradigmatic gap between law and society (Baier and Svensson, 2009: 15). Norms provide standards of conduct, which guide expectations and coordinate action and interactions, thus engendering normativity, behavioural regularities and social order (Durlauf and Blume, 2008). Since social order constitutes the central concern of socio-legal research, legal sociology should therefore investigate the sources of norms, their relationship with rules, and how they govern human behaviour (Hydén, 2011: 140). But what if norms do not govern social behaviour and are not the source of normativity? What if norms, as Judge Posner (2002: 34) insists, are 'endogenous', labels that we attach to regularities and patterns of behaviour which were initially caused by various social processes? What if normativity can emerge independently of norms and provide a basis for articulating norms? Where does that leave legal sociology? These questions set the backdrop against which this chapter will explore the ability of legal sociology to account for the normativity of law.

Although Hydén focuses on norms because they exert normativity which translates into social order, he nonetheless keeps his empirical distance from them. Norms, he emphasises, must be studied empirically and not normatively (Hydén, 2011: 131). This mirrors what is regarded by some legal sociologists (see Black, 1972) and many legal theorists (see Kelsen, 2002; Tuori, 2006; Zamboni, 2006) as the methodological limit of legal sociology – that is, legal sociology as an empirical science should engage with the external aspect of norms, which generate observable regularities, and leave the internal aspects of norms, which deal with the 'ought' dimension of the norms and the sense of obligation, to legal and moral philosophers. The central aim of this chapter is to examine this assumption by exploring the disciplinary discourses emerging from studies of the law. Therefore, what follows is as much an investigation into the methodological scope of legal sociology as it is an inquiry into how academic discourses (belonging to various fields of social and legal studies) position themselves in respect to each other in an attempt to reproduce specific epistemes and disciplinary identities.

Part One starts by briefly considering the relationship between norms and normativity, arguing that normativity is generated by the system as well as lifeworld and is not necessarily reducible to the effects or functions of individual norms. Part Two develops this point by making a case for justice as law's source of normativity *par excellence*. It maintains that, although the relationship between law and justice is often discussed in terms of norms, the normativity that justice exercises on law depends on the broader context of the legal system, which is defined differently by different theories. Part Three draws attention to the methodological constraints of socio-legal research, according to which social scientific studies of law should apply themselves to the external empirical or factual properties of the relationship between law and society, and leave the internal and normative matters to doctrinal scholars and moral philosophers respectively. The chapter concludes by arguing that the sphere of socio-legal research is not, and cannot be, limited to an examination of the factual characteristics of law. Moreover, the assertion that legal sociology should apply itself to the study of the empirical aspects of law, and leave the normative dimensions to other legal scholars, is a normative stance and part of on-going attempts at demarcating the disciplinary boundaries of various branches of legal studies.

Part one

What if norms are not the source of normativity?

Looking at the works of the founders of legal sociology, such as Eugen Ehrlich and Emile Durkheim, we note that norms have played an important role in socio-legal theorising and research,[2] partly because they allow us to address the materiality of the law (institutional facts and practices) as well as its ideal dimensions (values, autonomy, legitimacy and authority).[3] Norms also loom large within legal theory (see, for example, Kelsen, 1967 and 2002), even though the discourse which bestows weight upon the concept of norm in legal theory is more concerned with 'ought' statements and is thus different from sociology's interest in behavioural regularities.[4] These two understandings of norms are interrelated and are discussed by Hebert Hart (1994) as the internal and external perspectives on social rules. I shall use Hart's internal/external distinction liberally to discuss 'social norms', which may be regarded as a category broader than 'social rules'. The discussion which follows is therefore more in line with the distinction made between descriptive and injunctive norms by Carl Kallgren et al. (2000: 2002, see also Elek et al., 2006).

The external or descriptive aspect of a norm is revealed through tangible and observable behaviour, and can be studied by employing empirical methods.

2 I should hasten to add that neither Durkheim nor Ehrlich advocated a norm-based methodological approach to the study of law.

3 A note of caution is in place: A norm-based approach to the study of law is *likely* to promote consensus-oriented research. Its explicit or implicit focus on conformity and social integration, which treat the *normalisation* of certain practices and discourses as desirable or necessary, emphasise the stabilising role of law in society, rather than highlighting social conflicts or exploring forms of political domination through law. It suffices here to point out that the studies of law conducted from a conflict perspective often depart from the experience of injustice or structural inequalities and not from norms. The extent to which one can depart from norms and explore forms of domination from a conflict perspective is a topic for another paper.

4 Both sociology and legal theory consist of diverse theoretical perspectives, each propagating its own brand of epistemology. At the risk of making a sweeping generalisation, we could say that various methodological approaches within legal theory are either normative or analytically tuned. These can be contrasted with various socio-legal perspectives, which, despite their differences, are 'brought together by a common epistemology that views law as a social construct and argues that law and all its manifestations should be studied empirically and contextually'. See Banakar, 2011.

Some people follow norms, or the standard patterns of behaviour, more or less unreflectively, doing what is commonly done. By contrast, the internal or evaluative aspect of norms involves the agency's reflective commitment to them (that is, a commitment to what should be done and to what is commonly approved). This aspect of norms is intangible and, as such, does not have a factual expression that can be studied using empirical methods of investigation. The intangible dimension of norms nevertheless does possess a cognitive element, in that it involves thought processes and also requires confrontation with 'facts', which are external to the agency's cognition. One can form a general idea about the evaluative aspect of norms by studying the perceptions (attitudes, opinions and beliefs) of various groups, but social scientists are aware of the limitations of this method, as attitudes and perceptions do not necessarily translate into action.[5] Whether the agency's perception of the validity of a norm (that is, the subject's belief that the norm should be obeyed) translates into an actual behavioural response in accordance with that norm is determined ultimately by a host of social factors belonging to the context of the action. We shall return to the methodological limitations of social sciences in respect of the study of norms (and law and justice in particular) in Part Three; but, for our immediate purposes here, we need to take a closer look at law's normativity and consider the extent to which the normative force of law is linked, or can be traced back, to norms or a collection of norms which constitute the context of social action.

Normativity beyond social norms?

'Normativity' is used when exploring why, under certain circumstances, we feel obliged to act in specific ways (for a recent contribution to the debate on normativity, see Raz, 2011; Turner, 2010; Wedgewood, 2007; Delacroix, 2006). The notion of an 'obligation to act in a particular way' requires conscious commitment to a norm, and is thus linked to the internal (non-empirical) aspect of norms discussed above. The normative efficacy of a norm can, in turn, be explained by reference to the authority of the source of the norm (who said that we should act in a particular way?) and/or the social functions thereof (we might follow a rule because it fulfils certain social functions or upholds certain values such as justice, equality or fairness). In other words, norms in general, but the internal aspects of norms in particular, provide reasons to act in particular ways.[6] The reason itself (that I, for example, pay council tax because I would like to make a contribution to the community where I live, or I follow certain traffic

---

5 As I have argued elsewhere, it 'is now a social psychological commonplace that a discrepancy between attitudes and behaviour can exist. The fact that a person expresses a belief does not necessarily mean that that person will act in accordance with that belief'. See Banakar, 2003: 201.

6 As Raz (1999: 113) points out, reason (or rationality) in itself can have a normative dimension, therefore suggesting that normativity is not restricted to social norms.

rules because I care about other people's safety) is articulated consciously, while its underpinning values (why I should care about my community or the safety of other people) can be intersubjective, taken for granted, and rooted in the culture or customs of a group of people.

Limiting our discussion to the normativity of law and its implications for legal sociology, we are led to ask one of legal philosophy's classical questions: Why does law provide the majority of people with a reason for action? Moreover, why do some people comply with the letter of the law, even when there is no threat of sanctions against their non-compliance, and even though they know that following the law is not in their self-interest and will cost them in material and other terms?[7] The answer to this question takes us to the heart of law's normativity. For natural lawyers, such as Cicero, the normative force of law resided in some form of 'higher law'; while, for legal positivists, such as Austin (1967), it was to be found in the intimate relationship between legal norms and coercion. Subsequent legal positivists, such as H.L.A. Hart,[8] Hans Kelsen (2002) and Joseph Raz (1979), questioned the centrality of coercion in upholding the normative force of law, and maintained that coercion was neither an essential part of what constituted all the aspects of the law nor an indispensable requirement for what it did. Some laws are brought about to empower and facilitate social action, rather than coercing people into acting in particular ways.

From a sociological standpoint, people comply with the law for a number of empirically ascertainable reasons, which are not necessarily related to the threat of violence or whether the law is morally justifiable. Following Max Weber's forms of action (1978), we can say that one might follow a legal norm as a force of habit or custom (that is, Weber's 'traditional action', which we described above as descriptive norms). Alternatively, one might abide by the law for emotive reasons (that is, Weber's 'affective action'). Then again, one might believe that the law represents foundational values, such as rights and justice (this would correspond with Weber's value rational action), or one might follow the law because of the way it was enacted (that is, because of the authoritative source of the law). Finally, one's fidelity to the law might be motivated by purposive rationality, the belief that it accomplishes certain tasks which are required for an efficient governance of society. These ideal types of reason for action suggest that normativity can emerge out of system imperatives (purposive or instrumental rationality) as well as lifeworld (value and rationality), and that normativity can be the source, rather than the effect, of norms. To develop this point, we need to return to Hydén's

7 This is not to suggest that law (or the threat of violence) necessarily deters people from committing crime. Although the legal system does deter crime generally, the relationship between individual criminal action and the law (or the threat of sanctions) remains contingent on a host of factors. See Robinson, 2004.

8 Hart (1994: 82) criticises Austin's predictive model (namely, that the subject follows rules because he or she predicts sanction) and instead argues that the normativity of legal rules resides in their ability to provide reasons or justifications for action.

'science of norms', according to which a norm can emerge out of economic and political systems as well as the community:

> [B]oth moral and social norms are challenged by norms following from the construction or the structure of systems built up for the purpose of organising the production and distribution of material goods and services … Rationalities are thus bound to systems, and the more unambiguously the system is constructed, the stronger the normativity that follows from analysis of the systems relationship to a given empirical reality. The normativity is even more pronounced in systems that are associated with the laws of nature. (Hydén, 2011: 134–5)

Thus, system imperatives exert a normative force by urging and guiding action at societal (macro) and institutional levels. Norms then become labels that we use to refer to the normativity generated by system imperatives which can provide reasons for action, but not a sense of obligation. The sense of obligation (that is, the feeling that one is morally obliged to act in particular ways) emerges instead out of lifeworld (that is, the sphere of spontaneously generated values and worldviews) which are taken for granted by social actors and out of which 'system' is born (cf. Habermas, 1984). In that sense, lifeworld (and not system) provides the values which underpin the internal aspect of norms. This means not only that normativity can have other sources beyond social norms, but also that normativity *per se* can be a source of norms. In other words, system imperatives on the one hand, and lifeworld on the other, guide conduct, giving rise to repeated patterns of behaviour which are identified as social norms. These norms are not the cause of normativity, but equally they are not mere labels either, for they feed back into the system and lifeworld, thus strengthening systematic imperatives and community values respectively. We should bear in mind that normativity generated by social systems and the community (lifeworld) are based on different types of rationality and, following Habermas (1975 and 1984), coincide with system and socio-cultural integration respectively (see also Banakar, 2003: 291–2). One of the functions of modern law may be described in terms of its ability to mediate between the two types of normativity generated by system and lifeworld. However, the fact that law is a social system – defined variously by diverse philosophical and sociological approaches in terms ranging from a body of legal rules, norms and principles, to communications, practices and processes – exerts its own normativity. The uniqueness of the legal system's purported normativity is not captured by Weber's ideal types of action sketched above. Moreover, legal theory and legal sociology deal with law's normativity using epistemically incompatible terms. What mainstream legal scholarship regards as the principal values of the legal system, such as law's autonomy, objectivity and commitment to the rule of law, become the primary focus of critical inquiry within legal sociology.

What is unique about the law?

Whereas Weber sought an explanation for the normativity of law in reason, calculations and motivations that the agency employs to justify his or her actions (in this case, following the law), others have tried to find the normativity of the law in the law itself, in its specific form of reasoning or discourse, and thus implicitly attribute it to the law rather than to the subject's use of the law or to the agency's cognition or thought processes. Robert Alexy's theory of legal discourse is a case in point (Alexy, 1998). According to Alexy, besides a factual side, law also comprises 'a critical or ideal dimension', which is internally defined by a 'claim to correctness' (Alexy, 2000; see also Bulygin, 2000), a claim which, when made by law, also entails making a claim to justice. Alexy means that 'there are moral elements active in law', that adjudication (at least in hard cases) requires making moral judgements, and that 'legislation claims to be morally justifiable even in the case of political compromise' (Alexy, 2000: 143). Law is occasionally unjust, yet it remains and is recognised as law, as long as it aims to serve justice. Denis Galligan (2006), whose take on law and society is fundamentally different from Alexy's, also suggests that there is something unique about the law as a social formation. Paraphrasing Galligan, had law not been a social formation distinct from the other social phenomena with which it interacts, and had it not possessed its own very specific social properties and mechanisms, it would have long since collapsed into polity, economy, religion, morality or culture (Galligan, 2006; for a discussion, see Banakar, 2011b). Galligan (2006: 244) lists several aspects of the law which, by creating legal frameworks for security and stability, 'direct society in order to achieve social goods'. Galligan, who follows Hart's concept of law, does refer to the role of officials and citizens in determining what the law is; but, in the final analysis, it is the law which empowers officials and citizens to play an active role in realising socially desirable values. The institutional facts of the law are, in a sense, being transformed into values, suggesting 'a projective movement of sorts from the "is" to "ought"' (Minkkinen, 1999: 39).

From Mauro Zamboni's sober positivistic vantage point, the normative movement is in the opposite direction, from values to facts. Zamboni (2007: 172–85) identifies the specific property of the law in its ability to transform values entrenched in political decisions into legally relevant concepts and categories. While Zamboni describes how values and moral rights and concerns are transformed into (some would say 'reified' as) legal codes and rules, Radbruch contends that, for legal concepts to become law, they need to be translated back into the language of values. Although Zamboni conceptually separates law from values, one cannot but wonder if a part of the normative force legal rules does not retain the link to their underpinning values or social sources (or the normativity which emanates from system and lifeworld). It is reasonable to assume that laws which are generated by transforming political decisions based on existing community values or system imperatives continue to bear the legitimising seal of the community or the administrative system which initially generated them, and can more easily be translated back into a language that can be used by system or lifeworld to realise 'social goods'. By contrast, laws which are not rooted in community or system imperatives, and are brought about to modify common usages and *mores*, have to fight an uphill battle.

Zamboni, the ardent adherent of legal positivism, and Alexy, 'the apologist or polemicist in defence of the law' (see Goodrich, 2008: 105), conceptualise law and normativity in different ways, and yet their approaches belong to the discourse of legal theory (that is, they take for granted certain values and ideas belonging to legal theory). To tease out their disciplinary distinctiveness, we can contrast their take on law's normativity with Pierre Bourdieu's sociological exposition of the binding force of law. Bourdieu (1986: 843–4) maintains that law's 'symbolic power' extends itself beyond the circle of 'believers' (in other words, jurists, law's officials, law professors and others, who have internalised the values of the legal system, such as law's objectivity and autonomy not to mention its ability to deliver 'social goods'):

> The specific property of the symbolic power is that it can be exercised through the complicity of those who are dominated by it. The complicity is all the more certain because it is unconscious on the part of those who undergo its effects – or perhaps we should say it is more subtly extorted from them … [One] of the functions of the specifically juridical labor of formalizing and systematizing ethical representations and practices is to contribute to binding lay people to the fundamental principle of the jurists' professional ideology – belief in the neutrality and autonomy of the law and of jurists themselves. (1987: 844)

What was described above by Alexy as the 'claim to correctness', by Galligan as 'social goods', and by Zamboni as the transformative capacity of positive law, which turns values into legal rules, is reduced by Bourdieu to (and demystified as) the power of the jurists' professional ideology. This reveals the epistemic gap between Bourdieu's legal sociology and mainstream legal theory.[9] Perhaps understandably, from the standpoint of legal philosophers, such sociological explanations miss the target by miles, and at best trivialise law's *sui generis* normative property.

Although arguing for a *sui generis* normative legal content for law is reminiscent of natural law theories, those who evoke 'normativity' in this way often do not appeal to the metaphysics of natural law tradition. Instead, according to Stephen Turner, they maintain that this binding quality is neither natural, mystical nor empirical, and yet it is necessarily inherent in law and moral norms (Turner, 2010: 5). 'Normativists', as Turner calls them, do not deny 'the empirical sociological phenomenon of normativity', but insist that sociological explanations, such as

9 Bourdieu's point, that the force of law requires 'the complicity of those who are dominated by it' reminds us of Michel Foucault's discussions of power, knowledge and discipline (for a discussion, see Gustafsson, 2011).

the one produced above by Bourdieu, are 'not enough to explain what needs to be explained' (Turner, ibid.). The sociologist can explain that law rhetorically engenders its binding (symbolic, ideological or normative) power by, on the one hand, claiming to be an objective or an impartial arbiter of disputes, while conflating legality and justice on the other. In the English language, for example, the word 'justice' is frequently employed as a synonym to law. We refer to lay magistrates in English courts as 'Justices of the Peace' and to Supreme Court judges as 'Justices of the Supreme Court'. Similarly, we talk about 'access to justice' when we mean access to courts and legal services, 'the criminal justice system' when we mean the penal system, 'bringing offenders to justice' when we mean prosecuting suspects or sentencing offenders, and 'delivering justice' when we mean deciding cases. Although, following Bourdieu, one could say that these are examples of how law exercises its symbolic power, the 'normativists' would still demand an explanation as to why justice remains such a compelling force in public political discourse, not to mention in the mind of individual citizens, despite legal positivism's attempts to sharply distinguish it from legality.

Part two

Justice as law's primary source of normativity

Justice has been defined as a virtue or a moral value of the highest order. Its sources range from divine command to the practices of the wise ruler, and from the law of nature to the living law of the community. For our immediate purposes here, we will depart from the understanding of justice formulated as a general norm in Justinian *Institutes* as 'the constant and enduring will to render to each what is due' (Barden and Murphy, 2011: 5); a will which involves an unconditional, and arguably asymmetrical, responsibility to recognise and respond to the singularity of the Other (Derrida, 1992; see also McVeigh, 2002). 'Rendering to each what is due', most people would concede, should be one of the key considerations when determining how society is organised and how the activities of individuals and social groups are regulated. Some would even argue that it is one of the defining characteristics of a functioning human community and harmonious society. Nonetheless, few would agree on what 'rendering to each what is due' amounts to, and how it ought to inform human affairs in practice. This renders debates and discussions on what constitutes justice inevitable, even though, as pointed out by Alasdair MacIntyre (1981: 6), we know that 'they apparently can find no terminus' and, as argued by Derrida (ibid.), they require making an infinite, incalculable and ultimately impossible judgement. Nevertheless, law is required to be just, and unjust law is never recognised or accepted as a legitimate exercise in political and legal authority. This does not imply that law is expected to deliver justice in every case, but it should be committed to the principle of justice and not produce 'grossly unjust' outcomes, to borrow from Alexy again (this point is made in reference to Alexy's appropriation of Gustav Radbruch's legal theory; see Alexy, 2002). Expressed differently by Nigel Simmonds (2007: 197), '... while justice and legality are distinct and can compete with each other, legality can only fully be achieved where justice is achieved also'. By extension, any society not governed in accordance with the principle of justice is prone to social conflict and political upheaval; in such a case, the society will be no more than a precarious social order maintained over time purely through coercion, oppression and the threat of violence.[10] On this basis, justice becomes the source of law's normativity *par excellence*. This view is, however, not shared by legal positivists, who argue that there is no necessarily specific connection between law and morality, and they locate justice (which involves making an ethical judgement) beyond the legal system, in that it becomes not an integral part of the law's operations but a moral judgement about the law. For them, justice is not an intrinsic attribute of legal decision-making, but a normative benchmark which exists independently of the law and legal institutions. This allows legal positivism to construct a rule-based theory of law independently of morality,[11] while at the same time drawing a disciplinary borderline between themselves and others, such as natural lawyers and legal pluralists who conflate 'is' and 'ought' (for the debate between Kelsen and Ehrlich, see Van Klink, 2006).

Niklas Luhmann (2004) is one of the few scholars to have elaborated the essence of legal positivism's separation thesis into a sociological theory, according to which morals belong not to the systems, such as law, polity or law, but 'to the environment of all subsystems of the society' (Dallmann, 1998: 89). It is important to note that Luhmann's unit of analysis is not norms but communication – his social systems are communication systems which continuously objectify 'meaning'. The normativity of a legal system is generated internally by law recursively referring to its own previous communications or operations. In this way, the system excludes the diversity of its environment while reducing its own complexity (Luhmann, 1986 and 1990). The normativity which is generated internally within the legal system has no direct impact on how other systems operate or on social action,

10 Admittedly, lawyers, lawmakers, policymakers and ordinary people employ the law as a tool to protect and promote their own interests, if necessary at the expense of others and without consideration for the principles of justice or the rule of law. Nonetheless, Brian Tamanaha (2006) maintains that the instrumental attitude to the application of the law reduces it to a tool without any intrinsic value of its own or moral properties capable of promoting the common good. The fact that law is an instrument for achieving particular ends is not a problem in itself – it becomes a problem, and a threat to a democratic and just society, once the institution of law is divorced from considerations of the public good.

11 Tracing the development of legal positivism back to the critique of natural law in the sixteenth century, the separation between law and morality was initially a method for circumventing the contingency of law-making practices. As Delacroix explains: 'Montaigne invited us to proceed *as if* any inquiry into the context of social interaction giving rise to law were irrelevant to accounting for its normative dimension' (Delacroix, 2006: x).

and it produces 'juridical justice', which is a watered-down version of justice as discussed above.

Justice as law's contingency formula

Luhmann's systems theory conceptualises justice as the contingency formula of the legal system (Luhmann, 2004: 213–15). The law does not, according to Luhmann, 'recognise' but reacts to normative demands and other 'irritations' in its environment. Justice is neither internal nor external to law, but is instead generated within the internal constraints of the legal system as 'a programme of all programmes on the level of the programmes of the system' (Luhmann, 2004: 213),[12] which guides the operations of the law from the outside. According to Teubner's reading of Luhmann, this means that:

> Within the boundaries of law, justice cannot be weighed against anything. In this respect juridical justice differs from its counterparts in morality, politics and economics. For them justice is one normative programme among many – legitimacy, welfare, efficiency – while within the law, justice is invoked as the central non-contestable orientation formula. (Teubner, 2009: 9)

Although Teubner acknowledges the importance of justice within the legal system by describing it as law's 'central non-contestable orientation formula', his 'juridical justice' remains nevertheless limited in its practical scope and normative claims. The strengths and weaknesses of Luhmannian justice lie in its simplicity which, first, reduces justice to 'an individualisation process that looks for the (in)equality of new cases with old cases' (Teubner, ibid: 7) and, secondly, refuses to provide any substantive criteria for evaluating the justness of law's internal operations. Whether or not the binary distinctions made inside the law succeed in realising justice constitutes an effect observable only from the outside. This notion of 'juridical justice' can be criticised for being an abstract version of formal or procedural justice, essentially confirming the trivial claim that, inside the law, justice is reducible to the equality of cases before the law ensured by due process. It also fails to generate a specific legal value associated with justice and does not produce a set of substantive standards which can be employed to evaluate the correctness of individual decisions. Teubner recognises the critique directed at 'juridical justice' but dismisses it for ignoring Luhmann's point regarding 'adequate complexity' (Teubner, ibid: 9) – that is, according to Luhmann, justice requires 'adequate complexity of consistent decision-making'

---

12 For Luhmann (2004: 213), the normative closure of the legal system excludes morality as a valid criterion for decision-making within the legal system, but this exclusion is compensated by law internally constructing 'programmes' (such as justice, legitimacy, welfare and efficiency), which, by definition, cannot recognise, accommodate or address all moral issues and points of view (Luhmann, ibid.: 214).

(Luhmann, 2004: 219). This suggests that full realisation of 'juridical justice' requires a broader normative context produced by the legal system's 'adequate complexity of consistent decision-making'. It is also noteworthy that, although Luhmann departs from a positive concept of law (law in terms of state law), he nevertheless constructs a theory of justice fundamentally different from that of mainstream legal studies. Luhmann's application of a specific set of concepts and systems to theoretical ideas demarcates not only a disciplinary border between his sociological approach and mainstream legal studies and natural lawyers, but also between systems theory and other socio-legal theories of law, such as legal pluralism or Bourdieusian legal sociology.

The inter-connectedness of law and justice

For Barden and Murphy, justice is explained neither by reference to 'irritations' external to the juridical system nor by the ethical properties of legal discourse. Instead, they find it in the emergence of the human community and the functional necessity of maintaining social order over time. The relationship between law and justice evolved historically, Barden and Murphy (2011: 3) maintain, through what they call 'the living law'[13] – that is, 'a set of communally accepted norms that express how in certain types of situation members of the community are obliged to act'. They argue that the living law 'constitutes the commonly accepted rules of the community' and, conversely, that 'the communal moral law is the evolving principle of those who live together' (Barden and Murphy, 2011: 4–5). Barden and Murphy do not refer to the role of lifeworld and system in generating communal moral law, but their analysis corresponds with the discussion above, in that lifeworld can be a source of normativity and generate a sense of obligation (or moral law) underpinned by intersubjectively shared values. In short, law and justice emerged historically as an integral part of the cohesive moral force which holds the human community together. Through their interplay, they foster social integration, which is the prerequisite of an orderly modern society and gives rise to a normative context. MacCormick calls this 'a normative order' and writes:

> There is a shared or common sense of the "right thing to do", but this does not at all depend on there being one single officially formulated rule that each person can recite or learn by rote. For indeed the practice is an interpretative one, in which each party "reads" the situation as s/he thinks others are reading it and forms an opinion with regard to the opinion he/she thinks others hold, though this is not necessarily any kind of reflective deliberation about others' opinions. (MacCormick, 2007: 16–17)

13 Barden and Murphy's use of 'the living law' should not be confused with Eugen Ehrlich's 'living law' (see Ehrlich, 2002).

This normative context (or normative order) is rich in history and culture, provides reasons for action (reasons for obeying norms and rules), possesses 'adequate complexity', to use Luhmann's terminology, and as such is not reducible to specific norms or the collection thereof. It is, to borrow from MacCormick again, about a shared and unreflective sense of 'the right thing to do'; and, as such, it is a form of sensibility embedded in lifeworld. Once this taken-for-granted sensibility becomes intersubjective (that is, commonly shared among a group of people), it generates the foundation for a social institution – it creates a rational basis for repeated patterns of behaviour, while at the same time it is reproduced over time by the institutional practices it supports.[14] It also means that all sociological studies of law, which deal with issues of institutionalised order and social or system integration, are potentially studies of forms of normativity. Why is it then, one cannot help wondering, that the roots or sources of normativity are often placed beyond the scope of social sciences?

Part three

Dealing with the normativity of justice

In *A Treatise of Human Nature*, published in 1739, David Hume pointed out that norms and values could not be derived from 'facts' (see Hume, 1986). Empirical methods of research do reflect this insight and sharply distinguish between 'is' and 'ought', a distinction which also acts as one of the defining criteria of legal positivism (cf. Black, 1975: 1092). Perhaps understandably, most socio-legal researchers who rely on empirical methods – with few exceptions, such as the works of Leon Petrażycki (1956) and Philip Selznick (1992) – have avoided probing the normative core of rights and justice, leaving it to moral and legal philosophers to deal with the normativity of law conceptually and analytically (see also Nonet and Selznick, 2001). However, Emile Durkheim's identification of 'social facts' as the primary domain of sociological inquiry has undoubtedly played a more decisive role than Hume's facts/norms distinction in determining the methodological scope of legal sociology. As Lydia Morris (2006: 1) points out, Durkheim's 'insistence on the analysis of social facts as things ruled out a consideration of normative concerns'. Although Morris's view of sociology's treatment of rights is shared by many scholars, there are other notable readings of classical sociology which strongly suggest a more complex picture of the relationship between the normative and the empirical. One such interpretation is found in the work of Roger Cotterrell (2010), discussed below. It suffices to point out here that Durkheim was drawn to

14 Social institutions are more than aggregates of repeated patterns of interaction. They permit and entail the concentrated reflexive monitoring of social relations across indefinite time/space distances, thus constituting highly dynamic expert systems of social control (Giddens, 1991: 16).

the study of law precisely because he sought a sociological method of grasping the normative phenomenon.[15]

Max Weber, to mention another founder of the sociology of law, distinguished between three ways of thinking about the law informed by: 1) the method of dogmatic jurisprudence; 2) a sociological/empirical approach; and 3) the moral attitude towards the law which sharply differentiates between legal and moral standards, applying itself to the study of the latter (for an overview, see Kronman, 1983: 7). However, Weber also explained that these were ideal types – that is, 'exaggerated or one-sided descriptions that emphasised particular aspects of what is a richer and more complicated reality' (Kronman, 1983: ibid.). The 'unreality' of this distinction, Kronman explains, was supposed to assist us in 'disentangling the different elements that existing practices and institutions invariably involve' (Kronman, 1983: ibid.). Otherwise, Weber never intended to reduce the complexity of the operations of the legal system in respect of other social systems or spheres of action to simple distinctions between the internal and external operations of the law, for such sharply drawn distinctions abstract and differentiate law into parts which are otherwise interconnected and should be understood in terms of ongoing processes.

Notwithstanding what Weber intended, a three-fold division of labour is largely in force within contemporary legal studies, according to which: 1) legal scholars will study positive law's internal processes; 2) legal sociologists will investigate the empirical manifestations of the law, such as its efficacy in regulating behaviour and its impact on social relationships, and vice versa; and 3) legal philosophers will investigate the moral foundations of the law, which include justice.[16] As suggested above, this division of labour is maintained over time through the internal disciplinary discourses of various fields of legal research, and as part of these fields' attempt to reproduce specific epistemic identities. As I have argued elsewhere (Banakar, 2009), these discourses compete simultaneously for 'scientific stakes' (see Bourdieu, 1975) such as academic prestige and scarce resources. While various branches of legal studies, such as doctrinal research and legal philosophy, compete externally with each other and with legal sociology, they are at the same time constituted internally by their own competing discourses (that is, by the internal debates between their various schools of thought). In this scheme of things, socio-legal studies and legal positivism focus on positive

15 With reference to the sociology of human rights, Somers and Roberts also question the belief that sociology is incapable of studying normativity. They maintain that the sociology of human rights must transcend, negotiate or deconstruct the methodological barriers within social sciences which hold back sociology's engagement with the normativity of rights. See Somers and Roberts, 2008.

16 Legal theorists and philosophers will also clarify the general framework of legal ideas, and formulate general and abstract descriptions of legal systems. For a discussion, see Galligan, 2006: 7–12.

law, writes Marianne Constable (2005: 9), while employing a broadly conceived empirical approach, thus converging around a cluster of characteristics:

> Most texts of and about law take law to be a social phenomenon … Even scholars interested in what they call the "normative" aspect of law situate law in an empirical social world. That "society" is real, that "reality" is social and empirical, holds such sway that one wonders what else law could be. (Constable, 2005: ibid.)

Subsequently, according to Constable, we run the risk of forgetting that the empirical understanding of law is a relatively new insight generated to describe the operations of modern legal systems. Otherwise, law has not always been positivist, empirical or sociological, even though viewing it as a positive phenomenon has become the norm – the only reasonable way of comprehending and describing what actually constitutes law. It should therefore come as no surprise if the dominance of positivism within legal scholarship and socio-legal research comes at a price, namely the relegation of 'connections between law and justice, if any, to the empirically contingent social realities' (Constable, 2005: 10). Modern law and its socio-legal partner are thus both silent about justice, argues Constable. This does not mean that justice is absent in the discourses of legal positivists and socio-legal researchers; however, it can be sought in places where they are silent.

It is worth noting that injustice, rather than justice, prompts – not least of all amongst 'law and society' researchers – most debates and research on the impact of law on society. While the debate on justice is always shrouded in conceptual ambiguity and uncertainty, its opposite, injustice, is deliberated with some degree of conviction. The debate on justice is often marked by fundamental disagreements because it concerns itself with how things ought to be and with how to bring about and ensure basic rights, fairness and equal treatment, whereas debates on injustice generally, and miscarriages of justice in particular, are often concerned with actual cases pertaining to the abuse of power, existing unfair practices and the experience of wrongs and harm being perpetrated against oneself or others. We tend to respond to injustice more readily perhaps because, as Douzinas and Geary (2005: 28) point out, it has the power to stir us emotionally. In the context of socio-legal research, the emphasis placed on injustice is not only emotive (or, as Tamanaha (1997) has suggested, part of a political commitment),[17] but also partly due to its 'facticity' – that is, it offers an empirically tangible starting point for the study of the interaction between law and various social forces. Among these social forces, power looms large, for injustice is often about the abuse of power through law, and power is, unlike justice, treated as an empirical phenomenon.

---

17 The Law and Society scholarship has been criticised for focusing on the interests of marginalised groups and, subsequently, on injustice in society. Brian Tamanaha, for example, regards this tendency as proof of the politicisation of Law and Society research. See chapter 1 in Tamanaha, 1997. For a discussion, see Banakar, 2009.

Justice is therefore left to the legal philosophers, who are generally concerned with clarifying the general framework of legal ideas and formulating general and abstract descriptions of legal systems (for a discussion, see Galligan, 2006: 7–12). As a result, they tend to discuss the law at a level of generality and analyse its operations in terms of either its *sui generis* normative properties or judge-made law and court judgments – that is, justice becomes dependent on the judge's virtue and on the social interactions between the judge and other actors (for an overview of such an approach, see Andersen, 2011). By contrast, a sociological approach to how justice is delivered often departs from a much broader understanding of law, treating legal phenomena in view of their institutional properties, for example as empirically observable clusters of social practices or repeated patterns of behaviour which produce a sense of legality. One empirical aspect of the law, which affects the delivery of justice and yet stands out by its absence in most traditional moral philosophical treatments of law, concerns the impact that the socio-cultural identity of officers of the law (that is, identity in terms of gender, class, ethnicity, religion and so on) has on their practices. Traditional legal theory often works with an idealised concept of the judge, existing apparently beyond the constraints of sociological factors such as gender or class, and independently of problems arising out of the polycontexturality of late modern societies. The issue at hand can therefore be summarised in the following way. Legal sociology neglects the normativity of justice (or is 'blind' to the normative possibilities[18] and constraints of law), traditional legal philosophy overlooks the empirical dimensions of the legal system and practices (or processes) which reproduce law and its institutions, while doctrinal studies reduce them to rule-based reasoning. This makes traditional legal philosophy and doctrinal studies blind to the possibilities of, and constraints imposed by, the institutional settings within which the search for justice unfolds.

Facts and values in social and legal research

The presumed inability of social sciences in general, but sociology in particular, to address the normative cores of rights and justice is caused by their 'scientific' methodology, which makes them resistant to normativity on two different levels. It makes them suspicious of foundationalist and universalist claims inherent in (human) rights and justice (see Somers and Roberts, 2008; Deflem and Chicoine, 2011), and urges them to remain 'objective' in respect of the aims of their study, describing and analysing how things are, rather than speculating on how they ought to be. This means that they refuse to take at face value the normative claims made by social actors (including institutions of law and polity) while abstaining from making value judgements themselves. This is linked closely to another characteristic of sociology, which requires researchers to stay empirically grounded – seeking and exploring empirically tangible phenomena. In his essay

18 Following Norrie (2005: ix), I argue that 'law plays a central role in structuring, shaping and limiting the ethical possibilities in Western liberal societies'.

Science as Vocation, Max Weber states that 'historical and social sciences teach an understanding of social and political phenomena, but give no answer to the question as to how to judge activity in these realms' (Morris, 2006: 4). Similarly, Donald Black (1972: 1092), echoing Hume, maintains that 'value judgements cannot be discovered in the empirical world' and are therefore irrelevant to the sociology of law. Instead of speculating on the nature of a good life, social sciences should describe how people use values in their practices, how they employ moral arguments, and how they experience justice and deal with injustice using the law or other means available to them. In this sense, social sciences do study normativity, but they do so using a non-normative language, in order to comply with the methodological standards of (social) sciences. In short, legal sociology's inability to deal satisfactorily with the normativity of justice must be placed in the context of social scientific debate on the relationship between facts and values – or the is/ought problem – and the basic observation that 'ought' cannot be logically inferred from 'is'.[19]

This conclusion – that sociology as a primarily empirical science can describe and analyse what there is, but not what ought to be – is accurate yet deceptively simplistic, if not erroneous, once it is extended to legal sociology's ability to account for normativity. First, not all sociologists endorse or apply a positivistic methodology, and legal sociology is arguably influenced more by interpretive (qualitative) than by positivistic (quantitative) methods of inquiry. In debates where non-sociologists criticise the limits of socio-legal theory (see, for example, Constable, 2005 and Tuori, 2006: 28), the works of positivists such as Donald Black or Niklas Luhmann[20] are somewhat misleadingly taken to represent mainstream socio-legal research on law (Luhmann's work is often also misrepresented).[21]

19 Some legal sociologists such as Black, who have written on justice, limit their analysis to the *administration* of justice, to the empirically observable and measurable aspects of what is done in the name of justice (Black, 1998; for a discussion. see Banakar, 2003: 55–7). Black's theory of justice is constructed sociologically and supported empirically by data gathered from the outcomes of legal cases. Although his conceptualisation of the social structure of legal cases is socio-legally useful, it nonetheless avoids evaluating justice as a normative or emotional experience inseparable from the internal operations of the law and the legal system. In essence, it does not tell us if the right decision was made and justice done. As a result, in Black's final analysis, justice is reduced to the exercise of power and authority through the medium of law and legality, in the sense criticised by Constable.

20 Luhmann is a positivist, but only in the narrow sense of identifying law with state law. Otherwise, as we saw in connection with his discussion on justice, he distinguishes himself from mainstream legal positivists.

21 Black is a double positivist. He is a positivist in the social scientific sense of searching for aspects of social life which lend themselves to measurement; he is also a positivist in the legal sense of restricting law to the legal rules issued by the state or generated through the operations of the legal system. This cannot be said in Luhmann's case. Although his concept of law is positivistic, his methodological approach draws on a number of traditions that defy a simple classification as positivist. Also, Luhmann does

Subsequently, the theoretical diversity of the field and sociological debates on rights and justice are neglected (see, for example, Cotterrell, 2010 and Travers, 2010; for a classical example, see Gurvitch, 1947).

More importantly, most sociologists would readily admit that a combination of personal and professional values determines the angle from which they view social problems. Expressed differently, the way sociologists 'problematise' a particular issue is often determined by their values, some of which are rooted in their personal experience of social life and the position they occupy in society. Closely related is the argument that sociology's empirical data do not qualify as 'facts', if by 'facts' we are referring to entities existing independently of the observer. Alternatively, sociology's empirical data are located theoretically and are thus dependent on, and a function of, sociologists' basic theoretical (or rather epistemological) assumptions. Even when a study is conducted inductively in search of viable working hypotheses, the sociologist cannot avoid employing certain preconceptions about valid knowledge and how to locate and collect data (this point draws our attention to conceptual, empirical and analytical limits of sociology as a vantage point of social reality). It also means that the choice of perspective in social research (that is, deciding from whose standpoint a particular study is to be conducted) qualifies as a value judgement. I should hasten to add that the dependency of researchers' perspectives on values is not limited to sociology and applies to all social research, including doctrinal research, which is driven by the concerns and taken-for-granted values of the researcher or those who have commissioned the research, such as policymakers.[22] Expressed differently, deciding which perspective provides the correct point of departure for studying a social or legal problem entails making a value judgement, which in turn impacts upon the outcome of our research. This choice of perspective largely determines our method of inquiry.[23] In a study of hate speech, for example, we can produce very different results depending on whether we approach the problem from the standpoint of those who become the target of racist violence or from the vantage point of those who consider themselves the custodians of free speech and argue that legitimate public debates must be protected at all costs, even when this debate concerns issues which are deemed politically incorrect or offensive.

---

not adhere to legal positivism's sharp distinction between law and morality; instead, he proposes a sociologically sophisticated description of law's autonomy.

22 Sociology tries to cast light on the taken-for-granted values and concerns of sociological research. In this sense, sociology possesses a form of reflexivity which we do not find in, for example, doctrinal studies. For a discussion on doctrinal methods, see Banakar, 2011b.

23 If we depart from the authorities' conception of a problem, we are likely to use a top-down approach, while departing from the ordinary people's understanding of the same problem will most probably lead us to employ a bottom-up approach. Whether we use a top-down or a bottom-up approach can, in turn, have implications for the particular techniques we need to gather data. See Banakar, 2011.

There is yet another way of considering facts and values, or the relationship between empirical research and normative evaluation; one which can be traced back to the founders of American Legal Realism. An understanding of what law could do in actual fact would assist us when negotiating and determining what law should do (see Llewellyn, 1931). Expressed differently, law can benefit from the social scientific studies of the world that it tries to govern by employing empirical knowledge to improve its normative judgements (see Nonet, 1980: 58). Although values cannot be generated out of facts alone, accurate accounts of the relationship between law and society can lay the basis for addressing normative issues arising out of law's operations in society. This point has recently been elaborated in Cotterrell's reading of Durkheim:

> [S]ociology cannot reveal *universal moral truths* ... Any criteria governing what is morally appropriate will relate to the sociological character of the particular type of society concerned. Durkheim claims that sociology can study social life objectively as a matter of "social facts". In doing so it can identify moral principles and practices compatible with (or even necessary to) stable social relations in particular kinds of societies. To this extent sociology can provide guidance on moral issues. It is not limited to describing what people think in moral terms and what moral choices they actually make. To some extent it can also provide criteria to evaluate and criticize those choices. Thus, sociology can sometimes advise on what law should prescribe or permit. When sociology reveals the fundamental importance of certain moral principles, in particular social conditions, the question of whether these should be expressed and defended through law will need to be faced. (Cotterrell, 2010: 5)

Last but not least, sociology is the study not only of social norms, moral principles and legal rules, but also of the normative contexts which give reasons for following norms, rules and principles and bestow meaning upon the sense of obligations and responsibilities towards others. The main point of this chapter, which was developed in Part Two, is that some of the central concerns of sociology with, for example, social integration are ultimately concerns with justice and normativity. Legal sociology's ability to capture normativity in general, and the normativity of law in particular, has not been recognised for two reasons. First, normativity is often understood in the narrow, rule-based sense of making a moral judgement (a process which may be decontextualised and reduced to the application of norms and values to the facts of a case), thus ignoring the possibility that normativity may emerge from socio-historical contexts of law and other institutions. In this latter sense, norms become labels which we use to describe already existing regularities and normativities and not the cause of regularities or source of normativity. Secondly, sociology, being a different 'language game' from moral philosophy, studies normativity using social scientific terms rather than concepts employed by moral philosophy. Bourdieu's study of the symbolic power of law and Luhmann's theory of justice were used above to exemplify how sociological analysis distinguishes itself from mainstream legal theory using different concepts to discuss normativity. Closely linked to this point is the need for various fields of legal study to produce and reproduce an academic identity. Thus, legal sociology, legal philosophy and doctrinal studies identify themselves discursively by reference to specific ideas and interests. Legal sociology consists of a host of various theoretical perspectives and epistemologies (see Banakar, 2011a), but a broadly conceived commitment to the study of the empirical aspects of the law and legality, which often leads to an understanding of law in terms of institutional practices and social processes rather than a system of rules, principles, judgements and doctrines, brings these together under the same discursive/disciplinary order and distinguishes them from legal philosophy and doctrinal studies. As part of the attempt to define the boundaries of fields of legal research, many legal sociologists, as well as legal scholars, from Hans Kelsen (2002: 13–14) to Kaarlo Tuori (2006) and Mauro Zamboni (2006), have used the distinction between normative and empirical research as a marker for disciplinary inclusion and exclusion, and a building block upon which part of their disciplinary identities may rest (for a discussion on the disciplinary boundaries of legal studies, see Gustafsson, 2011).

Concluding remarks

Sociology in general and legal sociology in particular are concerned with and study the normative contexts of social action. Many of the studies of law conducted from a social scientific point of view are, for example, driven by a concern with (in)justice, but they focus on the institutional relationships and practices through which (in)justice materialises rather than evaluating the normativity of legal decisions. However, since socio-legal engagement with normativity is couched in the empirical language of social sciences, rather than the normative language of moral philosophy, it appears incapable of addressing the normativity of law. The methodological requirement of socio-legal research to remain empirically grounded admittedly restricts its mode of expression and the way it deals with the normativity of law – some studies tend to reduce law to the exercise of power, thus overlooking what distinguishes it from other forms of social regulation – but it does not exclude normativity from socio-legal analysis. Hence, the second argument of this chapter is that any analysis of law, which goes beyond the mere study of the technical aspects of positive law and tries to throw light on how law operates as an integral aspect of the social order, necessarily involves the study of justice, which (as argued above) is the primary source of law's normativity and an integral element of social integration. There might not be a conceptually necessary link between the factual and the moral dimensions of the law, as legal positivists claim, but justice and law emerged together historically as inseparable parts of the common moral force which integrated the human community.

Constrained by its scientific conceptual lenses, sociological analysis cannot unearth the inner reality of law's normativity, but it can analyse and explain how the various expressions of law's 'being' are generated discursively and produced and reproduced over time. Moreover, by studying law's normativity from specific angles – for example, by emphasising people's experience of injustice, or alternatively emphasising norms at the expense of social conflicts – it does, indirectly as it might be, take a stance on the nature of a good society.

References

Alexy, R. 1998. *Theorie der juridischen Argumentation. Die Theorie des rationalen Diskurses als Theorie der juridiscen Begründung* (1983), translated by Neil MacCormick as *A Theory of Legal Argumentation: The Theory of Rational Discourse as Theory of Legal Justification*. Oxford: Clarendon Press.

Alexy, R. 2000. 'On the Thesis of a Necessary Connection between Law and Morality: Bulygin's Critique', *Ratio Juris* 13(2), 138–47.

Alexy, R. 2002. *The Argument from Injustice*. Oxford, Clarendon Press.

Alexy, R. 2004. 'The Nature of Philosophy', in *Ratio Juris* 17(2), 157–67.

Andersen, S.S. 2011. 'Justice and other Judicial Virtues', in *Retfaerd* 134(3), 58–98.

Austin, J. 1995[1832]. *The Province of Jurisprudence Determined*. Cambridge: Cambridge University Press.

Baiers, Matthias and Svensson, M. 2009. *Om Normer*. Malmö: Liber.

Banakar, R. 2003. *Merging Law and Sociology: Beyond the Dichotomies of Socio-Legal Research*. Berlin: Galda + Wilch.

Banakar, R. 2009. 'Law Through Sociology's Looking Glass', in Denis, Ann and Kalekin-Fishman, Devorah (eds) *The New Handbook in Contemporary International Sociology: Conflict, Competition and Cooperation*. London, Sage. E-copy at: http://papers.ssrn.com/sol3/papers.cfm?abstract_id=1327025.

Banakar, R. 2011a. *The Sociology of Law: From Industrialisation to Globalisation*. Sociopedia.isa. E-copy at: http://ssrn.com/abstract=1761466.

Banakar, R. 2011b. 'Having One's Cake and Eating It: The Paradox of Contextualisation in Socio-Legal Research', in *International Journal of Law in Context* 7(4), 487–503. E-copy at: http://papers.ssrn.com/sol3/papers.cfm?abstract_id=1777165.

Barden, G. and Murphy, T. 2011. *Law and Justice in Community*. Oxford: Oxford University Press.

Black, D. 1972. 'The Boundaries of Legal Sociology', *Yale Law Journal*, 81 (May), 1086–1100.

Black, D. 1998. *Sociological Justice*. Oxford: Oxford University Press.

Bourdieu, P. 1975. 'The specificity of the scientific field and the social conditions of the progress of reason', in *Social Science Information* 14(6), 19–47.

Bourdieu, P. 1987. 'The Force of Law: Toward a Sociology of the Juridical Field', in *Hastings Law Journal*, 38(5), 814–53.

Bulygin, E. 2000. 'Alexy's Thesis of the Necessary Connection between Law and Morality', *Ratio Juris* 13(2), 133–7.

Constable, M. 2005. *Just Silences: The Limits and Possibilities of the Modern Law*. Princeton: Princeton University Press.
Cotterrell, R. 2010. 'Justice, Dignity, Torture, Headscarves: Can Durkheim's Sociology Clarity Legal Values?', in *Social and Legal Studies* 20(1) 3–20.
Dallmann, H-U. 1998. 'Niklas Luhmann's Systems Theory as a Challenge for Ethics', in *Ethical Theory and Moral Practice* 1(1) 85–102.
Deflem, M. and Chicoine, S. 2011. 'The Sociological Discourse on Human Rights: Lessons from the Sociology of Law', in *Development and Society* 40(1) 101–115.
Delacroix, S. 2006. *Legal Norms and Normativity: An Essay in Genealogy*. Oxford: Hart.
Derrida, J. 1992. 'Force of Law: The "Mythical Conditions of Authority"', in Cornell, Drucilla et al. (eds) *Reconstruction and the Possibility of Justice*. London: Routledge, 3–67.
Douzinas, C. and Geary, A. 2005. *Critical Jurisprudence: The Political Philosophy of Justice*. Oxford: Hart.
Ehrlich, E. 2002[1913]. *Fundamental Principles of the Sociology of Law*. New Brunswick: Transaction Publications.
Elek, E., et al. 2006. 'Influences of Personal, Injunctive, and Descriptive Norms on Early Adolescent Substance Use', in *Journal of Drug Issues* 36(1), 147–72.
Galligan, D. 2006. *Law in Society*. Oxford, Clarendon Press.
Giddens, A. 1991. *Modernity and Self-Identity: Self and Society in the Late Modern Age*. Cambridge: Polity.
Goodrich, P. 2008. 'Alexy ad Iustitum', in *Social and Legal Studies* 17(1), 105–108.
Griffiths, A. 2002. 'Legal Pluralism', in Banakar, Reza and Travers, Max, *An Introduction to Law and Social Theory*. Oxford: Hart Publishing, 289–310.
Gurvitch, G. 1947. *Sociology of Law*. London: Kegan Paul.
Gustafsson, H. 2011. *Dissens: Om det rättsliga medvetandet*. Göteborg: Juridiska institutionens skriftserie, Skrift 9.
Habermas, J. 1975. *Legitimation Crisis*. Boston: Heinemann Education.
Habermas, J.1984. *The Theory of Communicative Action*. Vol. I. Boston: Beacon Press.
Hart, H.L.A. 1994. *The Concept of Law*. Oxford: Clarendon Press.
Hume, D. 1896[1739–1740]. *A Treatise of Human Nature*. Oxford: Clarendon Press.
Hydén, H. *Normvetenskap*. Lund: Lund Studies in Sociology of Law.
Hydén, H. 2011. 'Looking at the World through the Lenses of Norms', in Papendorf, Knut et al., *Understanding Law in Society*. Zurich: LIT Verlag.
Kallgren, C.A. et al. 2000. 'A Focus Theory of Normative Conduct: When Norms Do and Do Not Matter', in *Personality and Social Psychology Bulletin* 26(8) 2002–12.
Kelsen, Hans. 1967. 2nd ed., *Pure Theory of Law*, trans. M. Knight. Berkeley: University of California Press.

Kelsen, H. 2002[1934]. *Introduction to the Problems of Legal Theory*. Oxford: Oxford University Press.

Llewellyn, K.N. 1931. 'Some Realism about Realism', in *Harvard Law Review* 44(8), 1222–64.

Luhmann, N. 1986. 'The Self-Reproduction of Law and its Limits', in Teubner, Gunter (ed.) *The Dilemma of Law in the Welfare States*. Berlin: Walter de Gruyter, 111–27.

Luhmann, N. 1990. 'Meaning as Sociology's Basic Concept', in Luhmann, Niklas (ed.) *Essays on Self-Reference*. New York, NY: Columbia University Press.

Luhmann, N. 2004. *Law as a Social System*, trans. K.A. Ziegert. Oxford: Oxford University Press.

MacCormick, N. 1991. Foreword to the English Edition, in Amselek, Paul and Neil MacCormick (eds) *Controversies about Law's Ontology*. Edinburgh: Edinburgh University Press.

MacCormick, N. 2007. *Institutions of Law*. Oxford: Oxford University Press.

Madsen, M.R. and Dezalay, Y. 2002. 'The Power of the Legal Field: Pierre Bourdieu and the Law', in Banakar, R. and Travers, M. (eds), *An Introduction to Law and Social Theory*. Oxford: Hart Publishing, 189–207.

MacIntyre, A. 1981. *After Virtue: A Study of Moral Theory*. Notre Dame: University of Notre Dame Press.

McVeigh, S. 2002. 'Postmodernism and Common Law', in Banakar, R. and Travers, M. (eds) *Introduction to Law and Social Theory*. Oxford: Hart, 268–83.

Minkkinen, P. 1999. *Thinking Without Desire: A First Philosophy of Law*. Oxford: Hart.

Morris, L. 2006. 'Sociology and Rights: An Emerging Field', in Morris, L. (ed.) *Rights: Sociological Perspectives*. London: Routledge.

Nonet, P. 1980. 'For Jurisprudential Sociology', in Evan, W.M. (ed.) *The Sociology of Law: A Social-Structural Perspective*. New York: Free Press.

Nonet, P. and Selznick, P. 2007[1978]. *Law and Society in Transition: Toward Responsive Law*. New Brunswick: Transaction Publishers.

Norrie, A. 2005. *Law and the Beautiful Soul*. London: GlassHouse Press.

Petrazycki, L. 1956. *Law and Morality*. Harvard: Harvard University Press.

Posner, E. 2002. *Law and Social Norms*. Cambridge, Mass.: Harvard University Press.

Raz, J. 1979. *The Authority of Law*. Oxford: Clarendon Press.

Raz, J. 1999. 'Explaining normativity: reason and the will', in *Engaging Reasons: On the Theory of Value and Action*. Oxford: Oxford University Press, 90–117.

Raz, J. 2011. *From Normativity to Responsibility*. Oxford: Oxford University Press.

Robinson, P.H. and Darley, J.M. 2004. 'Does Criminal Law Deter? A Behavioural Science Investigation', *Oxford Journal of Legal Studies* 24(2), 173–205.

Selznick, P. 1992. *The Moral Common Wealth*. Berkeley and Los Angeles: University of California Press.

Simmonds, N.E. 2007. *Law as a Moral Idea*. Oxford: Oxford University Press.
Somers, M.R. and Roberts, C.N.J. 2008. 'Toward a New Sociology of Rights', in *Annual Review of Law and Social Sciences* 4, 384–425.
Tamanaha, B.Z. 2001. *A General Jurisprudence of Law and Society*. Oxford: Oxford University Press.
Tamanaha, B.Z. 2006. *Law as a Means to an End: Threat to the Rule of Law*. Oxford: Oxford, Oxford University Press.
Teubner, G. 2009. 'Self-subversive Justice: Contingency or Transcendence Formula of Law?', in *Modern Law Review* 72(1), 1–23.
Travers, M. 2010. 'A Sociological Critique of Rights', in Banakar, Reza, *Rights in Context: Law and Justice in Late Modern Society*. Aldershot: Ashgate.
Tuori, K. 2006. 'Self-Description and External Description of the Law', in *2 No Foundations: Journal of Extreme Legal Positivism* 2, 27–43.
Turner, S.P. 2010. *Explaining the Normative*. Cambridge: Polity.
Van Klink, B. 2006. *Facts and Norms: The Unfinished Debate between Eugen Ehrlich and Hans Kelsen* (2006). Available at SSRN: http://ssrn.com/abstract=980957.
Wedgewood, R. 2007. *The Nature of Normativity*. Oxford: Clarendon Press.
Weber, M. 1978. *Economy and Society* (eds G. Roth and C. Wittich) (2 vols). Berkeley, University of California Press.
Zamboni, M. 2007. *A Policy of Law: A Legal Theoretical Framework*. Oxford: Hart.
Zamboni, M. 2006. 'A Reply to Reza Banakar's Review of "The Policy of Law"', in *Retfærd: The Nordic Journal of Law and Justice* 29(2), 81–5.

Chapter 3
Norms in Law and Society: Towards a Definition of the Socio-legal Concept of Norms

Måns Svensson

Introduction

During the last century, the concept of norms has kept a central position within the behavioural, social and legal sciences (see some examples from the extensive literature: Kelsen, 1967; Coleman, 1994; Pound, 1996; Ehrlich, 2001; Ross, 2002; Lewis, 2002; Ajzen, 2005; Bicchieri, 2005; Sugden, 2005; Hechter and Opp, 2005; Sumner, 2007; Posner, 2007; Fishbein and Ajzen, 2009). Although this multidisciplinary focus on norms has produced a variety of theoretical discussions, the need for clarification regarding the definition of the concept has remained significant. Different disciplines have formulated their own perspectives, and so the concept of norms has not developed into the unifying force that is its potential.

The aim of this chapter is to present a model for creating a more coherent concept, designed to meet the demands of the multidisciplinary field of sociology of law (hereafter shortened to 'SoL'). This model is built on an ontological analysis that can incorporate different perspectives. The suggested analysis is mainly founded on the Aristotelian concepts of 'essence' and 'accident.' Thus, the method is concerned with distinguishing between the 'essential' attributes that lie in the nature of the norms (together they form the general definition of the socio-legal concept of norms) and other 'accidental' attributes that are characteristic within certain groups of norms (such as social and legal norms). The result of this model for creating a definition – and the actual definition itself – has been tested in a number of research projects within SoL at Lund University (for example, Hydén and Svensson, 2008; Svensson, 2008; Baier and Svensson, 2009; Svensson and Larsson, 2009 and 2012; Leo, 2010; Hydén, 2011; Urinboyev, 2011; Larsson, 2011a; Naujėkaitė, 2011; Svensson and Urinboyev, 2012; Svensson et al., 2013; Larsson, Svensson, and de Kaminski, 2013; Leo and Wickenberg, 2013).

One of the advantages of this particular definition is its ability to adapt to different scientific perspectives. Each of the suggested essential attributes can be focused on individually, and a certain project might choose to apply only one of the essences (for example, pure legal science tends to focus on the normative aspect of the norms). SoL, however, being preoccupied with questions concerning relations and interactions between law, society and behaviour, tends to include multiple dimensions (attributes) of the norms. The essential attributes (of the norms) let us know what aspects of the norm concept are shared by all norms. The accidental attributes, on the other hand, are specific to each category of norms. In this chapter, the focus is on the two categories that are most relevant to SoL; namely, legal and social norms. However, one could imagine a research project focusing on 'fashion norms', for example, and then it would be necessary to identify the accidental attributes specific for norms that influence fashion (in addition to their essential attributes that are shared with all other norms).

An important final introductory remark is that the model for norm research presented in this chapter is not an unconditional support for the consensus theory within social science. Nor does it represent a presumption that norms are always functional within society. On the contrary, one important role of the empirical socio-legal research on norms is to unveil and explain conflicts and tensions in society, and to expose the manifest and latent dysfunctions of norms. The 'spirit' of the empirical research projects during the last decades, conducted within norm theory, in fact often resembles the ambition and tradition of critical theory (compare, for example, Horkheimer and Adorno, 1969; Marcuse, 1986; Adorno et al., 1993; Habermas, 1996), even though norm research is theoretically more inspired by functionalism within social science (compare, for example, Merton, 1949; Comte, 1988; Durkheim, 1997; Herbert, 2009). A striking example of that dual approach is the work of the research group Cybernorms, within the field of SoL, which aims to critically explore norm structures (social and legal) that appear in the wake of changing information technology (for example, Hydén and Svensson, 2008; Svensson and Larsson, 2009 and 2012; Larsson and Svensson, 2010; Larsson, 2011b and 2012; Larsson, Svensson and de Kaminski, 2013; Larsson, Svensson, de Kaminski et al., 2013; Svensson et al., 2013).

The socio-legal need for a multidisciplinary concept of norms

Whenever SoL is described in a general manner, the presentation revolves around some variation of the following theme: 'deals with the relationship between law and society'[1] – a description as pedagogically efficient as it is hazardous. While this description makes SoL seem concrete and easy to grasp, it also runs the risk

1 For example, Thomas Mathiesen, Professor of Sociology of Law at Oslo University, with reference to the classical Scandinavian legal scientist Ragnar Knoph (1894–1938), has demarcated Sociology of Law as the study of three basic questions: (a) to what extent, and how (when applicable), does the rest of society influence legal rules, legal decisions and legal institutions; (b) to what extent, and how (when applicable), do legal rules, legal decisions and legal institutions influence the rest of society; and (c) to what extent does there exist a reciprocal action between legal rules, legal decisions and legal institutions on the one hand and the rest of society on the other.

of hiding the core question: what aspects of law and society are comparable? One consequence of neglecting this particular question is the constant difficulty arising from trying to make SoL legitimate to both legal and sociological academics. David Nelken has discussed this problem in terms of identifying different 'truths about the law' (1993), and Roger Cotterrell comments:

> In a rich discussion of relationships between law and scientific (including social science) disciplines, David Nelken describes the efforts of these disciplines to tell "the truth about law" as being confronted, now, with law's own "truth". In other words, law has its own ways of interpreting the world. Law as a discourse determines, within the terms of that discourse, what is to count as "truth" – that is, correct understanding or appropriate and reliable knowledge – for specifically legal purposes. It resists scientific efforts to describe consequences (for example, in economic cost-benefit terms, psychological terms of causes and consequences of mental states or sociological terms of conditioning social forces). None of these interpretations, it is claimed, grasps law's own criteria of significance. (1998)

However, in the concept of norms lies the potential to supply a term that is accepted within both the legal field and the social sciences. A prerequisite for this, however, is that the concept is formulated so that it corresponds to the basic ontological presumptions of each respective field. In this text, I will assert that the concept of norms is crucial when trying to understand the relationships between law and society, and that the concept of norms is as central to SoL as, for example, the concept of attitudes is central to social psychology. The idea of norms as a cardinal phenomenon in society is older than empirical social science itself. David Hume has been described as the first thinker who, in a serious fashion, described the importance of norms. He did not, however, use the term 'norm'. Instead, he recognized 'mutual rules' as the natural solution to problems that emerged when different shortages limited the access to resources in demand, given that morality is essentially a product of human selfishness (Young, 2007).

SoL, as a science, takes its departure mainly from two distinct scientific traditions. First and foremost, SoL is a social science and has a sociological foundation. This gives SoL a solid anchorage in empirical and inductive method. Secondly, the discipline is, of course, closely tied to the legal sciences. It is impossible to attain a deeper knowledge of the law without acknowledging the internal nature of the legal system. It is becoming increasingly evident, however, that SoL, in order to grasp a phenomenon such as obedience, also needs to incorporate a behavioural (social psychology) perspective.

Being multidisciplinary, SoL must be able to take both an internal deductive and an external inductive approach when handling norms (for example, legal rules). In a sense, it could be said that SoL is supposed to explain logically normative statements from their material (empirical) context, something often argued as impossible by scientific philosophy. David Hume, the Scottish philosopher (1711–1776), established the basic philosophical 'law' that the 'ought' can never logically be derived from the 'is'. Hume's law had a considerable influence on modern legal thinking and created a fundamental divide between legal scholars, who came to consider norms (legal) essentially to be normative statements (without tangible connotations), while sociologists came to consider norms to be equal to 'things' that interacted with other phenomena in society and that could be studied empirically.

Hans Kelsen (1881–1973), Emilie Durkheim (1858–1917) and Muzafer Sherif (1906–1988) are all three considered to be classical thinkers, dealing with the norm perspective within their respective field (law, sociology and social psychology). They also represent opposite solutions to the is/ought problem of norm studies. Their respective perspectives illustrate the problem of combining research on normative statements with empirical research. However, their perspectives can also symbolically serve as 'suppliers' of one 'building block' each for the proposed socio-legal definition of the concept of norms.

Identifying the essential attributes of norms

The world-renowned Professor of Philosophy Irving M. Copi (1917–2002) wrote a chapter (1954), that is often referred to, called *Essence and Accident*. He argued that the notions of essence and accident, introduced by Aristotle (384BC–322BC), still play important, unobjectionable roles in pre-analytical thought and discourse, especially when creating definitions and categories.

'Essence' and 'accident' are two types of attributes that a phenomenon can have. Essential attributes form the phenomenon's existence, and the different essential attributes of a certain phenomenon together constitute its definition. If an object is lacking one or more of a phenomenon's essential attributes, it is a privation (and an exception). Hence, the definition of the concept of norms can be viewed as a number of essential attributes, and the challenge is to identify which attributes are common for all norms (legal, social and so on), and thereby essential. Accidental attributes, on the other hand, are variations within the phenomenon. For example, it is the accidental attributes that separate different kind of norms into categories (such as legal and social). The definition of legal norms will be the essential attributes (common for all norms) plus the accidental attributes specific for legal norms; and the definition of social norms will be the essential attributes (common for all norms) plus the accidental attributes specific for social norms, and so on.

In this chapter, I will argue for three essential attributes (based on the three dominating scientific perspectives on norms: law, sociology and social psychology) that can be considered to form the foundation for a definition of the norm concept (Hydén and Svensson, 2008; Svensson, 2008). I will not take upon myself to specify the accidental attributes that separate legal norms from social norms in this text, even though I will reflect on some of the consequences of making such a differentiation.

The evasive boundary between law and social norms

Since SoL emerged as a scientific discipline in the early twentieth century, one of the central tasks has been to define law, and thereby also to distinguish law from other norms in society. Eugen Ehrlich (1862–1922), however, in his ground-breaking book *Fundamental Principles of the Sociology of Law* (2001), pointed out that there is no real ontological difference between law and other norms:

> The legal norm, therefore, is merely one of the rules of conduct, of the same nature as all other rules of conduct. For reasons readily understood, the prevailing school of juristic science does not stress this fact, but, for practical reasons, emphasizes the antithesis between law and other norms, especially the ethical norms, in order to urge the judge at every turn as impressively as possible that he must render his decision solely according to law and never according to other rules.

This indicates that the difference between legal and social norms (in fact, all norms, including legal, are social, according to Ehrlich) does not lie in the nature of them, but rather in how they are practised. Consequently, the essential attributes of law are the same as for all other norms in society; and the accidental attributes of law are context-dependent and vary between different societies, and between different types of law within the same society. In order to complicate matters even further, law is ultimately an abstract term; and, as Julius Stone pointed out (1964; Vago, 2009): '… the definer is free to choose a level of abstraction; but by the same token, in these as in other choices, the choice must be such as to make sense and be significant in terms of the experience and present interest of those who are addressed'. Given that the attributes that differentiate law from other types of norms in society are highly context dependent, and that every attempt to define law must include a choice of level of abstraction, it is not hard to understand why Steven Vago comes to the conclusion (2009) that there are almost as many definitions of law as there are theorists (even though probably more scholarship has gone into defining and explaining the concept of law than into any other concept still in use in sociology and jurisprudence). For reviews of the literature dealing with the definition of law, see, for example, Ronald L. Akers and Richard Hawkins (1975); Robert M. Rich (1977); Lisa J. McIntyre (1994); Steven Vago (2009).

On a general level, following the suggested structure of this chapter, all norms in society are essentially of the same basic nature. Within SoL (and other legal sciences), for practical reasons, law is singled out and described through context-dependent accidental attributes. Consequently, we have a basic categorization between legal norms and (other) social norms. On a more detailed level, it is of course also possible to identify (through their specific context-dependent accidental attributes) other categories of social norms, such as ethical, technical and economic. Hence, the preferred terminology within SoL is: (a) 'societal norms' (or just norms) when referring to all varieties of norms; (b) 'legal norms' (singled out as the social norms that are the main object of study); and (c) 'social norms' (actually, all non-legal forms of social norms).

The sociological functionalistic perspective

Emile Durkheim was the first scholar to formulate and practise an empirical science that had its point of departure in the understanding of normative structures in society. His use of the concept of 'social facts' works as a guide to many scholars who are interested in social norms. The American sociologist George C. Homan (1910–1989), for example, claimed that there are indeed social facts as Durkheim described – and that they do apply a significant force on individuals and their actions. He also claimed that the best example of a social fact is a social norm, and that norms within a specific group undoubtedly force individuals to a degree of uniform behaviour (1969). Durkheim himself argued that[2] 'the first and most basic rule is to consider social facts as things' (1982), and that '[t]o treat phenomena as things is to treat them as *data*, and this constitutes the starting point for science' (1982). By doing so, Durkheim avoided the impediments of Hume's law. His position was that norms (although he did not name them so) are facts that can be studied, as they interact with other facts in society (material and non-material); a position that leads away from the study of human beings as mental figures. 'Social phenomena must therefore be considered in themselves, detached from the conscious beings who form their own mental representations of them. They must be studied from the outside, as external things, because it is in this guise that they represent themselves to us' (Durkheim and Lukes, 1982). Durkheim, in other words, places the forces of social life in an external (compared to individuals) structure of society. Furthermore, he makes an ontological statement through which he declares that the forces exist as things and that they, in that sense, are objective. The 'ought' is thus linked to an individual level, and falls outside any sociological or social analysis. Durkheim's concept of social facts is broader than the modern concept of norms. However, it is clear that Durkheim's ontological and methodological analysis of social facts is highly relevant when trying to understand the concept of norms: not solely because that would be a recipe for success in terms of finding a scientific method that could capture norms, but because it would be the way to understand the ontology of the norms. However, when claiming that norms are things, it is also understood that the most essential characteristic of those things is as carriers of normative messages. In other words, norms in this perspective are objects (things) containing messages of how reality 'ought' to be.

2 Durkheim himself was of the opinion that it was Montesquieu who, through his philosophy, cleared the way for Saint-Simon who was the first to start the real work on formulating a science about the social reality. Furthermore, Durkheim pointed out Comte as the one who brought order into the work of Saint-Simon.

The legal positivistic perspective

One of legal positivism's leading representatives, Hans Kelsen, introduced the word 'norm' to the legal discourse as a central concept. When explaining his pure theory of law, he argues that law is a system of norms, norms being 'ought' statements describing certain modes of conduct. The legal system is in that sense a structure of legal 'oughts', rather than social facts, as described by Emile Durkheim. Kelsen formulated his theory in polemic with the dominating discourse at the time; a discourse that he found to be hopelessly contaminated with political ideology and moralizing, on the one hand, and with attempts to reduce the law to natural or social sciences, on the other hand (Marmor, 2002). He considered these approaches to be reductions in a way that he could not accept. Instead, he argued that jurisprudence should be the pure theory of law, because it aims at cognition focused on law alone. Kelsen was convinced that, if the law is to be viewed as a unique normative practice, methodological reductionism should be avoided entirely. But this perspective is not only a question of method. Reductionism must be avoided because the law *is* a unique phenomenon, quite separate from morality and nature (Marmor, 2002). Furthermore, Kelsen was influenced by Hume's law and firmly believed in the distinction between 'is' and 'ought', and in the impossibility of deriving 'ought' conclusions from factual premises alone. The consequences of this reasoning are intriguing. Kelsen was convinced that law cannot be reduced to the natural actions or social and political contexts that give rise to it. The procedure of arguing, voting and so forth is not the actual law. The legal system consists essentially of 'ought' statements, and, as such, they cannot be deduced from factual premises alone (Marmor, 2002). This perspective forced Kelsen to explain how law is possible. If it does not emerge from human actions and societal substances in a direct manner, there must be another source. Kelsen's solution is the notion of an 'ought' presupposition in the background, rendering the normativity of law.

As opposed to moral norms, which, according to Kelsen, are typically deduced from other moral norms by syllogism (e.g., from general principles to more particular ones), legal norms are always created by acts of will. Such an act can only create law, however, if it is in accord with another 'higher' legal norm that authorizes its creation in that way. And the 'higher' legal norm, in turn, is valid only if it has been created in accordance with yet another, even 'higher', legal norm that authorizes its enactment. Ultimately, Kelsen argued, one must reach a point where the authorizing product is no longer the product of an act of will, but is simply presupposed. This is what Kelsen called the Basic Norm. More concretely, Kelsen maintained that in tracing back such a 'chain of validity' (to use Raz's terminology), one would reach a point where a 'first' historical constitution is the basic authorizing norm of the rest of the legal system, and the Basic Norm is the presupposition of the validity of that first constitution. (Marmor 2002)

Whereas Durkheim avoided breaking Hume's law by claiming that social facts (such as legal norms) adhere to the 'is', Kelsen chose to claim that the law should, in its entirety, relate to the 'ought', and that the law takes its source, not from a concrete context, but from a basic norm that belongs to the social 'ought'. In this chapter, I argue in favour of a norm concept that is capable of capturing the 'ought', as well as the 'is', and thereby can work as a link between the two dominating 'truths' concerning the legal system. By agreeing with Durkheim, as well as Kelsen, it is possible to avoid abuse of Hume's law. Since norms are bearers of characteristics that represent both the 'ought' and the 'is', it is possible, through norm analysis, to derive the 'ought' of the legal system from the 'is' of society. Furthermore, we will present a third, basic characteristic of norms related to their relationship with cognitive processes. Unless the individual level is taken into consideration, it will not be possible to understand, for instance, enforcement and obedience.

The social psychology perspective

Muzafer Sherif (1906–1988) is considered one of the founders of social psychology. His focus on social norms and social conflict forms the base of modern social psychology, and his book (1966) is still valued as one of the key works in the field. To Sherif, norms are psychological phenomena that occur when individuals perceive reality together with their social surrounding (for example, group). To Sherif, the social was closely related to the mental figures of individuals, and he often carried out experiments involving actual people.[3] Hence, the starting point for the social psychology perspective on norms is neither that they belong strictly to the 'ought', nor to the 'is', but rather to the 'individually perceived reality'. Another characteristic of the social psychology perspective on norms is that the behaviours they comprise are goal-directed and can be interpreted as purposive (but not necessarily conscious) (Cialdini and Trost, 1998). Further, social psychology tends to focus on norms that are primarily social in nature. According to Cialdini and Trost (1998), social norms can be considered as rules and standards that are understood by members of a group, and that guide and/or constrain social behaviour without the force of norms. These norms emerge out of interaction with others; they may or may not be stated explicitly, and any sanctions for deviating from them come from social networks, not the legal system.

The definition of norms

As showed, the concept of norms has maintained a central position within the behavioural, social and legal sciences (all perspective necessary to SoL);

3 One of his most famous experiments was the Robber's Cave experiment, where Sherif let two groups of young boys live for some weeks in a remote area and develop mutual norms and compete for desired resources.

subsequently, SoL must create a norm concept that adopts influences from these three academic fields. And, as a result, the socio-legal concept of norms, presented here, acknowledges three essential attributes that define the nature of norms. The first two relate to the dual ontological existence/shape of norms (see the matrix in Figure 3.1 below); and the third to the importance of acknowledging the behavioural dimension. Hence, all types of norms (for example, social and legal) have two ontological attributes and one behavioural. Accordingly, norms are:

1. imperatives (the 'ought' dimension of the norm; ontological);
2. social facts (the 'is' dimension of the norm; ontological); and
3. beliefs (the psychological dimension of the norm; behavioural).

These three essential attributes can also be described as norms, being (a) normative statements that (b) are socially reproduced and (c) represent the individual's perception of the expectations surrounding their own behaviour. The first essential attribute (the 'ought' dimension) is best represented by the positivistic legal science, where norms (and law) are considered to be essentially 'ought' statements (normativities) that should be studied deductively (Kelsen, 1967). The second essential attribute (the 'is' dimension) is tied to sociology and structural functionalism, which argues that norms (social facts) should be considered as things or data that can be studied empirically (Durkheim and Lukes, 1982) and inductively. These two dimensions ('ought' and 'is') can be applied to legal as well as social norms.

The 'ought' and 'is' of legal and social norms describe the most basic societal tensions that have been identified by scholars within the field of SoL. In law (legal norms), there is a tension between what is often referred to as 'law in books' and 'law in action', first described in those terms by Roscoe Pound (1910). These terms could, in many respects, be translated to what in Figure 3.1 is found in the normative and the factual dimension of legal norms respectively. This perspective emphasizes that a legal code by no means equals its intended practice in its implementation. The social, economic and cultural context that the law addresses

	The normative dimension	The factual dimension
Social norms	**'ought'**	**'is'**
Legal norms	**'ought'**	**'is'**

Figure 3.1 The Four Dimensional Socio-Legal Model (FDSL-model) – modified from Svensson, 2008

in practice will also shape, contribute to, and explain its outcome.[4] In society (social norms), there is a tension between the normative and factual dimensions as well. This tension (for example, deviance) has been discussed and analysed by scholars such as Robert Merton (1936 and 1949) in his strain theory and in his writings about manifest and latent functions and dysfunctions in society (Larsson and Svensson, 2010; Larsson, Svensson, de Kaminski et al., 2013; Svensson et al., 2013). Finally, there is a tension between legal and social norms that is of particular relevance to SoL. Many socio-legal scholars focus their studies on 'the gap' between the law and the intentions of the policy makers, on the one hand, and behaviour and social norms on the other (Nelken, 2009; Banakar, 2011). The third essential attribute of norms is that they are also beliefs; therefore, social psychology is needed in order to understand them fully. Following the logic of the 'theory of planned behaviour' (TPB) within social psychology (Ajzen and Fishbein, 1980; Ajzen, 2005; Fishbein and Ajzen, 2009), norms can be understood as a belief in the form of the individual's understanding of the surrounding expectations regarding his or her own behaviour. This attribute must be considered in order to explain the connection between norms in 'law and society' and human behaviour.

Robert C. Ellickson, a professor at Yale Law School, was one of the first legal scholars to fully recognize the importance of socially enforced norms. He states that 'much of the glue of a society comes not from law enforcement, as the classicists would have it, but rather from the informal enforcement of social norms by acquaintances, bystanders, trading partners, and others', and 'informal systems of external social control are far more important than law in many contexts, especially ones where interacting parties have a continuing relationship and little at stake' (Ellickson, 1998); and Drobak (2006) claims that social norms guide people's actions and social interaction to a greater degree than does the law.

Norm theory and legal pluralism

Even though legal pluralism, as a scientific field, perhaps has its most recognized roots within research of colonial and post-colonial societies (for example, Malinowski, 1926), it has since the 1970s been of increasing interest among SoL scholars for applying the classic concept of legal pluralism to western societies of, for example, Europe and the US (Merry, 1988). However, since SoL emerged

4 The 'law in action' perspective means focusing on law and its relationship to society, as 'a tool to better understand law and its operations, to improve the science of law and legal education and to develop law as a more effective instrument of social engineering' (Banakar, 2011:6). For Pound, valid law consists of legal rules laid down by authorities, and the distinction between law in books and law in action served 'to highlight the social nature of the legal process, a process which, once grasped sociologically, could be engineered to manufacture a tighter fit between law and the social reality it tried to regulate' (Banakar, 2011:7).

as an academic field in the early twentieth century, scholars have laid down the theoretical foundation for a pluralistic view on social control and norms. This is, to some extent, a separate path from what is normally described as legal pluralism, and it started with classicists such as Eugene Ehrlich (1862–1922), *Fundamental Principles of the Sociology of Law* (2001); Leon Petrazycki (1867–1931), *Law and Morality* (2011); Karl Renner (1870–1950), *The Institutions of Private Law and Their Social Functions* (2009); Nicholas Timasheff (1886–1970), *An Introduction to the Sociology of Law* (1939); and George Gurvitch (1894–1965), *Sociology of Law* (2001) (see Cotterrell, 1992).

Following that tradition, norm science can be used for studies within legal pluralism (or norm pluralism). One of the main advantages of the norm concept presented here is the possibility of identifying norms via the three-fold definition built on essential attributes, and then the possibility of classifying different types of norms via their accidental attributes (identified through empirical studies). A recent example of a study that uses this socio-legal norm concept in order to examine what could be described as legal pluralism (Svensson et al., 2013) focuses on social norms online versus traditional legal development. In that study, more than 90,000 respondents answered questions on their views and practices regarding file sharing. The result showed a striking gap between traditional law and online living law.

Conclusions

In this chapter, I have argued that the norm concept is central to sociology of law and could be held to be equally important as, say, the concept of attitude to social psychology. It will probably never be possible to fully bridge the classic gulf between the two dominating academic perspectives on law – namely, sociology and legal science. However, the norm concept, defined via the essential attributes, tells us that all norms (legal and other social norms) have three properties in common: they are imperatives ('ought'), yet social facts ('is'), and, in the end, always subjective beliefs.

References

Adorno, T.W., Frenkel-Brunswik, E., Levinson, D.J. and Sanford, R.N. 1993. *The Authoritarian Personality*. W.W. Norton Company.

Ajzen, I. 2005. *Attitudes, Personality and Behaviour*, 2nd ed. Open University Press: Maidenhead.

Ajzen, I. and Fishbein, M. 1980. *Understanding Attitudes and Predicting Social Behaviour*. Prentice-Hall, Englewood Cliffs: London.

Akers, R.L. and Hawkins, R. 1975. *Law and Control in Society*. Prentice-Hall, Englewood Cliffs: N.J.

Baier, M. and Svensson, M. 2009. *Om Normer*. Liber.

Banakar, R. 2011. *The Sociology of Law: From Industrialisation to Globalisation*. SSRN eLibrary.
Bicchieri, C. 2005. *The Grammar of Society: The Nature and Dynamics of Social Norms*. Cambridge University Press.
Cialdini, R.B. and Trost, M.R. 1998. 'Social influence: Social norms, conformity and compliance', in *The Handbook of Social Psychology*, Vols. 1 and 2 (4th Ed.), edited by D.T. Gilbert, S.T. Fiske and G. Lindzey. McGraw-Hill: New York, US, 151–92.
Coleman, J.S. 1994. *Foundations of Social Theory*. Harvard University Press.
Comte, A. 1988. *Introduction to Positive Philosophy*. Hackett Pub Co.
Copi, I.M. 1954. 'Essence and Accident', *The Journal of Philosophy* 51, 706–19.
Cotterrell, R. 1998. 'Why must legal ideas be interpreted sociologically?', *Journal of Law and Society* 25, 171–92.
Cotterrell, R.B.M. 1992. *The Sociology of Law: An Introduction*. Butterworths.
Drobak, J.N. 2006. *Norms and the Law*. Cambridge University Press: Cambridge, New York.
Durkheim, E. 1997. *The Division of Labor in Society*. Free Press.
Durkheim, E. and Lukes, S. 1982. *The Rules of Sociological Method and Selected Texts on Sociology and its Method*. Macmillan: London.
Ehrlich, E. 2001. *Fundamental Principles of the Sociology of Law*. Transaction Publishers: London.
Ellickson, R.C. 1998. 'Law and Economics discover social norms', *The Journal of Legal Studies* 27, 537–52.
Fishbein, M. and Ajzen, I. 2009. *Predicting and Changing Behavior: The Reasoned Action Approach*. Psychology Press, New York: Hove.
Gurvitch, G. 2001. *Sociology of Law*. Transaction Publishers.
Habermas, J. 1996. *Between Facts and Norms: Contributions to a Discourse Theory of Law and Democracy*. MIT Press: Cambridge, Mass.
Hechter, M. and Opp, K.-D. 2005. *Social Norms*. Russell Sage Foundation Publications.
Herbert, S. 2009. *The Principles of Sociology*. BiblioBazaar.
Homans, G.C. and Sigeman, U. 1969. *Upptäckt och Förklaring i Samhällsvetenskaperna*. Argos: Uppsala.
Horkheimer, M. and Adorno, T.W. 1969. *Dialectic of Enlightenment*, First ed. Continuum.
Hydén, H. 2011. 'Looking at the world through the lenses of norms', in Papendorf, K., MacHura, S. and Andenaes, K. (eds), *Understanding Law in Society, Developments in Socio-legal Studies*. LIT Verlag GmbH & Co: Hamburg, 120–59.
Hydén, H. and Svensson, M. 2008. 'The concept of norms in Sociology of Law', *Scandinavian Studies in Law* 53, 15–32.
Kelsen, H. 1967. *Pure Theory of Law*. University of California Press: Berkeley.
Larsson, S. 2011a. 'Metaphors and norms: Understanding copyright law in a digital society', *Lund Studies in Sociology of Law*. Media-Tryck: Lund.

Larsson, S. 2011b. *The Path Dependence of European Copyright*. SCRIPTed.
Larsson, S. 2012. *Conceptions in the Code: What "The Copyright Wars" Tell Us About Creativity, Social Change and Normative Conflicts in the Digital Society*. Societal Studies.
Larsson, S. and Svensson, M. 2010. *Compliance or Obscurity? Online Anonymity as a Consequence of Fighting Unauthorised File-sharing*. Policy & Internet 2.
Larsson, S., Svensson, M. and de Kaminski, M. 2013. 'Online piracy, anonymity and social change – Deviance through innovation', forthcoming in *Convergence: The International Journal of Research into New Media Technologies*.
Larsson, S., Svensson, M., de Kaminski, M., Rönkkö, K. and Alkan Olsson, J. 2013. 'Law, norms, piracy and online anonymity – Practices of de-identification in the global file sharing community', forthcoming in *Journal of Research in Interactive Marketing*.
Leo, U. 2010. 'Rektorer bör och rektorer gör', *Lund Studies in Sociology of Law*. Lunds universitet: Lund.
Leo, U. and Wickenberg, P. 2013. 'Implementation of education for sustainable development – with a special focus of the role of principals in change efforts', submitted to *Journal of Educational Change*.
Lewis, D. 2002. *Convention: A Philosophical Study*, 1st ed. Wiley-Blackwell.
Malinowski, B. 1926. *Crime and Custom in Savage Society*. Rowman & Littlefield.
Marcuse, H. 1986. *Reason and Revolution*, 2nd ed. Routledge.
Marmor, A. 2002. *The Stanford Encyclopedia of Philosophy*.
McIntyre, L.J. 1994. *Law in the Sociological Enterprise*. Westview Press: Boulder CO.
Merry, S.E. 1988. 'Legal pluralism', *Law & Society Review* 22, 869–96.
Merton, R.K. 1936. 'The unanticipated consequences of purposive social action', *American Sociological Review* 1, 894–904.
Merton, R.K. 1949. *Social Theory and Social Structure: Toward the Codification of Theory and Research*. Free Press.
Naujėkaitė, J. 2011. *The Implementation of the Kyoto Targets in Lithuania from a Perspective of Multilevel Governance*, Dissertation. Mykolos Romeris University: Vilnius.
Nelken, D. 1993. 'The truth about law's truth', *European Yearbook of the Sociology of Law* 93.
Nelken, D. 2009. 'The "gap problem" in sociology of law: A theoretical review', in Nelken, D. (ed.), *Beyond Law in Context. Developing a Sociological Understanding of Law*. Ashgate Publishing: England.
Petrażycki, L. and Trevino, A.J. 2011. *Law and Morality*. Transaction Publishers.
Posner, E.A. 2007. 'Social norms, non-legal sanctions, and the law', *Economic approaches to law* 4. Edward Elgar: Cheltenham.
Pound, R. 1910. 'Law in books and law in action', *American Law Review* 12–36.
Pound, R. 1996. *Social Control through Law*. Transaction Publishers.
Renner, K. and Treviño, A.J. 2009. *The Institutions of Private Law and Their Social Functions*. Transaction Publishers.

Rich, R.M. 1977. *The Sociology of Law: An Introduction to its Theorists and Theories*. University Press of America: Washington, D.C.

Ross, E.A. 2002. *Social Control: A Survey of the Foundations of Order*. University Press of the Pacific.

Sherif, M. 1966. 'The psychology of social norms', 1st Harper torchbook. ed, *Researches in the Social, Cultural, and Behavioral Sciences*. Harper & Row: New York.

Stone, J. 1964. *Legal System and Lawyer's Reasonings*. Stanford University Press: Stanford.

Sugden, R. 2005. *The Economics of Rights, Cooperation and Welfare*, 2nd ed. Palgrave Macmillan.

Sumner, W.G. 2007. *FOLKWAYS: A Study of Mores, Manners, Customs and Morals*. Cosimo Classics.

Svensson, M. 2008. 'Sociala normer och regelefterlevnad', *Lund Studies in Sociology of Law*. Media-Tryck: Lund.

Svensson, M. and Larsson, S. 2009. *Social Norms and Intellectual Property. Online Norms and the European Legal Development*. SSRN.

Svensson, M. and Larsson, S. 2012. *Intellectual Property Law Compliance in Europe: Illegal File Sharing and the Role of Social Norms*. New Media Society.

Svensson, M., Larsson, S. and de Kaminski, M. 2013. 'The Research Bay – Studying the global file sharing community', in Gallagher, B. and Halbert, D. (eds), *IP in Context: Law and society perspectives on intellectual property*, forthcoming in *Cambridge Studies in Law and Society*. Cambridge University Press: Cambridge.

Svensson, M. and Urinboyev, R. 2012. 'Welfare as a means for political stability: A law and society analysis', *EJSS* 14, 64–85.

Timasheff, N.S. and Treviño, A.J. 1939. *An Introduction to the Sociology of Law*. Transaction Publishers.

Urinboyev, R. 2011. 'Law, social norms and welfare as means of public administration: Case study of Mahalla institutions in Uzbekistan', *The NISPAcee Journal of Public Administration and Policy* 4, 33–57.

Vago, S. 2009. *Law and Society*, 9th ed. Pearson Prentice Hall: Upper Saddle River, N.J.

Young, H.P. 2007. 'Social norms', in Durlauf, S.N. and Blume, L.E. (eds), *The New Palgrave Dictionary of Economics*. Nature Publishing Group: Basingstoke, 647–51.

Chapter 4
Relations between Social and Legal Norms

Matthias Baier

Introduction

The relevance of a norms perspective was discussed in the introductory chapter of this book. It was shown that norms are a main part of societal issues in general, and normative issues in particular, with an obvious central point in the various research fields connecting law with society. The argumentation for a revitalization of a norms perspective was quite sketchy, and it mainly served the function of making this point. This book proposes that norms have the ability to integrate the plurality of the socio-legal field to a large extent; a proposition that will be elaborated in this chapter. One main argument for this strategy is that norms integrate the two strands of law and sociology. The concept of norms is a crucial part of law, as well as an important part of society. A second main argument is that, in social sciences, the concept of norms is a fundamental concept, with a strong ability to connect with other concepts (Baier and Svensson, 2009). A third argument is that the concept of norms also connects the micro and macro levels. For a further elaboration of arguments, see Hydén (2010). This chapter aims to follow up the introduction. It thereby seeks to answer the question of what it means (and can mean) to use a norms perspective in law and society studies, and thus argues further for the potential of research and studies undertaken within a norms perspective.

The introduction made it clear that such a norms perspective is quite broad and theoretically complex. This follows from the fact that norms are part of the fundamentals of a *homo sociologicus* perspective (Elster, 1989). Along with the increasing interest for norms in the disciplines of law and economics, norms also become important for the *homo economicus* perspective. Consequently, there is a risk of arguing for a perspective that might turn out to be incoherent and thereby not living up to its integrative and analytical potential. Thus, one challenge lies in determining the concept in a way that includes several theories or perspectives of the concept without risking the fallacy of losing its core idea. The obvious strength of the concept for sociology of law lies, however, in the fact that it forms the fundamentals of both the social and the legal spheres. A second challenge lies in the fact that sociology of law has the distinctive feature of being multidisciplinary and dealing with law. Therefore, sociology of law is claimed to be a theoretically disintegrated subject of research (Banakar, 1998) but also having problems with sociology's ability to address law's truth – see preferably Cotterrell (1998) and

Nelken (1998). There is even more plurality within the field of law and society (including also law and psychology, law and anthropology, law and economics, demography of law, law and political science, and criminology). Some argue, however, that this plurality within sociology of law is a distinctive and positive feature of the field (Mathiesen, 1998).

A third challenge lies in structuring the concept of norms so as to cover both the social and the legal aspects. There has been a long debate about the many differences between these two (see further this chapter), and several of the contributions in this book depart from and address these differences. There are differences in the way the concept of norms is defined, the way it is used, its genesis and its social functions – just to mention some problem areas. These notorious differences between how law and social sciences conceive norms, however, stress the need for a more integrated approach. As noted by Reza Banakar in Chapter 1, one difference between law and social sciences lies in the fact that, while certain perspectives within social sciences tend to focus on the gap between laws and norms, traditional legal theories tend to take norms for granted and treat them as socially neutral. The differences between law and social sciences tend to focus on conflicts between laws and social norms. An integrated approach would instead allow for an understanding of social and legal norms not just as producing conflicts, but also producing consensus. It would be dysfunctional if the two major systems of norms in western societies tend to be conflicting in most cases. Instead, we would assume the opposite. This does not, however, mean that I argue for a strict consensus perspective and, consequently, the norms perspective presented in this book allows for an approach that does not necessarily depart from one of these perspectives. The main argument for such a neutral position is that norms do integrate society, but they also exert power, and are therefore prone to conflict (Coleman, 1990). Instead, normativity in a socio-legal sense is made up by the combinations between the social and the legal spheres, be that conflicting or consensual manifestations. This position calls for an approach with the ability to cover various combinations between social and legal norms making up different kinds of normativity.

The basic idea of this chapter is to further elaborate the norms perspective by connecting it with a specific understanding of norms. This is the strategy to overcome some of the problems described above. Certain aspects of theory, but surely also empirical research, must eventually apply or relate to certain definitions of the concepts used. Here it means that, when getting closer to empirical aspects of the norms perspective, the question of what definition of norms is used cannot be avoided, and sometimes even becomes critical. Therefore, the proposed understanding of norms will also be connected with a definition of norms.

The chapter will proceed in the following way. First, I will account for an understanding of norms that departs from and analyses traditional definitions of norms. Secondly, I will connect this understanding with the definition of norms presented by Måns Svensson in Chapter 3. This understanding of norms is quite broad, but also adapted to a socio-legal discourse, and focuses on two essences of norms: norms are i) imperatives that are ii) socially reproduced. Norms thus connect the 'is' and the 'ought'. Thirdly, an assumption is made that it is possible – at least for analytical reasons – to distinguish between social and legal norms. I will do that by discussing the general concept of 'societal norms'. It is then recognized that the properties of 'is' and 'ought' can be attributed to social and legal norms respectively. Applying the two essences of norms to the two types of norms makes up four categories, labelled 'social norms', 'legal norms', 'social practice' and 'legal practice'. These four categories of societal norms provide the basis for a further elaboration, where the ambition is to unfold different relations between these categories. It is concluded that 12 relationships can be identified between these four categories. Most important is to identify and shortly comment on each relation. The chapter concludes with a discussion of the relevance of these relationships. It is also suggested that these 12 relationships can be looked upon as a heuristic tool in understanding, conducting and designing research within the norms perspective.

Understanding norms

There are a variety of ways of defining norms in the vast literature dealing with norms. It is probably not possible to define norms without employing and accounting for a particular interest, or a particular perspective, or a particular theory. Legal theorists, for example, tend to focus on the (formal) imperatives, and accordingly tend to omit aspects of regularities or social functions. For social psychologists, norms are connected to the ways in which meaning is constructed. For economists and game theorists, norms are connected to patterns of actions and thus explain features such as cooperation. Although contested, there is a sufficient amount of consensus about the basics of the concept. Without this consensus, it would not be possible for so many scholars from so many different scientific disciplines to communicate scientifically about it. As put by Bicchieri and Muldoon (2011):

> There is no necessary and sufficient condition for being a norm, just a cluster of characteristics that any norm can display to a greater or lesser extent. Norms refer to behavior, to actions over which people have control, and are supported by shared expectations about what should or should not be done in different types of social situations.

It should also be noted that the concept has a popular use, which coincides quite well with the scientific use. When looking into various encyclopaedias, dictionaries and handbooks defining norms, a certain formula can be discerned, which can be summed up as follows (Baier, 2003):

- consensual standards – describe – behaviours
- rule, standard or pattern – for – action

- shared expectation – connotes – desirable and appropriate
- cultural rule – associates – behaviour
- rules or expectations – regarding – behaviour
- shared expectations – constitutes – desirable conduct
- prescriptions – serving as common guidelines – social action
- general precepts – induce conformity – actions, ethical judgements

It is clear that the norm formula contains three aspects. The first concerns the normative expression. It can manifest itself as norms as such – that is, what we traditionally conceive of as norms, namely utterances that tell us how to behave or what to do, be that in terms of precepts, prescriptions, standards, rules and so on. This normative expression can also manifest itself as normative patterns of behaviour or expectations. Norms, being out there as social facts or individually conceived of as expectations, are still normative. The second aspect concerns the connection or even mechanism between the normative expression and the latter aspect (namely, actions). The second aspect is clearly the one which is least developed here. But somehow it seems to cover how, why and under what circumstances normative expressions tend to induce or otherwise result in actions. In a recent contribution (Bicchieri and Muldoon, 2011), there are three theories dealing with why normative expectations induce conformity: socialization, social identity and rational choice. However differently, these three theories seem to give an explanation of the normativity of norms. The last aspect seems to be the most coherent one. Normative expectations result in conformable behaviour that is also desirable. What is perhaps not common to all definitions, but widely recognized, is the sanction that follows if norms are not followed. Sanctions are often important in different theories, but they are not always necessary conditions.

This very brief introduction reveals that, at an overall level, there is a common agreement about norms, yet certain aspects of norms can still be contested. As is often the case with fundamental concepts common to several scientific disciplines and quite common in everyday usage, we know what we mean by them until we try to define them. This nature of the concept calls for a definition of norms that somehow has an essential core, but is still open to aspects that are not necessary, albeit of importance. Måns Svensson has elaborated on such a strategy for relating to the concept, which is presented in Chapter 3.

A socio-legal definition of norms

Svensson's strategy when dealing with the definition of norms is to use the concepts of essence and accidents. In short, the essences of a concept are necessary, while the accidents are not, even if they can be very informative. For instance, the fact that a statement appears in a code of laws does not necessarily mean that it is a legal norm, but it gives us useful information about the statement. A second strategy for Svensson is to argue for a definition of norms that can join or even settle the often different perspectives on norms in Law and Sociology respectively.

Along these lines, Svensson argues that the first essence of a norm is the imperative content of norms. Not surprisingly, this essence is to be understood symbolically, and what counts is if an utterance or a statement is interpreted as an imperative. The second essence tells us that norms are intersubjective. Norms that are not shared among the community are not norms – at least, not in this sense. The third essence is that norms are the individuals' understanding of the surrounding expectations regarding their own behaviour. This last essence is needed if we want to understand how norms influence our behaviour, Svensson points out. A note can be made of what happens if a norm actually lacks one or two essences. For example, a statute might be completely out of date, but for strange reasons still officially in the code of laws. In that sense, the statute is an imperative, but it is not reproduced. Since law puts up certain criteria of how to recognize law, it is still officially a statute with legal status. To explain this situation, we label the statute as obsolete. According to the philosophy of essences, this is labelled a privation.

Having established the three essences, Svensson also elaborates on the accidental attributes. Norms can, for instance, belong to a certain category and this might be of interest for different reasons. What makes us talk about 'medical norms', 'technical norms' or 'legal norms', and how do we distinguish between them? This question can be asked by analysing the accidental attributes pertaining to different categories of norms. Accidental attributes, such as sanction, origin, and arena, might then tell us if a norm can be categorized as legal, social or technical. But Svensson's strategy also allows for the opposite way of analysing norms. The claim that a certain norm exists is followed by the responsibility to state its accidental attributes. The attributes remind us of taxonomy in natural sciences. But this way of reasoning might also help us understand what role sanctions play for norms.

Societal norms

This definition seeks to cover all forms of norms. To avoid conceptual ambiguities, I will follow Mathieu Deflem (2008: 198) and refer to this general level of norms as 'societal norms' (cf Baier and Svensson, 2009). This prefix makes up a comprehensive concept, covering all other forms of norms. This is indeed not the place to try to account for all different types of norms, but there are reasons to comment shortly on the issue. Such an endeavour can be carried out in very different ways. Jack Gibbs (1966) tried to form a logical matrix of norms based on 'definitional' and 'contingent' attributes of the norm. In this way, he logically discovered 20 different types of norms, of which five were not logically possible. A more inductive way of discovering different norms results in other types. It is, for example, possible to ascribe importance to the sources of norms (Hydén, 2011). Hydén advocates the differentiation between moral, social and systemic norms, arguing that, empirically, conscience, social community and societal systems make up different sources of norms. Legal norms would then be norms originating from the legal system.

This discussion about different categories of norms brings to the fore whether we can talk about social and legal norms. Such a categorization assumes that we know the differences between the differing setups of these two concepts in terms of accidental attributes (given that they can be qualified as norms according to the essences). 'Legal' is an attribute that requires clarification but, as with the concept of norms, defining law is not all that easy, even though these categories are pivotal for the field of Law and Society and are therefore very often taken for granted but also used. The question of how to define law is also changing over time, and within different legal cultures, as a result of the fact that law itself can change. Again, practitioners might define law differently compared to legal theorists or social scientists. It suffices here to say that, when defining law, some characteristics are often used. Typically, law is described as a system of norms, it emanates from the government, it has a universal character, it is enforceable and binding, and it is associated with a certain form.

In most cases, there are no problems identifying law; due to its coercive character and due to principles of the rule of law, a great deal of effort is spent setting the limits of law. Social and cultural norms can be coercive. However, coercion alone does not turn them into law. The essence of legality (the specific normativity of law) is thus not a function of coercion. As a system of norms closely connected with power but also money, professions and institutes such as courts help to identify the limits of law. But, as with the example of law that is obsolete, there are many reasons to qualify and label different forms of law with a prefix – such as informal law, soft law, indigenous law, and living law. These examples can be viewed as instances of 'law' deprived of one or more of the essences of law. Soft law relates to measures which are not binding on those to whom they are addressed but still can produce some legal effects (see Eurofound). As society changes, there will always be reasons to re-evaluate what law is, but more often to evaluate new forms of normative orders. For the purpose of this chapter, it is not necessary to provide a clear-cut definition of law. But, following Svensson's line of argumentation, from a socio-legal perspective, law is (a formalized, binding and enforceable system of) imperatives, socially reproduced, expected as norms, and stemming from the political system.

Having distinguished legal norms from the overall category of societal norms, it is necessary to comment on the category of social norms. The main focus of this book is to highlight relationships between social and legal norms in general. The more empirical contributions to this book offer more detailed examples of these relations. Still, few of them need to elaborate particularly on the concept of social norms. Perhaps Ulf Leo's and Lars Persson's contributions dealing with the scholastic profession would benefit from such a differentiation. The main point with this book is to provide a coherent set of examples of these relationships. They all fit well into the concept of social norms, though. Social norms should therefore be understood as the remaining category, given that legal norms have been separated out. For these reasons, I will not elaborate on or define moral norms, professional norms and other, similar, categories. For an attempt to do this, see Gibbs (1965); cf Baier and Svensson (2009).

Unfolding relations between social and legal norms

Trying systematically to understand the relationship between social and legal norms requires some kind of conceptual platform, for analytical reasons as well as for administrative reasons. Above, I have distinguished between social and legal norms, a distinction that naturally provides the first dimension of this platform. What is then needed is one or more analytical aspects to guide how the relationship can be unfolded. Many questions can, of course, be asked about the relationship between social and legal norms. It is, for example, possible to proceed from the different institutional arrangements within law and social norms. But this comparison would rather highlight differences between the two, and thus conceal a possible relationship. Of interest is instead an analytical aspect that does not restrain the analysis too much, but still captures the socio-legal essence of social and legal norms.

From the previous account of definitions of norms, it is clear that societal norms are imperatives and/or expectations that somehow guide actions and/or behaviour, or result in conformity. This means that there is consensus about the fact that norms have two essential properties: one that we can refer to as the property of 'ought', and one that can be referred to as the property of 'is'. These aspects go well together with the two first essences of the norm definition discussed earlier. What is claimed here is consequently that norms can be looked upon as a coin with two sides, where both sides are necessary, even if the two sides seem to be incompatible. Indeed, what is argued here is that the very 'idea' of norms is to connect these two sides. Norms do transform 'ought' to 'is'. Norms are the nexus between 'is' and 'ought', and 'is' and 'ought' fuel each other within this nexus. Norms are about this transformation (Baier and Svensson, 2009). The analytical aspects chosen are simply those that make up the core of societal norms, and confer the arguments in Svensson's contribution. For the purpose of this level of analysis, these two categories of norms with the two properties make up a quite simple platform, yet with the ability to provide richness in the analysis. Invoking more categories of norms or more analytical aspects brings the risk of resulting in a platform that is too complex. It is wise to avoid the kind of affluence of different categories inherent in Jack Gibbs' matrix (1965: 591).

Given that social and legal norms both have the properties of 'ought' and 'is', we now have two aspects of legal norms and social norms. To make sense of the result of this, the following labels will be used. The 'ought' property of law is labelled 'law', referring to the dogmatic view of legal norms, often referred to as 'law in books'. The 'is' property of law is labelled 'legal practice', which can be seen as the aggregate of each and every decision where law is actually applied in different contexts and in different situations and under different circumstances, often referred to as 'law in action'. The 'ought' property of social norms is labelled 'social norms', referring to the imperative aspect of norms that indeed can be under debate and scrutiny as with legal norms, even though this takes place within civil society. Within socialization processes, for example, or due to changes in society's social norms, changes in their content and their relationship with other norms always takes place. The 'is' property of social norms is labelled 'social practice'. As with law, social norms will always be applied, and this manifestation of social norms can often be very important for the existence of social norms.

The two properties of the two categories of norms can be illustrated in a very simple matrix (see Figure 4.1). The matrix serves an entirely pedagogical function, by facilitating an overview of the relationship between social and legal norms. In the following, I will comment on and account for the four different fields and the relationships between them. Some relationships are quite well known, and some are less so. As far as possible, I will try to relate the relationships to existing research, preferably empirical findings.

Figure 4.1 Matrix with Categories and Properties of Norms

It goes without saying that 'law as such' is normative; this is the assumption *par excellence* within theories on law, but also within legal culture in a broader sense. Law deals with normative problems in a normative way. Legal practice, as an empirical phenomenon, is normative in another sense. Traditionally, 'law as such' makes a point of distinguishing between the two, even though the relationship between them is crucial. Social norms 'as such' are also unproblematic. Social norms are recognized as normative, though lacking law's formal character, lacking the formal connection with politics, and so on. Social practice is perhaps the least normative within law and society studies. Social practice has its importance when interfering with and disturbing the application of law. Mostly, it is treated as an empirical phenomenon, since it lacks a clear manifest relationship with law and legal practice. As the dashed lines indicate, I do not treat these four categories as logically exclusive. Instead, the platform illustrates societal norms with four normative nodes.

Relationships between social and legal norms

Going anti-clockwise round the matrix and starting in law, the first relationship is that between law and legal practice. For the sake of clarity, I label this relationship 'legal deduction'. This relationship is about enforcing law and maintaining law's coherence. The point with law is that it should be observed intact within the limits of law, and the content of law must be transformed into actual decisions. Simply put, this relationship is about multiplying law as such. Legal education and legal procedures are examples of means to ensure this multiplication. This is probably the most investigated relationship in law and society studies, and numerous studies have come to the conclusion that legal practice is not necessarily the same as what the law states. Even though law assumes fidelity to the law, a lot of legal (as well as extra-legal) factors intervene in the deductive process.

Given that we have a legal practice with a certain normative content, the overall idea of law and legislation is to provide guidelines for action that are applicable to both existing practices (to the actual existing behaviour) and practices which are in the process of being shaped. This is the general idea of all norms. Legal practice is therefore assumed to have effects on social practice. By means of different sanctions, or the threat of sanctions, compliance with the law is supposed be the result. I label this relationship 'legal efficiency'. This relationship is part of the general realization of the content of law. But, as with the previous relation, the fidelity to legal practice might differ considerably. Here, law interpreted by legal practice risks meeting a quite different normative reality. The legal efficiency is dependent on several factors. The actual number of cases decided plays an important role, within certain limits. If more people are corrected, the social practice would change accordingly. Monitoring and sanctioning speeding, for example, changes the way in which people drive. The question is, however, whether this observance will last beyond the actual corrective activity. One problem of legal practice is that social practice in most cases 'outnumbers' legal practice. Furthermore, legal practice and surveillance are expensive. The critical issue is whether legal practice has an indirect effect on social practice due to the normative message. Do people change their behaviour as a result of others being sanctioned? This legal efficiency is clearly necessary when it comes to criminal matters. But for other areas of law, this efficiency looks different. The welfare systems administered by law often rely on agencies distributing the legal outcome in terms of subsidies. For private law, legal efficiency works in yet another way. Since the content of law in many instances is optional, the difference between legal practice and social practice cannot be viewed as a problem, as with criminal law.

From a legal, dogmatic point of view, this relationship is of less interest. Furthermore, law lacks theories and methods for understanding and studying this process. The effects of law and its practice are studied by scholars within law and society but, surprisingly, there is no systematic evaluation of the effects of law and legal practice. The state is, of course, interested in the effects of law and the legal practice in terms of a cost benefit analysis, including political costs. This is the case in highly regulated areas where the state spends a lot of money and which, therefore, are politically controversial. But, for parts of society that are less regulated, such as contract law, there is little knowledge about the effects of law and its practice. Very often, people tend to solve problems by themselves.

The relationship between social practice and social norms seems quite obvious. Basically, it is about the generation of norms. In contrast to legal norms, some social norms tend to emerge spontaneously, due to different needs, such as the need for coordination or integration. Descriptive norms, such as etiquette, emerge and are maintained through patterns of behaviour. But this might be the case also for behaviour with more 'normative weight'. The example of file sharing (see Chapter 18) illustrates quite well that the actions of many people can also foster normative beliefs. Karl Dieter Opp (1982) argues that an evolutionary emergence of norms starts with recurrent behaviour, which, through the development of preferences, ultimately results in the acceptance of norms. Stroll (1987) takes it one step further when claiming that norms, basically, are descriptions of average behaviour, and 'normal' and 'normally' bear the logical weight in this connection. I label these relationships 'norm generation'. From a legal point of view, we are now in the social field as such, and thus in another normative strand. Nevertheless, to change social norms politically by changing social practice (through legislation and legal practice) does encounter problems. This is not to say that it never happens, but to plan such 'top-down' change seems challenging. Some aspects of reflexive law do, however, assume links between legal practice and social practice. If reflexive law 'restricts itself to the installation, correction, and redefinition of democratic self-regulatory mechanisms' (Teubner, 1983), social practice must obviously be of importance for such mechanisms. Worth mentioning is the concept of 'souls of fire' by Per Wickenberg (see Chapter 13). It is clear that such norm entrepreneurs operate with hindsight to changing behaviour in an empirical sense.

The last relationship is between social norms and legal norms. Given the direction, we can describe this relation as social norms influencing legal norms. We can also look upon this relationship as an aspect of the social basis for law (Cotterrell, 1992). Law needs to derive normative content from somewhere, and social norms are one major source of this content. Normally, this is done through the medium of politics, and then such a normative transformation is known as legislation. Within the process of legislation, normative standpoints are negotiated empirically through certain procedures, including organized referrals, surveys, lobbying, civic protests, and so on. But, since the ambition is to find relationships in a more pure sense between social and legal norms, the question is whether there are unmediated relationships between the two. Again mediated, the public sphere provides a channel for social norms into the legal system. But it is possible that social norms influence law in a less institutionalized way. Part of law is only to a limited degree politically decided. In Sweden, tort law has a manifestation in the code, but most of its normative content is produced by decisions by courts with precedent power, but also by legal doctrine. Apart from arguments about coherence in the legal system and political arguments, there is a substantial space for reasoning about moral principles and effectiveness (that is, fidelity to social norms).

Having gone around the matrix in one direction, it is now time to go round in the opposite direction. I will again start with the legal dimension. There are several relationships between legal practice and law. Of interest here is the formation of law based in legal practice. Legislation is not the only source of law, and in fact there are many areas of law that are quite dependent on legal practice to form new law. If a dogmatic view assumes a deductive perspective on law and legal practice, this relation can be labelled 'legal induction'. Through cases close to practice law, new and unforeseen conflicts or even new problems can be picked up. Normally, this is done through the appeal system. Case law and similar systems can be said to grow from below to a much greater degree than civil law systems. But new forms of governance in civil law systems are seldom normatively negotiated through the appeal process. 'Law' is thus actually located in legal practice, due to its numbers that have never been subject to scrutiny from doctrinal law. This is the case in Sweden regarding the regulation of genetically modified organisms (Baier, 2009).

The opposite relationship of legislation is the influence that law has on social norms. It was argued above that social norms 'law-forming norms' emerge through social practice. But social norms may also emerge through discourses about how to act. This is more probable with norms that carry more normative weight. The public sphere provides the forum for such discourses. Often, controversial cases serve as the catalyst for these normative discourses, which might previously have been latent. In these cases, representatives of the law might participate. Another example is legal education within, for instance, law faculties. Again, different cultures pay more or less attention to the law in this sense. US discourses on basic rights seem to be the opposite of Sweden, where law in this sense has been equated with politics to a high degree. Lacking relevant terminology, I label this relationship 'law forming norms'.

As with the legal dimension, the very idea is that social norms should actually influence social practice. However, although there has been some criticism, there is consensus about the fact that social norms have effects. This relationship has been much investigated. Still, norms are not natural laws, and there are many examples where norms and effects cannot be described in terms of simple causation. Mere recurrent patterns are not necessarily the result of norms and, equally, norms (as 'ought') do not necessarily result in behaviour. The different mechanisms, which in different ways explain why norms are followed or not, are socialization, social identity and rational choice. Sometimes, people learn social norms and internalize them; sometimes they are more exogenous, but might still be effective. This relationship might be labelled 'effectiveness of norms'.

Social practice influences legal practice. Generally, in civil law, law offers standard solutions that are optional. People are free to choose other solutions according to different normative practices and beliefs. In this way, normative change can easily be picked up by legal practice close to social practice. Major trends, which are stable over time, will eventually influence law through legislation or legal doctrine, but much of the plethora of different normative practices will just oscillate between the legal and social practices. In Swedish contract law, trade custom and similar practices are considered as law, which means that, when it is possible to lay down such a normative content, it is not necessary to codify it through legislation. Even in criminal law, there are examples of this relationship, although rule of law principles limit the existence of this relationship. Swedish criminal doctrine recognizes generally accepted social practices as a justification for freedom from responsibility under certain conditions. Physical sport, such as ice hockey or football, is one example. For precisely this reason, it is not likely that prosecutors would bring to court an action implying assault for an injury sustained in these sports. Of importance here is that, besides the fact that, for example, circumcision is a practice that is governed by cultural and religious norms (social norms), it is also a widely adopted social practice. I label this relationship 'socio-legal induction'.

Having ended this second turn around the matrix, there are still four more relationships remaining, going diagonally across the matrix. Again starting in the legal field and law, there is one relationship left with social practice. This is the influence that law has on social practice (as compared to social norms). In criminal law, it is possible to refer to general prevention or deterrence. The underlying idea is that people treat law as a normative phenomenon, which can thus have direct effects on behaviour. The content of law becomes known through mass media, for example, and this knowledge about the normative content exercises an influence on future behaviour. This relationship is also commented on in other areas of law. But normative discussions about the (ideological) content of law might also influence behaviour directly. From a policymaker's perspective, the existence of this relationship would be of great value, but there are few examples that confirm it. It is sometimes argued that prohibiting violence against children in Sweden during the 1960s had this effect to some extent. I label this relationship 'general prevention'. (See also Cotterrell, 1992: 142).

The opposite relationship between law and social practice concerns whether and how social practices are normative in relation to law. From a legal dogmatic view, this is not the case. Still, it cannot be ruled out that common practices do have an impact on law-making or legal doctrine. The Supreme Court in Sweden ruled on three cases concerning the value of pets. The issue was that the veterinary costs for a cat injured by a dog exceeded what was considered reasonable. Pets are 'things' in a legal sense, and the principle is that an object cannot be repaired at a cost exceeding the cost of replacing the object. No exceptions applied, but the court still granted the veterinary costs. Over the last decades, a shift has taken place in Sweden concerning the standing of pets. In several television series about veterinary surgeons, we have seen people treating pets like humans, and sparing no medical efforts. Allowing for a shift in these cases is, of course, in line with these practices and, in that sense, justice is done. The Swedish Supreme Court has also ruled on the case of circumcision (see the previous relationship), which means that law itself is sensitive to social practice. I label this relationship 'socio-legal influence'.

There are also two relationships between social norms and legal practice. The case that social norms can influence legal decision-making is not a valid influence according to legal dogmatics. Ideally, a case is decided through the application of law to the facts presented in a particular case. Problematic issues mostly concern how to value evidence. The norms against which the case is tried are legal norms, and the axiom '*jura novit curia*' tells us that the content of law is known by the judge. But, depending on the ambition to administer 'justice', other normative standpoints can, however, be taken into consideration. There might, of course, be many reasons to refer to non-legal norms, such as moral principles or social norms in a particular case. A pure application of the letter of the law is not always possible, and might lead to unjust decisions. Doing justice might involve some kind of factual or normative mitigation. With reference to the particular circumstances in the case, such mitigation might be done without reference to non-legal sources. This susceptibility is most easily detectable in controversial cases, where mass media exert pressure on the court. Mass media might serve as the platform where such normative standpoints are brought out in public, but with the purpose of influencing the court. This relationship can also be labelled socio-legal influence, but I will distinguish it from the previous one by labelling it 'normative influence'.

The last relationship covers the normative discourses that might arise in the social field as a result of concrete cases. Through various channels and in various social contexts, it is reasonable to assume that legal decisions result in various discourses about the normative status of certain issues. In Sweden, mass media often refer to non-controversial court decisions in small announcements. These cases belong to some kind of steady flow of normative reminders, which are always stimulating the social system. These days, new social media provide interesting channels with evidence of these discourses. The discourses then channel around questions of justice involving different normative standpoints. Court cases might also be chosen as examples in schools or other educational settings, but also more instrumentally by professional and industrial organizations. This relation is labelled 'adjudication as democratic practice' – see Resnick and Curtis (2011).

Concluding discussion

In the above discussions, the word 'influence' was often used to characterize the relationships between social and legal norms. However, this word denotes a power relationship. Conflict seems logical within normative systems and, not surprisingly, relationships between social and legal norms are often referred to in terms of conflict. Understanding law as autonomous and exercising power entails a conflicting view of other, non-legal norms 'interfering' with law. The coherence of law needs to be maintained, thus limiting flexibility in this sense. Law, in this capacity, can also dominate or suppress people or groups who, in different ways, hold social norms that are in conflict with law. Much, perhaps most, research has for various reasons taken this perspective – see Banakar in Chapter 2. It is, of course, true that much of the institutional design of state law is geared towards autonomy. Legal science (for example, through education) provides the legal profession with the ability to distinguish between legal and non-legal norms. This function is, of course, necessary in a state governed by law, where legitimate power is executed through law. However, law being autonomous does not mean that law is isolated; law needs to be normatively 'fuelled'. This last remark calls for a more functional perspective, to which the word 'interdependence' alludes.

From the introduction, it was argued that treating law as autonomous must be complemented with other perspectives on law. There are many arguments for law being a much more disintegrated system of norms today. There are also more systems that are normative, and law today seems to be best understood as partially autonomous and interdependent with other normative systems in different ways (for examples, see the concluding chapter of this book). Differing governance regimes are good examples of this. When the political system fulfils its legitimacy to a lesser degree, law cannot rely on legislation as the foremost normative source. Instead, law seems to be increasingly left with open-ended clauses, programs, procedural arrangements and similar quasi-laws that call for recourse to other normative sources (or greater autonomy). But it is not appropriate to consider such normative influences just as an 'invasion'; they should rather be considered as a functional normative negotiation; hence the word 'interdependence'. I therefore propose that the relations that exert influence properly should be understood in terms of a normative interdependence.[1]

But, as was argued earlier, the theoretical base for the platform is designed to cover both conflict as well as consensus perspectives. It is clear that some relationships cannot easily be understood as examples of conflict. The two relationships going 'downwards' from the norms fields to the practice fields are both about power. Legal as well as social norms are supposed to exert influence on practice. But the relationships between social and legal norms in the upper fields cannot be treated as power relationships in the same way. These latter relationships are rather about normative competition, or normative interdependence. It is also clear from empirical research that the influence that law has directly on social practice is quite weak. It is even argued that law

1 In theory, it would be possible to provide the platform with two different layers, one showing conflict relationships, another showing consensus relationships. This would, however, be to take the analysis too far and also risk the intended simplicity of the platform.

is powerless in such indirect relationships. One possible reason is that several of the relationships are mediated through different systems, while others are mediated through the public sphere. For example, legal norms do not influence social norms through their system properties. Such relationships could instead be realized discursively in a Habermasian sense.

It is also clear that a certain set of relationships covers the process that can be labelled the 'production of law', and another set of relationships covers the process labelled the 'application of law'. But the platform also allows for – at least theoretically – a description of the corresponding production and application of social norms. These processes seem, however, less adequately phrased in such terms, and instead the label of 'interdependence' fits better.

Another aspect that needs to be commented on is the significance of each of the 12 relationships. Obviously, some of the relationships described above seem more significant than others at first sight. But it is also possible to suppose that this difference might be a result of a scientific focus on some of these relationships. For very good reasons, research has been carried out within Sociology of Law that reveals how law relies on, and reproduces, gender differences, ethnic differences or class differences (see Schömer in Chapter 15 of this book). But this kind of research might also point to the fact that law is dependent on other normative systems. More research on some of the less significant relationships might therefore shed light on how law achieves its normative content. One problem is, of course, methodological. For instance, it is sometimes problematic to describe scientifically how legal decisions are influenced by social norms. The reason is that legal decision-making puts much effort into accounting for the decision in a normatively rational way. It might be possible to conclude statistically that a certain group is treated differently from others, for instance, but it is often problematic in a single case to detect how this is done. One problem is that the argumentation presented in, for example, the verdict might not reflect the way in which the decision actually came about (Andersson, 2012). The strength of the platform is that it allows for a structured review of possible normative interdependencies between social and legal norms.

A note has to be made regarding different subject matters. The previous account of relationships between social and legal norms was done *prima facie*. But, as indicated, different cases result in different normative set-ups in terms of the relationship between social and legal norms. Some relationships seem more typical in civil law cases, and others in criminal law. One explanation is that the production of law varies between criminal law, civil law and public law, and that the application of law correspondingly varies between these areas. This follows from the fact that law has developed as a result of differing societal needs during differing societal conditions (Habermas, 1996). We can even say that law has developed differing paradigms, operating with differing rationalities. Accordingly, different areas of law develop different relationships with, for example, social norms. Civil society's norms are more directly connected to law in civil law matters, while politics mediate society's norms in welfare law. Again, it would be possible to enhance the platform according to this aspect, but that would make it inaccessible.[2]

Until now, I have explored the possible relationships between social and legal norms. I will end by saying something about the use of this kind of platform. Elsewhere, the argument has been made for a norms perspective in sociology of law (Hydén, 2011). Such ambitions eventually have to be tested in terms of their compatibility and practical usefulness. Using norms as an important concept in sociology of law is not new, and there exist a number of studies following this line of inquiry. Considering just some examples, these can easily fit under the general perspective as well as under the platform. There is thus a considerable amount of research in this field that can be further analysed.

There is an interest in the interplay between social and legal norms. Some studies take an interest in how social and legal norms build up institutions (West, 1997; Mccgraw and Scholz, 1988). For a comparison between norms and institutions, see Susanna Johansson's contribution in Chapter 7. There are also examples in criminology, where the role of social norms is explored within the concept of social control (Mellish and Collis-Squires, 1994; Heckathorn, 1994). Todorova (2000) investigates the capacity of law to achieve 'moral changes' in the social field. Many studies use norms as a measure of the effectiveness of law – for example, in welfare law (Hyman, 2000), corporate law (Sarra and Nakahigashi, 2002) or legal culture in general (Galligan, 2003). Dorothy Thornton (2009) asks why social norms apply for large business firms, but not for small, in environmental regulatory settings. There are studies that focus on the dependency that law has on reciprocity norms for welfare regimes (Mau, 2004) and the importance of social norms for the possibility of the deterrent capacity of law (Wenzel, 2004).

There is always a need for some kind of heuristic that can guide and clarify research questions when conducting empirical research. Research that starts with interesting cases needs some kind of structured thinking, which provides an understanding of the problem at stake. In that sense, there are 12 possible questions that can be put to the case in question. When measuring social and legal norms, the platform provides a heuristic tool in the process of transforming (operationalizing) theories into measurable entities. The main advantage of the platform is the ability to supply a kind of language and to produce questions relevant to the problem or empirical material.

Quite a number of existing concepts within law and society studies can be related to and understood in terms of norms. The autonomy of law can be understood as the ability of law to distinguish between social and legal norms. Civil disobedience can mean upholding social norms in spite of law and its sanctions. Legal culture can be interpreted as the form and degree of how law relates to social norms.

2 A similar note has to be made regarding different legal cultures. Despite the ambition to use a standard definition of law, law's institutions, professions and procedures vary between different legal cultures and over time. Institutions such as jurors, lay judges and justices of the peace may be of importance for the normative set-up. The same is true for legal-administrative bodies of different kinds.

The same reasoning can be used regarding discretion in legal decision-making, legal education, the functions of law, law in everyday life, honour, informal law, the legitimacy of law, penetration of law, popular culture and law, reflexive and autopoietic law, social change and law, just to give some examples.

References

Anderson, B. 2012. 'Context of discovery, context of decision and context of justification in the law'. *IVR encyclopedie*, Online. Retrieved 13 October 2012. http://ivrenc.info/index.php?title=Context_of_Discovery,_Context_of_Decision_and_Context_of_Justification_in_the_Law.

Baier, M. 2003. *Norm och rättsregel: en undersökning av tunnelbygget genom Hallandsåsen*. Diss. Lund: Lunds universitet.

Baier, M. 2009. 'Law and participation', *Comparative sociology* 8(4), 580–601.

Banakar, R. 1998. 'The identity crisis of a "stepchild". Reflections on the paradigmatic deficiencies of sociology of law', *Retfaerd. Nordic journal of law and justice* 21(81), 3–21.

Bicchieri, C. and Muldoon, R. 2011. 'Social Norms', *The Stanford Encyclopedia of Philosophy*. http://plato.stanford.edu/archives/spr2011/entries/social-norms.

Coleman, J.S. 1990. *Foundations of social theory*. Cambridge, Mass.: Harvard University Press.

Cotterrell, R. 1989. 'Why must legal ideas be interpreted sociologically?', *Journal of Law and Society* 25(2), 171–92.

Cotterrell, R. 1992. *The sociology of law: an introduction*. 2. rev. ed. London: Butterworth.

Deflem, M. 2008. *Sociology of law: visions of a scholarly tradition*. Cambridge: Cambridge University Press.

Elster, J. 1989. *The cement of society: a study of social order*. Cambridge: Cambridge University Press.

Eurofound. Soft law entry. Retrieved at www.eurofound.europa.eu/areas/industrialrelations/dictionary/definitions/softlaw.htm.

Galligan, D.J. 2003. 'Legal failure: Law and social norms in post-communist Europe', in *Law and Informal Practices: The Post-Communist Experience*, edited by Denis J. Galligan and Marina Kurkchiyan. Oxford University Press.

Gibbs, J. 1965. 'Norms: the problem of definition and classification', *American Journal of Sociology* 70(5), 586–594.

Habermas, J. 1996. 'Paradigms of Law', *Cardozo Law Review* 17(4–5), 771–85.

Heckathorn, D.D. 1994. 'Collective sanctions and compliance norms: A formal theory of group-mediated social control', in *Contemporary Criminological Theory*, edited by Cullen, F.T. and Burton, V.S. Aldershot: Dartmouth.

Hydén, H. 2011. 'Nine reasons for norms', in *Understanding Law in Society. Developments in Socio-legal Studies*, edited by Knut Papendorf, Stefan Machura and Kristian Andenaes. Hamburg: LIT Verlag.

Hyman, D.A. 2001. 'Health care fraud and abuse: Market change, social norms, and the trust "reposed in the workmen"', *Journal of Legal Studies* 30(2), 531–67.

Korsgaard, C.M. 1992. *The Sources of Normativity.* The Tanner Lectures on Human Values Delivered at Clare Hall, Cambridge University, 16 and 17 November 1992.

Mathiesen, T. 1989. 'Is it all that bad to be a stepchild? Comments on the state of sociology of law', *Retfaerd. Nordic journal of law and justice* 21(83), 67–76.

Mau, S. 2004. 'Welfare regimes and the norms of social exchange', *Current Sociology* 52(1), 53–74.

Mccgraw, K. and Scholz, J. 1988. 'Norms, social commitment and citizens' adaptation to new laws', in *Lawyers in Psychology and Psychologists on Law*, edited by van Koppen, P.J. et al. Lisse: Swets & Zeitlinger.

Mellish, M. and Collis-Squires, N. 1994. 'Legal and social norms in discipline and dismissal', in *Social Control: Aspects of Non-State Justice*, edited by Henry Stuart. Aldershot: Dartmouth.

Nelken, D. 1998. 'Blinding insights? The limits of a reflexive sociology of law', *Journal of Law and Society* 25(2), 407–26.

Opp, K.-D. 1982, 'The evolutionary emergence of norms', *British Journal of Social Psychology* 21(2), 139–49.

Resnik, J. and Curtis, D.E. 2011. *Representing justice: invention, controversy, and rights in city-states and democratic courtrooms*. New Haven: Yale University Press.

Sarra, J. and Nakahigashi, M. 2002. 'Balancing social and corporate culture in the global economy: The evolution of Japanese corporate structure and norms', *Law & Policy*, 24(4), 299–354.

Shone, M.A. 1995. 'Social norms, judicial decision-making and low income status in Canada', *1995 Annual Meeting of the ISA Research Committee on Sociology of Law 'Legal Culture: Encounters and Transformations'*, section meetings supplement 1, 1–4 August 1995, The University of Tokyo, Sanjo Conference Hall, Tokyo, Japan.

Stroll, A. 1987. 'Norms', *Dialectica* 41(1–2), 7–22.

Teubner, G. 1983. 'Substantive and reflexive elements in modern law', *Law and Society Review* 17(2), 239–85.

Thornton, D. 2009. 'When Social Norms and Pressures are not Enough: Environmental Performance in the Trucking Industry', *Law and Society Review* 43(2), 405–436.

Todorova, V. 2000. 'Family law in Bulgaria: Legal norms and social norms', *International Journal of Law, Policy and the Family* 14(2), 148–81.

Wenzel, M. 2004. 'The social side of sanctions: Personal and social norms as moderators of deterrence', *Law and Human Behavior* 28(5), 547–67.

West, M.D. 1997. 'Legal rules and social norms in Japan's secret world of sumo', *Journal of Legal Studies* 26(1), 165–201.

Chapter 5
Parallel Norm Creating Processes

Karsten Åström

Introduction

Taking its starting point in the theoretical and empirical work in Sociology of Law, the aim of this chapter is to present and discuss the concept of 'parallel norm creating processes' (PNCP) in the light of theoretical developments on legal and social norms. The chapter restricts itself to dealing with normative processes concerning the implementation of administrative law, and empirical examples will primarily be taken from the field of social welfare. The chapter argues that using the concept of PNCP, with theoretical references to contemporary developments regarding the understanding of legal and social norms, can form a link between theory and empirical investigations of implementing regulations in the social field related to administrative law. It will also be concluded that the process of implementing legally defined norms in a milieu where strong social norms, in particular professional norms, compete with the legal ones is neither linear and successive, nor does it result in a homogeneous application of legally defined goals or aspirations.

Socio-legal research on the implementation of legal regulations in various fields has revealed considerable divergences between legal requirement (the 'ought') and the actual outcome of legal implementation (the 'is'). One aim is to break from an instrumental or top-down approach to studying legal implementation, to develop an understanding of the mixture of legal and social norms working side by side, not always coordinated, in the field of societal sectors regulated by administrative law. Another aim is to conduct empirical studies on the formation of normative practice in fields with strong influences from both legal norms and social norms of different kinds: family norms, professional norms and general social norms.

Ehrlich's (2002) important concept of 'living law' allows for a theoretical understanding of legal decision-making ruled by norms other than formal legal decision-making norms, such as ethnic or social. We do not want to get trapped in the so-called 'gap' problem, the gap between law in books and law in action. The work of Pound has been of great importance to identify the problem, and also to formulate a form of social engineering perspective pointing to the fact that legal norms are the result of political decision-making answering to the identification of conflicts to be solved by law. However, I agree with Nelken (1984) that the use of the concept of 'living law' rather than Pound's concept of 'law in action' opens up for a more sociological understanding of norms. 'Living law' was defined by Ehrlich as

> law which dominates life itself even though it has not been posited in legal propositions. The source of our knowledge of this law is, first, the modern legal document; secondly, direct observation of life, of commerce, of customs and usages, and of all associations, not only those that the law has recognized but also of those that it has overlooked and passed by, indeed even of those that it has disapproved. (Ehrlich, 2002: 493)

In principle, I agree with this definition, but we do face a problem researching implementation of legal interventions in social life if we want to separate legal norms from social norms. As pointed out by Nelken (1984), Ehrlich's concept of law is regarded rather as an outcome of social processes and social change than as a tool of intervention. This is a matter that I will come back to later in this chapter. Nevertheless, we do have to consider the relationship between legal and social norms to be able to conduct Sociology of Law research into the implementation of administrative law.

We also draw from writings on legal pluralist views on the character of law. As stated by Griffiths, and others, legal pluralism means the presence of more than one legal order in a social field (1986). Anthropological use of the concept of legal pluralism has, in most cases, dealt with either non-legal social orders or societies with more than one legal order – for instance, in a colonial situation with one system of customary law and one legal system enforced from the outside (see Malinowski, 1926; Merry, 1988). Later, Griffiths has presented a pluralist theory of legislation by schematically mapping out variables in a way that they indicate relationships between independent variables and how they influence the individual's behavioural choice (Griffiths, 1995: 224).

Legal pluralism has, on the one hand, gained a lot of support and has often been referred to in socio-legal studies. The concept has, on the other hand, also been questioned, by, among others, Teubner (1997) and Tamanaha (1993, 1997 and 2000). As Teubner has claimed: 'legal pluralism is at the same time both: social norms and legal rules, law and society, formal and informal, rule-orientated and spontaneous. And the relations between the legal and the social in legal pluralism are highly ambiguous, almost paradoxical: separate but intertwined, autonomous but interdependent, closed but open' (Teubner, 1997: 120). In other words, the concept comprises several (and contradictory) elements, and there is a need to refine entities like social and legal norms in order to develop concepts that it is possible to systematize and operationalize in empirical studies.

Cotterrell has pointed to the possibility for a re-establishment and intensification of legal pluralism to grasp 'the complex interplay of different, relatively autonomous, regulatory systems whose interactions constitute legal order' (Cotterrell, 1995: 281). So, without rejecting legal pluralism as a useful concept, I shall in this chapter try to frame a complementary, or an alternative, way of combining the ambition to study the role of both legal and social norms in a process of implementing legally regulated social programs without being trapped in the Pound conception of comparing 'law in books' with 'law in action' under the belief that the two shall perfectly coincide.

Before elaborating on the concept of PNCP, we shall present a model for empirical research on legal implementation related to legal and social norms – namely, a model of legal regulation of social conflicts.

In order to understand the relationship between legal norms and social norms, we need a clear understanding of the very special characteristics of legal norms. Following Svensson (see Chapter 3 in this volume), law is singled out as separate from other societal norms through context-dependent accidental attributes. However, legal norms cannot be identified according to who is actually applying the norm, as it is an empirical question what norms are guiding a specific decision. We cannot take for granted that a court decision is based on a legal norm, or that a decision by a court is closer to what can be regarded as the legal norm than a decision made by, for instance, a local welfare service. To further confuse the normative situation, legal norms often refer to social norms complementing legal ones. This is the case with legal norms such as '*bonus pater familias*' in family law, 'sound business practice' in contract law, and 'reasonable standard of living' or 'the best interest of the child' in welfare law. Here, the legal norm points out a social norm to guide the application of the law in courts and other governmental agencies. This also complicates the possibilities of comparing 'law in books' with 'law in action', or identifying the gap between the legal formal system and its factual implementation, or (in terms of Baier and Svensson in this volume) the relation between law and legal practice. One remedy could be to study legal and social norms in relation to the distinction between the 'ought' and the 'is'. As legal norms are related to legal practice, on the one hand, social norms relate to social practice on the other. However, empirical research on, for instance, the implementation of welfare law has clearly shown that we cannot identify a relationship between law and legal practice without also considering social norms and social practices. On an abstract theoretical level, this is basic socio-legal knowledge, but we still need theoretical concepts and models to investigate these relationships in specific situations and contexts.

Legal regulation of social conflicts

One way to understand, and explore, the gap between 'law in books' and 'law in action' is to relate norms to the process, starting with the identification of conflicts initiating law-making and the social norms that already exist in relation to this conflict or these conflicts. The model of legal regulation[1] presented below

1 This model was first elaborated by Hydén, H., Stridbeck, U., and Åström, K. in the early 1980s and published 1984; and, in a later edition, Hydén, H., Stridbeck, U.,

does not pretend to explain social reality, but to form a base for researching and understanding legal norms as political instruments for social change. The model is also supposed to structure the interplay between legal and social norms, as well as between legal practice and social practice, although the model primarily takes its starting point in legal regulation.

The first step of analysis is therefore to empirically, and theoretically, produce knowledge about underlying conflicts of interest and conflicts of norms. The second step is to make out how politics grasp the conflict, balancing different interests and norms, and formulate policy strategies, primarily in the form of legislation. Of special interest is whether (most often) the Parliament has a firm understanding of the conflict and if there is a true interest in actually solving the conflict and taking existing social norms into consideration.

The third step is to analyse how a political policy is transformed into a legal form to be analysed in terms of different types of legal norms. Legal norms can mainly be divided into three different types of norms: material norms indicating an imperative; procedural norms; and norms that constitute power to apply and implement the law. In turn, material norms can either directly impose a specific action, or define a goal or object to strive towards. These two types of material norms indicate two different forms or rationalities of decision-making (that is, norm rationality and goal rationality). Norm rationality corresponds to traditional legal decision-making, characterized by deduction from a legal norm. Goal rationality requires knowledge of the means to make a decision that promotes the fulfilment of the legally defined goal.[2] Law built up of norms indicating goals (as in so-called 'frame laws') gives more room for competing or supporting social norms in the process of implementation or application of the law.

To give significance to law in social life, agencies for application of the law are needed. Analysing how these are organized, professional qualifications and prospects constitutes the fourth step of analysis.

The sixth step is to empirically survey the consequences of the legal implementation and, finally, the seventh step must relate these consequences to whether the conflict of interests or norms has been affected or not. Since legal implementation does not exist in a societal vacuum, there is also the fifth step that must be taken into consideration – namely, the extent to which external factors or mechanisms influence the process.

Åström, K. (2008). Later, the model has been used in a number of doctoral dissertations, for example, Wickenberg, P. (1999); Svensson, L. (2006); Friberg, S. (2006); Svensson, M. (2008); Leo (2010).

2 Compare the Weberian concepts of '*Zweckrationalität*' and '*Wertrationalität*' (Weber, 1968). Teubner early on elaborated the concepts of formal, substantive and reflexive law. As formal law could be characterized by a rule-oriented type of decision-making, substantive and reflexive law followed a rationality related to the purpose behind the law and a rationality orientated to the procedure and its institutional structures respectively (Teubner, 1983).

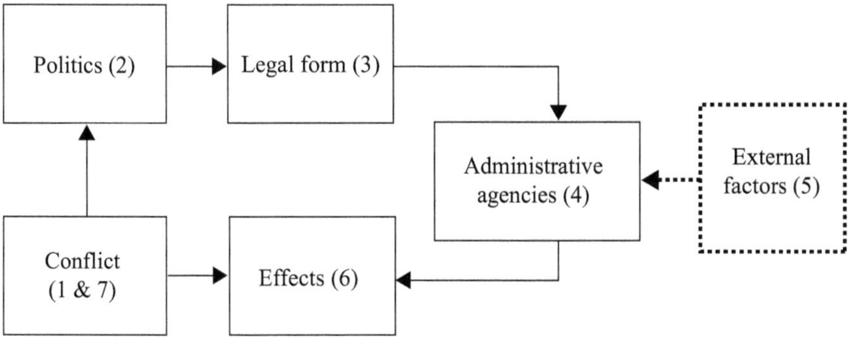

Figure 5.1 An Analysis Model of Legal Regulation – modified from Åström, 1988

Legal application of welfare law focusing on local municipalities

We shall now turn to some research findings concerning welfare legislation and its implementation. Since the early 1980s, there have been major changes in legislation, regulating different forms of means-tested welfare benefits, geriatric care, child care and care for people addicted to the use of alcohol and drugs. Local municipalities primarily apply these laws, although most decisions can be appealed to administrative courts. Since the mid-1980s, research has been conducted, with the model of legal regulations presented above as a starting point (Åström, 1988, 2002, 2005 and 2010; Åström and Bengtsson, 2005). What is common to all of these research findings is that they so clearly demonstrate that legal and social norms are mixed and cannot easily be classified in the four categories of law, legal practice, social norms and social practice. One might have imagined either that there should have been a successive normative process towards more precise legal norms, or that courts ultimately develop a more precise norm generated by social practice, but that is not the case.

The Swedish Social Services Act (SFS 2001:453)[3] constitutes a clear example of the framework legislation technique. At the same time, it must be stressed that this law also incorporates many prominent features that are characteristic of the classic positivistic law of a bourgeois rule of law state. Even if the material legal norms are vague and predominantly formulated as goals rather than actual delineations, the procedural structure has been strengthened considerably in relation to previous social laws in force. General administrative law principles (such as case-handling routines, documentation and formal requirements) have

3 The Social Services Act was first passed in 1980 (SFS 1980: 620) and revised 2001. The revision includes some degree of less-open material norms, although the essence of the legislation is still the same. These changes have no direct or significant influence on the empirical findings in relation to the analysis in this chapter.

been clarified, and the right of appeal through administrative procedures has been widened to cover a more extensive range of decisions than was previously the case. The integrity and position of the individual with regard to public authority has a stronger legal foundation than it had before (Åström, 2000).

The law is a goal-oriented framework law, meaning that the law contains norms stating general objectives. On the other hand, the law also contains norms in a more traditional sense, with ultimate facts and legal consequences. This means that the possibilities for social norms to influence legal decision-making are built into the law. In the case of a goal-oriented material norm, factors outside the law are supposed to form the base of the decision. Legislation does not give us an ultimate normative imperative. Rather, facts as theoretical and professional knowledge of social work, social policy on the municipal level, and practical experience in the field must necessarily be used in legal decision-making. According to the law, every single decision should be based on circumstances specific to the particular case.

The first study to be referred to was conducted in four municipalities located in different parts of Sweden (Åström, 1988). Although they are not statistically representative of the 284 municipalities (at that time), they are claimed to represent four typical types of municipalities. They were chosen in the light of two variables (namely, political representation and financial situation), so there is one socialist-governed poor municipality and one rich, and one poor bourgeois and one rich bourgeois municipality. To these four has been added one sub-district in Stockholm, to cover the most urban part of Sweden. All records from the welfare boards, and a selection of individual cases decided by the board, have been investigated, as well as a sample of cases delegated to social workers. A total of 500 individual cases are included in the study, and all politicians on the boards and about three-quarters of the employed social workers have individually answered questionnaires. A sub-sample of politicians and social workers has been interviewed orally. In addition, the study also includes documents from the National Board for Health and Welfare and the county administrative boards. Appealed cases have been followed up by studies of court decisions and files. The way in which social conflicts have been dealt with is based on studies of governmental and parliamentary preparatory documents in the legislative process.

Following the model of legal regulation presented above, the *first step* was to analyse conflicts behind the law. Social conflicts are basically, to put it simply, structural conflicts between classes or groups of individuals competing for limited resources. Conflicts could also be between individuals in sub-groups, such as the family. In the *second step*, we can, from parliamentary documents (especially Government Bill 1979/80:1) conclude that there is a clear ambition to promote welfare, both as supplementary benefits and as social services and treatments. The Swedish Parliament identified both structural and individual conflicts, and the bill for new legislation contained legal norms on both levels of conflict. However, the Parliament primarily considered social problems as matters concerning the individual, and therefore suggested legislation based on the relation between the individual and the municipal social welfare agency. Most forms of welfare benefits and services are regarded as individual social rights or societal obligations in relation to individuals (Åström, 1988 and 2005; Government Bill 1979/80:1; Government Bill, 2000/01:80). It must also be regarded as a sign of political realism that fundamental conflicts of interest related to the distribution of wealth and income cannot be solved in such a piece of welfare legislation.[4]

Moving to the *third step*, we shall consider how the Social Services Act is constructed. As indicated by the Parliament, the law regulates welfare on two levels: a structural level, and an individual level. The structural level does not solve basic conflicts, but includes material norms defining goals on a general level (that is, goals that the municipal welfare agencies shall endeavour to fulfil). These rules do not involve individuals, but groups of individuals, such as young people, elderly people, handicapped people and drug and alcohol addicts, and these norms are open in relation to what actions should be undertaken. Neither do these rules indicate how to give priority to one group in relation to another or the extent to which resources should be invested (see also Åström, 2004).

Among the material individual norms, there are both goal-orientated norms and more traditional norms that, in this case, state prerequisites defining a specific right to economic or social benefits. These prerequisites are vague – for instance, stating that you are entitled to a benefit that shall provide you with a 'reasonable standard of living'. This character of the material norms makes the procedural norms (and the norms that constitute power to different agents) extremely important. The material norms are the same, but the decision-maker could be a politician in the local welfare boards, who has the main responsibility to apply the law both on the structural level and on the individual level, a professional social worker, or a judge in the administrative courts. The material norms do not really solve the underlying conflicts, but rather pass them on to be solved in the municipal practice. The normative legal construct leaves considerable room (both in the municipalities and in the courts) for pluralist practices or, in the scope of this chapter, parallel norm-creating processes or possibilities.

Concerning the *fourth step*, we have already pointed to the fact that different actors (such as elected representatives (laymen), professional social workers and judges) apply the very same legal norms. Municipal welfare boards have the main mandate to implement the legislation. Members of the welfare boards are all politically elected, and so have neither legal nor social education. However, in practice, almost all decisions, at least in individual cases, are made by professional social workers by delegation from the political committee. In terms of institutional contexts, courts differ dramatically from local municipalities. The decision-making power in municipalities lies in the hands of the politically elected laymen in the first instance, and is almost always delegated to professional social workers. Although the legal norms are the same, the contextual conditions are substantially

---

4 The matter of what forces promoted the development of Swedish welfare legislation is considered in Svensson, Urinboyev and Åström (2012). It is claimed that welfare was a means for political stability in the case of Sweden.

different, not only between laymen and social professionals but also in relation to legally educated judges.

When questioned about what type of knowledge or skill is the most important in order to apply the legal norms, 16 per cent of the politicians stated that knowledge of the legal norms is of great importance, in comparison with 22 per cent of the professional social workers. Only about half of both groups declare that they often use the wordings of the Act, and that the more important sources behind their legal application are guidelines from the National Board of Health and Welfare, and most often internal guidelines produced in the local municipality itself. These guidelines are, of course, based in law and offer interpretative assistance, but are not established in any hierarchical or successive order and leave the way open for parallel norm formations. From questionnaires and interviews with board members and professionals in the municipalities, it follows that legal decision-making does not primarily follow a 'norm rational' logic but rather a 'goal rational' logic. In other words, decisions are not being argued by deduction from legal norms but from political or professional assessments based on material norms stating parliamentary defined goals. Without absolute knowledge about causes of, and remedies for, social problems, there is obviously considerable scope for different or parallel normative developments.

What we further detected was that normative processes in courts are substantially divergent from practices established in municipal social services. We also found significant differences between practices in different municipalities. Further, we could see deviating normative processes within the National Board of Health and Welfare (which is tasked with giving advice and guidance to harmonize legal application), the different municipalities and administrative courts.

It was the study carried out during the mid-1980s that led to formulating the concept of PNCP (Åström, 1988). One could say that the concept was developed from empirical findings, following from investigations of the six steps illustrating how conflicts become politicized, dressed in a legal form and implemented in different state and municipal bureaucracies, resulting in changes influencing the original conflict, but also influenced by external factors. Later research, not only in the field of welfare regulation, has confirmed that implementation of administrative law does not produce homogeneous and successive normativity, but various parallel norm formations, where a clear separation between social and legal norms can seldom be identified (Åström, 2002, 2005 and 2010; Åström and Bröchner, 2006 and 2007; Åström and Carlsson, 2005; Leo, 2010). Thus far, we have discussed these phenomena on a local municipal level. In the next section, we shall turn to the level of local administrative courts.

Legal application of welfare law focusing on administrative courts

The Swedish Social Services Act also includes individual rights to domestic services (among other social services) – that is, household help or special accommodation for service and care for elderly people. If the local welfare board rejects an application, the decision can be appealed to the county administrative court. This example of legal practice is based on an empirical study (Åström and Werner, 2002) including cases where the applicant was 65 years old or older. The overall aim of the study was to find out to what extent, by whom, in what cases (and with what result) the possibility to appeal a decision is being used, and to identify differences in the application of the law between one municipality and another, and between municipalities and the district administrative courts. The empirical material consisted of a sample of 500 judgments from all county courts in Sweden. The study was a comprehensive investigation of judgments during a six-month period (1 September 2001 to 28 February 2002). Studies of court documents were complemented with telephone interviews with 200 applicants. The decisions, and motivations, of the court cases were compared with the original decision made by the local welfare boards in the municipalities.

In this chapter, we shall focus on one sub-theme of this study – namely, on differences in legal application between municipal welfare boards and the courts. First, it shall be pointed out that, in qualitative terms, a limited number of cases actually reach the courts. Secondly, and this is the main object of this chapter, differences in the way that municipal boards and courts express themselves (in terms of motivating the decisions) shall be analysed. The aim of this analysis is to shed light on whether we can identify parallel norm-creating processes between municipal legal application and application by administrative courts.

Before presenting and analysing the empirical findings, we shall say some more words about the legal context. According to the Social Services Act, elderly people who need social services, in the form of help at home or as special accommodation for service and care, have the right to receive such help. There have been recent changes in the Social Services Act, and the studied cases are based on the legislation from 1980 and 1997. This, however, does not matter in the case of this study, because the law has not changed concerning elderly people and these forms of services. Law is constructed in terms of legal rights. If the applicant has a need, and this need cannot be fulfilled in other ways, he or she has a right to receive the service. These services are not free of charge; they have to be paid for according to a municipally decided schedule of rates, differentiated in relation to income. There are also goals formulated in the law, stating the purposes behind these services:

> The social welfare committee shall endeavour to ensure that older people are enabled to live independently, in secure conditions and with respect shown for their self-determination and privacy. The social welfare committee shall endeavour to ensure that older people obtain good housing and shall provide support and assistance in the home and other readily available services for those in need of the same.

We shall now turn to the application and functioning of the law. To be able to relate the appealed cases to the total number of cases decided at the municipal level, the number of applications in all Swedish municipalities in October 2002 was recorded as follows: 135,120 applications for home services and 61,614 applications for special accommodation for elderly people were filed and registered. The percentage of rejection was rather low. Only 1 per cent of all applications for home services were rejected, and the corresponding percentage for special accommodation was 17 per cent. One explanation as to why so few cases of home services were rejected by the municipalities is that legal decision-making in such cases is often very informal, and that municipal civil servants often do not live up to basic legal procedural rules (Åström, 1998). Frequently, formal decisions of refusal are not made. This is an example of the fact that not only are material norms subject to parallel norm-creating processes, but also procedural norms are developed in parallel tracks.

Of the rejected home services applications and the special accommodation cases, 5 per cent and 10 per cent respectively were appealed to the county courts, and these are the cases that we shall take a closer look at. We shall only raise two or three specific questions in this discussion. Having read the courts' judgments with special reference to the reasoning in support of the judgments, some conclusions can be drawn on the differences between the way that municipal officials, on the one hand, and judges, on the other, come to their conclusions and final decisions.

In the cases concerning special accommodation for elderly people, the most commonly stated reason for the rejection of an application was that the need could be fulfilled in another way by services in the applicant's home. Even if the applicant did not have the ultimate right to choose one form of service ahead of another, the welfare board could choose the most appropriate form of service corresponding to the needs of the applicant. The law actually states very clearly that there are two alternative forms of social services for the elderly, and the applicant may choose which one to apply for. In the decisions made by the municipalities in cases concerning special housing for the elderly, we often found expressions such as 'it has not been made obvious that the needs could not be fulfilled with services in the applicants home' or 'there are no medical indications making special accommodation necessary'. These formulations can be seen as examples of a misunderstood legal interpretation, or interferences by norms other than legal. The Social Services Act does not give support for a supplementary status for special accommodation in relation to help in the home. There is no legally accepted ground to reject an application for special accommodation based on the argument that the needs could be fulfilled with assistance in the home. It is obvious that the municipalities prefer giving help in the home rather than in special accommodation, and one explanation is that this is functional in economic terms. Building special houses to provide accommodation with special services is very expensive, and so is the running and administration of these institutions. In other words, decisions are made from a functional point of view in terms of local economical rationality according to municipally produced norms.

Some of these cases were, on appeal, reversed by the administrative court, but in many cases the court interprets and uses the law in the same way as the welfare boards. There are even cases where the court justifies a rejection by saying that the applicant has not shown that she needs permanent care day and night. The law does not state this need for care 24 hours a day, neither do the preparatory documents to the Act give support for this interpretation, and there are no precedents either. The 24-hour norm is developed on a municipal level, as a condition for the right to special housing. This is a municipally formulated norm and it could be regarded as a form of social norm. It does not follow from the legal norm; rather, it is in clear conflict with it. This is an example of a situation where municipal norm formation also influences the application of the norm in the administrative courts.

It is stated in the law that the welfare board shall, with service in the applicant's home, make it possible for elderly people to continue living in their own homes. This norm is often used by welfare boards to justify the rejection of applications for special accommodation. A norm in favour of the applicant is being used as a restriction of their possibilities to make a choice on their own or having their needs fulfilled. Also in this respect, the courts follow the legal application of the municipalities in more than half of the cases. Thus far, we can conclude that, even if the administrative courts are independent of the municipalities in terms of formulating their own motives behind the decisions, they do not always present a more elaborate discussion on, for instance, how to interpret the legally expressed concept of need, or how the right of services in the home and the right of special accommodation for service and care are to be related to each other. The county courts very often make use of the same simplified notion of 'need' as the municipalities do. The actual result is the same, and it must be concluded that the normative outcome of court decisions is often the same as that of the municipalities.

However, there are also clear differences between the legal application in municipalities and in the courts. In almost one third of the cases appealed to the administrative courts, the welfare board rejected the application with the justification that, although the need was not disputed, it had to be rejected due to the fact that, for the time being, the municipality did not have the resources to offer special accommodation for service and care. The administrative courts clearly stated that there was no support, in law, for lack of resources to be a legal ground for rejection. With this motivation, the county courts reversed almost all of the cases that had been appealed on this ground. This means that external factors influence legal application to a lesser extent than in the cases discussed above. There is a limit to the way in which external factors are being allowed to influence legal application in court.

One more empirical finding is relevant to the matter of factors influencing legal decision-making in this area. The legally defined criteria for the right to services for elderly people are social and psychological. It is legally undisputable that physical dysfunctions are only a secondary legal factor determining the right to services; social and psychological are the primary ones. Therefore, it is remarkable that social and psychological factors are, in practices, of minor importance in decision-making in the administrative courts. Only in one third of the cases in which the applicant has referred to such factors do the courts actually take this information into consideration when making the final judgment. From this we can conclude that there is a cognitive deficiency in courts. Judges are often not able, or willing, to take into account cognitive knowledge from another contextual field of knowledge and understanding. The legal framework clearly states that formal decision-making shall be based on social and psychological factors; these factors are supposed to rule the decision. Judges have not fulfilled legal requirements in this respect. Instead, judgments have been based on non-legally grounded criteria – that is, social norms, such as routines, municipal practice and economic rationality; in other words, social norms also play an important role in decision-making in the courts. It can be added that, in those cases where laymen have taken part, social and psychological factors have been taken into account to a greater extent.

One conclusion from this study of the appealed cases is that there is a limit where the administrative courts reject municipal decision-making grounded in, for instance, a lack of resources as a legally external factor influencing legal decisions. On the other hand, there are also shortcomings in the legal application of the courts. The use of indistinct legal material norms reveals imperfections in the way that administrative courts interpret and apply these vague material norms in individual cases. In terms of guiding legal decisions, it must be concluded that legally stated factors are often neglected. Municipalities, through elected representatives and professional social workers, are developing routines and practices that are shown to be significantly important motivating decisions, not only in the local welfare boards but also in the administrative courts.

Conclusions

From the analyses of the application of law in the field of social welfare, using the concept of parallel norm creating processes, the study reveals that legal application is not homogeneous or successive, but parallel in the sense that the outcome of legal decision-making is the result of the law deriving its content from implementation processes. Not even the courts produce a homogeneous practice. Processes involve norm conflicts between the different professions involved, and power relations between conflicting interests. The model of legal regulation is used in order to identify facts and mechanisms influencing the application or implementation of welfare legislation. With the help of this model, both legal norms and social norms can be put in context in terms of identified conflicts, politics, law-making, legal form and organization of the administration of legal implementation. Legal practice is to be found both in the administrative courts and in municipal welfare bureaucracies, and there is an interest in comparing legal application between courts and municipalities.

The application of norms is not strictly parallel, in the way that legal norms should be the base of legal practice and social norms the base of social practice. Parallel norm creating processes are interwoven in complicated patterns. To a certain extent, the legal norms stipulate that decisions should be based on social norms. However, legal norms also set the limit for social norms. Comparing the application of legal regulation between municipalities and courts, we have seen that administrative courts sometimes uphold legal norms and sometimes they do not. We have also seen that the bases for the normative content created in municipalities are not formal legal texts, preparatory work and precedential case law, but local politics developed in guidelines and professional norms.

Sociology of law studies of the application of administrative law cannot be regarded as a problem of 'law in action' being different from 'law in books'. To put it frankly, at least in relation to welfare law, there is no law in books. On the other hand, it is too vague to understand the situation in terms of a legal pluralism. The use of the concept of parallel norm creating processes, combined with a contextual understanding of legal regulation involving legal and social norms, is one way of overcoming a fundamental problem in sociology of law.

References

Åström, K. 1988. *Socialtjänstlagstiftningen i politik och förvaltning. En studie av parallella normbildningsprocesser*. Lund University Press.

Åström, K. 2000. 'Allmosor, skyldigheter och rättigheter i den sociala lagstiftningens historia', in Puide, A. ed. *Socialbidrag i forskning och praktik.* Centrum för utvärdering av socialt arbete. Gothia.

Åström, K. 2004. 'Prioriteringar i socialtjänsten: En analys av rättsliga förutsättningar', Research Report in Sociology of Law, Research Report 2004: 1. Lund.

Åström, K. and Bengtsson, H. 2005. 'Från politik till praktik', in Bengtsson, H. ed. *Politik, lag och praktik. Implementeringen av LSS-reformen.* 2u. Studentlitteratur.

Åström, K. 2005. 'Normbildning och beslutsfattande', in Bengtsson, H. ed. *Politik, lag och praktik. Implementeringen av LSS-reformen.* 2u. Studentlitteratur.

Åström, K. and Bröchner, J. 2007. 'Imitating Private Business in Public Procurement: Swedish "affärsmässighet"', *Journal of Public Procurement* 7(2) 213–27.

Åström, K. and Bröchner, J. 2006. 'Awarding Construction Contracts: Do Swedish Administrative Courts Support or Hinder Sustainability?', in CIB W92 Symposium on 'sustainability and value through construction procurement', Salford, UK, 26 November 2006.

Åström, K. and Carlsson, L. 2005. 'A Science of Norms and Decision-making – Public Procurement as a Tool towards Sustainable Development', in European Ways of Law: First European Socio-Legal Conference, Onati, Spain, 6–8 July 2005.

Åström, K. and Werner, C. 2002. *De äldre och besvärsrätten. Överklagade beslut om hemtjänst och särskilt boende.* Socialstyrelsen. http://www.socialstyrelsen.se/Lists/Artikelkatalog/Attachments/11132/2002-123-60_200212361.pdf.

Åström, K. 2010. 'Vad blev det av välfärdsstaten? Välfärdsrättens utveckling idag', in Lemann Kristensen, B. and Storgaard, A. (eds) *Nordisk rättssociologi. Status - aktuelle udfordringer - visioner*. Jurist- og Økonomforbundets Forlag.

Carlsson, L. and Åström, K. 2008. 'Court Decisions in Public Procurement: Delineating the Grey Zone', *Scandinavian Studies in Law*, 53 407–21.

Cotterrell, R. 1995. *Law's Community. Legal Theory in Sociological Perspective*. Clarendon Press.

Ehrlich, E. 2002. *Fundamental Principles of the Sociology of Law*. Transaction Publishers: London.

Friberg, S. 2006. *Normbildningsprocess genom brukarsamverkan*. Lund Studies in Sociology of Law 24.

Griffiths, J. 1986. 'What is Legal Pluralism?' *Journal of Legal Pluralism* 24, 1–55.

Grifffths, J. 1995. 'Legal Pluralism and the Theory of Legislation', in Petersen, H. and Zahle, H. (eds) *Legal Polycentricity: Consequences of Pluralism in Law*. Dartmouth.

Habermas, J. 1984. *The Theory of Communicative Action*. Vol. 1. Polity.

Habermas, J. 1987. *The Theory of Communicative Action*. Vol. 2. Polity.

Hydén, H., Stridbeck, U. and Åström, K. 2008 (first published 1984). *Rätten som administrativt instrument*. Sociology of Law Research Report 2008: 10, Lund.

Leo, U. 2010. *Rektorer bör och rektorer gör. En rättssociologisk studie om att identifiera, analysera och förstå professionella normer*. Diss. Lund Studies in Sociology of Law 34.

Malinowski, B. 1926. *Crime and Custom in Savage Society*. RKP.

Merry, S.E. 1988. 'Legal Pluralism', *Law and Society Review* Vol. 22.

Merry, S.E. 1992. 'Anthropology, Law, and Transitional Processes', 21 *Ann. Rev. Anthropology*.

Nelken, D. 1984. 'Law in action or living law? Back to the beginning in sociology of law', *Legal Studies*. Vol. 4, Issue 2.

Svensson, Lupita. 2006. *Häktad eller omedelbart omhändertagen? – en studie om akuta frihetsberövanden av unga lagöverträdare*. Diss. US-AB Print Center: Stockholm.

Svensson, M. 2008. *Sociala normer och regelefterlevnad. Trafiksäkerhetsfrågor ur ett rättssociologiskt perspektiv*. Lund Studies in Sociology of Law 28.

Svensson, M., Urinboyev, R. and Åström, K. 2012. Welfare as a Means for Political Stability: a Law and Society Analysis. *European journal of social security*. Vol. 14, No. 2.

Welfare as a means for political stability : a law and society analysis.

Tamanaha, B.Z. 1993. 'The Folly of the "Social Scientific" Concept of Legal Pluralism', *Journal of Law and Society*, Vol. 20. No. 2.

Tamanaha, B.Z. 2000. 'A Non-essentialist Version of Legal Pluralism', *Journal of Law and Society* Vol. 27. No. 2.

Tamanaha, B.Z. 1997. *Realistic Socio-Legal Theory. Pragmatism and a Social Theory of Law*. Clarendon Press.

Teubner, G. 1983. 'Substantive and Reflexive Elements in Modern Law', *Law and Society Review*, Vol. 17, No. 2.

Teubner, G. 1997. 'The Two Faces of Janus. Rethinking Legal Pluralism', in Tuori, K., Bankowski, Z. and Uusitali, P. (eds) *Law and Power: Critical and Socio-Legal Essays*. Deborah Charles Publications: Liverpool.

Weber, M. 1968. *Economy and Society. An Outline of Interpretative Sociology*. Vol. 1. New York.

Wickenberg, P. 1999. *Normstödjande strukturer. Miljötematiken börjar slå rot i skolan*. Lund Studies in Sociology of Law 5.

PART II
Norms in Perspective

Chapter 6
Norms about Norms: A Hartian Perspective

Karl Dahlstrand

Introduction

My purpose in this chapter is to make a contribution to what the legal philosopher H.L.A. Hart (1907–1992) has to say about providing a sociological understanding of law and to apply Hart's theory in relation to a specific area of law. The specific legal area consists of the compensation for violation of personal integrity that victims of crime can obtain from the Crime Victim Compensation and Support Authority in Sweden. The ambition in the following chapter is to relate Hart's theory to other theories that are usually of interest in sociology of law, in particular the relationship between legal and social norms in general, in order to stress the social and cultural basis of law (Cotterrell, 1992; Tuori, 2002), rather than to embellish Hart's theory as such.

For Hart, who is one of the most significant contemporary legal positivists with high relevance for socio-legal research, law is ultimately the outcome of institutional activity resulting from the individual and which law 'officials' recognize as legally valid (Galligan, 2007: 7; Friedrichs, 2006: 95). Hart's main contribution is that he stratifies legal rules into primary rules (mostly concerning orders and prohibitions, or rules of behaviour) and procedural secondary rules (specifying the criteria for legal validity and governing the use of the primary rules). The principal one of the secondary rules is labelled the 'rule of recognition' that determines which norms belong to (or do not belong to) a particular legal system. The recognition rule is therefore akin to a potent meta-norm, and its existence and authority is, for Hart, an open empirical issue about sociological facts regarding the social pressure among other things (Hart 1997: 94, 292). In this chapter, I will give some reflections about meta-norms and present Hart's key concepts.

Presentation of Hart's concepts

Hart, as a legal philosopher influenced by linguistic philosophy, works out a distinction between different rules and, in particular, pays regard to their social function. Perry (2006: 1171) has described Hart's view on rules in an interesting way:

> A rule is, according to Hart, a certain kind of complex social practice that consists of a general and regular pattern of behaviour among some group of

> persons, together with a widely shared attitude within the group that this pattern is a common standard of conduct to which all members of the group are required to conform.

The importance of the rule of recognition is evident, because it lays down the criteria for identifying the primary rules. In other words, the secondary rules have a procedural role. Secondary rules, including the rule of recognition, are not in themselves bound by authority, because they only make sense in relation to other rules. The primary rules of behaviour are social rules about a complex practice and the foundation of every legal system. To elucidate, Hart writes in the preface to *The Concept of Law*, first published in 1961, that 'the book may also be regarded as an essay in descriptive sociology' (Hart 1997: vi). This position or perspective can be seen in relation to his ambition to see norms as an issue of relationships among the internal and the external perspectives; what it means to follow a norm or a rule and the importance of different performative acts (Hart 1997: vi). Hart is doubtless under the influence of the contextualistic and anti-essentialistic tradition known as 'ordinary language philosophy' from Oxford, such as that put forward by J.L. Austin, G. Ryle, P.F. Strawson, P. Winch and Ludwig Wittgenstein, when he works out his combination of descriptive sociology and analytical jurisprudence (Lacey, 2004: 5). Judith Butler is probably the best-known developer of Austin's work and ordinary language philosophy in contemporary social science about how we use language to do things (Butler, 1997). Similar to Butler, Hart stresses the importance of the context, the social practice and 'the realities we use words to talk about' to sharpen our perception of the phenomena according to Austin (Hart, 1997: 14). 'Don't look for the meaning, ask for the use' and 'words are also deeds', two famous Wittgensteinian slogans, point out the important perspective of modern analytical jurisprudence, the tradition where Hart is one of the most influential writers (Cotterrell, 1989: 91). This also puts him in relation to a broader semantic and realistic tradition (Hart, 1983: 265–77; Lacey, 2004: 215–42; Stavropoulos, 2001: 59–98), which makes him still very powerful and inspiring.

Hart used the term 'rules' instead of 'norms' in his theory; but, since his theory has been called soft positivism because of his 'acknowledgement that the rule of recognition may incorporate as criteria of legal validity conformity with moral principles or substantive values' (Hart, 1997: 250), he includes more than formal rules in his theory to understand legal obligations. For Hart, law is about social rules, or rather about the social context of rules, as standards of behaviour, and, in contrast to some norms, they are expressed in language. Mostly, for Hart legal norm-governed behaviour is dependent on norm-guided behaviour, standards of conduct grounded in social practice (Shapiro, 2001: 154). Henrik Palmer Olsen has described the rule of recognition as a meta-rule, a rule about rules (Palmer Olsen, 2011: 184). In sociology of law, Hart's secondary rules have been described as 'norms for norms' (Baier and Svensson, 2009: 75). In jurisprudence, 'Hartian social rules' have been described as being 'clearly norms' (Perry, 2006: 1174), because they emanate from a complex social practice, form a certain pattern of general behaviour in a group, and there is a general demand for conformity to be insistent (Hart, 1997: 86–7; Perry, 2006: 1178). Deviations from the pattern, therefore, give rise to criticism related to the social pressure behind the rules, because they see them from an internal aspect, which involves some reflective critical attitude in relation to the present behaviour. Primary rules impose a duty and give rise to an obligation depending on some central conditions or characteristics of obligations, which Hart describes in the following way: (1) 'What is important is that the insistence on importance or *seriousness* of social pressure behind the rules is the primary factor determining whether they are thought of as giving rise to obligations'. (2a) 'The rules supported by this serious pressure are thought important because they are believed to be necessary to the maintenance of social life or some highly prized feature of it'. (2b) '[I]t is generally recognized that the conduct required by these rules may, while benefiting others, conflict with what the person who owns the duty may wish to do' (Hart, 1997: 87).

Thus, Hart connects the normativity of legal obligations to the social context and the practice: '[i]n this figure, which haunts much legal thought, the social pressure appears as a chain binding those who have obligations so that they are not free to do what they want' (Hart, 1997: 87). Hart's theory is close to the sociology of law description of the law, in that it sees law as a social practice, which revolves around the use and acceptance of social rules, whose existence is ultimately an empirical question (Hart, 1997: 292). The relevance of Hart, and his position described above, follows from his criticism of John Austin (1790–1859) and his description of causal connection between rules as based on command and behaviour, known as Austin's 'command theory'. For Hart, there is instead an action-language of interest, resting on normative rules and norms (Hart, 1997: 18–20). According to Hart, a legal act means that the action relates to a given norm, so Hart rejects Austin and his behaviourism and places the emphasis on the normative dimensions instead; that is, what it means to have an obligation (Hart, 1997: 50–61).

It is important to bear in mind that Hart is essentially a legal positivist, and that legal positivism is based on a desire to distinguish law from morality (or other normative systems), which leads to a paradox when Hart's sociological relevance is examined. Mauro Zamboni, for example, places Hart together with Kelsen as a representative of the 'autonomous model' of the relationship between politics and law, which 'produces' one distinctive feature, namely 'rigidity' of law (Zamboni, 2004: 30–54). The difference between Hart and Kelsen is somehow that Kelsen represents 'exclusive legal positivism', which stresses the separation thesis – that there is a conceptual separation between law and morality – and Hart represent the inclusive view on legal positivism, which stresses the social thesis – that the basic conditions of legal validity are derived from social facts (Zamboni, 2004: 28; Murphy, 2001: 379–80). For example, Colvin (1978: 197) writes that:

> [h]is treatment of rules of enforcement is only explicable as a reaction to the coercive theories of Austin and Kelsen, and against the background of his fear

> that sanctions may be supposed the standard motive for acting in accordance with legal rules. But Hart's correction risks distorting the image of law.

Some further reflections about meta-norms

There is a constant need for a better worked-out understanding of jurisprudential descriptions of valid law (for instance, the legal positivistic view) if sociology of law and jurisprudence are to learn from each other. In a society influenced by legal and cultural pluralism, this need is not only of theoretical interest. From a normative perspective on sociology of law, Hart is also interesting, as his theory highlights the importance of meta-norms in the determination of the law. Niklas Luhmann (2004: 125) relates to this meta-perspective about law when he describes the operative closure of the legal system:

> Even if the concept of sources of law is still used by lawyers, in legal theory it has long since been overtaken by instruments, which could be called the resolution of paradoxes (or unfolding of tautologies), with the tendency to externalize references. Following developments in logic and linguistics, this is the launch of a meta-level at which rules regulate the validity of rules. Hans Kelsen's "Grundnorm" (basic norm) offers a theory of this kind; Hart's "secondary rule of recognition" is another.

Luhmann's theory about the autopoietic character within law, by way of its reflexive, self-referential and self-regulatory dimensions, thus compares to Hart's concept of secondary rules. Luhmann writes a more or less potted version of Hart's theory regarding the operative closeness of the legal system:

> It is this point precisely that is the target of the concept of autopoiesis. What we are talking about here are the internally connected operations of the system, which could be called "practices of recognition", and even when the system externalizes reasons of validity such an externalization would still remain an internal operation of the system. (Luhmann, 2004: 130)

Luhmann takes further note of the circular motion of the second-order observation. In a similar way, Hart moves in circular movements when 'the officials' are likened to the rule of recognition, which provides the rules of adjudication, and the official's application of the rules, which is part of the rule of recognition in practice. Hart has also written about self-referentiality and paradoxes in law (Hart, 1983: 170–78; Teubner, 2006: 45). The way in which Hart uses his internal/external distinction has been criticized by key figures in both legal theory and socio-legal studies (Banakar, 2003: 6; Tamanaha, 1997: 153–70), in that it can be seen as a hermeneutic understanding of norms (Cotterrell, 1989: 101); in other words, for Hart, law is a 'self-regulating system rooted in social fact and convention' (Friedrichs, 2006: 95).

Legal self-descriptions from different perspectives

One interesting process, according to Hart, Teubner and Luhmann, is to understand when what Teubner calls 'socially diffuse law' – set by means of social norms and communication – becomes positive autopoietic law through pre-positivistic partially autonomous law (Teubner, 1993: 37). Here, Hart's idea of 'secondary rules' functions as something like a 'gatekeeper' for valid law (Teubner, 1993: 39–46). Given this description of these complex processes, we can try to empirically identify how social norms became legal norms and, finally, we can identify positive law as a central issue in sociology of law. In this respect, Hart points out both the legal autonomy and its dependence upon the context and its social function. Hart may be 'speculating about widely held attitudes to various kinds of rules' (Cotterrell, 1989: 95). Of course, there is no empirical evidence for Hart's arguments in his book, because it concerns legal theory, but there are many interesting and relevant topics within it that can be studied and analysed from a sociology of law perspective (MacCormick, 2007: 66). Sally Falk Moore (1978: 63), for example, has contributed a relevant perspective in her notion of different 'semi-autonomous social fields' in between law and social norms that are of interest. The semi-autonomous social field is defined by the procedural characteristic – generating rules and coercing or inducing compliance with them. Moore writes: 'This complex, the operation of the social field, is to a significant extent self-regulating, self-enforcing, and self-propelling within a certain legal, political, economic, and social environment' (Moore, 1973: 63).

In the light of Luhmann's ambition to create a really original theory of law in contrast to traditional legal positivism, including Hart, it is striking how Teubner, as one of the best-known developers of Luhmann's theory, relates to Hart in order to develop his system theory of law. Luhamnn (1987: 13) writes:

> [s]ystems theory is certainly not necessarily the only way of tackling the question of the unity of law. But as no other methods can be seriously contemplated at the moment, we will work on the assumption that the unity of law must be realized and we will therefore examine how the unity of the legal system is to be interpreted.

Teubner develops the theory of self-referential systems as a unity, and the closed nature of the legal system, by stressing the legal constitution of circular relationships through norms and actions about self-observation, self-constitution and self-reproduction in a broad sense. From my point of view, this is a development in the right direction, because it opens up the interface between sociology of law and jurisprudence, which I think is fruitful for both disciplines. How Teubner does this I will describe next in more detail, and I will also relate this discussion to a branch of law that has attracted much attention in the last few years.

Teubner (1993: 37) has presented a very interesting and competent figure about self-reference and 'hypercycle' in law, in my view. The figure shows how socially diffuse law, consisting of components that are socially produced, became partially autonomous law, consisting of self-referential constituted components and finally autopoietic law, consisting of hypercyclically coupled components. For Teubner, in contrast to Luhmann, there are degrees of autonomy (law produces itself), thus making autopoiesis a gradual process from social norms to self-referential legal norms. 'The thesis of autonomization through hypercyclical linkage also allows us empirically to identify critical threshold values – at least with the same degree of precision as Hart's theory of "secondary rules"', writes Teubner (1993: 36). From a sociology of law perspective, which is interested in norms, how norm-oriented social communication (and, for example, non-legal forms of conflict resolution) developed and became components of a legal system through self-description is a genuine key question. Teubner again states:

> The best-known example of legal self-description is Hart's idea of "secondary rules". According to Hart, we can speak of law only if the primary rules of conduct are overlaid and regulated by secondary rules of identification and procedure. For Hart, "the heart of a legal system … [is] the structure which has resulted from the combination of primary rules of obligation with the secondary rules of recognition, change and adjudication". (Teubner, 1993: 39)

In the light of all varying descriptions of how positive law is nowadays becoming more and more transnational, complex, diffuse and pluralistic, the sphere of interest shifts to self-referential and partially autonomous law instead of autopoietic law (de Sousa Santos, 1995: 114–22; Petersen, 1991: 91; Dalberg-Larsen, 1999: 324–31; Gustafsson, 2002: 150–69). As a consequence, questions arise about how the legal profession handles semi-legal norms and the process when socially diffuse law became more fixed than the formal legal norms as black-letter law (Peczenik, 1995: 147). Håkan Gustafsson has argued for a change and for adopting a new approach to the legal understanding, where the '*quid facit*' instead of '*quod est*' will be the centre of attention (Gustafsson, 2011: 65). So, even if Hart is a traditional legal positivist, his description of the secondary rules is very relevant and interesting from a sociology of law perspective, as it points out the importance of legal self-description and legal communication. This follows from Hart's plea for inclusive (soft) legal positivism and how he describes the connection between law and social facts. Teubner (1993: 41) writes about this in a way that opens up the dichotomy of an internal and external view on law:

> Legal techniques of norm identification may take their criteria from very different sources. These include religious texts, divine revelations, true cognitions of nature, long-established tradition, group-specific usages, or the straightforward exercise of power. This is an obvious case of the legal self-constitution of norms; but it is not yet autopoiesis in the full sense of the word. It is the legal itself which uses "secondary rules" to establish and use the criteria, even if the "substance" of the rules is determined by outside agents. The way in which the legal order refers to social norms in general clauses is an excellent example of this. Unlike socially

> diffuse law, social norms are not simply legal norms. It requires a secondary rule from either a legislator or a judge to make it possible for some social norms to become legal norms.

Teubner makes his further description with the emphasis on the importance of seeing action as a system-relative construction:

> Abstract legal thought, dogmatics, and construction as self-descriptions of the legal system have to become central to legal-sociological analyses in a way that would have appeared impossible in the wake of sociological disillusionment over law, be it in the tradition of ideological critique, that of legal realism, or in the "law and society movement". (Teubner, 1993: 44)

Self-description can also be seen in relation to an external description of the law, as Kaarlo Tuori does with reference to Luhmann and Hart (Tuori, 2006: 27–8). So, even if Hart is one of the sources of this separation between the internal-external distinctions, his theory can be used to both problematize and clarify the distinction. The distinction is usually criticized for its effects on the transdisciplinary nature of sociology of law (Cotterrell, 1998: 188). Ironically, there are some suspicions that Hart found inspiration in Max Weber's separation between an intra-juristic and an extra-juristic perspective on legal questions (Lacey, 2004: 230–31). Håkan Hydén (2011: 127) pointed out the problematic distinction between the internal (jurisprudence) and external (sociology) perspectives when he recently wrote about the implication of norms for the epistemology of sociology of law. But the most interesting perspective around this dichotomy arises in relation to Hart's own description of the secondary rules in his theory. Since, for Hart, the rule of recognition (as the most important of the secondary rules) is a social rule, he has been criticized for his use of social rules in his theory (Hart, 1997: 56; Dworkin, 1978). Dworkin (1978: 50) writes:

> [i]f we now ask why judges have a duty to follow social rules, after the fashion of our earlier quibbles, Hart will say that we have missed the point. It belongs to the concept of a duty, on his account, that duties are created by social rules of the sort he describes.

As seen above, Hart's type of positivism has been described as 'soft', as a consequence of his account of how the criteria of legal validity consist of social facts (Spaak, 2005: 414; Leiter, 2001: 357). Hart's description of rules as social has been of broad interest as such, but has also been regarded as a problem in relation to legal positivism, and his way of using secondary rules has been analysed from a sociological perspective (Perry, 2006: 1171; Groudine, 1980: 274; Colvin, 1978: 195–209). Hart writes (1997: 250): '… [t]he rule of recognition may incorporate as criteria of legal validity conformity with moral principles or substantive values; so my doctrine is what has been called "soft positivism" and not as in Dworkin's version of it "plain-fact" positivism'. As a matter of fact, Hart perseveres with normativity and morality ahead of validity (as Kelsen does, for instance, via his basic norm) when he uses concepts such as 'accepted' or 'satisfied' in relation to the rule of recognition (Hart, 1997: 103–4). This view is, in some ways, also closer to a common-sense perspective of what legal aspects deal with. Mauro Zamboni (2004: 34) describes it as follows:

> Hart grounds his investigation of the legal system and its constitutive parts on a more empirical analysis of the legal language. "Empirical" here simply means that Hart looks more at how the legal language actually appears in the space-time reality, instead of imposing its own categories, constructed *a priori*, as in the Kelsen's neo-Kantian approach.

So, to sum up, when we talk about law according to both Teubner and Hart, it cannot be separate from self-descriptions and social aspects. If the legal sources nowadays become more and more differential and with less monistic character, partially autonomous law and the rule of recognition also become of interest. This tendency increases the complexity in the legal field, and one way of handling this is to pay more attention to norms about norms, or meta-norms, so to speak. Meta-norms can, for example, be studied as a question about the legal profession (that is, self-descriptions); how lawyers view the world, legal action as a system-relative construct (Brante, 2010: 843; Hammerslev, 2008: 81) or legal culture and communication in general (Travers and Manzo, 1997; Nelken, 1997). The rule of recognition raises a question about identity that goes beyond the narrow understanding of legal positivism. The interest in legal self-descriptions and self-referentiality within law also points out the circularity in legal method that gives legitimacy from the internal point of view – that is, the perspective of the participants in the system (Hart, 1997: 88–90). For example, the rule of recognition has been described as a social and linguistic practice among lawyers, judges and citizens (Harris, 1997: 121; Cotterrell, 1989: 91). Here there is an echo from Wittgenstein and his practice-perspective, and the Wittgensteinian idea of 'meaning as use'; rules are understood just in relation to how they are used, and that means placing them in a wider social context and withholding other 'games' about rules and language (McVeigh, 2002: 279; Gustafsson, 2011: 71). Accordingly, their meanings and definitions follow from how they fulfil their function, but this also means that there is some room for different criteria of correctness (von Wright, 1965: 206–15; Nordin, 2011: 434–5). From a norm perspective, Hart's stress on the '"internal aspect" of rule-governed conduct' is an important contribution 'to a user-oriented understanding of norms' (MacCormick, 2007: 287).

Compensation for violation as a practical example

A person who seriously violates another person by means of a crime involving an assault on his person, liberty, peace or honour, shall compensate the damage that the violation causes (Swedish Tort Liability Act, Chapter 2, Section 3). The liability for the damage is accordingly linked to certain criminal acts – often some type of crime of violence or sex crime (an attack on a protected interest), but the damage is not in itself a punishment. This type of compensation, for non-financial (or non-pecuniary) damage, has been a growing phenomenon within Swedish tort law in recent years (Dahlstrand, 2008, 2011; Schultz, 2008; Friberg, 2010). The most important factor is probably the general focus on victims in criminal and social policy, which Henrik Tham, for example, has described thoroughly (Lernestedt and Tham, 2011: 23–6). As a consequence of the non-financial dimension of the damage, there is a problem and an uncertainty about how and when the damage is restored. There is, so to speak, a situation of incommensurability between this type of damage and the financial compensation, which means that the ambition to repair is perhaps impossible, but at the same time, the vagueness makes it difficult to prove incommensurability (Schultz, 2008: 82; Rabinowicz, 2009). The goal of the compensation is further to compensate for the victim's emotional state after the crime; it is important to remember that this is not a personal injury (such as 'pain and suffering') but a symbolic injury to human dignity. There has been a change in the wording of the Act, from 'suffering' to 'violation', which stresses the objective, typified violation more than the subjective, individualized injury (Government Bill 2000/01:68: 19, 51–52).

So, how should compensation for violation through crime be determined, in order for it to provide a form of redress of the individual's emotions (such as fear, shame and degradation)? The legislator has chosen to give a mandate to the person applying the tort law, in these cases, to make a discretionary estimate in relation to prevalent ethical and social values (Government Bill 2000/01:68: 51–2, 74). This wording goes back to an understanding of the lack of norms about how compensation for violation or other types of non-financial damages should be determined (Government Bill 1972:5: 121; SOU 1992:84: 133; SOU 1995:33: 320; precedent legal case of NJA 1991: 766; Ekstedt, 1977: 91–2). So, at the same time, the ambition is to provide complete redress for the victim – and the estimate of the compensation shall be based on and guided by objective factors (Government Bill 1975:12: 111; Ekstedt, 1977: 90; Government Bill 2000/01:68: 51). Over time, the focus has shifted from the level of violation of the person attacked to the protected interest, as in violations of rights (Friberg, 2010: 922; NJA 2007: 540). It is important here to remember that this type of compensation for violation is 'pure' non-pecuniary damage (Persson, 1995: 129) without any physical dimension. So, at the same time, the damages seem to consist of both compensation and a form of private law punishment (Friberg, 2010: 923). For example, the basis of the damage calculation is close to the process for meting out punishment and appraisal of a penal value. But this breaches the individualistic and subjective foundation of tort law, in that the calculation uses a more 'collectivistic' method and has a more objective ambition, so to speak. This method for working out the damages has also been criticized, because it is collective or general and not concerned with the unique victim and his or her situation (Schultz, 2008: 39–42). Tort law is civil law, and criminal law is public law; and, in general, tort law focuses only on the suffering (Schultz, 2008). But, in the case of damages for violation, the assessment of the damage is momentary, and not dependent on the resulting effects, as we have seen (Brottsoffermyndighetens referatsamling, 2009: 12). Sandra Friberg has argued

> that the principles governing how punishment is determined may be of guidance also in tort law when it comes to violations through crime. Application of the principles of proportionality and equivalence means that the damages should be proportionate to the degree of violation exhibited in the offence committed by the offender, and that damages should relate to other violations so that a serious violation is compensated with higher damages than a less serious violation. (Friberg, 2010: 926)

Swedish tort law has, by tradition, an ambivalent attitude towards this type of compensation because of the various uncertainty factors that strain traditional principles and dichotomies within tort law. The principal rule in Swedish tort law is that only economic damages can been compensated (Government Bill 2000/01:68: 17). This perspective has also been reflected in a judgment from the Supreme Court, as follows: 'Swedish law has by tradition assumed a restrictive attitude to the possibility of imposing entirely non-financial damages based on a violation of somebody's rights or interest' (NJA 2005: 462). As a consequence of the increased attention on this type of compensation, the question is what really constitutes a violation: 'the illegal or unlawful act, the personal responsibility of the offender or the attacked person's experience of being violated – and what is the ground for damages for violation through crime – compensation for a damage or a penalty for an offence – is vital to consider' (Friberg, 2010: 927; NJA 2007: 540). There are also several question marks surrounding the victimological perspective on the compensation. The situation is complex, and there is no unequivocal answer to whether the compensation finally really helps the victims (Rytterbro, Rönneling, Tham, 2009: 107–12).

Compensation from the Hartian perspective

Stefan Sciaraffa (2011: 609) has summarized the Hartian social rule-based account of secondary rules as follows:

> A key Hartian insight is that the secondary rules of a legal system, the system's rules of recognition, change and adjudication, are customary practices. Like all customs, such rules exist insofar as they are practised. In contrast, legally valid norms are not social rules. Rather, they are norms specified by certain social rules, the system's customary secondary rules.

Hart points out that the importance of customary practice, within the legal officials' attitudes and conceptions, gives him a realistic socio-legal approach which breaks up the general distinction between an internal and an external view of law. The different aspects on how to handle damages for violation, which were shown above, appear to fit well with Hart's idea about how formal legal rules are connected with social and informal norms 'as an empirical, though complex, question of fact' (Hart, 1997: 292). Other similarities among the two are the role of:

> a penumbra of doubt when we are engaged in bringing particular situations under general rules. This imparts to all rules a fringe of vagueness or "open texture", and this may affect the rule of recognition specifying the ultimate criteria used in the identification of the law as much as a particular statute. (Hart, 1997: 123)

Because of the uncertainty about how to calculate the non-pecuniary damage – even if the legal 'primary rules' impose a duty and lay down the obligation for the person applying the law – the rule of recognition confers power. This means that the rule of recognition, as Hart writes, is 'in a sense parasitic' on the first rules, because it is *procedural* and in various ways determines the second type of rules' incidence or controls their operations (Hart, 1997: 81; Colvin, 1978: 200). So this means that Hart can give us some understanding of how, even if there is a right to non-pecuniary compensation for damage in relation to a violation, this type of compensation is an exception in Swedish tort law and its status is ambivalent (Friberg, 2010: 927). From a general perspective, *predictability* is an important value in law; and, in the area of tort law, *mending* is the central goal – and both the value and the goal are difficult to fulfil with this type of compensation, as we have seen. But, as we also know, the basis for this type of compensation is the violation by means of a crime involving an assault on someone's person, liberty, peace or honour, and the damage can therefore be understood as an attack on a protected interest (Friberg, 2010: 529–32). The legal basis is actually similar to what Hart describes as 'the minimum content of natural law' (Hart, 1997: 193–200). Because of some truisms about the human nature and situation, such as we are all easily damaged and have limited altruism, 'there are certain rules of conduct which any social organization must contain if it is to be viable' (Hart, 1997: 194), and therefore legal sanctions are also required, according to Hart. So, what emerges here is a conflict between the legal profession – how the officials, from the internal point of view, 'apply' the rule of recognition – and the primary rule about the individual victim's right to redress. This conflict can be seen as a question about social pressure according to how Hart has defined the way in which primary rules maintain an obligation. From the sociology of law perspective, particularly in relation to the norm perspective successfully developed and pleaded for by Håkan Hydén for decades – about how sociology of law can become more adequate as a legal science and of greater relevance for legal practice (Hydén, 2011: 124) – this can be related to the essential attributes of norms (Hydén and Svensson, 2008: 25).

These essential attributes of norms are (a) behavioural instructions (imperatives), (b) socially reproduced, and (c) the individual's understanding of surrounding expectations regarding their own behaviour. Hart's description of when a primary rule imposes a duty is quite similar to the norm definition above. Sanctions, as a reaction when someone is breaking the norm, are said to be one of the accidental attributes of norms, and this is also the case when it comes to whether they have 'internal functions' or are 'system oriented' (Hydén and Svensson, 2008: 25).

As we have seen, as Hart does, when 'officials' are estimating the compensation for the damage that the violation has caused to the victim, they ought to do it from the victim's perspective – the starting point in the existing social values and norms. This perspective or 'method' has also been criticized because it is a collective or general one and not about the individual situation (Schultz, 2008: 39–42). In some respects, this method is more reminiscent of penal law and the way in which the court estimates the penal value. Because of this, and other problematic circumstances surrounding the compensation, there has been a restrictive attitude towards this type of liability of damages for violation by means of crime. The principal rule is still that a person should only receive compensation for financial damage, and the law must provide the possibility for non-financial damage. It is difficult to fix the boundary between the two types of damage in a legal context, and this situation is reminiscent of the generally uncertain language of rules and what Hart calls 'open-texture' (Hart, 1997: 128). Because of the great discretion that the legislator has given to the person applying the law when it comes to compensation for damage caused by violation by means of crime, the Swedish attitude has been more or less 'scant', and the application bears the stamp of far-reaching standardization. To sum up, it is unclear whether this type of compensation really is recognized as completely valid by the legal profession, because there are no clear norms for its estimation and, because its function is related to the right to personal integrity, this lack of norms increases. Or, from a different perspective, the secondary rules can be 'parasitic' on the primary rules about conduct and obligations (Hart, 1997: 81). I have previously referred to this situation of normative ambiguity or 'anomic' (Dahlstrand, 2008), because it also shows a potential mismatch between the formal norms (that is, how the legal profession handles this kind of question) and informal norms (that is, what people in general expect).

As Hart has described, the issue of the social pressure behind rules of obligation make them social, together with the question whether 'they are believed to be necessary to the maintenance of social life or some highly prized feature of it' (Hart, 1997: 87). From my survey, presented in my thesis (Dahlstrand, 2012), it is clear that there exists social pressure behind this type of compensation to victims of crime. But, more interestingly, the majority of the respondents succeed in the task of estimating these types of non-financial damages in monetary amounts in the vignette survey; and, even if the levels exceed the existing amounts of compensation, the proportionality was much the same. The respondents, consisting of both victims of crime who received criminal injuries compensation and a sample of ordinary people, were able to place themselves at an internal viewpoint of this area of law, like that of the person applying the law. Therefore, the rule of recognition relates to the social context as an empirical, though complex, question of fact, and 'it is a rule of the group to be supported by the social pressure it exerts' (Hart, 1997: 94). This means that the issue of estimating is an interesting example of secondary rules, because they are *about* the primary rule – thus meta-norms. At the same time, my empirical results show that there exists a 'common standard' (Dahlstrand, 2012), which follows from 'the internal point of view with its characteristic normative use of legal language' and is not confined to the world of officialdom (Hart, 1997: 117). The internal point of social rules is more than just social convention, but also a 'reflective critical attitude' which uses a '"normative" language' that can be used to criticize, for example, the legal application or demands for conformity with the general sense of justice (Hart, 1997: 56–7). Both rules and norms show reasons for action, they are reason-giving in the committed and internal point of view; the 'insider's perspective' is about the practical point of view among 'acceptors' producing the social practice that the rule of recognition consists of via internalized normative standards (Coleman, 2001: 110–11). The 'social fact thesis' shall not be seen as equal to a reductionist view, but rather, as Jules Coleman writes about Hart's description, 'that law *supervenes* on the relevant social facts' and therefore is still able to understand the internal point of view without reducing potential social norms to habits of obedience or predictions of behaviour (Coleman, 2001: 116). Paying attention, from this internal point of view, to meta-norms is also important from a sociology of law perspective, because otherwise, when just focusing on the external side and on primary norms of actual behaviour, there is, as Hart writes, a risk of being 'deplorably sheeplike; the sheep might end in the slaughter-house' (Hart, 1997: 117). Even more important is the ambition to see *both* perspectives, and in that sense break up the distinction between an internal and external view (Cotterrell, 1998; Dahlstrand, 2008) in the light of what Reza Banakar has written about 'misleading dichotomies' that reduces the sociology of law understanding of the actual pluralistic legal field (Banakar, 2003; Galligan, 2007).

Concluding words

From a norm perspective, norms about norms (or meta-norms) emphasize the normativity among norms. Given Hart's theory, the internal point of view is nearly connected to the secondary rule that specifies the condition for which rules that are valid (that is, these rules have meaning only in relation to other rules). The internal point of view, through the rule of recognition, is therefore closely connected to the normativity of social rules (Himma, 2001: 286). The issue is then 'what particular features a rule must have to be recognised as a rule of the society' (Cotterrell, 1989: 97). From a sociology of law perspective, defined as '[t]he systematic, theoretically grounded, empirical study of law as a set of social practices or as an aspect of field of social experience' (Clark, 2007: 1413), the key question is which of these norms and rules are of normative value, as meaningful guides for conduct. In Hart's theory, it is not necessary that citizens in general view the rules from an internal viewpoint; but, when we study social and informal norms, the internal view is of interest because that is where you will find the normativity and the critical reflections in relation to one's own (and others') norm- or rule-governed behaviour. At the same time, it is a central task for sociology of law to understand how the 'officials' – the legal profession – from the inside recognize and apply rules, to be able to understand the way in which rules and norms are used in various normative contexts. I also think it is fruitful to bear in mind Hart's criticism of John Austin's superficial and quantitative empiricism about normativity grounded in regularity; instead, normativity has to be understood 'locally', depending on the social context in all its variety and complexity. If rules are characterized by 'porosity' and 'open texture', as Hart considers, and if we also take into consideration Wittgenstein's 'private language argument' about what it means to follow a rule, there is even more reason for the need to go closer to the actual function and practice in order to understand normativity beyond convention and formalism. This chapter concludes, accordingly, in defence of the quantitative approach inspired by the 'ordinary language philosophy' – within a different complex of social practices that entails application, evaluations, judgements and criticism in relation to different rules and norms regarded from the insider's perspective, there appears a source of meta-norms (that is, norms about norms) in real life.

References

Baier, M. and Svensson, M. 2009. *Om normer.* Malmö: Liber.

Banakar, R. 2003. 'Merging Law and Sociology', *Beyond the Dichotomies in Socio-Legal Research.* Berlin: Galda + Wilch Verlag.

Brante, T. 2010. 'Professional Fields and Truth Regimes: In Search of Alternative Approaches', *Comparative Sociology*, 9(6), 843–86.

Brottsoffermyndighetens referatsamling, 2009. Umeå: Brottsoffermyndigheten.

Butler, J. 1997. *Excitable Speech: A Politics of the Performative.* New York: Routledge.

Clark, D.S. 2007. *Encyclopaedia of Law & Society.* Thousand Oaks: Sage Publications.

Coleman, J. 2001. 'Incorporationism, Conventionality, and the Practical Difference Thesis', *Hart's Postscript. Essays on the Postscript to the Concept of Law*, edited by J. Coleman. New York: Oxford University Press, 99–147.

Colvin, E. 1978. 'The Sociology of Secondary Rules', *The University of Toronto Law Journal*, 28(2), 195–214.

Cotterrell, R. 1998. 'Why Must Legal Ideas Be Interpreted Sociologically?' *Journal of Law and Society*, 25(2), 171–92.

Cotterrell, R. 1989. *The Politics of Jurisprudence: A Critical Introduction to Legal Philosophy.* 1st edn. London: Butterworths.
Dahlstrand, K. 2012. *Kränkning och upprättelse. En rättssociologisk studie av kränkningsersättning till brottsoffer*. Lund: Lund Studies in Sociology of Law.
Dahlstrand, K. 2011. 'How to compensate the irreplaceable? A socio-legal research project within victimology about the relation between formal and informal norms', in *Norms between law and society*, edited by H. Hydén. Lund: Lund Studies in Sociology of Law, 63–84.
Dahlstrand, K. 2008. 'Non-Pecuniary (Idealistic) Damages in Tort. How to break the Distinction between an Internal and External View of Law', in *Contribution in Sociology of Law*, edited by H. Hydén and P. Wickenberg. Lund: Lund Studies in Sociology of Law, 91–113.
Dalberg-Larsen, J. 1999. *Lovene og livet. En retssociologisk grundbog*. 4th edn. Viborg: Greensjura.
Dworkin, R. 1978. *Taking Rights Seriously*. London: Duckworth.
Ekstedt, O. 1977. *Ideellt skadestånd för personskada*. Lund: Juridiska föreningen i Lund.
Friedrichs, D.O. 2006. *Law in Our Lives. An Introduction*. 2nd edn. Los Angeles: Roxbury Publishing Company.
Galligan, D.J. 2007. *Law in Modern Society*. Oxford: Oxford University Press.
Groudine, A. 1980. 'H.L.A. Hart and the Problem with Legal Positivism', *The Journal of Libertarian Studies*, 4(3), 274–88.
Gustafsson, H. 2011. *Dissens. Om det rättsliga vetandet*. Göteborg: Juridiska institutionens skriftserie. Handelshögskolan vid Göteborgs universitet.
Gustafsson, H. 2002. *Rättens polyvalens. En rättsvetenskaplig studie av sociala rättigheter och rättssäkerhet*. Lund: Lund Studies in Sociology of Law.
Hammerslev, O. 2008. 'Skandinaviske studier af den juridiske profession', *Retfaerd*, 31(2), 81–100.
Harris, J.W. 1997. *Legal Philosophies*. 2nd edn. London: Butterworths.
Hart, H.L.A. 1997. *The Concept of Law*. 2nd edn. New York: Oxford University Press.
Hart, H.L.A. 1983. *Essays in Jurisprudence and Philosophy*. Oxford: Oxford University Press.
Himma, K.E. 2001. 'Law's Claim of Legitimate Authority', in *Hart's Postscript. Essays on the Postscript to the Concept of Law*, edited by J. Coleman. New York: Oxford University Press, 271–309.
Hydén, H. 2011. Looking at the World through the Lenses of Norms, in *Understanding Law in Society. Developments in Socio-legal Studies*, edited by K. Papendorf, S. Machura and K. Andenaes. Berlin: Lit verlag, 120–159.
Hydén, H. and Svensson, M. 2008. The Concept of Norms in Sociology of Law, in *Law and Society*, edited by P. Wahlgren. Stockholm: Stockholm Institute for Scandinavian Law, 15–32.
Lacey, N. 2004. *A Life of H.L.A. Hart. The Nightmare and the Noble Dream.* Oxford: Oxford University Press.

Leiter, B. 2001. 'Legal Realism, Hard Positivism, and the Limits of Conceptual Analysis', in *Hart's Postscript. Essays on the Postscript to the Concept of Law*, edited by J. Coleman. New York: Oxford University Press, 355–70.

Luhmann, N. 2004. *Law as a social system*. Oxford: Oxford University Press.

Luhmann, N. 1987. 'The Unity of the Legal System', in *Autopoietic Law: A New Approach to Law and Society*, edited by G. Teubner. Berlin: de Gruyter, 12–35.

MacCormick, N. 2007. *Institutions of Law. An Essay in Legal Theory*. Oxford: Oxford University Press.

McVeigh, S. 'Postmodernism and Common Law', in *An Introduction to Law and Social Theory*, edited by R. Banakar and M. Treves. Oxford: Hart, 267–83.

Moore, F.S. 1978. *Law as Process: An Anthropological Approach*. London: Routledge & Kegan Paul.

Murphy, L. 'The Political Question of the Concept of Law', in *Hart's Postscript. Essays on the Postscript to the Concept of Law*, edited by J. Coleman. New York: Oxford University Press, 371–409.

Nelken, D. 1997. *Comparing Legal Cultures*. Aldershot: Dartmouth.

Palmer Olsen, H. 2011. 'Britisk retspositivisme', in *Retsfilosofi – central tekster og temaer*, edited by O. Hammerslev and H. Palmer Olsen. Copenhagen: Hans Reitzels Forlag.

Nordin, S. 2011. *Filosoferna. Det västerländska tänkandet sedan år 1900.* Stockholm: Atlantis.

Peczenik, A. 1995. *Vad är rätt? Om demokrati, rättssäkerhet, etik och juridisk argumentation.* Stockholm: Norstedts juridik.

Perry, S. 2006. 'Hart on Social Rules and the Foundations of Law: Liberating the Internal Point of View', *Fordham Law Review*, 75(3), 1171–1209.

Persson, M 1995. 'Rent ideella skadestånd', in *Skada och ersättning*, edited by A. Ackebo, et al. Stockholm: Juristförlaget.

Petersen, H. 1991. *Informel ret på kvindearbejdspladser. En retsteoretisk og empirisk analyse.* Copenhagen: Akademisk forlag.

Rabinowicz, W. 2009. 'Incommensurability and Vagueness', *Aristotelian Society Supplementary*, 83(1), 71–94.

Rytterbro, L.-L., Rönneling, A. and Tham, H. 2009. *Brottsskadeersättning ur brottsofferperspektiv. En komparativ studie av Danmark och Sverige.* Stockholm: Kriminologiska institutionen Stockholms universitet.

Santos de Sousa, B. 1995. *Toward a New Common Sense. Law, Science and Politics in The Paradigmatic Transition.* New York: Routledge.

Shapiro, S.J. 2001. 'On Hart's Way Out', in *Hart's Postscript. Essays on the Postscript to the Concept of Law*, edited by J. Coleman. New York: Oxford, 149–92.

Scarafta, S. 2011. 'The Ineliminability of Hartian Social Rules', *Oxford Journal of Legal Studies*, 31(3), 603–23.

Schultz, M. 2008. *Kränkning. Studier i skadeståndsrättslig argumentation.* Stockholm: Jure.

Spaak, T. 2005. 'Kelsen and Hart on the Normativity on Law', in *Perspectives on Jurisprudence: Essays in Honour of Jes Bjarup*, edited by P. Wahlgren. Stockholm: Stockholm Institute for Scandinavian Law, 397–414.

Stavropoulos, N. 2001. 'Hart's Semantics', in *Hart's Postscript. Essays on the Postscript to the Concept of Law*, edited by J. Coleman. New York: Oxford University Press.

Teubner, G. 2006. 'Dealing with Paradoxes of Law: Derrida, Luhmann, Wiethölter', in *Paradoxes and Inconsistencies in the Law*, edited by O. Perez and G. Teubner. Oxford: Hart, 41–64.

Teubner, G. 1993. *Law as an Autopoietic System*. Oxford: Blackwell.

Tham, H. 2011. 'Brottsoffrens uppkomst och utveckling som offentlig fråga i Sverige', in *Brottsoffret och kriminalpolitiken*, edited by C. Lernestedt and H. Tham. Stockholm: Norstedts juridik, 23–49.

Travers, M., Manzo, J.F. 1997. *Law in Action. Ethnomethodological and Conversation Analytic Approaches to Law*. Aldershot: Ashgate.

Tuori, K. 2002. *Critical Legal Positivism*. Aldershot: Dartmouth Publishing.

von Wright, G.H. 1965. *Logik, filosofi och språk*. 2nd edn. Lund: Aldus/Bonnier.

Zamboni, M. 2004. *The Policy of Law. A Legal Theoretical Framework*. Stockholm: Stockholm University.

Chapter 7

Institutions and Norms in Collaboration: Towards a Framework for Analysing Law and Normativity in Inter-organizational Collaboration

Susanna Johansson

Introduction

During recent decades, collaboration on various issues between different organizations, in diverse areas of society, has become more and more common. Collaboration is justified in different ways, but most often involves the goal of achieving both greater efficiency and higher quality by exchanging perspectives, competences or resources among the organizations involved. For example, collaboration has been labelled 'the welfare state's new working method' (Danermark and Kullberg, 1999), highlighting the increase in (and need for) integrating measures from different human service organizations in relation to disadvantaged groups in society. At the same time, collaboration is common in many fields other than social welfare, both within and across sectors as well as nation states. Consequently, collaboration exists in many forms, with varying degrees of integration between the organizations involved. It can be seen as a modern form of governance, sometimes initiated or demanded by the state, and at other times voluntarily created by the organizations involved.

A common feature of collaboration is that it implies both the maintenance and the breaking of different organizational boundaries (Lindberg, 2009). Collaboration as an idea thus demands knowledge of one's own and each other's organizational conditions, as well as the ability to reach a balance between maintaining and breaking boundaries. This is, at the same time, a reason why dilemmas often occur in collaborative practice, not least in relation to different 'regulatory boundaries' (Johansson, 2011).

Scott (2004) emphasizes that boundaries of organizations have become more open and flexible in recent decades (that is, more permeable and less fixed). Among many other examples, the increase in inter-organizational collaboration can clearly be seen as an effect of this tendency. Following Scott, these developments do not imply the disappearance of boundaries, but rather 'changes in their scope, composition, duration, and enforcement mechanisms' (Scott, 2004: 11). These arguments can furthermore be compared with contemporary discussions on the transnationalization of law, the increase in soft law, self-regulation and governance – perhaps at the expense of state law and formal legal rules tied to separate organizations and/or nation states. Cotterrell (2012), for example, acknowledges the range and variety of regulation operating beyond nation state boundaries, implying that law increasingly has new sources, locations and bases of authority.

These developments raise critical questions that will be addressed in this chapter. If the organizational boundaries have become more flexible, what happens in inter-organizational collaboration, where different regulatory (and other) boundaries on different levels meet, collide and are negotiated? Which normative orders are established through collaborative practice? This chapter aims to discuss how an integration of perspectives from sociology of law and organizational sociology can be of use for analysing and explaining such phenomena. My ambition in this chapter is thus to contribute to this field of study by exploring a possible interplay between two rather seldom combined sub-disciplines.

Edelman and Suchman (1997) draw attention to the fact that classical social theorists, such as Marx, Durkheim and Weber, regarded legal and organizational sociology as intimately interconnected. They state that, in spite these early connections, later research within organizational and legal sociology has, to a large extent, developed independently. A few key theorists, such as Selznick (1948), aimed to bridge the gap, while most theorists within the respective traditions remained rather unaware of each other. According to Edelman and Suchman, this situation is changing. They argue that the conceptual separation between the two sub-disciplines has become increasingly difficult to maintain, since '(m)odern organizations are immersed in a sea of law' (Edelman and Suchman, 1997: 480). These authors have discussed socio-legal theory in relation to institutional theory of organizational sociology in two extensive articles: Suchman and Edelman (1996), and Edelman and Suchman (1997). Scott (2008a) similarly discusses the significance of a socio-legal perspective for institutional organizational analysis, mostly with reference to the same authors. Even though I might not have made an exhaustive mapping of the literature in this field, it can be noted that I have had difficulties finding more recent sources combining these sub-disciplines, although many other organizational researchers from disciplines other than sociology focus on regulatory aspects of organizations, not least within economics and management. This chapter has thus been inspired, to a large extent, by Suchman and Edelman's articles and can be said to 'pick up on the same track', although with a more specific focus on combining institutional theory (within organizational sociology) and a (sociology of law) perspective on norms, for the purpose of analysing contexts of inter-organizational collaboration.

Powell (1996) considers that three circumstances in particular bring about a need for an integration of sociology of law and of organizations, namely that:

> (1) Law is practiced in an organizational setting that shapes its conduct. (2) The law is carried out in an arena that is populated by multiple organizational

> jurisdictions, with competing claims of professional expertise. (3) The law serves as both a normative and a regulatory environment in which organizations operate. (Powell, 1996: 961)

Thus, my ambition here is to add to this sub-disciplinary integration by comparing, and proposing a possible combination of, a (sociology of law) perspective on norms and an institutional perspective (of organizational sociology). Both perspectives highlight relations and discrepancies between formal and informal structures and practices, which are of great interest for socio-legal research in general.

This chapter proposes a delimited but further developed framework that was first presented in my doctoral dissertation, where I analysed a specific model of inter-organizational collaboration between public agency organizations related to social services, law enforcement and health care concerning investigations of suspected crimes against children. The organizations involved formed a sort of 'hybrid organization', bringing together different institutional logics, in that case stemming from social welfare law, on the one hand, and criminal law, on the other (Johansson, 2011). In this chapter, I will relate to this context of inter-organizational collaboration at a few places in order to illustrate some of the theoretical arguments.

The overall purpose of this chapter is to contribute to both the norm perspective and the institutional perspective, in the sense of showing how they might complement each other. Due to space limitations, the chapter will only give brief descriptions of the theoretical perspectives as such. In relation to the more limited purpose of this chapter, I will pay special attention to the view on law and regulatory aspects within each perspective, as well as similarities and possibilities for combining them, rather than engage in a more critical discussion. Furthermore, I will focus on how the perspectives can be combined for analysis of inter-organizational collaboration in particular. More concretely, the aim of the chapter is to explore how these perspectives can be combined in an integrative framework, especially related to analysing law and normativity in inter-organizational collaboration.

The disposition of the chapter is as follows. By way of introduction, I will briefly describe and compare the institutional and norm perspectives, including the most central concepts of institutions and norms. In addition, views on law within the perspectives will be especially highlighted. Thereafter, I will propose an integrative framework in relation to analysing contexts of inter-organizational collaboration, including identifying some contributions of this framework to each perspective. Finally, I will have a closing discussion of what the chapter has concluded, and suggest future prospects for the field of study.

Institutional theory meets a norm perspective

Institutional theory has been highly influential during recent decades in several social science disciplines (Scott, 2008a). For example, Grape, Blom and Johansson

(2006) and Johansson (2009) discuss how the theory tradition has spread and developed from American sociology to Scandinavia, and especially Sweden, primarily within economics and management, but also within sociology and social work. Some other branches of neo-institutional theory have also been extensively used, for example within political science.

In contrast to traditional theories of organization (which focus on formal, rational and technical aspects of organizations), institutional theory emphasizes symbolic, informal, cultural-cognitive and legitimacy-seeking aspects of organizational life and practice. In this tradition, formal structures of organizations are seen rather as 'rational myths' (Meyer and Rowan, 1977), having little to do with what actually takes place in organizations. Hence, institutional theory highlights the discrepancy between institution and organization, as well as between formal and informal structures of organizing; in other words, between ideas and practices. The tradition has also developed away from emphasizing uniformity among organizations towards focusing on variation, as well as processes of organizing, not least in what is sometimes labelled 'Scandinavian institutionalism' (Eriksson-Zetterquist, 2009). Several such studies analyse how popular immaterial organizational ideas (such as reform policies or specific collaborative models) travel and spread among organizational fields, leading to a 'surface isomorphism' among organizations adopting the same ideas, and how these ideas – when materialized in local contexts of organizations – are being interpreted and translated (differently) into, sometimes, myriad varied practices (Czarniawska, 1997; Røvik, 2004).

A characteristic of institutional theory within organizational sociology is, among other aspects, the idea that organizations are not regarded as closed systems, but rather as influenced and permeated by different institutional environments. These environments (including legal regulations and other organizations) restrict and put pressure on, but also enable, a single organization's room for action and autonomy, and create interdependences between organizations. Organizations and their actors are considered as being wrapped in nets of ideas, values, norms, rules, beliefs and taken-for-granted assumptions – cultural institutional elements that define how the world is and ought to be (Barley and Tolbert, 1997). These institutional elements affect how organizations and actors both think and behave, and thus how organization and practice take shape.

The (sociology of law) perspective on norms, presented and discussed in this volume, is similarly interested in what is considered good or bad, right or wrong, in different situations, and how it influences actors' liabilities to behave in certain manners, but also in norm conflicts apparent in disparate societal phases or contexts. The perspective is specifically developed for the purpose of providing a bridge between legal and social science by focusing on norms – including both legal and social norms – as action directives (Hydén, 2002). Furthermore, a norm perspective pays special attention to relations between social and legal norms, as well as between norms and practice.

Both institutions and norms are much-debated and ambiguous concepts (Jönsson, Persson and Sahlin, 2011; Baier and Svensson, 2009). Norms constitute –

in resemblance to institutions – an abstract phenomenon, impossible to see or touch physically, but instead shown in their consequences, in the actions and behaviours to which they give rise (Hydén, 2002). Institutions are closely related to words such as 'customs', 'manners', 'routines', 'tacit agreements', 'traditions' and 'norms', all having in common that they make our days function largely unreflectively (Jönsson, Persson and Sahlin, 2011: 113). Hydén (2002) similarly states that norms function as complexity reducers, that it can vary how widespread they are and which strength they carry, whether norms are conscious or unconscious, or even internalized and thus simply taken for granted (Hydén, 2002). For example, norms have been defined as guidelines for action, as socially reproduced, and as comprehensions of expectations from the environment (Svensson, 2008; Hydén and Svensson, 2008; Baier and Svensson, 2009). Norms have furthermore been viewed as dependent on three dimensions: will/value; knowledge/cognition; and system/conditions. Hydén puts it as follows:

> A norm does not only consist of values and preferences. It also contains different cognitive elements. As a result of the norm being systemically tied, it is also dependent on the system conditions that prevail in the specific situation. (2002: 60, my translation)

Scott defines institutions in a particular helpful way in order to combine with a norm perspective:

> Institutions are comprised of regulative, normative and cultural-cognitive elements that, together with associated activities and resources, provide stability and meaning to social life. (2008a: 48)

The regulative elements are constituted by steering, controlling and sanctioning activities based on legislation, rules and administrative procedures. The normative elements are built up by values and expectations that have been negotiated and established socially; while the cultural-cognitive elements stress symbolic systems, such as underlying assumptions taken for granted and seldom questioned (Scott, 2008a and 2008b). Furthermore, Scott's division of institutions into three elements comprises both an 'ought' side and an 'is' side of institutions:

> [...] although institutional elements – rules, norms, beliefs – are primarily symbolic in nature, to be of interest these symbols must impact social behaviour: they must reflect in activities, relations, and resources. (2008b: 222)

Similarly, Baier and Svensson state that a characteristic of norms is to bridge the gap between the 'ought' and the 'is' – in other words, to transform values into actions (2009: 183).

Institutions and norms are thus quite similar, as they have been defined and used within the two perspectives, as well as the interest focus of the perspectives more generally, which speaks for a possible combination. Still, even though there have been shown to be obvious similarities between institutions and norms, there also seem to be differences (for example, regarding scope and their relation to sanctions), perhaps even as much within as between the two perspectives. In this chapter, I will not go too deep into a comparison of the concepts as such. This is because the aim of the chapter is to explore a possible combination of the two perspectives in relation to analysing law and normativity in inter-organizational collaboration, not to integrate the concepts as such. From my point of view, norms and rules are parts of broader cultural institutional environments of organizations. Hence, as I interpret and use it, the concept of 'institution' constitutes a more overarching concept than does the 'norm' concept, even though the meanings of the two (within an institutional and a norm perspective) have noticeable parallels.

Views on law within the perspectives

Even though norms and rules are considered as central components of institutions, the institutional perspective has been criticized for a simplified view on law, an almost 'legal formalist' view that stresses the nature of law as external, objective, rational and coercive (Suchman and Edelman, 1996; Scott, 2008a). As an example, DiMaggio and Powell's (1983) description of 'coercive isomorphism', a central concept within institutional theory, to some extent implies a rather simplistic understanding of the character of law, with statements such as 'organizational change is a direct response to government mandate' or '(t)he existence of a common legal environment affects many aspects of an organization's behavior or structure' (DiMaggio and Powell, 1983: 150). In my interpretation, this is related to a view on law as consistent and state-centred, while much contemporary legal sociology has pointed to a broader and more complex understanding of law than just state law, such as transnational, pluralistic, reflexive or hybrid characteristics of law. Furthermore, Suchman and Edelman acknowledge three important aspects of law: first, law is often uncertain, not determinate; second, law is often contested, not authoritative; and third, law is often constitutive, not coercive (1996: 930).

They are thus also highlighting the interpretative character of law, in which law acquires its meaning through social interaction, stressing that all legislation is subjected to various interpretations:

> The informalism of law, together with the cultural character of organizations, creates a dynamic interplay between the two arenas. Each helps to constitute the other. (Suchman and Edelman, 1996: 938)

In other words, organizations mediate and do not just respond to law. This can be compared with Hydén (1984) stating that the interpretation of legal rules, regardless of the type of legislation, is to a large extent determined by other than purely legal factors. This is because the context that surrounds the legislation –

in my understanding, the institutional environment and organizational setting of which the law is a part – plays a considerable role in determining the content of a specific piece of legislation, norm or rule (Hydén, 1984: 11). In a similar way, Scott acknowledges that socio-legal scholars have devoted attention to the fact that many regulations are controversial, imprecise or vague, and therefore do not provide clear guidelines for interpretation or action; in such cases, law is better understood in terms of meaning-creating processes and collective interpretation processes, supported by cognitive and normative institutional elements to a greater degree than coercive elements (2008a: 54).

Overall, a sociology of law-focused institutional perspective on organizing leads to a view on law that emphasizes the interpretative character of the law and the fact that the law acquires its content through social processes. Law is thus institutionally and contextually interdependent. Phrased in Powell's terms, such a perspective constitutes 'a law as process view for institutional analysis' (Powell, 1996: 961). Such nuancing of the institutional theory regarding the law's meaning(s) within institutional orders has the consequence that law becomes 'de-formalized' to a greater extent, and therefore that differences between legal rules and social norms are not emphasized to the same extent, since they co-exist and interplay.

This makes comparisons with a more specific (sociology of law) norm perspective interesting. Hydén (2002) views norms as a sort of generic term, which includes both legal rules and social norms. In principle, he considers that there is no difference between norms and legal rules, except that the latter have been 'elevated' in terms of status (to precisely legal rules) and, in that respect, strengthened as norms (by having a stronger system for sanctioning connected to them). Formal legal rules thus constitute a special category of norms. Hydén considers that the norm becomes less flexible when it adopts the form of a legal rule, and a consequence could be that the norm and the rule glide apart (that is, a discrepancy arises between the two). Furthermore, according to Hydén, formal rules are easier to observe, since they are written down and articulated (for example, in specific legislation), in contrast to social norms, which are rather taken for granted (Hydén, 2002). However, this appears to be a matter of which side (the 'ought' side or the 'is' side) of the rule that is considered.

By viewing norms as including both formal and informal rules, but still categorizing them differently (for example, in relation to their sources and connected sanctions), I consider the norm perspective as fruitful for an institutional analysis. On the other hand, the institutional perspective contributes to an understanding of norms and rules as parts of – and in interplay with – broader cultural institutions and institutional orders. I will further elaborate my point.

Suchman and Edelman express their socio-legal view on law in the following way:

> In short, law is much like other elements of organizations institutional environments: not an explicit, authoritative and coercive system of material

> constraints, but an ambiguous, contested, and constitutive system of cultural understandings. The New Institutionalism has taken great strides in bringing law into the organizational picture, but the lessons of sociolegal scholarship call for more careful attention to the law's pervasive informalism and malleability. (Suchman and Edelman, 1996: 938)

Even though I agree with their general statement above on the law's character, I consider that adding a more specific perspective on norms is useful for analytical purposes, by enabling distinction or categorization of different types of norms and regulations making up (parts of) institutions. In many cases, norms, rules and laws are used interchangeably. From a norm perspective, it becomes important to distinguish between them, not least in order to analyse the relationships among them, such as changes to, as well as discrepancies or mixes between, social norms and legal rules, in a specific context. They can then be analysed, for example, in terms of different characteristics (such as background, levels, and degrees of effect).

To sum up, by combining the institutional perspective with a norm perspective, I consider that a more nuanced understanding can be reached of the dependence of law on – and influence from – the contextual setting in which it is applied. Furthermore, the importance of social interpretation processes for the content that law gains in practice is acknowledged; in other words, a view on law that stresses both its formal and informal character, its relation to (and dependence on) social norms and practice. A norm perspective is also helpful for analytical purposes, in order to characterize more narrowly the relations between different types of norms and rules in a specific context. On the other hand, the institutional perspective helps to highlight the fact that regulative and normative elements are only some aspects of institutional environments surrounding organizations and actors in inter-organizational contexts. Cultural-cognitive processes (rooted in cultural traditions, ideas, routines and beliefs) are other central components, affecting how practice takes form, which is a valuable contribution to the norm perspective within sociology of law.

Towards an integrative framework

Powell and DiMaggio (1991), in their introduction, advocated a view on institutions focusing on the cognitive aspects at the expense of norms, as a way of contrasting the 'new' institutionalism from the 'old'. For example, they rhetorically stated that '(n)ot norms and values but taken-for-granted scripts, rules, and classifications are the stuff of which institutions are made' (Powell and DiMaggio, 1991: 15). This seems to be a one-sided focus which, in current developments of the perspective, is starting to converge more and more. Scott (2008a) is one example of this. He advocates a more integrated analytical framework for institutional analysis by defining the three elements (that is, rules, norms and beliefs), although pointing at different 'institutionalisms' focusing on the three elements to varying degrees (Scott 2008a). By combining an institutional perspective (of organizational sociology) with a (sociology of law) norm perspective, it is possible to move towards downplaying the gap between 'old' and 'new' institutionalism, and thus not only focusing on symbolic cultural-cognitive dimensions of institutions but also considering norms and rules as critical components.

Hence, in this chapter, I advocate an integrative analysis where cultural-cognitive meaning-creating processes are of great importance, not at the expense of norms and rules, but rather in relation or reference to them. Norms and rules are then central parts of institutions influencing organizational actors, but are at the same time interpreted and translated by them in cultural-cognitive meaning-creating processes of collaboration. This shows possibilities for a fruitful combination of the two perspectives, which in particular develops and elucidates how rules and norms interact with (broader) institutional environments, and thereby, to a varying extent, transform the meaning of law in inter-organizational collaboration.

In my understanding, the interaction and relations between regulative, normative and cultural-cognitive elements of institutions create patterns of thought and action in a certain context. The institutional structures that these elements constitute affect how organizations and actors think and behave. At the same time, organizations and actors interpret (and, to some extent, transform) the same institutional elements. Then, what Giddens (1984 and 1993) terms 'processes of structuration' occur, namely the reproduction and/or transformation of institutional structures. Hence, both institutional stability and change are taken account of, as well as the interplay between structure and agency of institutionalization processes. Institutionalization can thus be understood and studied as structuration processes, as on-going interplays between action and institution (Barley and Tolbert, 1997).

Institutionalization as structuration can be used as a basis for explaining both how established institutional patterns impact on the inter-organizational collaboration, and also how the inter-organizational collaboration between the actors involved in turn impacts on the reproduction or transformation of already established institutional patterns and/or the production of new institutional patterns; in other words, how normativity comes about in collaboration.

Phillips, Lawrence and Hardy (2000) argue that, when a context of inter-organizational collaboration spans multiple institutional fields – and thus covers several institutional rules and norms, which may be in conflict – the collaborative processes are made more complex (Phillips, Lawrence and Hardy, 2000: 30). Similarly, Scott states that:

> Varying, competing institutions and multiple institutional elements are often at work. Although they constitute new forms, they also interact with a variety of previously existing forms with varying characteristics and in differing locations. (Scott, 2008a: 153)

In collaboration, different regulative elements are thus at work, stemming from different institutional orders. Since contexts of inter-organizational collaboration often involve several organizations, governed by different regulations, it also implies that different regulations meet and collide. Furthermore, the regulations are often of differing characters: some are open and flexible framework legislations, others are specified legislations with detailed formal rules, while yet others have a more self-regulatory character. As an example, the context of collaboration studied in my dissertation spanned separate fields, connected to social welfare law (on the one hand) and criminal law (on the other), creating an inherent institutional tension between a treatment-oriented logic and a criminal-law-oriented logic for the organizations involved, as well as several norm conflicts between open and flexible (social welfare) norms on the one hand and specified formal (criminal law) rules on the other (Johansson, 2011). In collaboration, these differing regulations, norms and rules meet and are negotiated around, not only among themselves but also in relation to, and with the help of, other institutional elements surrounding them. These interactions finally determine the actual (and practical) meaning of law in collaboration. For instance, the collaborative practices that evolved between the organizations studied in my dissertation showed tendencies towards the more traditional formal legal rules (stemming from an institutional order of criminal law) gaining influence at the expense of the more flexible norms (stemming from an institutional order of social welfare law), which I labelled a process of 'juridification' (see further Johansson, 2011). Thus, the regulative elements of formal legal rules gained special influence in that specific context of collaboration, at that time, although this does not have to be the case in other collaborative contexts or periods of time.

In relation to contexts of inter-organizational collaboration, the processes are thus even more complex, since not only interactions between differing institutional elements emanating from one institutional order are at work, but also interactions between different, and frequently competing, institutional orders. In contexts of inter-organizational collaboration, multiple institutional orders and elements, such as rules and norms, therefore often collide. It then becomes an empirical and analytical question of which of the institutional orders and elements gain 'priority right of interpretation' and, in turn, what normativity the collaboration results in.

More concretely, when studying specific contexts of inter-organizational collaboration, it becomes an empirical and analytical question of which institutional elements gain influence, affect and become affected, and thereby which institutional changes and power balances between institutions take shape through collaboration; in other words, what normativity actually comprises in a specific inter-organizational context. Finally, this is a matter of power and legitimacy in interplay and negotiation between institutions and actions (Johansson, 2011; Phillips, Lawrence and Hardy, 2000; Hardy and Phillips, 1998). For such kinds of analysis, I consider that a combination of an institutional and a norm perspective would be promising for future socio-legal-oriented research on normativity and inter-organizational collaboration – where institutions, norms and rules are understood as co-existing and interplaying, and thereby creating (different) relations and normative orders.

Within the institutional perspective, several concepts have been developed that are useful for analysis of inter-organizational collaboration, such as 'organizational fields' (DiMaggio and Powell, 1983) and 'institutional logic' (Friedland and Alford, 1991). Nonetheless, these concepts do not say much about the more specific content of them in a certain context, or the relations between different institutional elements within a certain field or logic. The more specific content of the concepts must be filled contextually and empirically. This, on the other hand, is true (more or less) for all theoretical concepts, but my point is that a norm perspective can help in the direction of this 'filling out'.

The norm perspective within sociology of law has, in general, devoted limited attention to processes of organizations, which is a further argument for the proposed combination of perspectives outlined in this chapter. Several studies within the norm perspective have analysed perceived norm pressures or expectations of the individual. A combination with an institutional perspective instead directs attention to the norm pressures and perceived expectations of the organization from the broader institutional environment (including other organizations) by which they are surrounded and permeated.

In my understanding, out of a combination of institutional theory and a norm perspective, interactions between institutional orders and elements are of crucial importance for the understanding of 'normativity' in society. Institutional theory creates an overarching understanding, while a norm perspective is of help for a narrower analysis of the interaction between different elements, such as legal rules and social norms. It also contributes to a more nuanced understanding of the character of law as such.

Through a combination of these perspectives, it is possible to seriously explore the complex ways in which organizations – in collaboration with other organizations – negotiate and mediate the impact of regulations, norms and rules, stemming from differing institutional environments on different levels – and thereby negotiate, interpret, translate and construct the meaning of 'legal and social compliance' in a specific inter-organizational context. This is a way of broadly (and narrowly) exploring how law and normativity emerge in collaborative practice.

Concluding remarks

As pointed out in the introduction to this chapter, the boundaries of organizations are becoming more flexible and permeable. Inter-organizational collaboration in differing forms is an example thereof. Another related tendency acknowledged in the introduction, is that state law and formal legal rules are being challenged by other types of norms and softer forms of law. For example, collaborative rules (covering all or several organizations involved in an inter-organizational context of collaboration) are often of a more or less self-regulatory character, without specific formal sanctions connected to them. However, in many contexts of inter-organizational collaboration (at least involving the public sector), these norms are not replacing state law and legal rules tied to separate organizations, but rather adding to them. I posed the question how these tendencies affect law and normativity taking shape in inter-organizational collaboration, where the organizations involved are often governed by differing kinds of regulations and norm types, and thus which normative orders are established through collaboration.

I have argued for a broad understanding of law and, more specifically, for an understanding that focuses on the meaning that law gains in and through collaborative practice. This meaning – which continually undergoes negotiation and thus also varies between local contexts and over time – evolves through structuration processes, including negotiations between and around different types of norms and rules (that is, norms and rules on different levels, stemming from different sources). These could be state laws (which themselves can be of varying types, such as framework laws, coercive formal rules, or directives aiming more or less at self-regulation) but also social norms, agreements, guidelines, criteria, standards or contracts created through collaboration (see, for example, Johansson, 2012). These different kinds of rules and norms interplay with the broader institutional environments that they are part of (such as ideas, beliefs, traditions, routines, resources, problem definitions) and altogether affect, transform and create the institutionalization processes taking form in collaboration, and thus the creation of the meaning of law and normativity. This integrative framework, or 'institutions and norms in action in collaboration' perspective, can thus be said to analyse 'hybrid normativity'. The hybrid normativity could, in turn, be of different character – such as conflicting, contested, dominated or balanced – depending on contextual and power factors. This is also a way of locating state law and legal rules in wider normative and institutional orders.

As I see it, boundaries of organizations are of different character and on different levels in relation to inter-organizational collaboration, all together forming a mix of different norms and rules interplaying in a specific collaborative context, thereby leading to varied normative orders or hybrid normativity. So this is a matter of social and legal practice mixing and merging together through collaboration. Consequently, the institutional power balance can change through collaboration without being transparent, but on the contrary rather diffuse and hidden. Therefore, I see a need for future research in the field of study to pay particular attention to power aspects connected to inter-organizational collaboration and hybrid normativity, including further investigations into which types of norms and rules, stemming from which institutional orders, connected to which organizations, are becoming dominant in different inter-organizational contexts and collaborative practices in society, during different periods of time. I believe that the integrative framework outlined here, combining institutional theory (of organizational sociology) with a norm perspective (within sociology of law), can be especially useful for such analysis.

References

Baier, M. and Svensson, M. 2009. *Om normer*. Malmö: Liber.

Barley, S.R. and Tolbert, P.S. 1997. 'Institutionalization and Structuration: Studying the Links between Action and Institution', *Organization Studies*, 18, 93–117.

Cotterrell, R. 2012. 'What is Transnational Law?', *Law & Social Inquiry*, 37(2), 500–524.

Czarniawska, B. 1997. *Narrating the Organization. Dramas of Institutional Identity*. The University of Chicago Press.

Danermark, B. and Kullberg, C. 1999. *Samverkan: välfärdsstatens nya arbetsform*. Lund: Studentlitteratur.

DiMaggio, P.J. and Powell, W.W. 1983. 'The Iron Cage Revisited: Institutional Isomorphism and Collective Rationality in Organizational Fields', *American Sociological Association*, 48(2), 147–60.

Edelman, L.B. and Suchman, M.C. 1997. 'The Legal Environments of Organizations', *Annual Review of Sociology*, 23, 479–515.

Eriksson-Zetterquist, U. 2009. *Institutionell teori: idéer, moden, förändring*. Malmö: Liber.

Friedland, R. and Alford, R.R. 1991. 'Bringing Society Back In: Symbols, Practices and Institutional Contradictions', in *The New Institutionalism in Organizational Analysis*, edited by W.W. Powell and P.J. DiMaggio. Chicago: The University of Chicago Press.

Giddens, A. 1984. *The constitution of society: outline of the theory of structuration*. Berkeley: University of California Press.

Giddens, A. 1993. *New Rules of Sociological Method*. Polity Press.

Grape, O., Blom, B. and Johansson, R. 2006. *Organisation och omvärld: nyinstitutionell analys av människobehandlande organisationer*. Lund: Studentlitteratur.

Hardy, C. and Phillips, N. 1998. 'Strategies of Engagement: Lessons from the Critical Examination of Collaboration and Conflict in an Inter-organizational Domain', *Organization Science*, 9(2), 217–30.

Hydén, H. 1984. *Ram eller lag? Om ramlagstiftning och samhällsorganisation*. Stockholm: Liber.

Hydén, H. 2002. *Normvetenskap*. Lund: Lund University.

Hydén, H. and Svensson, M. 2008. 'The Concept of Norms in Sociology of Law', *Scandinavian Studies in Law*, Law and Society, 53, 15–32.

Johansson, R. 2009. 'Vid den institutionella analysens gränser: Institutionell organisationsteori i Sverige', *Nordiske Organisasjonsstudier*, 3, 5–22.

Johansson, S. 2011. *Rätt, makt och institutionell förändring. En kritisk analys av myndigheters samverkan i barnahus.* Diss. Lund: Lund University.

Johansson, S. 2012. 'Diffusion and Governance of "Barnahus" in the Nordic Countries: Report from an On-going Project', *Journal of Scandinavian Studies in Criminology and Crime Prevention*, 13(1), 69–84.

Jönsson, L., Persson, A. and Sahlin, K. 2011. *Institution*. Malmö: Liber.

Lindberg, K. 2009. *Samverkan*. Malmö: Liber.

Meyer, J.W. and Rowan, B. 1977. 'Institutionalized Organizations: Formal Structure as Myths and Ceremony' *The American Journal of Sociology*, 83(2), 340–63.

Phillips, N., Lawrence, T.B. and Hardy, C. 2000. 'Inter-Organizational Collaboration and the Dynamics of Institutional Fields', *Journal of Management Studies*, 37(1), 23–43.

Powell, W.W. and DiMaggio, P.J. 1991. *The New Institutionalism in Organizational Analysis*. Chicago: The University of Chicago Press.

Powell, W.W. 1996. 'Fields of Practice: Connections between Law and Organizations', *Law & Social Inquiry*, 21(4), 959–66.

Røvik, K.A. 2004. *Moderna organisationer: trender inom organisationstänkandet vid millennieskiftet*. Malmö: Liber.

Scott, R.W. 2004. 'Reflections on a Half-Century of Organizational Sociology', *Annual Review of Sociology*, 30, 1–21.

Scott, R.W. 2008a. *Institutions and organizations: ideas and interests*. 3rd edn. Thousand Oaks California: Sage.

Scott, R.W. 2008b. 'Lords of the Dance: Professionals as Institutional Agents', *Organization Studies*, 29, 219–38.

Selznick, P. 1948. 'Foundations of the Theory of Organization', *American Sociological Review*, 13(1), 25–35.

Suchman, M.C. and Edelman, L.B. 1996. 'Legal Rational Myths: The New Institutionalism and the Law and Society Tradition', *Law & Social Inquiry*, 21(4), 903–41.

Svensson, M. 2008. *Sociala normer och regelefterlevnad*. Diss. Lund: Lund University.

Chapter 8
Conceptions, Categories and Embodiment: Why Metaphors are of Fundamental Importance for Understanding Norms

Stefan Larsson

Introduction

An important point of sociology of law which is often brought up is law's social dependence (Aubert, 1972: 13; Mathiesen, 2005; Hydén, 1978: 26; Svensson and Larsson, 2012). This is also one of the key arguments for using the concept of norms to analyse society (Hydén and Svensson, 2008; Svensson, 2008). This chapter demonstrates how the fundamental lingual and conceptual meanings of metaphors and conceptions support this point. The propositions in this chapter are, to a large extent, drawn from an existing thesis (Larsson, 2011b), but with some important additions, not least concerning the implications of categorization. The chapter is explorative in bringing findings from cognitive linguistics into the quite common socio-legal task of studying norms. Its aim is not to debunk, but to assemble. The promise of cognitive theory is here found in its ability to make explicit the unconscious and cognitive operations that structure our conceptions of reality.

Emphasis is put on the importance of understanding how language, meaning and thought are connected. A main advantage of the metaphor-theoretical connection to general norm analysis lies in how language-based expressions and metaphors relate to the mind, how our thoughts are framed and thereby both controlled and enabled by how different conceptions are constructing metaphors. This goes for the most mundane and everyday events as well as law. This perspective indicates the significance of detailed studies of the surface structures, which have the potential to reveal underlying conceptions that may control a legal or social norm (Larsson, 2011b; Larsson and Hydén, 2010).

Cognitive linguistics is here argued to be of significance to norm studies. The important findings not only take into account the fact that metaphors play a much more fundamental role in thought and language than is traditionally acknowledged in the theory of law. The key findings concern how categorization is (really) done, the case of 'prototype effects' (that is, some members of a category are regarded as more 'true' representatives of that category than other members of the same category), and the framing aspects of conceptions and metaphors. This is further emphasized by the process of embodiment of metaphors, and, hence, law. In simple terms, law is in need of a reification in order to be talked and thought about. This process is therefore of great interest for anyone concerned with understanding law's place in society as a cognitive, lingual and cultural artefact. This chapter considers all of these contributions from cognitive linguistics, to see what may benefit the study of norms in sociology of law.

In the development of metaphor theories, Max Black (1962) has been influential, introducing a cognitive dimension. Black stated that metaphor is not just an aesthetic embellishment of language, but organizes and transforms our perception of the original term. The cognitive metaphor studies that have inspired this chapter started around 1980, with Lakoff and Johnson (1980).

Metaphors and policy

Of extra importance for this chapter is the analysis of law that has been made based on the work of Lakoff and Johnson (see Berger, 2004, 2007 and 2009; Blavin and Cohen, 2002; Herman, 2008; Hunter, 2003; Johnson, 2007; Joo, 2001; Larsson, 2011b, 2012b, 2012c and 2013a; Morra, 2010; Ritchie, 2007; Tsai, 2004; Winter, 2001, 2007 and 2008). Metaphor studies have found their way into policy research and political analysis. An example is the collection of chapters in Carver and Pikalo (2008). The anthology emphasizes the impact of our metaphoric language, and puts forwards the productive element of metaphors in the subtitle, 'interpreting *and* changing the world'. However, many of the contributors draw their theoretical foundation from the conceptual metaphor theory of Lakoff and Johnson, and inspiration is also found in Black (1962 and 1979) and the pragmatic philosophy of Schön (1979), for instance.

Metaphors and norms

Metaphors cannot only be studied in relation to legal norms, but in relation to social norms as well. It has been suggested that they may be fruitful when studying the imperative essence of social norms (Larsson, 2011b: 52–3, 65–8, 123–4), as defined by Svensson (2008) and Hydén and Svensson (2008). The major methodological difference between studying legal metaphors versus socially embedded metaphors affecting social norms is found in the formalized character of the legal norm. The legal formalization creates certain and fixed metaphors, and hence 'locked-in' conceptions, whereas the socially embedded metaphors and conceptions probably require another type of empirical evidence when studied (Larsson, 2011b: 85–7).

It has been shown that legal metaphors can allow rather substantial changes in meaning without necessarily changing concepts, as Larsson (2011b) has shown in relation to 'intellectual property' and the 'copy' in copyright law in a digital society (see also Larsson 2012a and 2012b). This means that the study of legal metaphors is a study of fixed metaphors, whereas the study of the metaphors that control a social norm needs to be separately formulated. For example, when Svensson and Larsson (2012) studied the strength of social norms corresponding to copyright among approximately 1,000 respondents in Sweden, they had to define the social norm in similar (but not exactly the same) terms as the legal norm. This means that the the understanding of the social norm, to a greater extent than the legal norm, is likely to be sensitive to and dependent on the choices of the formulator. This is the case especially where a study is made of social norms that do not correspond to legal norms (that is, that do not have a pre-formulated conception of a norm on which they are based).

According to Mark Johnson, a professor in philosophy, there is a Western moral tradition in which we make ethical decisions by applying universal laws to concrete situations. Contrary to this conception, Johnson (1993) shows how research in cognitive science undermines this view of normatively controlled and enlightened behaviour and reveals that imagination has an essential role in ethical deliberation. How we conceptualize and imagine how we can act not only has implications for how we actually act, but also for what we think is just and appropriate behaviour. These imaginative paths are probably not unforeseeable and random, as Winter puts it: 'Despite the fact that it is conventional to think of imagination as random, unpredictable, or indeterminate, it is actually orderly and systematic in operation' (Winter, 2001: 259).

It is a task for the sociologist of law, among others, to depict the implications of these systematic and orderly processes of imagination in terms of implications for behaviour and social norms. However, for us to understand these implications, we must turn to how metaphors operate in detail, as well as relate them to underlying conceptions.

Metaphors

The key idea of metaphors is that they are analogies which allow us to map one experience (the target domain) in the terminology of another experience (the source domain), and thus to acquire an understanding of complex topics or new situations. The metaphors often tend to be viewed as exclusively linked to linguistic structures, rather than to thinking and the mind. In contrast to this minimalist conception of metaphors, cognitive scientists George Lakoff and Mark Johnson (Lakoff and Johnson, 1980/2003: 3) showed that 'metaphor is pervasive in everyday life, not just in language but in thought and action. Our ordinary conceptual system, in terms of which we both think and act, is fundamentally metaphorical in nature'. This means that metaphors are not simply a figure of speech, but a 'figure of thought' (Lakoff, 1986) – that is, focusing on metaphors not merely as lingual features but as conceptual features. Consider the following examples:

Source Domain	Target Domain
Lion	My dad
Journey	Love

There is a major difference between these two metaphors. They both share the mapping from source domain to a target domain, which is the essence of metaphoricity, but the first one ('my dad is a lion') is an easily detected and figurative metaphor, whereas the other ('love is a journey') is a conceptual metaphor, from which a number of other metaphors relating to each other can be derived in a 'metaphor cluster' (see Larsson, 2011b: 60–61, 72–3; Larsson, 2012b; Loughlan, 2006).

The first example creates the figurative metaphor of 'my dad is a lion'. It is, as stated, pretty clear to most people that this is a metaphor for something, and that some aspects of the source domain are mapped onto the target domain in order to achieve some effect on the target domain. Since there are also cultural patterns involved in this, these aspects are likely to relate to something similar to the assertion that my dad is strong, fierce and perhaps something of a leader – in our culture, the lion is sometimes described as the 'king of the animals' (this bears evidence to how a lion is conceptualized, which emphasizes its cultural dependence). Consequently, the ordinary use of this metaphor would also exclude aspects from the source domain that could just as well be meaningful but are not, such as 'my dad is a lion – and is therefore covered with fur and eats antelope'.

For the other metaphor, which describes that 'love is a journey', there are a number of expressions that are connected to this metaphor according to Lakoff and Johnson: it is a conceptual metaphor, from which follows that it is meaningful to say, for instance, that 'our relationship has hit a dead-end street', 'we're going in different directions', or 'our relationship is at a crossroads' (Lakoff, 1986; Lakoff and Johnson, 1999: 123). It is meaningful to speak of several other related versions of the same conception of 'love is a journey'. This means that this is rather a cluster of metaphors derived from one conception of relationships. While some of the metaphors in the cluster may be clearly seen as metaphorical, others might not be perceived as so clearly figurative or metaphorical, such as 'this relationship isn't going anywhere'. This pattern of cross-domain mapping is of extreme importance here. There is one conception (in my terminology – see Larsson, 2011b) creating meaning for one cluster; not many completely unrelated metaphors. Such expressions can be part of everyday language, because the 'love is a journey' mapping is part of our ordinary, everyday way of conceptualizing love and relationships and how to reason about them.

The conception defines what is a socially meaningful use of language for a given phenomenon, and it does so through metaphor. By emphasizing the social aspects of meaning-making, the context-dependency and the 'situated' (cf Svensson, 2008: 52 onwards), the socio-cultural implications are of great importance. Winter expresses this in terms that '(m)eaning is a shared social phenomenon that constrains how we as embodied and culturally situated humans understand our world' (2001: 315). A further generalization that we can make regarding metaphor comprehension is that it is mandatory, in the sense that it is an 'automatic' interpretation made by us (Glucksberg, 2008). This means that literal meaning has no priority; the associative paths creating meaning are there anyway. The metaphor cluster – what Lakoff and Johnson call a 'conceptual metaphor' – highlights the question of what it is that conceptually ties the cluster together as one meaningful entity. How is it framed and delimited, and by what structures does it operate?

Conceptions

To focus the conceptions is to focus the framing structures of thought (Larsson, 2011b: 65–70, 130–32). They are seen as underlying metaphors and can be regarded as the acting fundamental behind, for example, legal statutes, or the basis for a metaphor cluster. The concept of conceptions that is proposed by Larsson (2011b) is inspired by both the conceptual metaphor theory (Lakoff and Johnson, 1980), including 'cognitive models' of cognitive linguistics (Lakoff, 1987) as well as the concept of 'figures of thought' from social science, stemming from Asplund (1979) and Foucault (2001). Views of conceptions have further been used in teaching and learning science, often to display student thinking and 'conceptual change'. It has played a significant role in this line of research since the late 1970s – for instance, speaking of conceptions as learners' mental models of an object or an event (Glynn and Duit, 1995; Treagust and Duit, 2008).

Conceptions focus the building blocks and frames for the mind and for thinking, rather than the pictorial of figurative aspects of them. The conception is seen here as a subsurface structure. The conception is, in this sense, not what is explicit (for instance, in a legal regulation), but what the legal regulation (often) implicitly emanates from. It forms its 'logic'. By studying legal metaphors, or metaphors in legal imperative formulations, it is possible to reveal the conceptions upon which they are formed. This is relevant because of what was just stated about metaphors – they are often not perceived as metaphors – their work is often hidden on a subconscious level and might erroneously be perceived as though we actually 'speak of Things as they are', as John Locke expressed it (Locke, 1975/1690). When the metaphors are not perceived as metaphors, the conceptions behind them will be perceived as the only possible alternative for the purpose of a given regulation. It does not seem possible to find any meaningful alternatives to a certain logic or thought structure, or – which may be even more important – there is no reason for even trying to find an alternative. This means that any attempted revisionary arguments will then be framed within the prevailing conception, no matter what arguments are being produced. That is, unless the conception is analytically unlocked and displayed via the metaphors that reproduce it. I will return to this issue below when studying norms.

Social norms and conceptions

A metaphor theory revealing conceptions can be used not only to analyse metaphors hidden in formulated legal norms. When a debate about an abstract relation develops, it needs some sort of conceptualization in order for the debaters to position themselves in relation to each other. Depending on this conceptualization, which can be contested or not contested by any party, based on conscious or unconscious choices, the frame is set for the debate, with the result that some aspects are easier to talk about than others. To bring this abstract talk into clearer relief, the example can be provided from the political debates that started in the mid-1990s in Sweden regarding professional household services (*hushållsnära tjänster*), and the possibility of deducting tax when employing these. Further back in Swedish history, it was common for households with well-ordered finances to employ a 'maid' (*piga*). In Swedish, however, the word '*piga*' signalizes the hierarchy between the maid and the members of the family, where the maid is subordinate. It implies a social structure of classes in a way that brought negative connotations to the political debate. Those who were against the political proposition of offering tax deductions for household services brought up this old concept and termed the debate the 'maid debate'. The concept struck a chord in the debate, and thereafter reframed the debate itself, forcing everyone who was in favour of tax deductions for household services to deal with the 'maid' conceptualization of the debate (see Platzer, 2004). In this particular context, this conceptualization was very advantageous to the critics of the proposal.

In more general terms, this could be described as the underlying conception setting the interpretative frames for what will seem like the logical consequences of any given debate surrounding a particular phenomenon. And those who manage to steer this framework, by applying particular metaphors, can also guide the development of debates. Yanow (2008) highlights the framing aspect of metaphor with the example of the American debate on abortion. By framing the issue as 'pro-life', the movement against abortion, by the logic of language use, forces the oppositional label 'anti-life'. Not wanting to be forced into such negative language, the 'for access to abortion' camp narrates itself as 'pro-choice' (Yanow, 2008: 228). In other words, the conception can be perceived as a frame of mind – a frame that we in no way have to be conscious about. However, when it is a conscious practice, this frame-like essence of conceptions is useful as a rhetoric skill. This applies also to the 'framing' of debates and arguments, of which legislative processes are not free from. As Lakoff explains:

> Remember, don't just negate the other person's claims; reframe. The facts unframed will not set you free. You cannot win just stating the true facts and showing that they contradict your opponent's claims. Frames trump facts. His frames will stay and the facts will bounce off. Always reframe. (Lakoff, 2005)

This is when the use of metaphors, and the framing of conceptions (although they are not necessarily perceived as metaphors and frames), have become a rhetorical strategy. Beginning from an opponent's metaphor is a difficult rhetorical stance, so choosing one's own metaphor or conception from which to begin is generally a much better strategy. The trick in a debate is to attach a metaphor to it that carries with it normative values that are beneficial to one's own position. However, the framing aspects of metaphors and their underlying conceptions probably apply to most abstract phenomena. The borrowing of a concept from one domain to another – considering our conceptual system as being 'fundamentally metaphoric in nature' – is often done with bodily operations, spatial relations or physical artefacts as source.

Embodiment

Embodiment, and what here to some extent may be called spatialization, is of great importance for the process of something becoming meaningful, according to the focused strand of cognitive science (Gibbs, 2005; Johnson, 1987; Lakoff, 1987; Lakoff and Johnson, 1999). In conceptual metaphor theory, this is often referred to as the embodiment of the metaphors (Kövecses, 2008; Lakoff, 1993; Winter, 2001). This follows from the fact that metaphors are so common and a fundamental part and process of language and the mind. This statement means that there is constant borrowing in progress, and interdependence on the surrounding context, in order for language to become meaningful. In short, metaphors are often based on our interaction with our physical and social environment. They are derived from bodily sensations, for instance found in image-schemas, such as that balance keeps you 'upright'; more is 'up', for when you add things to each other, you increase the pile upwards (Lakoff, 1993: 240).

The conceptual metaphor theories fitted well with the 'conduit metaphor' system first identified by Michael Reddy (Reddy, 1979; see also Winter, 2007: 884; Winter, 2001: 52–6). It is a systemic set of mappings from the source domain of physical objects to the target domain of mental operations:

Source Domain	Target Domain
PHYSICAL	MENTAL
object	ideas
seeing	knowing
container (vehicle)	words
content	ideational content
sending	communicating
grasping (receiving)	understanding
container	mind

These are conceptions that guide and also control how new metaphors develop, and they can be represented by the mnemonics 'Ideas are objects', 'Knowing is seeing', 'Words are containers', 'Communication is sending', 'Ideational content is (physical) content', 'Communication is sending', 'Understanding is grasping', and 'The mind is a container'. The 'conduit metaphor' system enables us to automatically extend the conceptual mapping by modelling other actions in the physical domain – as a result of embodiment. It is thus meaningful to speak of the 'content' of this chapter, trying to 'grasp' the concept of norms in sociology of law, or to 'see' the point I am trying to make here.

Expressing the dependency on the physical and spatial can be made in the words of Steven F. Winter:

> Thought is not primarily linguistic and propositional, but embodied and imaginative; language is neither entirely arbitrary nor merely socially contingent, but grounded in our embodiment and motivated by our interactions with the physical and social world. (Winter, 2001: 47)

We borrow constantly from the physical world, from the objects, the body and the spatial sphere, in order to describe and talk about the abstract. This is where we must be extremely attentive in relation to how our understanding is built. Many of the building blocks for how this works, even for much less obviously metaphorical concepts, can be found in cognitive linguistics, but also in the symbol- and language-oriented legal (critical) discourse. In terms of the ontological account, the embodiment should, however, probably not be taken as evidence that the values attached to specific metaphors or any language can be constructed completely unrestrained by patterns, as a more social constructionist perspective would imply, nor that they are 'natural' and completely rationally fixated (see Larsson, 2012c). There are patterns, and they can be strong patterns and be perceived as 'natural', but they are, to some extent, negotiated socially and culturally. A point here is not that a freedom exists in general, but that these patterns are probably often different from the rationalistically defined and outspoken patterns and categorizations (Johnson, 2007).

The metaphor researcher Ning Yu develops the dual connection of metaphor to both body and culture. Yu shows how an analysis of the distinction between primary and complex metaphors allows us to determine which aspects of metaphor are bodily or culturally based. This allows Yu to set up a hypothesis that primary metaphors, derived from bodily experience, are likely to be widespread and universal, while complex metaphors, based on conceptual mappings and cultural beliefs, are likely to be more culturally specific (Yu, 2008).

A consequence of this embodiment is that law is also constructed from embodied metaphor and linguistic operations, relying on the in-the-mind cognitive approach (Johnson, 2007; Larsson, 2012b and 2013a and 2013b; Winter, 2001: 22–42). These findings question the 'objectivist' approach in law (Johnson, 2007). As law is an abstract social phenomenon, it is more the case that the need for metaphors is greater than ever. We need to 'reify' and embody law in order to talk about it, think about it and understand it. As a result, Winter claims that law can constantly be found in a dependent position, which requires object-making, a reification, where we talk about law as something physical (Winter, 2001 and 2008). This is particularly noticeable in clear metaphors: 'as the long arm of the law' (Berger, 2009: 262–6) and how we 'take law in our own hands', but perhaps slightly less clearly in how we 'break' the law, sign a 'binding' contract or 'trespass' when sharing files that we are not authorized to share. We speak of a *corpus juris*, and how we understand law is depending on this reification (Larsson, 2011b: 64–5; Larsson, 2012b; Winter, 2001: 334).

Norms and embodiment

The embodiment of metaphors probably also means that norms are dependent on the same processes of embodiment. When norms emerge and are formulated (as with legal norms), they do so in interplay with the surrounding culture, milieu or architecture, in 'interactions with the physical and social world' (Winter, 2001: 47). They are somehow 'cognitively situated', as Måns Svensson describes the norm concept in sociology of law, outlined above (Svensson, 2008; see also Svensson and Larsson, 2012). This means that the focus should not be on the individual's cognition, but on the context that the individual is in. As Svensson explains:

> Cognition is basically about how people perceive their environment – in an extension of perception, memory, concept formation, reasoning, problem solving and attention. All these processes are active in some way when people create an impression of societal norms and how their surroundings expect that they should relate to different phenomena in everyday life. (Svensson, 2008: 52, author's translation)

The point of view of situated cognition sees knowledge as inseparable from social, cultural and physical contexts. It is the shared expectations, social norms and social control that, to a large extent, control the cognitive processes (Svensson, 2008). The situated cognition can possibly work as a link between conceptions on the one hand, and social norms on the other, connecting the two, adding to the explanation of the social processes that contribute to makes us share conceptions. This means that, if cognition changes from being situated (that is, if the embodiment is processed under new constraints of a changing reality), the norms may change as well (Larsson, 2011b: 124–6; cf Larsson, 2013a; 2013b).

Further, embodiment supports the argument of Stanley Fish, namely that the distinction between text and context is impossible to maintain because there can be no such thing as a non-contextual sense (Fish, 1989: 329). This means that it is not the focus on the text that is of essence, but the bundle of tacit assumptions that organize the world for us, for our thinking, our actions and, hence, our norms.

Metaphors and law

If art is the 'legitimate paradigm of unconscious activity' (Kofman, 1993: 31), then law, it seems, is often hailed as the complete opposite. The legal concepts are presented in an 'objectivist view', with 'strict, fixed boundaries defined by necessary and sufficient conditions' (Johnson, 2007: 847). There is a growing field of research into interpreting legal metaphors. Many persons interested in legal analysis, influenced by this school of metaphor theory, start their presentation with the conflicting perspective on metaphors in law. They often do that by citing the early American legal realist, Justice Cardozo, who observed that 'metaphors in law are to be narrowly watched, for though starting as devices to liberate thought, they end often by enslaving it' (see Berger, 2004; Herman, 2008; Patry, 2009; Winter, 2008). Ironically enough, and as is often pointed out, this statement by Cardozo uses at least two important metaphors – liberation and slavery (Loughlan, 2006). Cardozo's view follows in the same tradition as the famous enlightenment philosopher, John Locke, who condemned metaphor and other figurative speech as 'perfect cheat' and insisted on literal prose 'if we speak of Things as they are' (Locke, 1975/1690). Conceptual metaphor theories collide with a more formal approach to meaning and truth. A formal approach underlines the objective, literary and linear thinking, whereas metaphors are considered only as colourful, figurative linguistic symbols or expressions, used to express a point clearly. This includes law and legal thinking. Robert Tsai writes:

> Legal scholars have traditionally understood metaphor as, at worst, a perversion of the law, and at best, as a necessary but temporary placeholder for more fully developed lines of argument. On this view, metaphors are vague and inherently manipulable, appealing to base instincts, whereas explicit legal argumentation represents the rigorous, authentic core of law. (Tsai, 2004: 186)

This conception in the legal field has been durable and strong. The British philosopher Jeremy Bentham (1748–1832) thought that metaphors were the anti-thesis to legal reasoning (Bentham and Ogden, 1931). The traditional legal perception of the unimportant place and function of metaphors in law is, in other words, completely at odds with what language and cognition research has shown from 1980 onwards. The philosophy professor and cognitive scientist Mark Johnson is using these insights to study the language-based judicial system and to ask how we can gain a better understanding of how legal knowledge and reasoning works, and sees part of the answer in cognitive legal research, in a 'cognitive science of law' – that is, how thinking works in relation to legal concepts and legal decision-making (Johnson, 2007). Johnson argues that legal reasoning and legal concepts are based on a sort of self-image of objectivity. This 'objectivist view' includes the idea that concepts have strict limits and are defined by necessary and sufficient conditions, which contradicts the empirical findings in cognitive and linguistic research (see, for instance, Winter, 2001). Johnson's main point for including cognitive science in the study of law is that the legal 'objectivist view' is based on an incorrect understanding of how thinking and language works (Johnson, 2007: 847).

Metaphors in law

Linda Berger, an American professor of law, has successfully used metaphor theory to analyse the judicial decision-making in custody disputes (Berger, 2009), rhetorical choices in (the US) Supreme Court Decisions on campaign finance regulation (Berger, 2007), and to help lawyers shape the law (Berger, 2004). Her conclusion is that lawmakers cannot avoid being affected in their decision-making by myths, metaphors and symbols. Berger analyses cases involving determining which parent is best suited to have custody, when there is often no rational basis for choosing one parent over another. Decisions must, however, be taken, and Berger argues that there are 'embedded knowledge structures' that influence judicial decision-making in a negative and unconscious way. This is sometimes a disadvantage to individual families which are not constituted according to a more traditionally rooted picture of what families ('should') look like. Berger makes what she calls a rhetorical analysis in order to 'uncover the symbols and stories that affect judicial decision-making and then to construct arguments that may overcome deeply rooted constraint, help individual clients, and persuade policy makers' (Berger, 2009: 260):

> The rhetorical analysis indicates that the best interests of the child standard fails to explain child custody outcomes, and the analysis suggests that the cognitive setting for custody disputes – cluttered with outmoded metaphors, simplistic images, and unexamined narratives – interferes with the ability of judges to attend to complex and radical transformations of parent-child relationships. (Berger, 2009: 260)

In this sense, she argues that better understanding of the cognitive role of metaphor can help display how law is dependent on symbols and metaphors, which is of extra importance when these are 'outmoded' or perhaps not in line with those of the rest of society.

Categorization

Categorization is a fundamental activity in language, thought, decision-making – and, not least, law – which probably correlates with how norms affect behaviour. How we categorize – be it socially reproduced or neurologically connected – probably determines which social norms are alerted in a given situation and which legal norms should apply for a specific case. There is a classic Aristotelian approach to categorization that sees it as based on grouping objects on the basis of their similar properties. According to the classical view, categories should be clearly defined, mutually exclusive and collectively exhaustive (Lakoff and Johnson, 1999: 373–414). However, a cognitive approach following Lakoff and Johnson (1999) renounces the classic approach, in that it accepts that natural categories are graded (they tend to be indistinct at their boundaries) and inconsistent in the status of their constituent members. It is not that the classic view is entirely wrong, according to the cognitive approach; it is just that the categorization based on shared properties only displays a (small) part of the story (Lakoff, 1987: 5). This means that even categories are, to some extent, culturally biased, and connected to embodiment. This has implications for the study of norms in the sense that, whenever it concerns categories, the study should include an empirical approach to the categories that the norms are dependent on, instead of an ideal or analytic definition of the category. How we categorize (in practice) probably has implications for how we reason about and justify behaviour. For example, Goodenough and Decker (2008) studied neurological aspects of how people experience property in relation to intellectual property by looking at neurological functions. They concluded that traditional approaches to property, in particular those relating to tangible objects, are supported, at least in part, by functional neurological structures or networks in the brain that help to recognize property-related choices and to link them to emotional, inhibitory processing. Further, they state that these property-related primitives and/or networks are not readily elicited and mobilized by concepts of intellectual property. Following the point made by Goodenough and Becker, this could be expressed as the way in which we experience reality has something to do with defining what we find right and wrong. The Goodenough and Decker conclusion, in the field of 'cognitive jurisprudence', suggests that people do not experience illegal file sharing as stealing, in its physical sense. This is supported by studies which have found the social norm corresponding to copyright to be extremely weak (Svensson and Larsson, 2012; see also Larsson et al., 2013) – regardless of the letter of the law.

A common practice in law-making and legal decision-making is to form categories. The legal categorization is often viewed in a conventionalist standard view, which states that categories are descriptive, definitional, and have exact delimitations. It follows from this view that any example chosen from within a category will represent the category equally well. In contrast to this view, cognitive science claims that there is a pattern, and it is empirically detectable, but it is often not the same pattern as the conventionalist or rationalist view. From this practical approach to categorization follows that certain members of a category are generally regarded as more representative members of that category than others. For instance, when speaking of furniture, 'chair' is more frequently cited than 'stool' (Rosch 1975 and 1978; see also, for instance, Lakoff, 1987). 'Prototype theory' is a departure from the Aristotelian logic – that categories are logical, clearly bounded entities, whose membership is defined by an item's possession of a simple set of criterial features, in which all instances possessing the criterial attributes have a full and equal degree of membership. Prototype effects mean a sort of graded categorization, again as opposed to a traditional objectivist view (Amsterdam and Bruner, 2000; Lakoff, 1987; Winter, 2001). In addition to this, the categorization that we do in our everyday lives, just as with the use of metaphors, is automatic and unconscious (Lakoff, 1987). This is a fact that makes any study of norms – which includes categorization of some sort – in need of at least some reflection upon how this categorization is being done.

Scientific categorization as ontological politics

There is a methodological difference between a legal scholar who wants to investigate existing law and a social scientist who seeks to state something about the circumstances of the world. To connect to the knowledge of categorization from cognitive science, there are more than just language-level reasons for broadening this presentation of how scientific work is being done. If we look at arguments in the theory of science, Brante (2008 and 2009) discusses the elements of scientific analysis, and claims that there is a third element which is often missed, which works as an intermediary between theory and empirical data as a condition for making it useful. Brante proposes what he calls 'fundamental categories'. By means of this, he highlights the extreme importance in science of defining categories, as the results are heavily dependent on them:

> In other words, classification is no innocent activity but, on the one hand, is a presupposition for a discipline's observation and identification of significant facts, and, on the other, provides the building blocks – basic concepts – between which associations and causal relations can be established. (Brante, 2008: 274)

This places the focus on what cognitive science claims regarding categorization in general. According to Brante, the first of the three elements of scientific work is the descriptive part, meaning measurements, calculations, observations, experiments, representations, narratives and so on. The second is the specific way in which a science divides the object of study into categories and subdivisions. In other words, categorization is a condition for scientific observations and identification of relevant facts. At the same time, the categorization supplies the science with the basic concepts between which connections and causal relations can be determined. This determination is thus the third element, which is not surprising; the explanations are the same as connecting concepts and categories to each other. A main point that Brante makes is that descriptions are category-dependent. The typologies and concepts that we use to sort facts, in order to determine relevance, can also sometimes 'produce' facts. Social science is highly dependent on categorizations – for example, Durkheim (organic/mechanic, repressive/restitutive), Marx (classes), Tönnies (Gemeinschaft/Gesellschaft),

Merton (dysfunctional/functional, manifest/latent), and how we as scientists use divisions of history such as traditional, modern, post-modern; industrial society/knowledge society, analogue/digital, classes, gender, ethnicity, globalization, non-globalization, humanist/post-humanist. And think for a moment about law – it is an 'empire' of categorization. How do you study such a categorized domain as sociologists of law? Generally, we trade these categorizations for others, hopefully more theoretically justified, but in a sense we are trapped in the categorizations that the domain brings. And these can be normative, producing aspects of reality and control of how we conceptualize the phenomena that they categorize.

Law and Urry make the case of hidden politics or world views in social science, and they claim that 'social and physical changes in the world are – and need to be – paralleled by changes in the methods of social inquiry' (Law and Urry, 2004: 390). First, they argue that social inquiry and its methods are productive, in the sense that they contribute in the making of social realities and social worlds. They do not simply describe the world as it is, but also enact it. Second, they press some of the implications of this claim. In particular, if social investigation makes worlds, then it can, in some measure, think about the worlds that it wants to help to make. It gets involved, in other words, in the business of ontological politics. At the same time, they argue that its methods – and its politics – are still stuck in, and tend to reproduce, nineteenth-century, nation-state-based politics. The problem is then naturally the question of how we move in social science from the enactment of nineteenth-century realities? The authors suggest that there are many possibilities. For instance, they suggest a commitment to what they call 'sociology of the elusive', and elaborate on the potential of a 'social science of complexity'. To return to Brante, categories are prerequisites for descriptions, but also for explanations. Categorization is a type of 'ontological model' that is chosen, derived or for some reason prevailing in a scientific tradition. When focusing on 'categorization' in social science, there is a risk of getting stuck in something of a surface phenomenon, which would miss the importance behind simply dividing descriptions and explanations under different titles. The category-dependency tells something more about how to reach a conclusion, and which conclusions will be perceived as proper in the scientific context. In search of his fundamental categories, Brante refers to concepts such as 'Denkstiel' (Fleck, 1979), 'paradigm' (Kuhn, 1997), and 'thought style' (Douglas, 1996) in order to focus on this 'third element' of scientific method. He refers to Walter Buckley, who writes: 'Scientific work, analytically speaking, goes on at three, not two, distinguishable levels: besides empirical and logico-deductive theory we have the equally important, though all too implicit, frameworks, models, or philosophies that inform our approach to both of the former' (Buckley, 1967: viii).

Speaking of this 'third level' is a way to acknowledge that part of scientific work which refers to some sort of choices of structurization, the moment where the scientist affects the explanations in the research. When studying norms (legal or social), this argument calls for an awareness of the steering capabilities of categorization.

Conclusion

Language is fundamentally metaphoric in nature, and the framing aspects of our perhaps surprisingly metaphoric language is of great relevance, not only to legal analysis in a way not generally spoken of or acknowledged, but also to analysis of norms other than legal norms. Metaphors in language, and law, do not passively describe reality better or worse. In fact, it is quite the opposite: metaphors in a sense produce (our construction of) reality, as they frame our conceptions in certain patterns, and categorize metaphors and concepts into seemingly necessary but often falsely indispensable categories. Much of this stems from the fact that our conceptual system is fundamentally metaphoric in nature, and thus relying on embodiment and the surrounding physical and cultural context. Further, although the metaphor and conception analysis is thankfully applied to legal norms due to their often text-based sources of interpretation, this type of analysis may also aid the understanding of the operation of other types of norms as well. For instance, a metaphor representing a particular social norm may reveal underlying conceptions that affect and are relevant for a particular behaviour without being spoken of or conscious to us. The analysis of metaphoric patterns is a way to outline what the underlying and ruling conceptions are. The theory's explanatory function works in just the same way, although the methodology is possibly different, due to the difference in how the norm types are represented.

A theory or elaborated concept of conceptions can help to deconstruct the frameworks or underlying cognitive models on which a norm is based or to which it correlates. A part of the necessity of this lies in the fact that we may not even be aware that a norm is based on a particular conception in the first place; we might perceive it as 'objectively' describing the circumstances when, in fact, it is framed within a particular conception. For example, metaphor analysis can both reveal hidden and automatically associated values in legal metaphors, as well as outline the conception on which a particular law or legal rule is based (and framed).

Recognition of metaphorical thought, and the methods of conceptual analysis, demonstrate how legislative statutes express significant aspects of our social reality which cannot be devalued by reductive approaches to legal reasoning (see Larsson, 2011b; Winter, 2008). A main point is that, although the meaning is very much bound to specific patterns, these patterns can be, and probably often are, different from the 'objectively' defined patterns of meaning. The concept of prototype effects clearly displays this in terms of categorization – in a general as well as a legal context (Johnson, 2007; Lakoff, 1987; Winter, 2001: 331). The approach of cognitive linguistics to norms offers a toolbox of deconstructive tools for norm analysis.

Categorization is a fundamental activity by which we make sense of the world. This activity is heavily dependent on metaphors, which are often embodied. It is an activity that therefore cannot be neutral or objective, but represents (ontological) 'choices' which have implications for norms, actions, law, as well as for scientific enquiry as a whole.

References

Amsterdam, A.G. and Bruner, J. 2000. *Minding the Law. How courts rely on storytelling, and how their stories change the ways we understand the law – and ourselves*. Harvard University Press.

Asplund, J. 1979. *Teorier om framtiden*. Stockholm.

Aubert, V. 1972. *Rättssociologi*. Stockholm: Aldus/Bonnier.

Bentham, J. 1931. *The theory of legislation*. Edited with an introduction and notes by C.K. Ogden. London: Trübner and Co.

Berger, L.L. 2009. 'How embedded knowledge structures affect judicial decision making: A rhetorical analysis of metaphor, narrative, and imagination in child custody disputes', 18 *S. Cal. Interdisc. L.J.* 259–308.

Berger, L.L. 2007. 'Of Metaphor, Metonymy, and Corporate Money: Rhetorical Choices in Supreme Court Decisions on Campaign Finance Regulation', *Mercer Law Review* 58, 949–90.

Berger, L.L. 2004. 'What is the sound of a corporation speaking? How the cognitive theory of metaphor can help lawyers shape the law', 2 *J. Ass'n Legal Writing Directors* 169–208.

Black, M. 1962. *Models and Metaphors: Studies in Language and Philosophy*. New York: Cornell University Press.

Black, M. 1979. 'More About Metaphor', in *Metaphor and Thought*, edited by A. Ortony. Cambridge: Cambridge University Press.

Brante, T. 2008. 'Explanatory and non-explanatory goals in the social sciences', *Philosophy of the Social Sciences*, 38(2), 271–8.

Brante, T. 2009. 'Kategorins makt', in *Den berusade båten*, edited by R. Eliasson-Lappalainen, A. Meeuwisse and A. Panican. Lund: Arkiv förlag.

Carver, T. and Pikalo, J. (eds). 2008. *Political language and metaphor, Interpreting and changing the world*. Abingdon and New York: Routledge.

Drulák, P. 2008. 'Identifying and assessing metaphors: discourse on EU reform', in *Political language and metaphor, Interpreting and changing the world*, edited by T. Carver and J. Pikalo. Abingdon and New York: Routledge.

Fish, S. 1989. *Doing what comes naturally: change, rhetoric and the practice of theory in literature and legal studies*. Oxford: Clarendon Press.

Foucault, M. 2001. *Order of Things: An Archaeology of the Human Sciences*. London and New York: Routledge.

Gibbs, R.W. 2005. *Embodiment and Cognitive Science*. Cambridge University Press.

Glynn, S.M. and Duit, R. 1995. 'Learning science meaningfully: Constructing conceptual models', in *Learning science in the schools: Research reforming practice*, edited by S.M. Glynn and R. Duit. New Jersey: Lawrence Erlbaum Associates.

Goodenough, O.R. and Decker, G.J. 2008. 'Why do good people steal intellectual property?', in Freeman, M. and Goodenough, O.R. (eds) *Law, Mind and Brain*. Aldershot: Ashgate, Berkman Center Research Publication No. 2008-2, 345–72.

Hedrén, J. 1994. *Miljöpolitikens natur*. Linköping studies in art and science 110.

Hydén, H. 2002. *Normvetenskap*. Lund: Lund University, Lund Studies in Sociology of Law.

Hydén, H. 1978. *Rättens samhälleliga funktioner*. Lund: Studentlitteratur.

Hydén, H. and Svensson, M. 2008. 'The Concept of Norms in Sociology of Law', in *Scandinavian Studies in Law*, edited by P. Wahlgren. Stockholm: Law and Society.

Johnson, M.L. 2007. 'Mind, Metaphor, Law', *Mercer Law Review*, 58, 845–68.

Johnson, M.L. 1993. *Moral Imagination: Implications of Cognitive Science for Ethics*. Chicago: University of Chicago Press.

Johnson, M.L. 1987. *The body of the mind: The bodily basis of meaning, imagination, and reason*. Chicago, IL, US: University of Chicago Press.

Knutagård, M. 2009. *Skälens fångar: Hemlöshetsarbetets organisering, kategoriseringar och förklaringar*. Lund: Egalité, Lund University.

Kofman, S. 1993. *Nietzsche and Metaphor*, translated by Duncan Large. London: The Athlone Press.

Kövecses, Z. 2008. 'Conceptual metaphor theory. Some criticisms and alternative proposals', *Annual Review of Cognitive Linguistics* 6, 168–84.

Lakoff, G. 1986. 'A figure of thought', *Metaphor and symbol*, 1(3), 215–25.

Lakoff, G. 2005. *Don't think of an elephant: Know your values and reframe the debate*, 115. Chelsea Green Publishing.

Lakoff, G. and Johnson, M. 1999. *Philosophy in the flesh: the embodied mind and its challenge to Western thought*. New York: Basic Books.

Lakoff, G. 1993. 'The Contemporary Theory of Metaphor', in *Metaphor and Thought* (2nd edition), edited by A. Ortony. Cambridge University Press.

Lakoff, G. 1987. *Women, fire and dangerous things: What categories reveal about mind*. Chicago, IL: University of Chicago Press.

Lakoff, G. and Johnson, M. 1980. *Metaphors we live by*. Chicago: University of Chicago Press.

Larsson, S. 2010. '459 miljarder kronor – om metaforer, flöden & exemplar', in *Efter The Pirate Bay*, edited by J. Andersson and P. Snickars. Stockholm: Mediehistoriskt arkiv, Kungliga biblioteket.

Larsson, S. 2012a. 'Conceptions in the Code: What "the copyright wars" tells about creativity, social change and normative conflicts in the digital society', *Societal Studies*, 4(3), 1009–30.

Larsson, S. 2012b. 'Copy Me Happy – The Metaphoric Expansion of Copyright in a Digital Society', *International Journal for the Semiotics of Law*, Vol. 26, online first.
Larsson, S. 2008. 'Den nya tidens hybrid. Människan och informationen', in FRAMTIDSBOKEN: Volym 1.0 *The Darling Conceptions of Your Time*, edited by H. Hydén. Lund: Lund University.
Larsson, S. 2011a. 'Den stigberoende upphovsrätten. Om konsekvenserna av rättslig inlåsning i en digital tid', *Retfærd, Nordic Journal of Law and Justice*, 4(135), 122–46.
Larsson, S. 2012c. 'Metaforerna och rätten', *Retfærd, Nordic Journal of Law and Justice* 2(137), 69–93.
Larsson, S. 2011b. *Metaphors and Norms. Understanding Copyright Law in a Digital Society*. PhD Thesis, Lund Studies in Sociology of Law, Lund University.
Larsson, S. 2013a. 'Metaphors, Law and Digital Phenomena: The Swedish Pirate Bay Court Case', *International Journal of Law and Information Technology*, Advance Access.
Larsson, S. 2013b. 'Rätten som Rum, Kropp och Kontext: Det Konceptuella Förtingligandets Rättsvetenskapliga Relevans', *Tidsskrift for Rettsvitenskap*, 126(3), 343–63.
Larsson, S. 2011c. 'The Path Dependence of European Copyright', *SCRIPT:ed. A Journal of Law, Technology & Society* 8(1), 8–31.
Larsson, S. and Hydén, H. 2010. 'Law, deviation and paradigmatic change: Copyright and its metaphors', in Vargas Martin, M., et al. *Technology for Facilitating Humanity and Combating Social Deviations: Interdisciplinary Perspectives*. Hershey, PA, USA: IGI Global, 188–208.
Larsson, S., Svensson, M. and de Kaminski, M. 2013. 'Online piracy, Anonymity and Social Change – Innovation through Deviance', *Convergence: The International Journal of Research into New Media Technologies*, 19(1), 95–114.
Lessig, L. 1999. *Code and other laws of cyberspace*. New York: Basic books.
Lessig, L. 2006. *Code version 2.0*. New York: Basic books.
Locke, J. 1975/1690. 'An Essay Concerning Human Understanding', in Nidditch, Peter N. (ed. 1975). Oxford: Oxford University Press.
Loughlan, P. 2006. 'Pirates, Parasites, Reapers, Sowers, Fruits, Foxes … The Metaphors of Intellectual Property', *Sydney Law Review*, 28(2), 211–26.
Mathiesen, T. 2005. *Rätten i samhället: En introduktion till rättssociologin*, [Original title: *Retten i samfunnet*]. Lund: Studentlitteratur.
Patry, W. 2009. *Moral panics and the copyright wars*. Oxford University Press.
Platzer, E. 2004. *En icke-lag i sökljuset: Exemplet hushållstjänster i Sverige*, Licentiate thesis in Sociology of Law. Lund: Lund University.
Rosch, E. 1975. 'Cognitive Representation of Semantic Categories', *J Experimental Psychology*, 104, 192–233.

Rosch, E. 1978. 'Principles of categorization', in Eleanor Rosch and Barbara B. Lloyds (eds). *Cognition and Categorization.* Hillsdale, N.J.: Lawrence Erlbaum, 27–48.
Schön, D.A. 1979. 'Generative Metaphor', in *Metaphor and Thought*, edited by A. Ortony. Cambridge: Cambridge University Press.
Svensson, M. 2008. *Sociala normer och regelefterlevnad. Trafiksäkerhetsfrågor ur ett rättssociologiskt perspektiv*, [*Social Norms and the Observance of Law*]. Lund University, Lund Studies in Sociology of Law 28.
Svensson, M. and Larsson, S. 2012. 'Intellectual Property Law Compliance in Europe: Illegal File sharing and the Role of Social Norms', *New Media & Society* 14(7), 1147–63.
Svensson, M. and Larsson, S. 2009. *Social Norms and Intellectual Property. Online Norms and the European Legal Development.* Lund: Lund University, Research Report in Sociology of Law, 2009, 1.
Treagust, D.F. and Duit, R. 2008. *Conceptual change: a discussion of theoretical, methodological and practical challenges for science education.* Cult Stud of Sci Educ, 3, 297–328.
Tsai, R.L. 2004. 'Fire, Metaphor, and Constitutional Myth-Making', *Georgetown Law Journal* 93(1), 181–239.
Winter, S.L. 2001. *A clearing in the forest: Law, Life, and Mind.* Chicago and London: University of Chicago Press.
Winter, S.L. 2008. 'What is the "color" of law?', in *The Cambridge Handbook of Metaphor and Thought*, edited by R.W. Gibbs Jr. Cambridge University Press.
Yanow, D. 2008. 'Cognition meets action. Metaphors as models of and models for', in *Political language and metaphor, Interpreting and changing the world*, edited by T. Carver and J. Pikalo. Abingdon and New York: Routledge.
Yu, N. 2008. 'Metaphor from body and culture', in *The Cambridge Handbook of Metaphor and Thought*, edited by R.W. Gibbs Jr. Cambridge University Press.

Chapter 9
Spatializing Social and Legal Norms: Street Vending Regulation in Acapulco, Mexico

Lucas P. Konzen[1]

Introduction

Think about a street, but preferably one visited just in thought, a street you have never been to before. Then imagine that the norms of conduct vary spatially, in such a way that an action which is perfectly permissible on one of its sidewalks is unacceptable on the opposite sidewalk. If you find this hard to conceive, just open your digital atlas and search for Joao Pessoa Avenue, dividing the neighbouring cities of Santana do Livramento and Rivera, along the border of Brazil and Uruguay. Take a look as well at Pio XII Plaza, just a few steps away from Saint Peter's Square in the Vatican City, the papal enclave within Rome, Italy. Or you might prefer to consider the much less notorious case of Azkuene Street, located in between the municipalities of San Sebastian and Pasaia, in the Basque Country, Spain. Examples abound, as lawyers thinking exclusively in terms of jurisdictions and legal norms would acknowledge themselves. Even official and formal definitions of law and space are sufficient for recognizing that actions might be treated differently according to the place where they are performed, and that the physical proximity between two places does not necessarily preclude normative distance.

For socio-legal scholars, however, the reasons why a certain behaviour is treated differently on the two sidewalks of a street might have nothing to do with jurisdictions and legal norms. Regardless of whether they live near the borders between countries, provinces, and municipalities, people are likely to experience in everyday life the normative distance between two places that are physically close to each other. First, this is due to the degree of discrepancy between legal norms and legal practice. Legal norms assumed to be valid in a jurisdiction tend to be unevenly enforced by the agencies of the state bureaucracy within its geographical limits, with individuals changing their perceptions accordingly about what is proper behaviour in a particular place. Second, this is because the content of legal

1 I would like to thank Karsten Åström, Matthias Baier, Ana Maria Vargas and Karl Dahlstrand for their comments on earlier drafts of this chapter, and also Antonio Azuela for his support during the fieldwork in Mexico. This publication is part of my research work at Lund University, thanks to a Swedish Institute scholarship.

norms does not always coincide with the content of social norms. Legal norms expected to be in force within a jurisdiction might be dismissed, due to variations from one place to another in terms of the social norms governing actions. Third, this is simply because people move between places. The interactions between legal norms, legal practice and social norms are unequivocally related to the spatiality that characterizes the social practice which they attempt to regulate.

Space matters for norms. Over the past two decades, following the spatial turn in social sciences (see, for example, the seminal works by Castells (1972), Harvey (1973) and Lefebvre (1974)), a growing body of literature in sociology of law has been concerned with understanding the mutually constitutive intersections between law and space. Challenging the notions of state-based spatiality which are central to legal dogmatics, so-called 'legal geography' became a research field of great interest in socio-legal studies (see, among many others, Blomley (1989 and 1994), the volumes edited by Blomley, Delaney and Ford (2001), Holder and Harrison (2003), Taylor (2006); F. Benda-Beckmann, K. Benda-Beckmann and Griffiths (2009)). Nevertheless, there is still much work to be done in exploring the theoretical, methodological and practical implications of the insights of legal geography into the study of norms and normative action. This chapter aims to contribute to strengthening the foundations of this relatively new scientific debate, arguing that there is a need of spatializing not only the study of legal norms in society, but also of social norms, in order to account for the interrelations of norms of different types with legal practice and social practice.

Starting with the empirical evidence concerning street vending in the city of Acapulco, Mexico, this chapter illustrates the extent to which this social practice is regulated through a dialectics among legal norms, legal practice and social norms (on the one hand) and jurisdictional spaces, spatial zoning and territorial spaces (on the other hand). Street vending is considered a highly controversial social practice, particularly in Latin America. Street vendors, to put it simply, are informal traders of goods and services who make use of public spaces to work. Street vending as an economic activity has a long history, but in recent decades it has been pointed out as a major urban problem. There are those who associate street vending with public health risks, tax evasion, unfair competition, pirated products, tourist harassment, traffic congestion, contamination, disorders of all kind, and even organized crime (for a review on the topic, see Bromley (2000)). Street vendors became a central target of legal norms regulating public spaces, in spite of the claims suggesting that such a traditional activity is not only socially relevant but also a manifestation of the human right to work.

Acapulco is taken as an empirical setting of interest to analyse street vending regulation, due to the degree of informality of the local economy and its almost complete dependence on activities directly or indirectly connected to tourism. Situated on the Pacific Coast and benefiting from its geographical proximity to the United States of America, Canada, and Valley of Mexico, the city of Acapulco is an icon of mass tourism in Latin America. Since the 1930s, its process of urbanization has been oriented towards the goal of building a tourist destination. Millions of tourists arrive in Acapulco every year to enjoy the high temperatures, the beauty of its beaches, and the nightlife. However, the growth of tourism attracted waves of national migrants just as much as tourists. With a population estimated at 790,000 inhabitants, Acapulco is the largest city in the State of Guerrero, one of the country's poorest regions. For many, Acapulco is nowadays a tourist destination in crisis. International tourism no longer provides the largest percentage of tourist arrivals, the consumption power of visitors is lower than ever before, and the city is at the centre of the drug wars ranging across much of Mexico. Street vending regulation can, therefore, be seen as an element of the city's strategy to strengthen its position within the highly competitive and globalized tourist market.

This chapter is divided in two sections. The initial section presents the main findings of a case study into street vending regulation conducted in Acapulco. The case study design relied on qualitative methods of research. Empirical data was partially assembled through fieldwork carried out in Acapulco during 2011, including extensive sessions of direct observation of public spaces and 16 semi-structured interviews, which involved mostly government officials. This material was supplemented by empirical data gathered from other sources, including a collection of planning documents, legal acts, newspaper reports, and tourist brochures. The subsequent section of the chapter briefly analyses the theoretical implications of the findings, discussing the results of the case study in the light of the literature in legal geography. As the debates in this emerging field suggest, street vending regulation in Acapulco can be analysed in terms of the interplay between legal norms and jurisdictional spaces, legal practice and spatial zoning, social norms and territorial spaces. Indeed, this set of analytical categories consists of a trio of conceptual pairs, grasping the two-way relationship between law and space, which are potentially useful for theorizing the spatiality of norms and normative action.

The example of street vending regulation in Acapulco

The tourist boom in Acapulco not only meant economic growth, but also spread the image of a charming big city, offering plenty of work opportunities and the promise of a better life. The opportunities for formal employment offered by the tourism industry, however, have been far from meeting the needs of the workforce. Thousands of women and men who decided to come to Acapulco from Guerrero's countryside were unskilled for the modern jobs available in the tourist zone. Most migrants succeeded in finding occupation as chambermaids, waiters, taxi drivers and shopkeepers, which are generally low-paid and temporary occupations. But many workers started to make a livelihood from the informal economy, which includes a wide range of activities, such as street vending. In Acapulco, street vending is often considered 'the last option that somebody from Guerrero has for making a living before migrating to the United States or engaging in criminal activities', as one interviewee put it. Informal economic activities are articulated with the modern ones taking place along the tourist zone and constitute the main mechanism providing for the consumption needs of the majority of Acapulco's inhabitants.

Not only local residents engage in street vending, but also seasonal migrants, who come to Acapulco from the mountains of Guerrero and other Mexican regions, to sell handicrafts, foodstuffs and all sorts of cheap goods and services. Every day, thousands of street vendors are working in Acapulco; they are seen almost everywhere, both in the tourist zone and the non-tourist zone of the city. Local authorities tend to think that street vending is 'a serious social problem' and 'a very complex one' to deal with; they also believe that this is 'an old problem' which increasingly affects 'Mexico and cities of the entire world', claiming that there is an urgent need to solve the problem, following the example of cities that have already done so. Government officials concede that the best solution consists of generating employment opportunities, but they claim that street vending in Acapulco must be controlled, ordered and regularized. As a local authority explained, 'When an individual does not find a job, he or she looks for alternatives of income and street vending is one of such alternatives. So this is what we do, we regularize it; we put some order into it, because we cannot eliminate it'. Under the current circumstances, government officials would not really support any sort of zero tolerance policy concerning street vending, because they are afraid of the explosive social consequences.

Controlling street vending has been considered an important goal for several reasons. According to government officials, street vendors obstruct sidewalks, affecting pedestrian and motorized circulation, and thus the freedom of movement. Also, street vending increases the demand for maintenance services, but does not generate tax revenues for the municipality. In addition, it consists of unfair competition *vis-à-vis* formal commercial establishments, since similar goods and services are sold at lower prices in the streets due to the absence of costs relating to the payment of taxes, labour rights and rents. Overall, local authorities believe that street vending makes tourists feel uncomfortable, damaging the image of Acapulco as a tourist destination. Some reactions of government officials to questions about this topic are as follows: 'Tourists get bothered, because for anyone who comes with the idea of taking a rest, it's very boring to say "No, thanks!", "No, thanks!" all the time, to hear "Hey my friend, look to me, why don't you buy me this?"'; 'Tourists do not want to be bored by vendors, you come to the beach and one arrives, then another one, and sometimes within one hour you have to give attention to ten vendors'; 'It's at stake the insecurity problem too, among vendors there are pickpockets looking around, checking what they can steal from tourists'.

If there is a general agreement among local authorities on the need for a policy to control street vending, how to implement it has been a matter of controversy over the years. Since the 1980s, the main approach to this issue in Acapulco has been the regularization of street vendors' activities through the construction of buildings dedicated to public markets. First, small markets were built in order to relocate street vendors, but they soon started to get bigger. Nowadays, there is an impressive number of markets of this kind in Acapulco. Even so, street vendors soon started to occupy the corridors between the stalls, as well as the sidewalks surrounding the markets. Those who benefited from stalls inside the markets brought their relatives to take their places in the streets. In fact, anyone who enters into these markets immediately notices that many of the stalls located inside are kept closed to customers and only used for the storage of goods. That is, regularized vendors realized that they could actually earn much more money when working outdoors. As a result, there are few doubts that the construction of public markets actually increased, instead of reduced, street vending in Acapulco.

The set of proposals to control street vending from the 1980s also included the creation of a permit system. It was seen as a way of balancing individual interests against collective interests, the right to work (Article 5, Constitution of Mexico, 1917) against the need to keep both an ordered image for tourists and to keep traffic flowing across the city. According to the Public Ways Act (1985) and the Street Vending Act (1990), the use of plazas, parks, streets and sidewalks for commercial activities is prohibited throughout the Municipality of Acapulco, except where it is carried on by street vendors authorized by the municipal government according to the conditions stipulated on temporary permits. The Public Ways Department was appointed the agency of the state bureaucracy competent to issue street vending permits on an individual basis, which may be valid for a period of one year, a couple of months, or even one single day. The permit conditions include the payment of a fee, as well as restrictions in terms of place, time, quality of the goods on sale, and personal circumstances of the beneficiary. The inspectors working for the Public Ways Department are responsible for enforcing the permit system by imposing sanctions on street vendors who are unable to prove that they have a permit, or who are not complying with the established conditions. The coercive means for obtaining compliance range from fines and the seizure of merchandise to the arrest of the transgressors.

Controlling street vendors on the beaches of Acapulco, however, is outside the jurisdiction of the Public Ways Department. Some governmental tasks are handled by the agencies of the state bureaucracy at higher levels of government than the municipal level, such as the management of the Maritime-Terrestrial Federal Zone (ZOFEMAT). According to the National Property Act (Article 119, 2004), a statutory text enacted by the legislative body at the federal level, the ZOFEMAT is defined as the 20 metre-wide strip of passable firm land parallel to the coastline within Mexico's national borders. The ZOFEMAT is considered to belong to the nation's patrimony, and it is under the jurisdiction of the federal government. Consequently, the National Secretariat of Environment and Natural Resources (SEMARNAT) and the Federal Environment Protection Agency (PROFEPA), both federal agencies, are responsible for sharing the tasks relating to the management of urban beaches.

According to the National Property Act, explicit authorization from SEMARNAT is required for any commercial use of ZOFEMAT, while PROFEPA is responsible for imposing sanctions for non-authorized uses. The possibility of creating a permit system for street vending on the beaches is mentioned in the legislation (Article 11, ZOFEMAT Decree, 1991); but, for this purpose, SEMARNAT must follow the technical criteria stipulated by the National Secretariat of Tourism (SECTUR). Indeed, permit systems for street vending on urban beaches have been created in other Mexican tourist destinations. Nevertheless, this is not the case in Acapulco, because SECTUR never provided the technical criteria for issuing permits. As one government official reported, 'Whenever this issue is discussed, someone claims that no permit system should be implemented at all, because if it ever happens that a single permit is issued, soon the authorities would have to deal with thousands of permits'. Thus, SEMARNAT does not issue any permits for street vending in Acapulco, while PROFEPA considers that all those who exercise this activity on the beaches are violating the federal legislation and are therefore potentially subject to enforcement actions.

The existence of two agencies at different government levels, with jurisdiction over contiguous areas, entails a coordination problem of considerable relevance. One government official explained such a curious situation by reporting a hypothetical dialogue between municipal and federal inspectors:

> On the beach, in the fringe of sand where street vending usually takes place, federal authorities have jurisdiction. But they don't intervene … "The problem of the street vendors is yours; you shouldn't allow them to be there!" – says the municipal inspector; "But how am I going to prevent them to enter? I can cover 1 km of beach, but not 20 km, help me!" – replies the federal inspector.

Another interviewee complemented the dialogue:

> The municipal inspectors say "Because this is federal zone, it is not under our competence". But when the federal inspectors catch street vendors, they tell them: "You know what? Move on, this is a public area"; and after they go and tell municipal inspectors: "Look! Now it's under your competence!" But then municipal inspectors tell street vendors: "No, go back there!" We play this game, it shouldn't be like this, but it is.

In addition, inspectors from PROFEPA and the Public Ways Department consider that imposing sanctions for street vending is far from being a simple task, due to the legal procedure that must be followed. As one government official commented:

> I found this vendor today on a certain beach, but tomorrow he is not going to be there anymore … How am I going to notify him? … If his legal residence is not there, I cannot apply the procedure properly. Sometimes it's already very complicated the task of sanctioning someone who is permanently established, so try to figure out how difficult it is when it's at stake an ambulant, it's much more complicated.

To these issues must be added the lack of human resources for controlling thousands of street vendors. The Public Ways Department has about 30 to 40 inspectors for the entire city, while only four inspectors of PROFEPA are in charge of controlling a diversity of uses in the ZOFEMAT across the coast of Guerrero. Government officials claim that the strict enforcement of statutes would require 'a person from PROFEPA in each access to the beach', 'at least one municipal inspector in each street, an army', and both agencies of the state bureaucracy acting in coordination.

Without the material means available for enforcing legal norms throughout their entire jurisdictions, and with different approaches to street vending permit systems, the agencies of the state bureaucracy follow distinct strategies. PROFEPA carries out enforcement operations in the area under its jurisdiction only sporadically, focusing mainly on the beaches of tourist interest. In addition, PROFEPA relies extensively on the action of ZOFEMAT concession-holders, such as hotel and restaurant establishments, whose concession contracts grant them territorial powers to prevent unauthorized vendors from using the parcels of the nation's patrimony which are under concession. ZOFEMAT concession-holders make use of this power through tactics of spatial control, such as roped-off beach areas, close-circuit television, and conspicuous presence of their own security personnel. The Public Ways Department clearly prioritizes some areas of the city to the detriment of others, and it is constantly encouraged to do so by off-street merchants, to say the least. In the words of one civil servant, 'the tourist zones, these are the main areas covered by us, it's impossible to cover the entire municipality'. This is confirmed by testimonies from different local authorities, quoted in Table 9.1. It is regarded as legitimate for thousands of street vendors to use the public spaces of Acapulco to work, except those public spaces located in the tourist zone.

The establishment of the tourist zone as the area where legal norms governing street vendors must be enforced by the inspectors finds echo in the legislation at the municipal level. The Policing and Governance Act (2002), one of the most significant statutory texts passed by the city council of Acapulco, is a clear example of such a process of turning an informal mechanism of street vending management into an official tool for controlling the appropriation of material sites by living bodies. This statute states that:

> Street vending is strictly prohibited in the tourist zone, which is understood for this purpose as: Las Naciones Boulevard; the Scenic Highway; La Costera; the main square; the streets of the Historic Center; and the tourist areas known as Barra Vieja, Diamond Acapulco, Revolcadero, Bay of Puerto Marques, Bay of Santa Lucia, La Quebrada, Caleta and Caletilla. Offenders will be severely sanctioned, and repeated violation entails 36-hour arrest and merchandise seizure. (Articles 111 and 203, Policing and Governance Act, 2002)

Even without making explicit use of a visual zoning map, the Policing and Governance Act relies on mechanisms for representing the space of the city which are similar to land-use administrative zoning. It has the same effect in terms of setting zoning districts with more or less well-defined boundaries.

The tourist zone is taken seriously by municipal inspectors as a zoning district concerning street vending. Nonetheless, plenty of unauthorized street vendors can be observed in the tourist zone. Apart from the problems regarding the enforcement of legal norms, much of the visibility of the street vendors in the tourist zone of Acapulco is related to collective action. Over the last decades, the official policy for controlling street vending has been facing fierce opposition. Street vendors argue

Table 9.1 Excerpts from interviews with government officials in Acapulco, 2011

'We don't prohibit street workers to make a living, as far as they don't make it in the tourist zone. They should go to the neighbourhoods and avenues where they don't obstruct that much the traffic of vehicles. Basically we tell them "not here, but there". Such option is given to them, it not like that we tell them "don't make it, simply because you shouldn't make it".'
'The city council has made agreements in order to make public spaces be respected. Across La Costera, the main tourist avenue, street vending is prohibited. In all avenue along, and also in some of the main streets of the Historic Centre.'
'In squatter settlements we don't have such kind of problem, because the neighbours dedicate themselves to this kind of commerce, and they know each other, so there is somehow a tolerance and we don't receive many complains, you know? … In squatter settlements there is no problem; it is not allowed only in the tourist zone, … where there is more traffic, more people walking around.'
'In the tourist zone we have this problem with street vending, and also in the rest of the city we have the same problem. In respect to the tourist zone, it is more regulated, because there are places which were given to the street vendors. In the other part of the city they establish themselves and we don't make anything but regulating them, whether or not they can use a particular street.'
'There is a special concern with the tourist zone, it is permanent, the 24 hours, 365 days per year, there are people who are taking care and making the norm be respected. Sometimes street vendors come with an one-meter cloth and run from one place to another, trying to evade from inspectors, but within some days they are identified, inspectors learn how they work, which spaces they use.'
'Street vending is a problem across the entire city, not only in the tourist zone. But what matters for my Department is that tourists are not bored in public spaces, such as the beach, such as the street.'
'We have been controlling street vending to avoid it to occur in La Costera. But, if you come to the Historic Centre, probably you have already seen them, if you go to the public markets, it's crowed with street vendors. We always tell street vendors "look, here in the tourist zone you cannot make it, but I'm going to send you over there".'

that they have the right to organize themselves to use public spaces for making a living according to their own ideas and criteria, even violating the legislation whenever they have no other means to survive. Episodes of open, face-to-face confrontation between street vendors and the agencies of the state bureaucracy are common in Acapulco. Massive demonstrations have been organized, including the blockade of avenues and sit-ins in plazas, in order to force the local authorities to start negotiations and make agreements over the content and enforcement of legal norms. That is, street vendors make use of public spaces not only as means of economic subsistence for their families, but also for political activism. Some politicians have seen conflicts of this kind as an opportunity to act as mediators and often make electoral gains from negotiations, by urging inspectors to be more flexible about the enforcement of legal norms.

There is another side to the street vendors' collective action in Acapulco. They do not form a homogenous social group and they do not always act together. At other times, they compete among themselves in the streets, and sometimes vendors who have got a permit assume the role of inspectors themselves and denounce unauthorized colleagues to the local authorities. More importantly, many street vendors find themselves compelled to take part in permanent organizations in order to get a permit, and thus start to work under the supervision of leaders who control a number of territories across the city, both in the tourist zone and in the non-tourist zone. However, this provides organized street vendors with more favourable conditions for resisting the local authorities' strategies of social control. If the organization is strong enough, it eventually succeeds in establishing privileged relationships with politicians, based on the exchange of political support for tolerance towards the territories which they make use of for their unauthorized commercial activities. On the other hand, leadership struggles within street vendor organizations and between leaders of different organizations often result in violence and corruption, contributing to undermine collective consciousness. Some interviewees went as far as to suggest that there are street vendor organizations in Acapulco operating under the control of mafias, indirectly related to the powerful Mexican drug cartels.

An additional issue to be taken into account is that street vending is still considered a socially legitimate economic activity, not only from the perspective of the majority of Acapulco's residents, but also from the perspective of most of the tourists who visit the city. Whenever tourists decide to buy a good which is being sold by a street vendor on the beaches and streets of Acapulco, they somehow legitimize social norms governing the consumption relationship, because they do not see such a problem about this. Tourists are aware that they can simply say 'No, thanks!' if they feel uncomfortable. There are plenty of tourists in Acapulco, particularly at the lower end of the income scale, who cannot pay to eat in restaurants and actually find the possibility of buying cheap foodstuffs and goods on the beach, directly from street vendors, very convenient. Also, whenever a group of persons decide to engage in street vending in Acapulco, they do not regard themselves as wrongdoers. Quite the opposite, when thousands of people are doing exactly the same, including their relatives and neighbours, the newcomers to such an economic activity assume that it is not a deviant behaviour. Besides, street vending is a longstanding activity in the history of Mexico, frequently depicted as an important part of the country's traditions.

The findings from the case study of Acapulco show that street vending regulation is both a matter of norms and space. Concerning the enforcement of legal norms, a permit system (combined with a zoning district) was settled to deal with street vendors. There is tolerance towards street vending throughout the city, except in the tourist zone. Nevertheless, even there, street vendors remain visible. This is partly due to the fact that streets vendors are too numerous. When deviation from legal norms is normal rather than exceptional behaviour, sophisticated systems for controlling behaviour may not be settled or strictly enforced because they are too difficult to manage. In addition, street vendors often succeed in taking advantage of enforcement problems, including conflicts of jurisdiction between agencies of the state bureaucracy. A less evident motive is that street vendors, regardless of being the target of legal norms, often act as norm-setters in respect to social norms. They organize themselves in order to force authorities to start negotiations and reach agreements relating to legal norm enforcement. Such a process is not exempt from ambivalence, since social norms developed within a street vendor organization to guide the behaviour of its members are likely to affect unorganized street vendors as well. They find themselves compelled to take part in a street vending organization, and start to work under the supervision of leaders who maintain territories under control throughout the city.

Theorizing the norms–space nexus

The example of street vending regulation in Acapulco suggests that space must be taken seriously if deeper understanding of norms and normative action in society is sought. This case study illustrates the conflicting interplay of a specific social practice with legal norms, legal practice and social norms. Agreed forms of regulation are rarely possible, since the interests of multiple groups collide. Social struggles determine the normative and spatial ways through which they are contested and negotiated in everyday life. In concretized social relations, normativity and spatiality are always intertwined. For many years, this fundamental insight has been encouraging scholarship in the field of legal geography. Yet, the theorization of the relationship between norms and space still lacks consistency. There have been calls for 'a conceptual language that allows us to think beyond binary categories such as "space" and "law"' (Blomley, 2003: 30) and at least one serious attempt to advance towards this direction (see Delaney, 2010). Nevertheless, the evidence from the case study of Acapulco indicates that at least a certain degree of analytical consistency can be achieved by relying on a fairly sophisticated trio of conceptual pairs for grasping the norms-space nexus: legal norms and jurisdictional spaces, legal practice and spatial zoning, and social norms and territorial spaces.

Legal norms and jurisdictional spaces

From the narrative concerning street vending regulation in Acapulco, two jurisdictional spaces can be clearly distinguished. On the one hand, there is the ZOFEMAT; on the other, the Municipality of Acapulco. Both are state jurisdictions in Mexico, formally defined by legal norms originating from different government levels. In the case of ZOFEMAT, the relevant norm-making process occurs at the federal level. The legal norms, found in a statutory text, defined that the 20 metre-wide strip of passable firm land parallel to the coastline is part of the nation's patrimony. In the case of the Municipality of Acapulco, the precise boundaries of the jurisdiction are defined by legal norms enacted at lower government levels. If the visual maps of ZOFEMAT and the Municipality of Acapulco are compared, it is possible to verify that these jurisdictions are partly overlapping (that is, the former includes an area also covered by the latter). Jurisdictional zones usually have multiple purposes. For the specific purpose of regulating street vending, however, legal norms are officially interpreted within Mexico's legal system in such a hierarchical way that it results in the conversion of ZOFEMAT and the Municipality of Acapulco into contiguous jurisdictions, subjected to the control of distinct agencies of the state bureaucracy.

Legal norms operate through the establishment of rigid and precise boundaries defining countries, provinces and municipalities, but also other spatial divisions organizing government, such as Mexico's ZOFEMAT. From a theoretical standpoint, the example of Acapulco illustrates how a given state, through its legislative agencies at different levels of government, is the settler of legal norms which are valid only within the boundaries of specific jurisdictional spaces. Legal norms, essentially, consist of socially reproduced instructions guiding social behaviour imperatively. They can be distinguished from norms of other types for several reasons – for instance, because they are state-made norms, explicitly articulated and formalized by means of official documents such as statutory texts and judicial decisions. This body of norms has the peculiarity of being reproduced within the legal system, which consists of a highly complex arena including a wide range of agencies of the state bureaucracy. Allegations of non-compliance can ultimately be submitted for judicial consideration, and the application of sanctions to violators is backed by the coercive force of the state. In any case, jurisdictional spaces frame social expectations about the geographical boundaries of state action.

Legal norms and jurisdictional spaces exist as a conceptual pair. Jurisdictional spaces are better conceptualized as a collection of legal norms emanating from the state, representing an abstract area with the deliberate purpose of organizing the exercise of its powers. For this reason, jurisdictions can, to a certain extent, be considered an arbitrary creation of governmental institutions; they are mainly policy-making tools for the sake of administrative convenience. According to an influential account in the field of legal geography (Ford, 1998), there are three basic characteristics which apply to the concept of jurisdictional spaces. First, a 'jurisdiction categorizes the elements over which authority is to be exercised primarily by area, and secondarily, if at all, by type' (Ford, 1998: 852). Second, the boundaries of a jurisdiction 'are not ambiguous or contested except in anomalous cases or in times of crisis or transition. If ambiguity arises, it is usually a source of concern and embarrassment and is settled as quickly as possible. The geographic boundaries of a jurisdiction are a "bright line" rule, never a flexible standard' (Ford, 1998: 852–3). Third, a jurisdiction is conceptually empty, abstract and homogenous, 'the space of a jurisdiction is conceived of independently of any specific attribute of that space' (Ford, 1998: 853).

Jurisdictions are discursive constructs which may precede legal practice and social practice and can even change dramatically from time to time; that is, they are representations of space. Arguably, the existence of jurisdictional spaces seems to be a timeless, natural and inevitable feature of social life, but to a large extent they are a modern invention (Ford, 1998: 929). Jurisdictions consist of mental models conceived with the purpose of orienting legal practice in everyday life. The learning process of individuals and groups with respect to jurisdictions is mainly based on verbal and graphical descriptions. Although other representations of space are possible, 'most refer to maps, such as the notation in a treaty between nations that refers to a cartographic grid of latitude and longitude, or the language in a property title that refers to an official chart of plots' (Ford, 1998: 853). Without a doubt, the advent of the science of cartography is a factor that contributed enormously to making possible the existence of the gapless maps of contiguous jurisdictional spaces which are today so familiar to bureaucrats around the world.

Legal practice and spatial zoning

The study of the case of Acapulco shows that the agencies of the state bureaucracy rely on informal mechanisms of spatial zoning for enforcing legal norms. There is tolerance towards street vendors across the city, except in the tourist zone. Under the current circumstances, street vending is managed and controlled by means of spatial tactics, because outlawing it altogether is out of the question. Government officials are aware that street vending is, in general, considered a socially legitimate economic activity in Mexico. They know that this is normal rather than exceptional behaviour in the context of Acapulco. Even if local authorities should decide that eradicating street vending is a worthwhile goal, they are unlikely to succeed, due to the fact that they lack the material means for making such a decision effective. The resources available are far from being sufficient to meet what is required for successfully controlling such an activity throughout the entire urban perimeter. Besides, government officials believe that there are good reasons – among others, the ordered tourist image, the flow of vehicle traffic, the pressure from off-street merchants – to concentrate the enforcement actions in the tourist zone to the detriment of other areas of the city. The state's repressive action is not the same everywhere in Acapulco. The zoning district settled by the Policing and Governance Act does nothing but give official status to an ongoing legal practice.

Thanks to the work of pioneers, such as Roscoe Pound, for nearly a century now, socio-legal scholars claim that 'If we look closely, distinctions between law in the books and law in action, between the rules that purport to govern the relations of man and man and those that in fact govern them, will appear' (Pound, 1910: 15). The abstract content of the statutory texts enacted by law-making bodies often contrasts with the concretized enforcement actions taken by the agencies of the state bureaucracy in everyday life. Since the exercise of the state's police power allows for a margin of discretion, there is a degree of discrepancy between legal norms and legal practice. Legal norms assumed to apply for a jurisdictional space are likely to be unevenly enforced by agencies of the state bureaucracy within its boundaries, with people changing their understandings about what is adequate behaviour according to the actual functioning of the mechanisms of spatial zoning. The spatial selectivity associated with the lack of correspondence between legal norms and legal practice is one of the angles of this phenomenon that merits a more careful analysis in socio-legal scholarship.

Spatial zoning and legal practice function as a conceptual pair. The enforcement officers from the agencies of the state bureaucracy may benefit directly from demarcating lines, coordinate grids and cartographic techniques alike to learn about the exact configuration of their jurisdictional spaces, responding accordingly to the task of making these abstract representations a concrete part of everyday life. But it is not like this in respect of spatial zoning. On the contrary, spatial zoning is often based on a geography defined by concrete landmarks, determined in narrative terms. Maps, where they exist, are merely of a schematic kind, because space is understood by the name of places, in much more concrete, less precise, and flexible terms. For instance, the tourist zone in Acapulco is a zone in substance only, not a formal one. It is the area of the city being publicized for tourist consumption, within which the tourist attractions are situated and where the majority of the visitors who arrive in the city actually circulate. The frontiers between the tourist zone and the non-tourist zone are better known through the descriptions found in tourist materials than by any graphical or written descriptions provided in the municipal legislation.

Legal practice is, to a large extent, about the informal action of the members of the agencies of the state bureaucracy who are officially authorized to use coercive means in order to obtain compliance with legal norms. For example, in Acapulco the official mechanisms for enforcing legal norms for street vending are diversified and very bureaucratic in character, ranging from the possibility of asking someone to 'move on' from a certain place to seizing merchandise, from imposing fines to arresting the transgressors. In every case, a considerable margin of manoeuvre is involved in the normative action of government officials. This means that the legal practice of local authorities is, in fact, much more a matter of starting negotiations, making agreements, being more or less tolerant towards individual and collective situations, mediating between the interests of distinct groups, and displacing social practices from certain places to others. Surely, the spatiality of the legal practice can be mapped as much as the spatiality of any social practice. But this mapping assumes special importance, as it reveals a lot about the extent to which the action of the state is capable of influencing social practice.

Social norms and territorial spaces

The example of street vending in Acapulco illustrates the role of social norms which arise within informal communities for supporting the livelihoods of their members in a context in which the state cannot cope with enforcement demands or with the most basic needs of people. Over the years, strong organizations of street vendors have settled social norms governing the appropriation of certain territories in the city by their members. Organized street vendors are able to work against legal norms without fear of sanction, by creating and defending spaces for themselves where a different normativity is in operation. These territorial spaces, which spread like islands of self-regulation across the urban perimeter, are to a large extent respected by the authorities, who consider that these organizations are powerful enough to create social unrest if enforcement efforts are undertaken. Social norms are of unequivocal importance as tools for granting the internal cohesion of communities and as means for controlling the territories which are used to carry out street vending. Nevertheless, from the standpoint of unorganized street vendors, social norms play a much more ambiguous role, and can also be perceived as exclusionary. These street vendors also fight for the right to work freely on the streets without fearing either the official control exercised by the state or the unofficial control imposed by street vendor organizations.

For a long time, which can be tracked back to Eugen Ehrlich's theory of the living law (Ehrlich, 2001), socio-legal scholars have been accustomed to distinguishing between legal norms and social norms. One key issue of debate in sociology of law is how social order is upheld in the absence of, or despite, legal norms – a discussion akin to the broader debate over legal pluralism. Indeed, there can be normative order without explicitly formulated and institutionalized norms (see, for instance, Macaulay, 1963; Ellickson, 1991). In particular, there is plenty of evidence confirming that close-knit communities develop a sense of membership and regulate themselves through social norms guiding the behaviour of their members. The concept of social norms is therefore closely associated with communities which are based on tight-knit relationships: the family, the workplace, the neighbourhood, the religious congregation. Individuals tend to follow certain social norms, as they know that their actions are subject to the approval and disapproval of the communities to which they belong. The enforcement of social norms is diffuse, the sanctions typically affect only an individual or a small group of individuals within the community, and gross violations may ultimately result in membership rejection and exclusion.

Social norms and territorial spaces also work as a conceptual pair. Communities which aim to present themselves as controlling the occupation of a territory must establish a set of distinctive social norms for monitoring its boundaries. Territorial spaces with more or less precise boundaries are defined and organized concretely, not abstractly, through daily practices of norm-setting and norm-enforcement within communitarian organizations. The social norms determine 'who socially belongs in a space and who is therefore transgressive' (Staeheli and Mitchell, 2008: 148). Therefore, social norms are fundamentally about the normative action of geographically based communities. The identity of a community is often dependent upon claims of autonomy, separateness, self-determination and cultural preservation. The community's social power relies on its ability to exercise control over a territory which is culturally or economically significant for its members. Membership of a community is presumably denied unless expressly granted, because there is a need to control who belongs to an organized group in order to preserve the specific interests of its members. Since social norms also affect insiders and outsiders unevenly, the question of how a community is defined is of crucial importance.

Conflicting and unequal relationships permeate social norms, communities and territorial spaces. Legal geographers have emphasized that '[social] norms and definitions of community are rarely critically examined or collectively agreed upon; more often, they are simply asserted' (Staeheli and Mitchell, 2008: 148). Besides, assertions about who belongs to a community are frequently backed by the police power of the state and cannot be isolated from the exercise of political and economic power by groups and individuals (Staeheli and Mitchell, 2008: 148). As the example of street vending in Acapulco suggests, social norms are a source of exclusion when seen from the perspective of outsiders (that is, from the standpoint of unorganized street vendors) as much as from the standpoint of other local residents. Not surprisingly, research in the field of legal geography found that territorial spaces might be seen as attempts 'to create a private or communal domain ... at the expense of other communities (and of community in general)' (Copper, 1996: 535). The implications of social norms and territorial spaces as counter-hegemonic ways of spatializing normative action cannot, therefore, be taken for granted. They can neither be condemned as oppressive forms of order without law, nor celebrated as emancipatory forms of collective action; instead, they must be critically addressed, focusing on their interrelations with the hegemonic spatiality represented by legal norms and legal practice.

Conclusion

Norms matter for space, and the other way around. In everyday life, actions are treated differently according to the place where they are performed, and even the physical proximity between two places does not necessarily preclude a degree of normative distance. There is indeed a spatiality which characterizes legal norms as much as social norms, and legal practice as much as social practice. Therefore, space must be taken seriously in the scientific task of understanding norms and normative action in society. In order to theorize the norms-space nexus, this chapter engaged with a fairly sophisticated set of analytical tools: legal norms and jurisdictional spaces, legal practice and spatial zoning, social norms and territorial spaces. These operational categories provide for a trio of conceptual pairs of unequivocal utility for grasping the two-way relationship between norms and space. Such a framework for studying the spatiality of norms and normative action was empirically grounded on the discussion of the findings from a case study into street vending regulation in the city of Acapulco, Mexico; and theoretically informed by interpretations from the scholarship in legal geography, a relatively new but promising disciplinary field within sociology of law.

References

Benda-Beckmann, F., Benda-Beckmann, K. and Griffiths, A. (eds) 2009. *Spatializing Law: An Anthropological Geography of Law in Society*. Farnham: Ashgate.

Blomley, N. 1989. 'Text and context: rethinking the law-geography nexus', *Progress in Human Geography*, 13(4), 512–34.

Blomley, N. 1994. *Law, Space, and the Geographies of Power.* New York: Guilford Press.

Blomley, N. 2003. 'From "what?" to "so what?": law and geography in retrospect', in *Law and Geography*, edited by J. Holder and C. Harrison. Oxford: Oxford University Press, 17–33.

Blomley, N., Delaney, D. and Ford, R. (eds) 2001. *The Legal Geographies Reader: Law, Power, and Space*. Oxford: Blackwell.

Bromley, R. 2000. 'Street vending and public policy: a global review', *International Journal of Sociology and Social Policy*, 20(1/2), 1–29.

Castells, M. 1972. *La Question Urbaine*. Paris: Maspero.

Copper, D. 1996. 'Talmudic territory? Space, law, and modernist discourse', *Journal of Law and Society*, 23(4), 529–48.

Delaney, D. 2010. *The Spatial, the Legal and the Pragmatics of World-making: Nomospheric Investigations*. London and New York: Routledge.

Ehrlich, E. 2001. *Fundamental Principles of the Sociology of Law*. New Brunswick: Transaction Publishers.

Ellickson, R. 1991. *Order Without Law: How Neighbors Settle Disputes*. Cambridge: Harvard University Press.

Ford, R. 1998. 'Law's territory: a history of jurisdiction', *Michigan Law Review*, 97, 843–930.

Harvey, D. 1973. *Social Justice and the City*. London: Edward Arnold.

Holder, J. and Harrison, C. (eds) 2003. *Law and Geography*. Oxford: Oxford University Press.

Lefebvre, H. 1974. *La Production de l'espace*. Paris: Anthropos.

Macaulay, S. 1963. 'Non-contractual relations in business: a preliminary study', *American Sociological Review*, 28(1), 55–67.

Pound, R. 1910. 'Law in books and law in action', *American Law Review*, 44, 12–36.

Staeheli, L. and Mitchell, D. 2008. *The People's Property? Power, Politics, and the Public.* New York: Routledge.

Taylor, W. (ed.) 2006. *The Geography of Law: Landscape, Identity and Regulation.* Oxford and Oñati: Hart and IISL.

PART III
Norms and Actors

Chapter 10
Social Workers Linking Together Family Norms and Child Protection Norms

Eva Friis

Introduction

Legislation exists everywhere in the West which, in varying ways, regulates when and how society should protect and support abused children (Sundell et al., 2007). Notwithstanding the variations, two positions may be seen: either legislation is of a preventive nature, and aims to prevent children from being subjected to serious abuse and neglect; or it is more reactive in nature, and aims to protect children where there are indications of abuse (Gilbert, 1997). Swedish legislation is based on the preventive model, meaning that problem families should be identified and supported at an early stage so as to avoid future harm or injury to the children (Wiklund, 2006). This family service-oriented model (Gilbert, 1997) is based on collaboration between the social authority and parents, and aims to resolve the family's problems voluntarily (Friis, 2003). The model also contains elements directed towards child protection, which are of a more controlling and coercive nature (Coccozza, 2007; Olsson Hort, 1997; Sundell et al., 2007; Wiklund, 2006; Östberg, 2010). There is a trend towards the expansion of the protective elements in the legislation (Wiklund, 2006), which creates a tension in practical social work. From a sociology of law perspective, this can be explained as a tension between two different ways for the legal system to intervene in the family: according to the service-oriented model, the aim of the intervention is to help the family get back to a functional life, but the law cannot accomplish this through its own means. The aim of the intervention under the protective model is to 'save the child' (Gilbert, 1997), which the law can achieve by its own means, for instance, through the power of legislation on compulsory care of children.

The question whether an intervention in a family in accordance with the service-oriented model will be successful is basically a question of whether the intervention will be accepted by the family or not. There may be many reasons why a family might accept an offer of support, or refuses to participate in the social authority's investigation into the child and the family. Among these reasons are expectations of (and attitudes towards) the social authority, which are related to social and legal norms concerning the family's autonomy and independence versus the state and its agencies. Underlying this is the ideology of liberty, which expresses the idea of the individual's right to freedom from interference by the state and the law (see Cotterrell, 1996).

There is, thus, a tension between legal and social norms in the family service-oriented model, which indicates the need of a mediating actor. From this point of view, the task for the social authority's representative is to mediate between two groups of norms: one group consists of legal norms that aim for child protection, while the other consists of both social and legal norms which aim to protect the family's integrity and self-determination. In accordance with the logic of the family service-oriented model, the mediation is performed through collaboration with the family. Such mediation through collaboration will not occur if an intervention in the family is made strictly in accordance with the child protection-oriented model, where the law operates solely in the power of its legal status.

In the family service-oriented model, the tension between the integrity-norms and the norms on child protection is evident in cases where children are exposed to violence and abuse within the family. At the same time, in such situations the ability of the social authorities to link together legal and social norms through collaboration with the family will be put to the test. The questions to be dealt with in this chapter are, first, how this mediation is performed in cases where the parents are suspected of having maltreated their children, and, secondly, what outcomes this mediation is leading to: will it lead to a change in the parents' priorities between norms on family integrity and norms on child protection? Since the aim of the mediation in the end is to improve the situation for the children concerned, a follow-up question is how the change (or lack of change, as applicable) in the parents' normative priorities affects the conditions for a change for the better in the children's situation?

In the next sections, there follows, first, a description of the norm-theoretical points of departure, and then a description of the part of the legal norm system that is relevant to the mediation. After this follows a section in which problems and aims are developed.

Norm-theoretical points of departure

The term 'norm' can be defined and analysed in many different ways, as discussed by Baier in the introduction to this book. This chapter will be based on an ontological definition of norms. A norm has 'essences' of the following kind: it expresses an imperative, it is socially reproduced, and it is related to expectations. A norm is also connected to accidental attributes, which in turn are related to factors such as its background and context, including the presence of sanctions, the origin of the norm, and the arena in which the norm is socially reproduced (Baier and Svensson, 2009; Hydén and Svensson, 2008; Svensson, 2008).

In this case, there are two normative arenas of specific interest for the mediation. One arena is localized to a micro level of civil society, namely the family. This part of society can be described as a 'self-regulating' system, where the individuals are regulating their obligations and rights through contracts (Cotterrell, 1992; Hydén, 2002). The other arena is related to the social authority, which is a part of the public administration or, if seen from a system perspective, the 'planned' system (Hydén, 2002). This part of the society is localized at the political-administrative level of society (ibid.). As will be described in the section below, the task of the social authority is to perform the state's obligations towards children and their families, in accordance with the legal norms that regulate this area in society.

The family's norm system consists of social norms, which it shares with other people and families in the society. Compared to legal norms, which have been formalized in a juridical and political process, and are therefore relatively easy to identify as 'written' law (Hydén, 2002; compare with Cotterrell, 1992), it may generally be more problematic to find out what the social norms are, since they have a more informal character than legal norms. In this case, however, it is a question of a social norm that is of great importance for the understanding of parents' reactions to interventions by social authorities in the family sphere; and that social norm is protected by legal norms. It is well known from sociological research that parents want to be treated with respect for their own (and the family's) integrity and self-determination (see, for instance, Drake, 1994; Dumbrill, 2006). Such research indicates both that the conception of the family's autonomy is deeply anchored in society, and also that there actually are social norms on the family's integrity. These social integrity-norms are defended by legal norms, as will be illuminated in the next section. It should, however, be noted here that it is well known within the social and family-related political arena that the legislation on child protection must be balanced with both the social and legal norms on the family's right to privacy (Socialdepartementet, 1986; see also Lundström, 2000).

This takes us to the relationship between social and legal norms, which can be explained in terms of a distinction between 'living law' and 'state law' (Cotterrell, 1992, with reference to Ehrlich, 1936). 'Living law' consists of social norms, which emerge from the core of society and which people spontaneously follow, and these norms regulate social relations by means of people experiencing (from within) that they have certain moral rights and obligations. Meanwhile, 'state law' is a political control instrument for those in power (the political state), which controls social relations from 'the outside'. As described in the literature (see, for example, Cotterrell, 1992; Habermas, 1987; Hydén, 2002), the modern legal development can be characterized as a juridification process, meaning that, increasingly, more types of social relations are subjected to legal regulation. There are, however, certain limitations on the relations and areas of society that 'state law' can direct. One example is the relationships in a family: the social agencies have a responsibility for welfare of the children and the family, but they are 'incapable of substituting for or enforcing natural ties and moral duties of family life' (Cotterrell, 1992: 52). This incapacity to substitute or repair social relationships also means a limitation on the effectiveness of the law.

When this perspective is applied to social child welfare, it means that the legal norms cannot by their own force keep children and parents together – that is, repair damaged relations (if this is best for the child). The state can only, by its own force, carry out actions which are of a coercive character. This limitation on what the law itself can do in the family's sphere justifies the model on which the Swedish social welfare legislation is based (namely, the family service-oriented model), which aims to accomplish voluntary solutions in collaboration between the authority and parents. It is in this collaboration that we can find the prerequisites for the authority's mediation between social norms on integrity, which are being reinforced by legal norms, and the legal norms on child protection.

Legal norms in the field of social child welfare

In Sweden, public services and social support for families and children in vulnerable situations are dealt with by the municipal social services agencies. The agencies' activities are regulated by the Social Services Act, which is a part of the special administrative law. This law is complemented by a law on compulsory care of young people (Act on the Care of Young Persons). Legal norms within this field have two target groups: children who fare badly or are at risk of faring badly, either because of shortcomings in parental care, on the one hand, or because of the children's own behaviour, on the other. It is legal norms concerning the first group of children that are of interest in the following sections. The legal norms within this area can be divided into two groups.

First, there are norms that can be defined as 'norms for norms' (Baier and Svensson, 2009). These are norms which regulate the power balance between the state/public authorities and individuals, and therefore they can also be defined as 'power-norms'. They are related to a higher level within the public legal norm system, such as the constitution and, hierarchically above this, the conventions on human rights and the rights of the child respectively. For instance, the European Convention for the Protection of Human Rights and Fundamental Freedoms contains norms on the state's actions towards individuals – for example, that the state shall respect the individual's right to privacy and family life. This kind of 'power-norm' can be said to be based on the idea of the right to freedom, which is closely related to the idea of 'individualism – as an assertion of the sanctity of the autonomy and dignity of the individual and of tolerance of individual diversity' (Cotterrell, 1996: 233). This 'power-norm' is also mirrored in one of the norms in the Social Services Act, according to which the authority's activity is founded on respect for the individual's self-determination and integrity. In conformity with this 'integrity-norm', the basic norm for the social services' interaction with the family is cooperation.

However, the state also has obligations towards the child, such as the child's right to have its needs met, which give legitimacy to a group of 'child protection-norms'. According to the 'norm for norms' within this group, which is the norm regulating the power relationship between the state and the child, the child's interests, if they collide with those of the parents, shall be given precedence. In the first place, it is the parents who are responsible for the child and its wellbeing (according to the civil legal norms in the Parental Code); but, if the parents cannot fulfil their responsibilities, and if this means that the child might be harmed, the state takes over the responsibility for the child's protection and security. These obligations of the state are carried out by the social services.

Secondly, there are norms that can be said to be 'norms for acts and decisions' (Baier and Svensson, 2009), which regulate the authority's actual and decision-making activities.

This category contains two types of norms: one group concerns aid and support to families based on voluntariness, and the other group concerns coercive measures. The latter includes norms which aim to control the families. The first group of legal norms is, thus, related to the family service-oriented model, while the second group is related to the child protection-oriented model. Each group of norms is supported by its 'power-norms' at a higher level, but the child protection-oriented norms have the highest priority. This indicates an imbalance in the power relationship between the social authority and the parents.

An example of this imbalance is the norm on compulsory care, which means that, if the social services assess that it is in the child's best interest to receive care and upbringing in a foster home, this can be arranged without the parents' consent. Another example is the legal norms on mandatory reporting for certain occupational groups, in cases where they have reason to believe that the social services may need to provide protection for the child. This can activate another legal norm, whereby the social services, if they have reason to believe that intervention is required for a child's protection, shall open and carry out an investigation. In such a case, the social services do not need the parents' consent to start and complete an investigation. These legal norms, which aim to protect the child, do not exclude the norm on collaboration, which aims to find a voluntary solution to the family's problem.

The social services' mediation activities, which are related to the norms on collaboration, are carried out by public servants, usually professional social workers (see, for instance, Friis, 2003). They use a method which 'ideally involves workers and parents formulating goals in a partnership process' (Dumbrill, 2006: 36). This partnership process can also be defined as a 'cooperation between client and social worker for problem solving', which aims to improve the conditions for the client in accordance with the goals for social welfare (Socialdepartementet, 1974: 350, my translation). As a method for mediation, it presupposes a willingness of the client/parents to cooperate. However, as shown in research, many parents whose families are the subject of social interventions do not feel any confidence in the social authorities. This can be related to the legal imbalance in the power relationship between the parents and the social worker (Dumbrill, 2006), which in turn can explain why most parents do not call on social services voluntarily, but are referred to them (Sundell et al., 2007; Wiklund, 2006). It is also related to circumstances such as parents often being anxious and under stress regarding the report, and that they seldom have a positive attitude towards the investigation (Andersson, 1995; Drake, 1994; Dumbrill, 2006; Lindell, 2005; Rasmusson, 2008; Sundell et al., 2007). This is a problem, since the parents' attitudes towards the social authority influence their willingness to collaborate with the authority's representatives in the investigations (Drake, 1994; Dumbrill, 2006). Thus, research indicates that the imbalance in the power relationship, which is founded on legal norms that aim to protect the child, may have a hindering effect on the mediation. The trend towards the expansion of such norms within the field of social child welfare indicates that this imbalance is growing.

One example of the expansion is related to such cases where the social services suspect that the child has been subject to and/or witnessed violence in the home. This activates norms which belong to the authority's general guidelines, which do not have the status as legal norms but are binding on those to whom they relate. One of the guidelines is a recommendation to the social services to promptly report to the police any suspicion of crimes against children, if it is for the good of the child (Socialstyrelsen, 2006a and 2006b). This is an 'old' norm that has been reformulated into a more distinct imperative. A comparison between two studies made at different times (Friis, 2008; Socialdepartementet, 2001) shows that this norm has been applied in different ways, and that the social services nowadays are more inclined than previously to report suspicions about violence against children within the family to the police. This is an indication of a normative change in the field of social child welfare, which implies an increase in the power of the state/public authorities over the individuals/parents, and which might also have implications for the mediation processes at the individual level. This aspect has been taken into consideration in the coming analysis, as will be described in the next section.

Problem and aim

The problem to be explored is related to the tension between the two groups of power norms in the legislation, which are supporting different interests – on the one hand, the family's right to privacy and integrity, and on the other, the child's right to protection and security. The first group of legal norms, the integrity-norms, are deeply anchored in people's conception of family autonomy and the right to self-determination in its own matters, as is mirrored by expressions such as 'my home is my castle'. This includes the idea that it is the parents' right to decide on matters concerning their children, because they know best what their children need and what is best for them. These conceptions are anchored in both social norms and civil legal norms (in family law). There are, however, also certain limits to the parents' freedom, which are defined by legal norms, such as the prohibition against using physical or mental violence against the child, which is supported by other child protection-norms in different areas of the legislation (in social welfare, family and criminal law).

The family service-oriented model in the Social Services Act can be seen as an attempt to balance these different interests against each other. The model offers opportunities for solving the family's problem in a voluntary way, through collaboration between the authority and the parents. The success of this interaction is dependent on the authority's representative, the social worker, and the parents managing to establish an effective working relationship (Drake, 1994). If this is possible, the social worker can act as a mediator between social and legal norms – that is, between the integrity-norms and child protection-norms, and together with these, societal and legal norms for child upbringing.

It may be assumed that the mediation is carried out by means of the communication between the social worker and the parents. Through this, the social worker can influence and motivate the parents to change such forms of behaviour as contravene legal norms and related social norms, which define the good or acceptable methods of child upbringing, and to move closer to these norms. Such a normative change would also imply that the situation for the child is about to change in a positive direction.

The aim of this chapter is to find out how the social services mediate through collaboration in cases involving suspicions of child maltreatment, and if this leads to a normative change in the family's life, and with what implications for the family's children. The study will be restricted to cases where the suspicions of maltreatment are based on weak or vague information, which is reported to the police by the social services. A reason for this is that it highlights the tension between the integrity-norms and child protection-norms, at the same time as the social worker's ability to mediate is put to the test: a vague suspicion about a child being abused does not usually constitute enough grounds for coercive measures, which is why the social worker must try to encourage the parents to take active part in collaboration with the worker, since this is the central mechanism in the mediation.

The investigation in this chapter will be based on a previous study (Friis, 2008) of social investigations into abused children, which is described in the next section. This study and similar research are also of relevance for this chapter, since they illuminate some of the ways in which the legal norms on child protection are expanding within the field of social child welfare.

The expansion of legal norms on child protection

The trend towards the expansion of the legal child-protection norms is apparent from, among other things, stricter rules on violent and sexual crimes against children (see, for instance, Kaldal, 2010), collaboration among agencies concerning children who fare badly or are at risk of faring badly, and mandatory reporting to the social services (see, for instance, Socialdepartementet, 1997, 2001 and 2009). Recent research shows that there have also been changes in the practices of social child welfare, which are related to these legal changes.

The application of the new legal norms, on collaboration between authorities involved with children who fare badly or are at risk of faring badly, was studied in an evaluation of a pilot project concerning a new form of collaboration between authorities regarding suspected crimes against children (physical and sexual abuse). Representatives of the social services, police, public prosecutor and healthcare and medical services are working together in Barnahus,[1] primarily during the initial stages of the preliminary police investigation and the social services' investigation. The aim of the collaboration in Barnahus is, among others, to improve the quality of the investigations and to provide a better overall basis for the judicial process (see Johansson, 2008 and 2011; Kaldal et al., 2010; Åström and Rejmer, 2008).

The evaluation contained several studies, one of which was a study of the social services' investigations into suspected crimes against children in 19 social services areas during 2006 and 2007. According to the study, the social services reported the majority of the cases to the police, even cases where the suspicions were weak or vaguely formulated (Friis, 2008). The result can be compared with an earlier study of the number of reported suspicions of child abuse to the social services in an administrative county (Östergötland) in 2000. Here, the social services did not report the majority of the cases to the police – for example, because the report was unfounded, or for the good of the child, or because the grounds were considered insufficient for various reasons (Socialdepartementet, 2001). Thus, the result indicates that the social services are more inclined nowadays to make reports to the police than previously.

The evaluation covered six Barnahus and two comparison locations without Barnahus. One of the other studies concerned the police's preliminary investigations (Rejmer and Hansen, 2008; Åström and Rejmer, 2008). The result indicates that the social services in Barnahus locations report suspected child abuse to the police more frequently than the social services in locations without Barnahus. However, the evaluation study did not find any difference between Barnahus and the comparison locations in terms of the number of cases reported to the police that had resulted in legal proceedings. Approximately 20 per cent of the cases reported to the police ended up in court (Åström and Rejmer, 2008). The result was about the same in a later evaluation study that covered eight Barnahus and four comparison locations during 2009 and 2010 (Kaldal et al., 2010). These results can be compared with a study of police reports regarding child physical abuse in one police district during 1986–1996, in which approximately 20 per cent of the cases went to court. It was only severely injured children, or children who had been subjected to severe violence, who had their cases prosecuted (Lindell, 2005).

The relatively wide gap between the number of cases reported to the police and the number of reports leading to prosecution is related to the function and logic of the norms in the criminal legal system. The task of the police and the court system is to deal with crimes, but legal proceedings against a suspected perpetrator can

1 Barnahus is a Swedish version of a Children's Advocacy Centre (CAC), a number of which were established in the USA during the 1980s. In Sweden, the first Barnahus was established in 2004, and six years later there were 22 of them (Kaldal et al., 2010).

only be taken if the suspected criminal action has been made concrete (in terms of place, time, every element of the action, the effects of the crime, and so on), and a sentence of guilty can only be passed if there is evidence of each element of the deed description[2] (Kaldal, 2010). This logic is probably an important part of the explanation of the discrepancy between the number of cases reported to the police and reports which lead to prosecution.

Another part of the explanation is related to the function and logic of the norms in the social child welfare system. The task is to detect and give help to children in vulnerable situations as early as possible, in order to prevent the problems within the families from escalating to the detriment to the children. The system is built on mandatory reporting, and this leads to a large inflow of reports to the social services. Research shows that the most common reasons for a report to the social services regarding a child are vague and directed towards lack of care, which cannot be directly related to physical or sexual abuse or repeated neglect (Wiklund, 2006). This, in turn, influences the social services' investigations, which are, to a great extent, based on a tentative concern about the child's situation in relation to the parents' lack of care, and more seldom on suspicion of physical and sexual abuse (Sundell et al., 2007). According to the author's study (Friis, 2008), reports to the social services regarding suspected child abuse often concerned abuse that had occurred in the past, and therefore any signs of possible injuries had disappeared, or the reports were often vaguely formulated and/or concerned abuse which had not left any physical traces. As already mentioned, a majority of the cases reported to the social services was also reported to the police, but few of them ended up in court.

To sum up the research: it gives clear indications that, first, there is an on-going expansion of the legal norms aimed at child protection within the social child welfare system; and, secondly, the logic of the criminal law system is becoming ever more dominant in the work of social child welfare. This development raises many questions, above all, whether it might mean that mediation will come to lose its importance as a tool for preventive work in the family service-oriented social work in the future. At the end of this chapter, after the relevant mediation issues have been analysed, we will return to this question for a brief discussion.

Methods and material

The foundation for this chapter is the author's study of the social services' investigations into child abuse within the family (Friis, 2008), which have been described in the section above.[3] The study was based on documentation from social

2 What the prosecutor claims must 'be beyond reasonable doubts' (see Kaldal, 2010: 54, my translation).

3 The aim of Friis' (2008) study was to describe and compare the social services' target group, handling methods and measures, on the one hand, and the child perspective,

services' investigations into cases where it was suspected that a child had been subjected to physical or mental abuse or sexual abuse by an adult (thus not crimes against children committed by other children) and comprised 236 investigations.[4]

The initial study consisted of two parts: 1) a quantitative section with a compilation of statistics, and 2) a qualitative section in which a randomized sample, comprising 27 investigations, had been analysed in depth on the basis of formal regulations for handling (see method description in Friis, 2008: 25–9). This sample of investigations forms the foundation for this particular study, but a second sample has been made on the basis of the following considerations.

In the analysis of the 236 investigations, which in most cases had been initiated because of suspected child abuse within the family (but also, in some cases, sexual abuse), it was clear that many of the cases were based on vague or indistinct suspicions of excesses against the children. Another observation was that, in these cases, it often seemed as if the underlying reason why the families had been reported to the social services was related to conflicts and aggressions within the family (that is, between biological parents, or between parents and their partners). A further observation was that this kind of family problem is not limited to any special social group or category of people, nor is it typically related to a certain kind of personal problem (for instance, that the parents have drug problems or are unemployed, or are criminals). However, at that time it was not possible, for various reasons, to make a more in-depth investigation of these observations. The focus for this study will, therefore, be on families in conflict.

The sample of investigations is based on the first sample of 27 investigations (see above) which, in this study, has been reduced to five cases. These cases can be considered to be typical of families in conflict, and they also illustrate this kind of family problem in a clear way.

Further characteristics of these cases are that it is plain from the documentation that the social services have filed a report to the police, and that this report is based on weak or ambiguously worded suspicions of child abuse.

The documentation of the investigations in these cases has, thus, been examined for the purpose of shedding light on the mediation processes and their outcomes. The starting point for this has been the assumption that the authority must mediate between the family's social norms on integrity and the legal norms on child protection, for the purpose of encouraging the parents to pay more consideration to the latter group of norms. The underlying 'object' for the mediation – the conflicts and aggressions between the adults – can be described in terms of 'risk behaviours' in the families. The term 'risk', when used in social

---

on the other, in investigations concerning suspected child abuse in the evaluation municipalities, to find out if there were qualitative differences in the investigations carried out in municipalities which practise or do not practise the collaboration model.

4 The case officers were asked to send in the investigations in cases related to suspected crimes against children under the third, fourth and sixth chapters of the Criminal Code, to the author at her workplace at Lund University.

child welfare work, refers to the probability that a child will fare badly in the future. 'Assessment of risk' is a central part of social child investigations, which is anchored in theories about risk factors in the environments of children growing up (see, for example, Lagerberg and Sundelin, 2000; Sundell et al., 2004 and 2007; Vinnerljung et al., 2007). According to these theories, certain kinds of behaviour in the family can be seen as indicators of a risk to the child's health and development. Such 'risk behaviour' in the families in question is related to conflicts and aggressions between the child's parents and, if applicable, their partners. It is known from research that children's well-being is affected negatively in families with high level of conflict (Lagerberg and Sundelin, 2000), and also that relationship problems between parents are one of the most common reasons for social interventions in families (Sundell et al., 2007). The cases in question here are, thus, not unique; rather, they belong to one of the most common client categories within the social child welfare system.

The mediation processes have been analysed on the basis of the descriptions in (the documentation of) the investigations.[5] The following three aspects of the mediation have been taken into consideration in the analysis.

One aspect is the parents' interactions with the mediator/social worker. As observed by research, parents can have a positive, neutral or negative attitude towards the social worker and, depending on the attitude, they can be more or less willing to cooperate in the investigation (Andersson, 1995; Drake, 1994; Dumbrill, 2006). The parents' attitudes towards the social worker should, however, also be understood in relation to the norms on integrity being challenged in these kinds of situations. To understand why some parents react in a more positive way and others in a negative way, it should be taken into consideration that these kinds of norms also regulate the power relationship between the parents and the authority. It has also been shown in research that it is of central importance how the parents perceive that the social worker uses his or her authority towards them (Dumbrill, 2006). For instance, parents can feel that the social worker is using his or her powers 'over' them or 'with' them, and they can react by 'fighting', 'playing the game' or 'collaborating' (ibid.). If they perceive that power is being used 'over' them, this tends to lead them to fight or play the game. If they experience that power is being used 'with' them, this tends to lead them to cooperate, and perhaps play the game at times.

5 It should be mentioned that there might be shortcomings in the documentation of the investigations – for instance, that it does not describe the entire case handling, but merely reflects what the social services know or believe to be relevant to write down (Sundell et al., 2007). On the other hand, an investigation text should not be written from the text author's perspective, but from the perspective of the legislation and the authority (Hydén, 1995). This means that the documentation of the investigation is also directed by legal and administrative norms (see Socialstyrelsen, 2006b and 2006c). According to these norms, the documentation of an investigation must give such information as is of importance for the outcome of the investigation.

In the light of the integrity-norms, it is understandable why parents react in these ways. The parents' experiences of the social worker's powers as being used 'with' them is based on their perceptions that the worker, among others, is operating in their interests, encouraging and supporting them, and using the social authority's resources to help the family (Dumbrill, 2006). Conversely, if the parents experience that power is being used 'over' them, it may promote negative emotions, such as fear of the social worker, and feelings of powerlessness and frustration in the interaction with the worker (ibid.).

The second aspect is related to the interactions of the investigator/social worker with the parents during the investigations. Social workers are obliged to 'defend' the legal norms on child protection, but also to take the integrity-norms into consideration. This balancing necessitates certain competences, above all, that the social worker has an ability to establish an effective working relationship with the parents (Drake, 1994). Competences that promote such a relationship are, for instance, the ability to treat the parents with respect, and to let them take part in the problem definition (ibid.). Again, in the light of the integrity-norms, it is understandable why such acts are successful in the mediation. This and the above-mentioned study are used in the analysis as a frame of reference for understanding the outcomes of the interactions between social workers and parents.

In the third aspect of the mediation study, the outcomes have been analysed in relation to a normative change in the family: if there is a shift in the parents' priorities, between the integrity-norms and the legal norms on child protection, this change might affect the conditions for a change for the better (or, if applicable, for the worse, or for no change at all) in the child's situation. The analysis of the normative changes has been based on the information in the investigations, which contain descriptions of the parents' attitudes, acts and behaviour (and changes in these factors) during the investigation process. The basis for the assessment of how a normative change affects the conditions for a change in the child's situation is the research into the conditions of children growing up, which has identified favourable and less favourable living conditions for children (Lagerberg and Sundelin, 2000).

Mediations and outcomes

The cases can briefly be described as follows: a common characteristic is that the children's parents are separated (but sharing custody of the child). It was evident from the descriptions in the investigations that the parents (and, if applicable, their new partners) were in conflict with each other, and that the families' everyday life seemed to have been permeated by the adults' quarrels and hostile communications. It was also clear from the descriptions in the investigations that the investigators and also the children concerned perceived the adults' quarrels and aggressive acts towards each other as being the main problem in the families. The parents' relationship problems also seemed, in a majority of cases, to have obstructed them from collaborating about the child. These problems were, thus, the underlying causes for the mediations. The task for the mediations was therefore to make the parents aware of the legal demands on them – for instance, that they as parents should ensure the children's security and a good and close relationship to both of the parents (according to the Parental Code, which is backed up with socio-legal norms on child protection), which presupposes that the parents can collaborate with the child's best interest in mind.

In two of the cases (C1, C2), the children's parents had separated, and were living with new partners. It is evident from the investigation that the parents and their partners often quarrelled, and that the children's parents had very hostile relations towards each other, which influenced their collaboration in relation to the children in a negative way. It is also evident that the child in each family did not like the fact that the parents quarrelled with each other and with their partners, and that they wanted the situation to change. The children's situations were assessed by the social services' investigators as a risk to their health and well-being, and this gave rise to the decisions to start investigations.

Both cases had been brought to the attention of the social services through a report by one of the children's parents about suspected child maltreatment. This indicates that (at least) one parent from each family had a positive expectation of getting help from the authority. It may be related to the fact that both families had long-standing problems with their finances, in combination with alcohol abuse, and had earlier received assistance and support from the social services. This may also explain why the other parents, according to descriptions in the investigations, seem to have taken an active part in the investigations. So, this indicates that the parents had a positive attitude towards the social worker and were willing to cooperate.

In both cases, the social services' investigators formed the opinion that the families had initiated a process of change and that the home environment for the children had improved during the investigation. The children had previously moved between the parents, but, in connection with the investigation, lived full-time with one of the parents (the children's mothers). It also seemed that the parents had gained better control over their drinking habits. Both investigations ended with a forward-looking perspective, in that the parents and the social services' investigators agreed on continued contact. In the light of this, it seems as if the children achieved a more secure and peaceful existence than they had before the investigation started. This indicates that these investigations had promoted conditions for a positive change in the children's situation.

According to the theory on parents' reactions (Dumbrill, 2006), the key to understanding the outcomes of interventions is centred on the parents' perceptions of how the social workers use their powers in their interactions with the parents. It seems as if the parents in these cases have perceived that the social workers used their power 'with' them – and, because of this, they wanted to cooperate with the worker. According to the descriptions in the investigations, the social workers managed to establish an 'effective working relationship' (see Drake,

1994) with the parents, built on trust. In both of these cases, the investigator had a more intensive contact with the child's mother than with the father. In one of the cases (C1), it was the conversations between the social services' investigator and the mother which, according to the investigator, led the mother to the insight that the child was in need of peace and quiet, and stability in its home conditions. The mother realized, also, that both she and the child's father needed help. They and the child were offered a support family, which they also accepted. In the other case (C2), it was the mother's wish that the social services should make home visits at regular intervals, because she wanted to show that the child's home conditions had improved. The investigator affirmed this, and also that the mother had improved her capabilities as a parent and was able to take both initiative and responsibility. The ways in which the parents changed their actions and attitudes in the two cases can be seen as an indicator of a shift in the parents' normative priorities – that is, a shift away from the integrity-norm towards the norms on child protection.

The mediation is, thus, anchored in the way that the social worker interacts with the parents. In these two cases, the mediation seems to have caused a normative change. The descriptions of the families' situations in the final stage of the investigations indicate that the previous risk behaviours, the parents' aggressive interactions, which also hindered them from collaborating in relation to their children, had been replaced with a behaviour that conformed better to legal norms in family law. The success of the mediations can be explained by the methods that were used by the social workers leading to the establishment of an effective working relationship, built on trust. The workers supported the families through conversations, but also through other kinds of assistance, which the families were in need of in order to accomplish the necessary changes in their ways of living. The social worker monitored the families in their change processes and encouraged them (for instance, praising them when they were making progress). It can be assumed that these kinds of acts made the parents feel that the social workers cared about them and were operating in the interests of the whole family.

Among the other investigations is one case (C3) where the child's school had reported suspicions of child maltreatment to the social services. The parents had divorced and were living with new partners, and the child was living alternately with each parent. According to the child, the stepfather had been heavy-handed when they were wrestling for fun, and that had only happened once. The child considered it was much more troubling that the mother and stepfather frequently quarrelled. The investigator/social worker assessed that the situation for the child was insecure, and decided to open an investigation.

In contrast to the previous cases, the biological parents in this case did not seem to have had any problem in cooperating in relation to the child. It also seems as if these parents had a more neutral attitude towards the social worker, compared with the previously reported cases. The child's mother and stepfather had contacted the family counselling service to get help with their relationship problems, and wanted no further help from the social services. According to the information in the investigation, the parents had not previously been in contact with the social services. This may explain the adults' reserved attitudes towards the social worker – it seems as if they would have preferred to solve the problems in the family on their own. However, they did take part in the investigation and had conversations with the social worker. According to the social worker's assessment, the investigation had been a turning-point for the family, which had resulted in a calmer home environment. So, this indicates that the investigation had promoted the conditions for a positive change in the child's situation.

To summarize the mediation in this case: it seems to have led to a change in the adults' behaviour that was better for the child, as well as conforming better to legal norms on children's upbringing. This might be seen as an indicator of a change in the parents' normative preferences – that is, a shift away from the integrity-norms towards the norms on child protection. However, the question is whether the change was the result of an honest collaboration or not. The parents' reserved stance toward the investigator/social worker might have been caused by the feeling that they had not asked for this contact with the authority, with the result that they had got into this situation involuntarily. This may indicate that they felt that the social worker was using power 'over' them. If so, it may also have been a hindrance to an effective working relationship (that is, a relationship that promotes honest communication). This could mean that the parents' and the stepfather's cooperation was not honest, indicating that they only 'played the game'.

On the other hand, the parents were, as it seems, sincerely concerned about the child, and the investigation gave them the opportunity to discuss the situation. The descriptions of the investigation indicate that the parents were treated with respect, and that their opinions and interpretations of the problem situation were taken seriously by the social worker. So, this indicates that the parents may have had the feeling that power was used 'with' them.

The remaining two cases also concern separated families, where the parents shared the custody of the children. All parents lived with new partners. In one of the cases (C4), the child was under review of the social services due to a report from the police that the child's parents had reported each other for threats. In the other case (C5), the father had reported to the social services that the mother had maltreated the child. The situation for the concerned children was assessed to be insecure, and the social services decided to open investigations. Both families had already experienced this kind of contact with the social services.

In both investigations, it was shown that the parents' relationships were characterized by deep-seated conflicts and difficulties in cooperation. According to the social workers, the children were deeply affected by the parents' conflicts, and they wished nothing more than that the parents would stop quarrelling. In both investigations, there also came a turning-point, where the parents realized that the children were suffering from the conflicts and that they must try to establish a neutral relationship between themselves and concentrate on the children's needs. Both investigations ended with the social worker's assessment that the child's home environment had altered for the better. This indicates that the investigations have promoted the possibilities for a positive change in the children's situations.

To summarize the mediation: at the beginning of the investigations, the parents in these two families seem to have been very occupied by their conflicts and aggressions. In light of this, it appears that the primary task for the social workers was to talk sense to the parents and get them to put their own problems aside and instead think about the children's well-being. The success of the mediation in these two cases can, therefore, be put down to the ability of the social worker to negotiate between the parents and help them to come to a shared understanding about the children's needs. This presupposes an effective working relationship built on trust. However, in situations like these, it can be difficult for the social worker to get both parents to trust her or him.

This problem was demonstrated in one of the cases (C4). The mother was critical towards the social worker, because she considered that the worker was on the other parent's side. However, the investigation led to a point where both the mother and the father could agree to the social worker's suggestions for arrangements that would improve the child's situation. So, this happened despite the mother having a critical attitude towards the social worker. The mother's attitude may have been related to a feeling that the social worker's power was used 'over' her. She cooperated with the worker, but it cannot be excluded that she simply 'played the game'. The father, on the other hand, seems to have had a more trustful attitude towards the social worker, which indicates that he felt that the worker used the power 'with' him. In this case, the social worker seems to have established an effective working relationship.

In the other case (C5), both parents had a more positive approach to the social worker. It seems as if there was no problem in the parent/social worker relationship, which is indicated by the parents telling the social worker about themselves and their problems in an open and direct way, for instance. This indicates that the parents experienced that the social worker was using her power 'with' them, which resulted in an effective working relationship.

At the end of each investigation, it seems as if the parents had changed their behaviour, and started to collaborate and communicate in a more constructive way with each other. So, this is an indication that the risk behaviours would change so as to conform better to legal norms in family law. It is also an indicator of a change in the parents' normative preferences, meaning a shift away from the integrity-norms towards the norms on child protection.

Conclusions

The analysis has illustrated the mediation process in five cases concerning families in conflict, which can be considered to give a typical picture of this kind of family problem. The result of the analysis cannot, however, be treated as valid for all kinds of mediations which are performed by the social authority in cases like these. What it is possible to say is, rather, that the analysis has shown a pattern for successful mediation in typical cases concerning families in conflict.

The starting point for the analysis of the social workers' mediations was the assumption that the task of the mediator in these kinds of case is to accomplish a normative change in the family. This means that the parents should become more inclined to accept and (perhaps even more important) to apply norms that promote the child's interest of a safe and peaceful home environment. A successful change is indicated by a shift in the parents' normative priorities, from social norms that shield their own and the family's integrity towards legal norms that aim to protect the child. On the basis of the information in the documentation of the investigations, such normative alterations can be observed as a change in the parents' attitudes and/or behaviour, which indicates that their new priority conforms better to legal norms that promote the child's interest. Such a change also promotes the conditions for an improvement in the child's situation. One conclusion from the analysis is that these mediations have contributed to such normative changes. A second conclusion is that this success may be explained by the fact that the social workers have used methods which are in harmony with the integrity-norms.

A pattern of conversations and dialogues between parents and social workers was evident in the documentation of the investigations. In each investigation, there was a description of the parents' perspectives and opinions about the family's problems, as well as the assessment by the investigator/social worker of the children's needs and the family's situation. These descriptions also indicated changes in the parents' attitudes, opinions and behaviour during the investigation process. In this way, the descriptions created a picture of a dialogue between the social workers and parents. The characteristics of these dialogues correspond to the criteria for effective communication (Drake, 1994). For instance, the social worker must show the parents respect, allow the parents to define the situation as they see it, and try to see the situation from the parents' point of views. It is apparent that such methods are in harmony with the integrity-norms.

The fact that some of the parents did not seem to have reacted in a positive way, despite being treated with respect, indicates that there might also be other factors that influence the parents' interactions with the social workers. In the cases in question, such a factor could be that the social worker had reported the parents to the police (which happened in all five cases, because of the initial suspicion of child abuse). Some of the parents might have experienced this as a repressive and insulting action, which could have influenced their interactions with the social worker in a negative way. Despite this, in most of the cases in question, there were clear indications that the parents, as a result of the mediations, had changed or were about to change their normative priorities.

A third conclusion of the analysis is that these normative changes were positive in terms of the children's situation. It is an empirical question whether the situation for those children actually did change for the better. One may at least assume that the mediations in question have contributed to prevent, or reduce, the risk that the child would develop in a disadvantageous direction. This is in clear conformity with the legal intentions of the family service-oriented model.

This chapter has focused on the normative changes in the field of social child welfare, which indicates that child protection-norms are gradually achieving an ever more prominent position. This can be seen as an expression of the juridification process – that is, 'the intrusion of law into fields that are ill-fitted to regulate' (Cotterrell, 1992: 52), such as social relations within the family. A final question to be discussed is how this process will influence the prerequisites for mediation in the future.

The activities in the field of social child welfare are regulated by two models for family services and child protection respectively, which are both products of 'state law', and, as such, aim towards social control and change. However, they perform this task in different ways, and according to different logic. Family service-oriented norms are working in a proactive way, to avoid problems occurring in the future. Mediation is an important tool in this work. Child protection-norms are functioning in the opposite direction, as a reaction to something that has happened in the past. This group of norms is connected with repressive sanctions and, related to this, with the assessment of guilt and punishment. This kind of consideration has no relevance to the first group of norms. On the contrary, if the mediator presents a judgmental attitude, this would be a hindrance to the aim. This kind of thinking does not have the same relevance for the child protection-norms. One conclusion of this reasoning is that, if the logic of the child protection-norms takes over in the work with cases that concern children who fare badly or are at risk of faring badly because of failings in the parents' care, it will impair the prerequisites of the mediation.

There are, however, also reasons that speak against such a development. They are based on the integrity-norms, and the fact that informal social relations are controlled by social norms, which have been internalized by people, through what people perceive as their moral duties and rights. The law cannot substitute the natural relationships within the family, but it does offer the possibility of repairing damaged relationships through informal interactions (collaborations) between social workers and parents, which is the basis of mediation. As indicated by the analysis in this chapter, this presupposes that the social worker can establish a situation of 'effective communication', which in turn presupposes that the worker can treat the parents as equals and meet them with respect for their integrity. If this condition is fulfilled, the social worker and parents can meet in a dialogue about the child's situation and needs, and in this way the worker can appeal to the parents' moral commitment to the child and, through this, promote a change in their normative priorities which is to the benefit of the child.

Ultimately, this is a question of the effectiveness of the two models. As indicated by this study and related research, the effectiveness of child welfare work that focuses on the logic of criminal legal norms may be questioned. It can be compared with the effectiveness of child welfare work that focuses on the logic of family service-oriented legal norms, which can adapt to and cooperate with social norms. As indicated by this study, mediation can be an effective tool to accomplish normative changes.

References

Andersson, G. 1991. *Socialt arbete med små barn.* Lund: Studentlitteratur.

Andersson, G. 1995. *Barn i samhällsvård.* Lund: Studentlitteratur.

Åström, K. and Rejmer, A. 2008. *'Det blir nog bättre för barnen ... '.* Slutrapport i utvärderingen av nationell försöksverksamhet med barnahus 2006–2007. Research Report in Sociology of Law 2008, 7. Lund: Sociology of Law, Lund University.

Baier, M. and Svensson, M. 2009. *Om normer.* Malmö: Liber.

Coccozza, M. 2007. *The Parenting of Society. A study of Child Protection in Sweden – from Report to Support.* Linköping: Linköping University, Faculty of Health and Sciences.

Cotterrell, R. 1992. *The Sociology of Law. An Introduction.* London: Butterworths.

Cotterrell, R. 1996. *Law's Community. Legal Theories in Sociological Perspective.* Oxford: Clarendon Press.

Drake, B. 1994. 'Relationship Competencies in Child Welfare Services', in *Social Work* 39(5), 595–603.

Dumbrill, G.C. 2006. 'Parental Experience of Child Protection Intervention: A Quality Study', in *Child Abuse & Neglect* 30, 27–37.

Friis, E. 2003. *Sociala utredningar om barn. En rättssociologisk studie av lagstiftningens krav, utredningarnas argumentationer och konsekvenser för den enskilde.* Lund Studies in Sociology of Law, 18. Lund: Sociologiska institutionen, Lunds universitet.

Friis, E. 2008. *Sociala utredningar om brottsutsatta barn. Målgrupp, handläggning och insatser.* Research Report in Sociology of Law 2008, 3. Lund: Sociology of Law, Lund University.

Gilbert, N. 1997. 'Conclusion', in N. Gilbert (Ed.), *Combatting Child Abuse. International perspectives and trends.* Oxford: Oxford University Press, 232–40.

Habermas, J. 1987. *The Theory of Communicative Action.* Volume 2. Boston: Beacon Press.

Hydén, H. 2002. *Normvetenskap.* Lund Studies in Sociology of Law. Lund: Sociologiska institutionen, Lunds universitet.

Hydén, H. 2008. 'Using Law as Model. Different Approaches to the Understanding of Normative Decision-making', in H. Hydén & P. Wickenberg (eds) *Contributions in Sociology of Law. Remarks from a Swedish Horizon.* Lund Studies in Sociology of Law, 29. Lund: Sociology of Law, Lund University, 11–36.

Hydén, H. and Svensson, M. 2008. 'The Concept of Norms in Sociology of Law', in H. Hydén and P. Wickenberg (eds) *Contributions in Sociology of Law. Remarks from a Swedish Horizon.* Lund Studies in Sociology of Law, 29. Lund: Sociology of Law, Lund University, 129–46.

Hydén, L.-C. 1995. 'Det sociala misslyckandet som berättelse. Att återställa den moraliska ordningen', *Socialvetenskaplig tidskrift* 2 (1995), 3, s 194–207.

Johansson, S. 2008. *Myndighetssamverkan i barnahus – organisering, innehåll och process.* Research report in Sociology of Law 2008, 4. Lund: Sociology of Law, Lund University.

Johansson, S. 2011. *Rätt, makt och institutionell förändring. En kritisk analys av myndigheters samverkan i barnahus.* Lund Studies in Sociology of Law, 35. Lund: Sociology of Law, Lund University.

Kaldal, A. 2010. *Parallella processer – en rättsvetenskaplig studie av riskbedömningar i vårdnads- och LVU-mål.* Stockholm: Jure förlag.

Kaldal, A., Diesen, C., Beije, J. and Diesen, E. 2010. *Barnahusutredningen 2010.* Stockholm: Jure förlag.

Lagerberg, D. and Sundelin, C. 2000. *Risk och prognos i socialt arbete med barn. Forskningsmetoder och resultat.* Göteborg: Gothia Förlag.

Lindell, C. 2005. *Child Physical Abuse. Reports and Interventions.* Linköping: Division of Child and Adolescent Psychiatry, Department of Molecular and Clinical Medicine, Linköping University.

Lundström T. 2000. 'Om kommunernas sociala barnavård', *Välfärd, vård och omsorg.* Socialdepartementet. SOU 2000:38. Stockholm: Fritzes offentliga publikationer, s 15–55.

Olsson Hort, S. 1997. 'Toward a Deresidualization of Swedish Child Welfare Policy and Practice?', in N. Gilbert (Ed.), *Combatting Child Abuse. International perspectives and trends.* Oxford: Oxford University Press, 105–24.

Östberg, F. 2010. *Bedömningar och beslut. Från anmälan till insats i den sociala barnavården.* Rapport i socialt arbete nr 134 – 2010. Stockholm: Institutionen för socialt arbete, Stockholms universitet.

Rasmusson, B. 2008. *'Det är ju inget dagis precis ...' Barns och föräldrars upplevelser av kontakter med barnahus.* Research Report in Sociology of Law 2008, 8. Lund: Sociology of Law, Lund University.

Rejmer, A., and Hansen, H. 2008. *'... känner du till skillnaden mellan sanning och lögn?' En analys av förundersökningar.* Research Report in Sociology of Law 2008, 5. Lund: Sociology of Law, Lund University.

Socialdepartementet. 1974. *Socialvården. Mål och medel. Principbetänkande av Socialutredningen.* SOU 1974: 39. Stockholm: Fritzes offentliga publikationer.

Socialdepartementet. 1986. *Barns behov och föräldrars rätt.* SOU 1986: 20. Stockholm: Fritzes offentliga publikationer.

Socialdepartementet. 1997. *Barnets bästa i främsta rummet. FN:s konvention om barnets rättigheter förverkligas i Sverige.* SOU 1997: 116. Stockholm: Fritzes offentliga publikationer.

Socialdepartementet. 2001. *Barnmisshandel. Att förebygga och åtgärda.* SOU 2001: 72. Stockholm: Fritzes offentliga publikationer.

Socialdepartementet. 2009. *Lag om stöd och skydd för barn och unga (LBU).* SOU 2009: 68. Stockholm: Fritzes offentliga publikationer.

Socialstyrelsen. 2006a. *Barn och unga i socialtjänsten. Utreda, planera och följa upp beslutade insatser.* Stockholm: Socialstyrelsen.

Socialstyrelsen. 2006b. *Socialstyrelsens allmänna råd om handläggning och dokumentation av ärenden som rör barn och unga.* SOSFS 2006: 12. Stockholm: Socialstyrelsen.

Socialstyrelsen. 2006c. *Socialstyrelsens föreskrifter och allmänna råd om dokumentationen vid handläggningen av ärenden och genomförande av insatser enligt SoL, LVU, LVM och LSS.* SOSFS 2006: 5. Stockholm: Socialstyrelsen.

Sundell, K., Egelund, T., Löfholm, C. Andrée and Kaunitz, C. 2007. *Barnavårdsutredningar. En kunskapsöversikt.* Stockholm: Gothia Förlag.

Sundell, K., Vinnerljung, B., Andrée Löfholm, C. and Humlesjö, E. 2004. *Socialtjänstens barn. Hur många är de, vilka är insatserna, hur ofta återaktualiseras de och vad händer dem i vuxen ålder?* FoU-rapport 2004: 4. Stockholm: Socialtjänstförvaltningen, FoU-enheten.

Svensson, M. 2008. *Sociala normer och regelefterlevnad. Traffiksäkerhetsfrågor ur ett rättssociologiskt perspektiv.* Lund Studies in Sociology of Law. Lund: Sociology of Law, Lund University.

Vinnerljung, B., Hjern, A., Ringbäck, G. Weitoft, Franzén, E. and Estrada, F. 2007. 'Children and Young People at Risk (Chapter 7). Social Report 2006', in D. Biterman (Ed.), *International Journal of Social Welfare* 16, 163–202.

Wiklund, S. 2006. *Den kommunala barnavården – om anmälningar, organisation och utfall.* Stockholm: Enheten för socialt arbete, Socialvetenskapliga fakulteten, Stockholms universitet.

Chapter 11
Meta-norms in Complex Situations: The Pedagogy of Recognition

Lars Persson

Introduction

Education has a central role in creating the foundation for democracy: participating and competent citizens. This democratic assignment is the basis for the schools legislation formulated in the Swedish Education Act and curricula. In order to fulfil this assignment, teachers have to transform the meaning and values of the legal texts into classroom actions. Teaching democracy is a challenge for teachers on all levels, from preschools to upper secondary schools, not least because the democratic issues are difficult issues, as they lie close to the meaning of life and society. In this chapter, I will discuss actions and norms in a professional setting by means of the example of how teachers transform school laws to actions in classrooms.

Teaching involves a close relationship between classroom[1] actions and reflections on these. While classroom action is mainly a process between the teacher and the child/student, the reflection is a process mainly between the teacher and her teacher colleagues. These two processes are very closely related, almost intertwined in each other. By analysing them separately in this chapter, it is my aim to extract the central characteristic norms of teaching democracy from the classroom actions, and further to discuss the reflection process as a process of developing professional norms.

Teaching takes place in social situations, where teachers confront situations in which they have to consider, on a daily basis, several different, and sometimes conflicting, interests and norms. I will suggest that such tensions can be handled by the professionals by developing meta-norms, which in turn can be related to the legal norms in the Education Act and the curricula. In a final discussion, I will also draw some conclusions about how the concept of norms can be useful when analysing actions in professional life.

This chapter is based on research into a democracy project in preschools, primary and secondary schools in the city of Lund (Persson, 2010). It deals with areas in society and social science where concepts like education, democracy and

1 Classroom action involves all forms of teaching and interaction between teachers and children/students.

professionality are frequently used. The use of these concepts is often problematic, however, which makes it desirable to construct a framework for them in some way.

Democracy and education

The concept of democracy has many definitions and interpretations, and it is, as Lundquist (2003) puts it, probably not even possible to clarify what democracy ought to be. Lundquist points out that democracy is related both to 'substantial values', such as freedom, equality, solidarity and justice, and to 'processual values', such as openness, mutuality, discussion and responsibility.

There is a close relationship between democracy and education. The Swedish educational system is based on democratic values formulated in national documents, such as the Education Act, curricula and syllabuses. Democratic aims and means are supposed to be included in all parts of teaching. The democratic assignment for the teachers, as it is formulated in the steering documents, is broad, and has:

a) a cognitive perspective concerning knowledge related to school subjects;
b) an ethical perspective concerning transformation of democratic values; and
c) a social perspective concerning building skills to act in the different forms of social and democratic life in society.

It supports ideas of empowerment, emancipation and equality. This includes becoming socialized into democratic society, learning how to act based on one's own convictions, and being able to treat others as equal individuals. Another dimension of democratic education is to support and enable participation in developing a better future, which is mainly construed as the discourse of sustainable development. The democratic assignment is, therefore, a difficult task for teachers and their professionality.

Professional action

We find an idealistic description of professionality in Talcott Parsons's (1939) words: 'The professional man is not thought of as engaged in pursuit of his personal profit, but in performing services to his patients or clients, or to impersonal values like the advancement of science'.

The concept of professionalism relates to professions involving specialized education and a special responsibility in their profession (Freidson, 2001) which, together with experience, develops into professional expertise (Dreyfus and Dreyfus, 2005). According to Molander and Therum (2008), there are two aspects of professionalism: the organizational aspect deals with power and control over the profession; and the performatory aspect deals with competences and is related to formal training and experiences. These competences are often related to a client, student or patient, and to situations involving uncertainty and risks concerning the result of the professional action (Molander and Therum, 2008). Many scholars stress the important central role of relationships in pedagogical professionalism (Frelin, 2008). Bergem (2000) discussed professionality and ethics of the relationships between teachers and children, students, parents, colleagues and the assignment set by society. To act ethically requires a competence to understand what is needed and to act on the basis of this, which corresponds to what Dreyfus and Dreyfus (2005) called 'proficiency' in their ladder of professional development. The final step of their ladder, 'expertise', included not only competence to assess, but also to have immediate access to a broad repertoire of possible actions.

Reflection is a commonly used concept in the discussion of professionality (Alexandersson, 1999). Professional reflection is central for the professional in understanding and developing his/her professional practice. Reflection is a concept with a history that leads back to ancient Greek philosophy and onwards to modern socio-philosophy. Donald Schön was a leading writer on reflection among professionals. He has analysed professional reflection and contributed to the discussion of professional reflection, where he draws a distinction between 'reflection in action' and 'reflection on action' (Schön, 1983 and 1987).

In conclusion, there are some general ideas for the concept of pedagogical professionalism. The central dimension in pedagogical professionality is, of course, to teach in a professional way, which is about competences to act both in immediate situations and with a planned, long-term view towards goals and aims. Teaching also requires competences to analyse and assess situations and individual needs. Teaching is the act where goals in the curricula and other steering documents are to be realized.[2] Another important dimension of pedagogical professionality is to be able to reflect on actions and to apply pedagogical theories and models in these as a means of further developing the practice of teaching. In this chapter, I will consider teaching and reflection on teaching as the two central activities of pedagogical professionality. The first is about doing a really good job, and the second is about doing an even better job. Professionality is a quality with more or less continuous development. This points to the importance of developing the competence through experiences and reflections, just as Dreyfus and Dreyfus describe it.

Professional actions, society and norms

Social sciences deal with human beings and their abilities and possibilities to act. The concept of norms, as used here, is based on the understanding that actions are grounded not only in individual values and knowledge, but also in social matters,

2 Lindensjö and Lundgren write about three arenas: the formulation arena, the transformation arena and the realization arena (Lindensjö and Lundgren, 2002).

such as group pressure and restrictions imposed by laws. By living in social contexts in a society, we seldom act as isolated individuals. Living and acting in modern society is complex, and most often involves being part of different social spheres. Sometimes, we speak of life-world as opposed to system-world. In most social situations, different values and norms meet. Åström (1988) has described this as situations with 'parallel norm systems', which easily cause tensions. Preschools and schools are social settings where the legal sphere interacts with the professional sphere and the life-world sphere. Accordingly, we will find norms and values from at least these three spheres when studying teachers in action. Norms from these different spheres can be in opposition. Sometimes, social norms (here in the meaning of life-world norms) can make it acceptable to break laws or regulations. A well-known example of this is breaking traffic laws, such as speeding, which has become acceptable in many groups (Svensson, 2008). The development of legal texts is often a way of finding compromises to solve ideological controversies. In a forthcoming article, Wickenberg and Leo (2012) present a study of how the legal regulation of the environment and sustainable development in Sweden has changed during the last 20 years.

Norms are socially supported ways of acting, and the concept of norms used in sociology of law has the following characteristics (Hydén and Svensson, 2008):

- norms are behavioural instructions;
- norms are socially reproduced; and
- norms are the individual's understanding of surrounding expectations concerning their behaviour.

The definition of norms might be elaborated into 'universal' and 'general' principles (Nussbaum, 1990). A general principle is applicable to all situations, but is formulated in a way that makes it possible to discuss the meaning; an example might be, 'You should not harm others'. A universal principle is formulated in a concrete way and applicable to all situations; an example would be 'You should not kill others'. When trying to detect norms, it is important to search for a proper formulation of them. According to the definition, a norm should have an imperative grammatical form. We speak of the 'dos' and the 'don'ts' when speaking of what is expected. Furthermore, norms can be formulated as 'must do' or 'ought to do'. A norm formulated as a 'must do' is stronger than a norm formulated as an 'ought to do'. Then, as mentioned above, a norm can have a general or a universal form. The formulation of the norm indicates the relationship between the norm and the actual action. Another aspect of norms, which is of special interest in this chapter, is the hierarchy of norms.

Professional groups can establish norms of their own related to the profession. Such 'professional norms' tend to be strategic or teleological norms, and not concrete instructions on what to do in specific situations (Grimen and Molander, 2008). The latter, as we encounter them in manuals or in top-down instructions, are consequently mostly considered to have a deprofessionalizing effect.[3] Professional groups are not autonomous and cannot act freely, but are controlled by state legislation. The legislation contains expectations of the teachers, and we can accordingly speak of 'legal norms'. The dynamics between the professionals and the state is not only a question of control, but also a question of democracy in itself, where the whole of society and its citizens are involved when we deal with professionals such as teachers. Studies in sociology of law have made contributions to the understanding of the development and processes in schools relating to conflicts of norms and the relationship between school laws and professional norms in schools (Wickenberg, 1999; Hallerström, 2006; Leo, 2010). Professional norms are dependent on collective reflections. This, in turn, needs to be supported by the surrounding structure (Wickenberg, 1999).

The study of democracy projects

In order to study how professional teachers handle the democratic assignments, a group of teachers was followed during their work as leaders of democracy projects (Persson, 2010). In the study, the teachers were interviewed on different occasions during their projects. The study contained both focus group interviews and individual interviews. Documents such as applications to carry out the projects and the final reports were also used in the analysis.

When studying the different projects that the teachers were engaged in, it was obvious that they focused on quite different matters. This was related not only to the fact that they worked at different educational levels – from preschools, primary schools and afterschool centres to upper secondary schools (gymnasium) – but also to different prioritizations and different assessments of factual situations. The situation in which the research was carried out was that the participating preschools and schools had received targeted financial support to carry out democracy projects. This allowed for and legitimized an extended freedom of action for the teacher, and subsequently a situation where pedagogic actions for democracy might be more clearly observable. From the start, it was clear that the teachers choose to plan for activities that are normally difficult to carry out. In order to enhance the democratic side of teaching, they favoured working with:

- interdisciplinary teaching combining different school subjects;
- active student participation, where students are learning by doing;
- esthetical methods, such as arts and drama; and

3 Recent leadership research give support to this, as transformational leadership – leadership based on empowerment and stimulation – had the effect of activating teachers, while transactional leadership – leadership based on rewards and compliance – resulted in teacher burnout to a significantly greater extent (Eyal and Roth, 2010).

- organized encounters and dialogues with people outside the students' normal social context.

This supports a need for teachers to expand their range of action when working with the democratic assignments, which was more evident at the more advanced levels, where the syllabuses are more regulatory than at the earlier stages of school and preschools, where these teaching methods are normally seen more frequently.

Interviews and documents showed, at first sight, a great variety of different actions and projects which seemed to consist of a multitude of actions and processes with little in common. Theories of recognition as a process towards equality and inclusion – which we find among writers such as Ricoeur (2005) and Honneth (2003) – produced a structure and meaning when analysing the material, and a pattern could be revealed. The pattern formed a set of strategic rules or intentions directing the teachers. This pattern seemed to be able to include variations in actions and to build a basis for future actions, which means that these rules form a set of meta-norms applicable to different pedagogical situations. As they were clearly connected to the relationship between the teachers and the children/students and satisfied the criteria of models of recognition, they are a structure for a 'pedagogy of recognition' (Persson, 2011). The meta-norms in this pedagogy of recognition[4] contain three dimensions illustrated in the figure below:

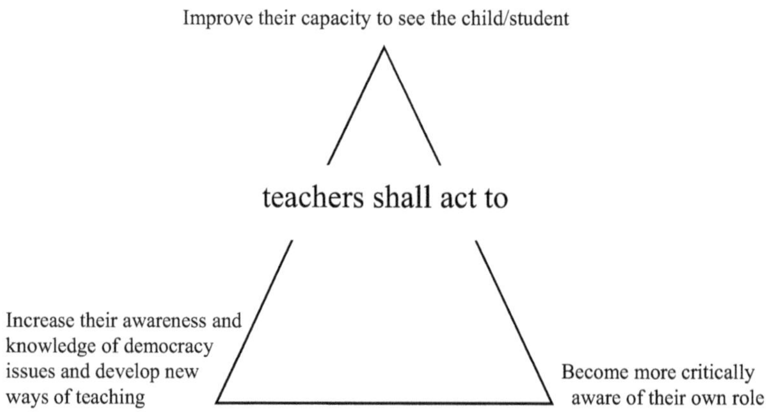

Figure 11.1 Dimensions of Meta-norms for Democratic Teaching

4 Nixon et al. (1997) use the term 'pedagogy of recognition' for a pedagogy based on recognition of differences and empowerment. In Germany, the concept of 'Pädagogik der Anerkennung' is presented in an anthology by Hafeneger et al. (2007) in a similar way.

Improving the capacity to see the child/student

This was seen among the teachers as a striving to listen to what the children and students say, and not to be governed by prejudices or to take children's opinions for granted. Teachers wanted to know more about the children they met, and to deepen the understanding of their ways of thinking. They tried to find those children that easily fall into silence and have difficulties being seen. Lefstein and Snell (2011) have elaborated the concept of professional vision in teaching. They argue that professional vision should be seen in terms of plural, competing visions, which (as social practices of seeing) involve social skills and sensitivities alongside dispositions to notice and capacities to reason.

Becoming more critically aware of their own role and behaviour

This intention is about understanding the importance of how you act as a teacher and to acquire the ability to be critical of your own acting. This includes accepting criticism from children and students, and even welcoming it as an opportunity for change. This is, of course, often difficult, but even more problematic is finding ways of helping colleagues by offering criticism and establishing enough trust in the team of colleagues to hold a critical discussion on sensitive matters. The problem of looking at yourself in a critical way is quite obvious for us, as are the difficulties when it comes to questioning the actions of others, which is often a very sensitive matter. I considered this as especially interesting, as it illustrates a dimension of recognition: becoming aware of oneself through another.

These two norms are directly related to teaching as a relationship between teachers and children/students, which I earlier labelled the process of teaching. The third meta-norm is related to the process of reflection.

Increase their awareness and knowledge of democracy issues and develop new ways of teaching

Through the deeper understanding of children and the experiences of their own practice, teachers also search for explanations and perspectives on this. They read books and articles and attend in-service courses, as well as external lectures. Increasing their own awareness and knowledge of democracy becomes an inspiration to make way for changes in their practice.

A strong emphasis on the need to participate in pedagogical discussions with colleagues was detected in the research. Such discussions contained a clearly reflective element for the working team. The concept of 'justification', elaborated by Boltanski and Thévenot (1999), is interesting here. They consider that justification is especially needed in social situations which contain disputes or discussions. They describe the social world as a set of different worlds, in a way which I find similar to the discussion of parallel norm systems. The justification is related to existing norms in situations where the act, in some way, could be interpreted as questioning or perhaps even breaking a norm. The justification process is a social process related to the norms, but much of it might be internalized in the mind and thinking of the actor herself. An example of this is that several teachers witnessed the impact that video observations of themselves had on their behaviour. The justification is, according to Boltanski and Thevenot, about bringing out arguments that are supported by moral statements, either from within the actual social world (internal argument) or from another social world (external argument). The result might be either support for the action or a future change in similar situations. A teacher can, for instance, use arguments from the Education Act, UNICEF's Convention on the Rights of the Child or similar steering documents to justify her action. When looking at reflection as a process of justification, we find in it the process where not only actions but also norms are discussed, and where there is a possibility of developing specific professional norms for teachers as a response to conflicts caused by difficult situations and parallel norm systems.

The concept of meta-norms and a hierarchy of norms, as a structure for solving norm conflicts, might serve as possibility for the researchers when analysing this kind of situation (Axelrod, 1986). For professionals, the existence of meta-norms produces an opportunity to overcome difficult professional situations. The establishment of a value-based professional ethic is a way to seek such guidance in actions, and to formulate functional meta-norms and make them known. Ethical guidelines are, at their best, a professional way of solving such complex social and professional situations.

Professional norms and legal steering documents

The teachers in the study strongly emphasized their responsibility for the relationships with the students. At the same time, they were conscious of the difficulties of creating good relations with all children and students. The concept of 'recognition' served as a model for the pattern found in the study of how the teachers described their work. In order to develop the social relationships among children, and between themselves as teachers and the children, they implied an intentional way of thinking by working towards the three distinguishable meta-norms.

These intentions were encouraged by (and, most often, dependent on) opportunities to carry out pedagogic discussions among colleagues. Professional and reflective discussions were important in order to develop an understanding of democracy issues and to elaborate interpretations of democracy values. The pedagogical discussions often contained normative questions, such as confronting daily events with ideas found in steering documents such as the curricula. An act carried through is open to scrutiny and criticism by others, and the actor might be drawn into a discussion about whether it was right or wrong. An interesting observation was that teachers could sometimes criticize the contents of the curricula. For instance, some of the teachers found that there might be a possible support for a radical and individualistic, bordering on egoistic, interpretation in some parts of the curricula, which they did not approve of. Such critical stances between professionals and the state governance produce a dynamic relation, with space for a professional arena. Wickenberg (in Chapter 13 of this volume) stresses the importance of ideological leaders, referred to as 'souls of fire' – that is, professionals who, with their own convictions, initiate and carry through changes that lead to new norms. Teachers' actions, and the norms behind them, can encounter both support and resistance, from both internal and external positions. This is sometimes a challenge to professional autonomy, with its extended freedom of action and questioning of professional responsibility. Support from colleagues and the headmaster is considered to be of great importance, if not essential. This includes encouragement to carry on with an idea or a project, but also more tangible support in the form of help to solve problems, to find inspiration, or to get started with what you set out to do. Headmasters could play an important role by challenging, taking notice, or supporting, such as allowing extra time or other types of resources. Teachers who received this kind of support appreciated it, and the others clearly pointed out that they also wanted it. Leo (2010) and Hallerström (2006) have studied norms related to headmasters in particular. Both studies found that headmasters had a difficult and, most often, a weak position, in-between teachers and the official system, where they had problems finding a role and an arena in which to act functionally as leaders of professionals.

Returning to Parsons (1939), professional norms are non-egoistic and directed to serving the well-being of others. A second characteristic, as I see it, is that professional norms are constructed in reflective discussions within the professional group, with an intention to develop the practice. Professional norms are, as a third characteristic, actively discussed in relation to the legal norms in official steering documents, and then often in an interpretative process of the actual texts and the realities in their own practice.

The relation between the legal sphere of education and the everyday life of teaching can be looked upon from different perspectives. One is the division between life-world and system-world, and another is the division between the arenas of realization and formulation. Both perspectives offer relevant views on this relationship. The professional meta-norms hold a position as the transformational means of communication between life-world and system-world, and between realization and formulation in the world of education law. Meta-norms can function as a framework for interpretation of legal rules issued by the state, and also as a protection of the right to a professional range of action. Meta-norms, created as a process in a professional environment, such as preschools and schools, are thus an important part of professionalization. This is probably partly because of their close link to ethical standpoints, sometimes even formalized into special ethical codes.

Discussion

How can we then understand the relationship between the legal norm, the professional norm and the actions that really occur? I have tried to describe teaching as both a process and a relationship between teacher and child/student, and also as a process and relationship between teachers. I have related teaching democracy to the concept of recognition and described it in three pedagogical norms.

Teachers shall act to:

- improve their capacity to see the child/student;
- become more critically aware of their own role; and
- increase their awareness and knowledge of democracy issues and develop new ways of teaching.

These norms were not bound to special situations or educational stages. Instead, they unified different actions and intentions, and thus had the character of meta-norms, around which there was consensus. Consequently, they presented an opportunity to overcome conflicting interests and tensions between parallel norm systems. Keeping such norms continuously alive demands, as the teachers stressed, a more or less permanent and qualified discussion in the team. As this is mostly an internal matter in the work team/preschool/school, it is vital that it is also open to the external world in the discussion. An active interpretative discussion of the steering documents is, of course, of crucial importance.

I have suggested that it is meaningful to view professional reflection as a process of developing professional norms. The concept of norms, as presented above, serves as a working tool in analysing situations and processes that people meet with different perspectives and interests, meaning that we can understand them as parallel systems of norms. Using the parallel norm systems as a model is, I believe, a fruitful way of handling the idea of complex systems. Professionals are supposed to be able to deal with situations of great complexity, where parallel norm systems exist and where the question of right or wrong might be discussed forever. The existence of meta-norms brings a way for teachers, and other professionals, to create solutions related to such situations. As meta-norms are constructed as general or universal principles, they form a strategic base for teaching, thus opening up for actions in the classroom. To a researcher, a meta-norm model presents a possibility of finding structures in complex social situations. Another advantage for the researcher is that meta-norms can be analysed and compared to the meanings found in the steering documents. This is important for the contemporary discussion, which has a tendency to focus on more anecdotal observations and single events. The interaction between legal norms, professional norms and teaching is a dynamic relationship, not only on a micro-social level, but it can also be analysed on a macro-social level. This is another possible area for future research into how professionals, legislators, politicians, media and other parts of society interact in social development.

References

Alexandersson, M.R. 1999. *Styrning på villovägar*. Lund: Studentlitteratur.

Åström, K. 1988. *Socialtjänsten i politik och förvaltning. En studie i parallella normbildningsprocesser*. Lunds universitet, Lund.

Axelrod, R. 1986. 'An Evolutionary Approach to Norms', *American Political Science Review*, 80/4.

Bergem, T. 2000. *Läraren i etikens motljus*. Lund: Studentlitteratur.

Boltanski and Thévenot. 1999. 'The Sociology of Critical Capacity', *European Journal of Social Theory* 1999 2, 359.

Dreyfus, H. and Dreyfus, S. 2005. 'Peripheral Vision Expertise in Real World Contexts', *Organization Studies*, 2005 (26).

Eyal, O. and Roth G. 2010. 'Principals' leadership and teachers' motivation. Self-determination theory analysis', *Journal of Educational Administration*. Vol. 49, Issue 3.

Freidson, E. 2001. *Professionalism, the third logic*. Chicago: The University of Chicago Press.

Frelin, A. 2008. 'Professionell närhet och distans', in C. Aili, U. Blossing and T. Ulrika (eds), *Läraren i blickpunkten – olika perspektiv på lärares liv och arbete*. Stockholm: Lärarförbundets förlag.

Grimen, H. and Molander, A. 2008. 'Profesjon og skjönn', in A. Molander and L.I. Terum (eds) *Profesjonsstudier*. Oslo: Universitetsforlaget.

Hafeneger, B., Henkenborg, P. and Scherr, A. (eds) 2007. *Pädagogik der Anerkennung*. Schwalbach: Wochenschau.

Hallerström H. 2006. *Rektorers normer i ledarskapet för skolutveckling*. Lund Studies in Sociology of Law nr 23. Universitet: Lund.

Honneth A. 2003. *Erkännande*. Göteborg: Daidalos.

Hydén, H. & Svensson, M. 2008. 'The concept of norms in sociology of law', in H. Hydén & P. Wickenberg (eds) *Contributions in Sociology of Law*. Lund Studies in Sociology of Law nr 29. Universitet: Lund.

Leo U. 2010. *Rektor bör och rektor gör*. Lund Studies in Sociology of Law nr 34. Universitet: Lund.

Lefstein, A. and Snell, J. 2011. 'Professional vision and the politics of teacher learning', *Teaching and Teacher Education* Vol. 27, Issue 3, April 2011.

Lindensjö, B. and Lundgren, U.P. 2002. *Utbildningsreformer och politisk styrning*. Stockholm HLS förlag.

Lundquist, L. 2001. *Medborgardemokratin och eliterna*. Lund: Studentlitteratur.

Molander, A. and Terum, L.I. 2008. 'Profesjonsstudier – en introduktion', in A. Molander and L.I. Terum (eds), *Profesjonsstudier*. Oslo: Universitetsforlaget.

Nixon, J., Martin, J., Mckeown, P. and Ranson, S. 1997. 'Confronting "failure": towards a pedagogy of recognition', *International Journal of Inclusive Education*, 1, 2, 121.

Nussbaum, M.C. 1990. 'Urskillning i förnimmelsen om privat och offentlig rationalitet' (am. originalets titel 'The discernment of perception: An Aristotelian conception of private and public rationality'), in M.C. Nussbaum (ed.), *Känslans skärpa tankens inlevelse*. Stockholm/Stehag: Brutus Östlings förlag Symposion.

Parsons, T. 1939. 'The Professions and Social Structure', in T. Parsons (ed.), *Essays in sociological theory*. New York: The Free Press.

Persson, L. 2010. *Pedagogerna och demokratin*. Lund Studies in Sociology of Law nr 33. Lunds Universitet: Lund.

Persson, L. 2011. 'Erkännandets pedagogik', in *Education and Sustainability* nr 4, 2011.

Riceur, P. 2005. *The course of recognition* (D. Pellauer trans.). Cambridge, Massachusetts: Harvard University Press.

Schön, D. 1983. *The reflective practitioner: How Professionals Think in Action*. New York: Basic Books.

Schön, D. 1987. *Educating the Reflective Practitioner*. San Fransisco: Jossey-Bass.

Svensson, M. 2008. *Sociala normer och regelefterlevnad*. University of Lund: Lund.

Wickenberg, P. 1999 *Normstödjande strukturer – Miljötematiken börjar slå rot i skolan*. Lunds universitet: Lund.

Wickenberg, P. and Leo, U. 2013. *Ett steg fram och ett tillbaka ... Statens styrning av miljö och hållbar utveckling genom skollag, läroplaner och kursplaner*. Sociology of Law research report 2013:1. Lunds universitet: Lund.

Chapter 12
School Principals' Norms: Between Law and Action

Ulf Leo

Introduction

This text is based on a study of the relationship between legal and professional norms guiding the education in elementary schools (Leo, 2010). The purpose of the study was to find out whether any special professional norms, generated in a professional system, exist with regard to principals' leadership of the democratic mission which is presented to the schools. At the same time, research methods were developed to identify professional norms, so that they can be discussed and, if necessary, developed or altered. The aim was to identify norms in order to be able to analyse and understand them. The basis for the study is described in terms of the following fundamental research questions:

- How do principals interpret the democratic mission which is presented to the schools?
- How do principals translate this mission into concrete actions?
- What professional norms for leadership are inherent in these concrete actions?

This study focuses primarily on principals as a group and, to a lesser extent, on individual principals or on principals as individuals. Norms exist in groups of various types and, by using the term 'norm', I am addressing the actions of principals, rather than their individual personal characteristics. I am using Sweden as a case study, and it is what principals should be doing according to the Swedish Education Act (2010: 800) that serves as the point of departure for the study. One purpose of education is to teach the students respect for human rights and democratic values (Education Act 2010: 800, Chapter 1, Section 4). The education shall be designed in accordance with fundamental democratic values and human rights, such as sanctity of human life, individual freedom and integrity and dignity, equality and solidarity between people. Everyone working in education should promote human rights and actively work against all forms of degrading treatment (Education Act 2010: 800, Chapter 1, Section 5). These fundamental values in the Education Act are transferred and transformed in the 'Curriculum for the compulsory school, preschool class and the leisure-time centre 2011', which guides all elementary education:

> Fundamental values
>
> The national school system is based on democratic foundations. The Education Act (2010: 800) stipulates that education in the school system aims at pupils acquiring and developing knowledge and values. It should promote the development and learning of all pupils, and a lifelong desire to learn. Education should impart and establish respect for human rights and the fundamental democratic values on which Swedish society is based. Each and everyone working in the school should also encourage respect for the intrinsic value of each person and the environment we all share.
>
> The inviolability of human life, individual freedom and integrity, the equal value of all people, equality between women and men, and solidarity with the weak and vulnerable are the values that the school should represent and impart. In accordance with the ethics borne by Christian tradition and Western humanism, this is achieved by fostering in the individual a sense of justice, generosity of spirit, tolerance and responsibility. Teaching in the school should be non-denominational.
>
> The task of the school is to encourage all pupils to discover their own uniqueness as individuals and thereby be able to participate in the life of society by giving of their best in responsible freedom. (Curriculum for the compulsory school, preschool class and the leisure-time centre 2011)

Democracy in schools

If the above values are reflected on, there are a lot of potential conflicts between these values. The democratic mission given to schools is complex and difficult to interpret. One example is that conflicts and tension between individual and collectivistic values must be handled in schools. There are also different ways of understanding concepts such as equality between women and men, solidarity with the weak, and so on.

The Swedish National Agency of Education (2000), in a policy interpreting the Education Act, states that the task of schools is to develop the democratic skills of children and young people, which is a task with several aims:

- to conduct activities in a democratic way;
- to help children and young people develop into democratic citizens; and
- to give children and young people an insight into the forms and substance of democracy.

The concept of democratic values in education is primarily about attitudes, communication and how people view one another. The term 'deliberative dialogue' is used here to describe discussion in which the participants express their own opinions and views and those of others (Swedish National Agency of Education 2000).

Dewey (1999 [1916]) wrote: 'A democracy is more than a form of government; it is primarily a mode of associated living, of conjoint communicated experience'. Englund (2006) is using the concept of deliberative communication when he links Dewey's views with Habermas's perspective of normative rationalisation. Habermas (1996) explains social integration as communicative and argumentative consensual processes. It is the good argument that creates validity, and this validity also has an integrative force (Habermas, 1996; Englund, 2006). My conclusion is that deliberative dialogue is perceived as the essence of democracy, according to the research of Dewey (1999), Habermas (1984 and 1996) and Englund (2000 and 2006). The policy from the National Agency of Education indicates the need for dialogue about tensions between democratic values, and this raises the question whether school principals have the knowledge and skills to initiate these kinds of dialogue.

The democratic mission given to schools by the legal norms in the Education Act and the curriculum provides for values and normative behaviour to develop in the interaction in schools, both in formal and informal education inside and outside the classroom. The conclusion is that work on promoting democratic values is a continuous process, for which all the adults employed in schools share responsibility, but in this study I have placed special focus on the role of the principal, who always has the ultimate responsibility in the school. The question is whether the legal norms are transformed into professional norms guiding the principals' work.

The responsibility of school principals

Since 1980, the Swedish school system has gradually transformed from being a centralised to a decentralised school system, with many responsibilities for implementation and school development given to the municipalities (Lundahl, 2002; OECD report, 2005; Werler and Claesson, 2007). According to Pierre (2010: 249), decentralisation is about transforming 'decision making and action competence from higher to lower levels of an organization – or, if you like, from the center to the periphery'.

This change has also gradually increased the responsibility of the principals in the school. In the 'Curriculum for the compulsory school, preschool class and the leisure-time centre 2011', the responsibilities of school principals are given as both pedagogic leader and head of the teaching and non-teaching staff in the school. The principal has overall responsibility for ensuring that school activities as a whole are focused on the national goals. The principal is responsible for the results of the school, and for following up and evaluating school results in relation to the national goals and the knowledge requirements, and has special responsibilities in several areas, such as ensuring that 'the working forms of the school are developed to facilitate pupils in exercising influence' (Lgr 11, 2.8).

The importance of school leadership

Research highlights the importance of school leadership for the development of the school, but also for the outcomes for the students (Hattie, 2008; Leithwood and Day, 2008). At the same time, there is a great problem with school leadership in many countries (Pont et al., 2008). Principals have heavy workloads, many are reaching retirement, and it is becoming harder to replace them. Many countries have moved towards decentralisation, making schools more autonomous in their decision-making, and holding the schools and the principals more accountable for results. As countries are adapting their education systems to the needs of contemporary society, expectations of schools and school leaders are changing. As a result, the function of school leadership across OECD countries is now increasingly defined by a new set of roles, which include financial and human resource management and leadership for learning (Pont et al., 2008). Principals have to lead change processes in their schools, and we can regard principals as 'culture builders' (Hallinger, 2005) or 'change agents' and 'norm entrepreneurs' (Ellikson in Hechter and Opp, 2001).

One common ingredient in many studies is the principal's ethical or democratic values, and the principal's purpose in the work for change (Fullan, 2001; Leithwood and Jantzi, 2002 and 2005; Starrat, 2004; Day, 2007). According to Johansson (2004), the democratic principal's most important tool for carrying out leadership tasks is the ability to decide the agenda. Johansson argues for a democratic, learning and communicative leadership involving 'the principal's guidance and determination of purpose of educational projects, discussions and debates that take place at the school' (ibid.).

Leadership is about handling complex situations in constant change, and a 'distributed leadership' is needed to be able to lead change processes in schools today. School leadership also has a greater influence on schools and students when it is widely distributed (Harris, 2004 and 2011; Hargreaves and Fink, 2006; Day, 2007). Distributed leadership is 'a form of lateral leadership where the practice of leadership is shared amongst organisational members. Here organisational influence and decision making is governed by the interaction of individuals rather than individual direction' (Harris, 2008: 174).

My conclusion, before I proceed, is that school principals are constantly facing a big challenge, dealing with the legal norms and other norms in the schools. Communication, distribution of leadership and a solid base of values seem to be important to enable school principals to lead the implementation of the democratic mission set out in the Education Act and the curriculum.

Theoretical framework

Organisations as cultures

I am using the image of organisations as cultures (Alvesson, 2002; Morgan, 2006) as a theoretical approach to support the study into identifying and analysing professional norms. Cultures are generally described as development patterns of the organisation in terms of knowledge, values, rituals, ideologies, actions, laws and norms (ibid.). Hemmelgarn et al (2006) refer to organisational culture as the shared norms, beliefs, and behavioural expectations that drive behaviour and communicate what is valued in organisations; organisational culture is often described as the 'way things are done around here'. Hoy and Miskel (2008: 177) give a general definition of organisational culture as a 'system of shared orientations that hold the unit together and give it a distinctive identity'. In this study, I have placed a special focus on the 'professional' norms guiding the democratic mission given to the principals. Professional norms are generated in a professional system, which means that teachers' norms are reproduced by the teachers, in teacher training, texts for teachers, meetings with other teachers, and so on. The same applies for school principals in education, by following and talking to other principals, and so on. The professional norms in schools often have their origin in a legal norm regulating or guiding the work and responsibilities of the profession.

Culture as shared norms

According to Alvesson, '(c)ulture is a tricky concept as it is easily used to cover everything and consequently nothing' (2002: 13). He considers that culture often refers to surface phenomena rather than exploring the meanings and ideas behind them. In this study, I am focusing on norms in school culture. I realise that the influence that culture has on the members of the organisation varies, and there are often several sub-cultures in an organisation. A problem with studying organisational culture, and the norms within it, is that norms and culture are often unconscious and covert (Rommetveit, 1955; Elster, 1992). Norms play an important role in human interaction: they reduce uncertainty about how to act in different situations; they set standards and specify what the appropriate behaviour is; and there are different expectations on different people (students, teachers and principals) in the organisation (Giddens, 1989: 31). Norms are usually unwritten, affected by informal expectations, and they directly influence behaviour. For example, norms determine the way in which people talk within the organisation, how participants respond to authority, conflict or pressure, and how they balance self-interest with organisational interest (Hoy and Miskel, 2008).

I consider that the norms of a work group define a big part of the culture of the organisation, and that it is important to be aware of the legal, social and professional norms that influence the organisation. An interesting feature is the intertwined relationship between culture and norms, as they are stated as 'functions of culture' (Robbins, 1998) and as 'functions of norms' (Elster, 1992; Alvesson, 2002; Baier and Svensson, 2009). Both culture and norms provide standards of behaviour, create distinctions among organisations, provide the organisation with a sense of identity, and enhance stability in the social system, as the social glue that binds the organisation together (Elster, 1992). Both strong cultures (Hoy and Miskel, 2008) and strong norm systems (Elster, 1992) can promote or impede development and change processes. The conclusion is that culture and norms are linked to each other; and, by identifying, analysing and discussing norms, we also identify, analyse and discuss parts of the culture.

One problem with the term 'norm' is that it is used in so many different ways, both scientifically and in everyday parlance. In response, I am working according to a line of reasoning concerning the ontology of norms and what norms are. I use a sociology of law-based definition of the concept of norms, a definition that can meet the needs of both the social and the legal sciences (Hydén and Svensson, 2008). This is also the definition I use to identify and to analyse professional norms in this study:

- Norms are action instructions. Norms are imperatives and thus directing actions – that is the very meaning of norms.
- Norms are socially reproduced. Elster describes it as follows: 'For norms to be social, they must be shared by other people' (1992: 99). Wickenberg highlights the importance of communication, and believes that the norms that are interesting to sociology of law are those that occur in a social context. They have social connections, social impacts, and they are communicated in a social community (1999: 292). The action instructions must be communicated and disseminated in a social community to live up to this essential attribute. In this case, it means that the professional norms are reproduced in a school context.
- Norms represent the individual's perception of the expectations surrounding their own behaviour. 'Social norms do cooperate expectations' (Elster, 1992: 97) and this is a widespread sociological starting point, also expressed as a social pressure on individuals (Durkheim, 1982; Rommetveit, 1955).

According to the sociologist Therborn, we may comply with a norm because of our identification with the norm source and its values (2002: 869). Ellickson refers to a person who supplies a new norm relatively early as a change agent (in Hechter and Opp, 2001: 41). In order to be able to make a change and establish norms according to the democratic mission in schools, there is a need for change agents and also for professionals with whom the children and young people can identify. The principals interviewed in this study often referred to themselves as role models, revealing their willingness to be someone for the students to 'look up to' in matters related to democracy.

Method

My research method has a pragmatic realistic approach (Pierce, 1905; Sawyer, 2000; Pawson, 2006), where I started from the theory of norms to construct the interview guide for the first round of interviews. The approach has always taken into account the interactions between empiricism and theory. I interviewed 14 school principals in four steps, where each step involved an extension of the empirical scope. In brief, the steps are:

- First round of interviews of elementary school principals with a primary emphasis on the question: 'What are you doing in your role as principal to ensure that the activities at your school are based on democratic values?'.
- Second round of interviews with the same elementary school principals to delve more deeply into problem areas identified, using the 'critical incident technique' (Flanagan, 1954).
- Focus group interviews with the same elementary school principals, with a view to identifying norms and obtaining a basis for analysis within problem areas.
- Second round of focus group interviews with the same elementary school principals in different groupings based on 'stimulated recall'.

Before and between each step, I have used the theories of norms to construct new interview questions and to perform analysis after each round of interviews. These analyses then led to a new understanding of the theory and new questions to the principals, in interplay between theory and empiricism. What is special about the method I have developed is that I have been coming back to the same participants for a number of years. The objectives have been the same throughout (that is, to identify norms in leading the democratic mission in schools, and to obtain a basis for analysing and understanding those norms). The process has involved various angles of approach, different groupings and varying focuses. I have analysed and interpreted, drawn conclusions, formulated new hypotheses and acquired new understanding after each round of interviews. This working method has enabled me to deepen and renew my understanding, and to confirm earlier findings in later interviews.

Results and analysis

What principals do

The first research question is: 'How do principals interpret the democratic mission for schools?' I interpret the responses of the principals regarding their actions as follows: they do not distinguish the democratic mission as a separate one, but rather view it as part of the whole process of leading the school. They describe this as an attitude; they want to serve as role models in their actions, and view themselves as representatives of a broad national mission. Most of the principals describe their management style as one that involves numerous dialogues, and they speak more about listening to others than about talking themselves. The principals also talk more about working with democratic processes that involve large numbers of people than about making quick decisions by themselves. This indicates that the principals are aiming at deliberative dialogues and distributed leadership.

The second research question is: 'How do principals translate this mission into concrete actions?' This question reveals that physical presence and different types of dialogue are central to how the mission translates into democracy in practice. Such presence and dialogue occur both in formal circumstances, such as when the principals participate in or chair meetings, and in informal ones, with activities involving both pupils and staff.

The final research question is: 'What professional norms for leadership are inherent in the principals' concrete actions?' This is the central issue in this study, and I have used the essential attributes of the identified norms in order to understand them. I have confirmed that there are many different action instructions for principals (that is, things that principals should do). I have found that one way to identify norms using the methods chosen is to start by looking for action instructions. What should principals do? This question puts the focus on principals as a group, and on their actions.

Action instructions

My step-by-step method has led toward action instructions that can also be viewed as general norms or meta-norms for a democratic principal. Meta-norms support the creation of more concrete sub-norms. 'The existence of a meta-norm can be an effective way to get a norm started and to protect it once it is established' (Axelrod, 1986: 1102).

The identified norms are the result of the principals' characterisations of an ideal democratic principal, obtained from the first one-to-one interview. The results in the items below point to the complexity of the mission, which is the focus of the group interviews. The items are intertwined, and they can also find themselves on a collision course, with the result that principals have to choose to follow the norm that fits the specific situation in question. Examples of identified norms are:

- Principals should be clear about standing up for their views, and have their own goals and visions.
- Principals should be patient and persistent.
- Principals should have good self-awareness, reflect, and know their strengths and weaknesses.
- Principals should listen to everyone, be sensitive, and reach out to other people.

- Principals should dare to make decisions.
- Principals should offer opportunities, and be tolerant and supportive.
- Principals should be humble and self-effacing.
- Principals should know the mission/framework/steering documents.
- Principals should be present and visible.

Social reproduction

It has been difficult to identify clear signs of any separate professional reproduction of norms among, or for, principals. There are few or no indications as to how principals' actions are spread or communicated. Most principals have been teachers and have, through their training as teachers, acquired special professional codes, which I interpret to mean that special teacher norms exist, and that principals retain many of them. But leading and managing adult staff and developing schools is not the same thing as leading teaching and learning processes in the classroom, or managing children and young people. In certain areas specific to principals, there is no reproduction of norms and, as I see it, this has consequences in terms of norm formation among principals. It is not possible for positive concrete examples to be disseminated or communicated if principals do not know what other principals are doing, or how they are doing it. This leads to grossly generalised norms, meta-norms such as 'principals should involve staff in democratic decision-making processes', but such norms provide insufficient guidance to reduce the complexity of the principal's role.

Surrounding expectations

We know from earlier research that principals are influenced by expectations from many different sources (see Leo, 2010). One finding of this study is that, in most cases, they are affected most strongly by their staff or, more specifically, the teachers. According to the 'theory of planned behaviour' (Ajzen and Fischbein, 1980; Ajzen, 1991), strong pressure deriving from social expectations creates a strong subjective norm. In the case of principals, they are heavily influenced by teachers' expectations, but little affected by the direct expectations of the pupils. The potential consequence of this is the forming of norms that favour staff over pupils, contradicting the intention of legal norms setting the pupils interests first. Additional research is needed to determine whether this is, in fact, the case. If it is true that there are norms that favour staff members, while at the same time disfavouring pupils, principals need to be aware of them. This may pertain to internalised, unconscious norms that need to be made visible.

Sanctions in the norms

Results and analysis indicate that sanctions are associated with legal norms, while also having a major influence on other norms. The principals have noted that, if they fail to follow the general norm that 'principals should know the mission', the responsible authority (in this case, the municipality) may impose a formal sanction, such as a fine for violating the Swedish Discrimination Act (2008: 567), for instance. The principals also want to prevent their operations from being criticised by the Swedish Schools Inspectorate or the National Agency for Education. However, it was the informal sanctions that most affected the principals in the study. One principal expressed this in the sense that violations of their professional norms have consequences for the school, and for how they feel.

Origin of the norms

There is a distinct correlation between the principals' view of the origin of their professional norms and new legal norms. The principals believe that the ways in which schools are governed, based on goals and results, constitutes a developmental mission that has led to a new role and set of professional norms for principals. These include the norms that principals should be patient and persistent; that principals should be clear in standing up for their views; that principals should have personal goals and visions; and that principals should offer opportunities, and be tolerant and supportive. According to the principals, these norms were not absolutely necessary when schools were governed based on rules and regulations, and this is especially clear when the principals assert that the following norms are very old: 'principals should know the mission/framework/steering documents' and 'principals should dare to make decisions'. Both of these norms are fundamental, and have been found in rules-governed schools, and in goals- and results-governed ones. This is yet another example of the complexity of the principal's work. The 'new' mission has to be interpreted, which takes time, and this leads to many different processes as well. I believe that the norm that 'principals should dare to make decisions' is relatively clear, compared to the vaguer 'principals should offer opportunities, and be tolerant and supportive'. One conclusion is that these new professional norms need to be discussed, clarified and concretised in order to form new sub-norms that are clear and more instructive in terms of actions. This could support the work done by principals moving forward.

Norms and action

The principals associate the vast majority of their professional norms and actions with some form of physical presence. According to the principals, these norms find expression in action within steering groups, in workplace encounters, or in other meetings involving staff, pupils, parents and administrators, rather than in the private sphere. I believe that the principals could analyse their actions by mapping their various arenas in which they are present, and how they act in these different arenas. This could lead to a greater understanding of, and more knowledge about, how their professional norms are formed.

Discussion and conclusions

The norm perspective

In this study, I have focused on professional norms as being a part of school culture. It has to do with understanding schools and, in this case, the leadership provided by principals, in what could be called a 'norm perspective'. Social and professional norms are formed and changed in the contexts in which they exist, and the norm perspective offers a possible way of understanding the actions and patterns of the actions of which the principals' activities consist.

One function of norms is that of reducing complexity, and I would point to the need for research in this area. The position as school principal is a complex one, as the identified norms also indicate. One conclusion is that more concrete norms are needed to reduce the level of complexity for principals. I view the identified professional norms as a form of meta-norm (that is, according to Axelrod who studied game theory, general norms that can protect existing ones). Meta-norms also enable the formation of sub-norms (Axelrod, 1986; see also Lars Persson's chapter in this book). Using the theories regarding norms presented here, not only researchers, but also practitioners, such as school principals, can deepen their knowledge of norms and identify, change or form more concrete sub-norms.

Reflection

One of the norms identified and analysed in this chapter is that principals should have self-awareness. The principals speak about the importance of reflection for greater self-awareness. This leads to a more concrete norm for the actions of principals: principals should reflect in order to acquire self-awareness. I believe that reflecting on their own actions and the actions of others offers the principals a means of achieving the distance that greater self-awareness requires. The principals turn inwards, toward themselves, to gain insight into their own actions. This also has to do with a more outward process, in which the principals think about something outside themselves, such as how other people have acted, or about the actual role of the principal. Schön (2003) used the notions of 'reflection in action' and 'reflection on action'. The former is described as 'thinking on our feet' and it involves looking to our experiences, connecting with our feelings, and attending to our theories in use:

> The practitioner allows himself to experience surprise, puzzlement, or confusion in a situation which he finds uncertain or unique. He reflects on the phenomenon before him, and on the prior understandings which have been implicit in his behaviour. He carries out an experiment which serves to generate both a new understanding of the phenomenon and a change in the situation. (Schön, 2003: 68)

The ‘reflection on action’ is done later, and enables us to spend time exploring why we acted as we did, what was happening, and so on (ibid.). Reflection enables us to think about what is happening beneath the surface, and this leads to greater personal understanding. To me, this means that we reflect by asking ourselves questions, and it gives an opportunity to understand the norms that are guiding the actions. Applying a norm perspective can support practitioners and enable the principals to acquire the linguistic terms and concepts to allow them to reflect on their own actions and those of others. Reflection creates distance and an opportunity to critically review the actions performed by the principals, and the norms by which they are governed. Through reflection, the principals could become more aware of their own actions.

Communication

Another identified norm was that ‘principals should listen to everyone, be sensitive, reach out, and invite others’. I am linking this to communication and the principals’ ability to communicate. Törnsén (2009) considers that principals are unaware of what good communication is about and, according to Ärlestig (2008), there is ‘organizational communication blindness’ affecting principals’ communication in the schools. The results from this study show that principals *want* to have deliberative communication, but we do not know how this works in practice, from the teachers’ or the students’ point of view.

Finally, there seem to be conflicting norms for leadership. Is it possible that ‘principals should be clear in standing up for their views, and have their own goals and visions’ and dare to make decisions, at the same time as they ‘should listen to everyone, be sensitive, reach out, and invite others’ and ‘be humble and self-effacing’? Perhaps this is what democratic leadership is about? On the one hand, principals have to stand up and defend democratic values as representatives of a national mission; and, on the other hand, they need to distribute leadership in their organisations by means of deliberative dialogue. I consider that professional judgement and actions are based on knowledge of legal norms, and these are often mediated by professional norms. There is a need for better understanding of these relations among researchers as well as practitioners.

References

Ajzen, Icek, and Fishbein, Martin. 1980. *Understanding attitudes and predicting social behaviour*. Englewood Cliffs, NJ: Prentice-Hall.

Ajzen, Icek. 1991. ‘The theory of planned behaviour’, *Organizational Behaviour and Human Decision Processes*, 50, 179–211.

Alvesson, Mats. 2002. *Understanding Organizational Culture*. London: Sage.

Ärlestig, Helene. 2008. *Communication between principals and teachers in successful schools.* Diss. Umeå: Umeå University.

Axelrod, Robert. 1986. 'An Evolutionary Approach to Norms', in *The American Political Science Review*, Vol. 80, No. 4, 1095–1111.

Baier, Matthias and Svensson, Måns. 2009. *Om normer.* Malmö: Liber.

Day, Christopher. 2007. 'What Being a Successful Principal Really Means', *Educational Leadership and Administration,* Vol. 19.

Dewey, John. 1999 [1916]. *Democracy and education: an introduction to the philosophy of education.* [New ed.] New York: Free Press.

Discrimination Act of Sweden (SFS 2008: 567).

Durkheim, Emile. 1982[1895]. *The Rules of Sociological Method and Selected Texts on Sociology and its Method.* New York: Free Press. *Les règles de la méthode sociologique.*

Education Act of Sweden (SFS 2010: 800).

Ellickson, Robert, C. 2001. 'The evolution of social norms: a perspective from the legal academy', in Hechter, Michael and Opp, Karl-Dieter (eds). *Social Norms*. New York: Russell Sage Foundation.

Elster, Jon. 1992. *The Cement of Society, a study of social order*. Cambridge University Press.

Englund, Tomas. 2006. 'Deliberative communication: a pragmatist proposal', *Journal of Curriculum Studies,* 2006, Vol. 38, No. 5, 503–20.

Englund, Tomas. 2000. 'Rethinking democracy and education: towards an education of deliberative citizens', *Journal of Curriculum Studies*, 2000, Vol. 32, No. 2, 305–13.

Flanagan, John C. 1954. 'The Critical Incident Technique', *Psychological Bulletin* Vol, 51, No. 4, July 1954.

Fullan, Michael. 2001. *Leading in a culture of change.* San Francisco: Jossey-Bass.

Giddens, Anthony. 1989. *Sociology*. Cambridge: Polity Press.

Habermas, Jürgen. 1996. *Between Facts and Norms.* London: Polity Press.

Habermas, Jürgen. 1984. *The theory of communicative action. Vol. 1, Reason and the rationalization of society*. Cambridge: Polity Press.

Hallinger, Philip. 2005. 'Instructional Leadership and the School Principle: A Passing Fancy that Refuses to Fade Away', *Leadership and Policy in Schools,* 4, 3, 221–39.

Hargreaves, Andy and Fink, Dean. 2006. *Sustainable Leadership*. San Francisco: Jossey-Bass.

Harris, Alma. 2004. 'Distributed Leadership and School Improvement: Leading or Misleading?', *Educational Management Administration Leadership* 2004, 32, 11–20.

Harris, Alma. 2008. 'Distributed leadership: according to the evidence', *Journal of Educational Administration*, Vol. 46, Issue 2, 172–88.

Harris, Alma. 2011. 'Distributed leadership: implications for the role of the principal', *Journal of Management Development*, Vol. 31, Issue 1, 7–17.

Hattie, John. 2008. *Visible Learning – A Synthesis of Over 800 Meta-Analyses Relating to Achievement*. London: Routledge.

Hemmelgarn, Anthony L., Glisson, Charles and James, Lawrence R. 2006. 'Organizational culture and Climate: Implications for Services and Interventions Research', *Clinical Psychology Science and Practice*, Vol. 13, No. 1.

Hoy, Wayne & Miskel, Cecil. 2008. *Educational Administration, Theory, Research, and Practice.* New York: The McGraw Companies.

Hydén, Håkan & Svensson, Måns. 2008. 'The Concept of Norms in Sociology of Law', in *Law and Society, Scandinavian studies in Law*, Vol. 53.

Johansson, Olof. 2004. 'Democracy and leadership – or training for democratic leadership', *Journal of Educational Administration* Vol. 42, No. 6, 620–24.

Leithwood, Kenneth and Day, Christopher. 2008. 'The impact of school leadership on pupil outcomes', *School Leadership & Management* (formerly *School Organisation*), 28, 1, 1–4.

Leithwood, Kenneth & Jantzi, Doris. 2005. 'A Review of Transformational School Leadership Research 1996–2005', *Leadership and Policy in Schools*, 4, 3, 177–99.

Leo, Ulf. 2010. *Rektorer bör och rektorer gör*. Lund: Lund University.

Lundahl, Lisbeth. 2002. 'From Centralisation to Decentralisation: governance of Education in Sweden', *European Educational Research Journal*, Vol. 1, No. 4.

Morgan, Gareth. 2006. *Images of Organization.* Thousand Oaks, CA: Sage.

National Agency of Education. 2000. *Democracy in Swedish Education: A thematic presentation of basic Values.*

National Agency of Education. 2011. *National Curriculum for the compulsory school, preschool class and the leisure-time centre 2011.*

OECD report. 2005. *Equity in education, thematic review.*

Pawson, Ray. 2006. *Evidence-based Policy, a realist perspective.* London: Sage.

Peirce, Charles. 1905. 'What Pragmatism Is', *The Monist*, Vol. 15, No. 2, April 1905, 161–81.

Persson, Lars. 2010. *Pedagogerna och demokratin.* Lund: Lund University.

Pierre, Jon. 2010. 'Decentralisering, governance och institutionell förändring', in Rothstein, Bo (ed.) *Politik som organisation. Förvaltningspolitikens grundproblem*. 4e upplagan. Stockholm: SNS, 245–70.

Pont, Beatriz, Nusche, Deborah and Moorman, Hunter. 2008. *Improving School Leadership, Volume 1 Policy and Practice.* OECD Report.

Robbins, Stephen. 1998. *Organizational behaviour*. Englewood Cliffs: N.J. Prentice Hall.

Rommetveit, Ragnar. 1955. *Social Norms and Roles, Explorations in the psychology of ending social pressures*. Minnesota: University of Minnesota Press.

Sayer, Andrew. 2000. *Realism and Social Science.* London: Sage.

Schön, Donald A. 2003 [1983]. *The reflective practitioner: how professionals think in action.* [New ed.] Aldershot: Arena.

Starratt, Robert. 2004. *Ethical Leadership.* Jossey-Bass.

Therborn, Göran. 2002. 'Back to Norms! On the Scope and Dynamics of Norms and Normative Action', *Current Sociology*, November 2002, Vol. 50(6), s. 863–80.

Törnsén, Monika. 2009. *Successful Principal Leadership: Prerequisites, Processes and Outcomes*. Diss. Umeå: Umeå University.

Werler, Tobias and Claesson, Silwa. 2007. In Hörner et al. (eds), *The Education Systems of Europe*. Springer, 741–57.

Wickenberg, Per. 1999. *Normstödjande strukturer: miljötematiken börjar slå rot i skolan*. Lund: Lund University.

Chapter 13
'Souls of Fire', Change Agents and Social Norms

Per Wickenberg

Introduction

The aim of this chapter is to focus on the significance of 'souls of fire' that have been found in different research projects over the years. The main aims are to explore the concept of 'souls of fire' and its connections to change agents, and the creation of norms in organizations, and to explore the need and kind of support required when creating new norms. These empirical research projects are studying implementation processes of new legal norms at the very local level in different professional organizations:

- implementation of new legal norms on the environment and sustainable development in local schools;
- implementation of new legal norms on public participation in a local large-scale construction project; and
- implementation of new legal norms on the Convention of the Rights of the Child in local schools in developing countries.

Implementation at the very local level in society, studied from the perspective of sociology of law, is adding new knowledge to the understanding of norm creation and the vital question of norm support from actors or norm support, seen in a structural perspective.

Sociology of law at Lund University has a special interest in and focus on the relationship between norms, law and society and how the norms are communicated and socially reproduced. Legal norms or laws are linked to the state and have a background in the political system. Social norms are based on relationships among people, and have a background in the interaction and communication that takes place between people. This sociology of law and norm approach have been applied and developed in studies of implementation in education (Wickenberg, 1999 and 2004; Hallerström, 2006; Persson 2010 and Chapter 11 of this volume); Leo 2010 and Chapter 12 of this volume; Wickenberg and Leo, 2013; Leo and Wickenberg 2013). These studies have contributed new knowledge about norms and also about the role of education as an arena for the formation of norms. They have also contributed to the further development of the methodology of how to identify norms in organizations (Leo, 2010) and how to measure the strength of the norms and the expectations (Svensson, 2008; Svensson and Larsson, 2012).

'Souls of fire', change agents and norms

'Souls of fire' are very dedicated and enthusiastic persons in organizations, who are figuratively burning for some particular cause in which they strongly believe.[1] They could be studied as key actors, as they are acting in and influencing processes and, in that, they are carrying on an actorship. Åke Philips (1988) studied 16 'souls of fire' in nine case studies in three big Swedish companies, and his definition of those actors is: '... a limited number of deeply involved individuals [that] seems to have had an important impact on the development and viability of the new organizational solutions. These individuals were often referred to as "souls of fire"' (Philips, 1988: 173). Philips did his study of actorship in work organization development efforts, and within a tradition of organizational development. His work is connected to Scandinavian work organization experiences which started in the early 1970s. Philips also makes international research references to social science and human resource researchers, such as Kurt Lewin, Donald A. Schön, Chris Argyris, David Kolb and Gareth Morgan.

The concept of 'souls of fire' was used in the research (Wickenberg, 1999: 452) to understand the role of project leaders in local schools working with implementation of new legal norms on the environment (see further below). Evert Vedung, a political scientist, writes about 'souls of fire' in his book on evaluation, with a chapter on 'Explaining evaluation of processes'. In this, Vedung mentions eight factors which he has found influence results in the public sector from a political science perspective. Under the heading of 'Addressees', Vedung mentions 'souls of fire', and he has the following view of 'souls of fire':

> The personal element can play a role. The direction can have a greater impact among some recipients due to the presence of *souls of fire*, people with a strong commitment to the practice of politics at stake. Exchange of individuals within a collective actor such as a municipality can be important. If the souls of fire disappear, perhaps the desirable outcome peters out, if souls of fire enter, it takes off. (Vedung, 1991: 188; italics in original – author's translation)

Dedicated individual persons, 'souls of fire', can influence a result. Furthermore, they are, on the one hand, an asset with their presence in an organization; on the other hand, they are a loss if they leave it.

---

1 'Souls of fire' is a straight translation of the Swedish concept 'eldsjälar'. A search on the Internet shows that it is quite well-known internationally. Nevertheless, it works as a valid concept in this context, given the definitions as above.

Other Swedish social science research on the theme of 'souls of fire' has been carried out by Gun-Marie Frånberg (1994 and 1996); Tore Brännberg, (1996 and 1998); Barbro Lewin (1998); Urban Markström (2003) and Kristina Palm (2008).[2] A common theme in this research is that it is about deep commitment, dedication, burning interest and enthusiasm. Philips (1988) is a commonly used reference for 'souls of fire' to most of these researchers, and they are exploring different aspects of public or private organizational work and the role of key actors in this. Other references for 'souls of fire' found in the broader search in databases are connected to music and art, voluntary associations and NGOs, leaders, gender issues in organizations, welfare and health care, churches and religious organizations, and local work (for example, in home districts). But none of the previous research work has a reference or links to norms, or to the role of norms in organizations.

Læssøe (2012) has also been inspired by using this concept to explain what is happening at local level in Denmark in the ongoing work on Local Agenda 21. Læssøe is talking of 'fiery souls' or enthusiasts:

> It is a person who is burning for a case ... there is, so to speak, an inner relationship between person and case: The case is not something superficially ascribed to the person but an integrated part of the person's project towards the world. This burning engagement means that enthusiasts often take initiatives in order to influence their socio-cultural context.

Another, very connected concept in this norm context is 'change agent', and that concept is used by Robert C. Ellickson when referring to a person who is relatively early in supplying a new norm as a 'change agent' (Ellickson in Hechter and Opp, 2001: 40; and see Ulf Leo in this volume). There are evidently interesting links between these two concepts: from 'souls of fire' to 'change agents' in terms of when new norms are created in organizations. Bringing about change in schools, such that new norms are established, requires enthusiasts[3] or change agents who challenge old norms, who want to stake out new paths and establish new norms. There are three subcategories of change agent according to Ellickson: self-motivated leaders, norm entrepreneurs, and opinion leaders. The first ones, self-motivated

2 In the search in Swedish research databases, the Swedish word for 'souls of fire' ('eldsjäl/eldsjälar') was used. It was then found that the concept was translated in many different ways in the English abstracts or summaries: for example, enthusiasts, (committed) champions, change agents, aficionado, devotee, fan, buff. The concepts 'souls of fire' and 'change agents' are defined in very similar ways, and the conclusion here is to use them in that way. 'Change agents' is a somewhat broader concept including 'souls of fire', but here it is also noted that the concept 'souls of fire' puts more weight on a value background or an emotional dimension of the actor's motives or driving forces.

3 They could be very dedicated, enthusiastic and deeply involved persons in organizations burning for some cause that they strongly believe in; sometimes, they are called 'souls of fire'. We can compare this with the concept 'charismatic authority' from Weber (1947: 358–63).

leaders, favour changes and do not need special esteem rewards to challenge the existing norms. They could be seen as charismatic change agents, with their own internal driving forces working for social change, and with unexceptional leadership abilities supplying the establishment of new norms. They are acting, from the start, in the supply of a new norm in the forefront. The enthusiasts or change agents could also, in the study, be seen as vital links – or even a 'putty' – between the legal norms and the new local professional norms in schools. They are often acting as forerunners and norm setters, bringing their personal commitment from their lifeworld into the professional role in the system, to use the wordings and concepts of Jürgen Habermas (1986: 13, 342, and 1987: 113). In this way, the processes are going the opposite way to that of the system which is colonizing the lifeworld. This would not have been easy or possible without norm-supporting actors and structures. It further connects to Reza Banakar's chapter in this volume, exploring the ability of legal sociology to account for the normativity of law, and analysing relations between social norms and normativity. Normativity can have other sources which are beyond social norms, but normativity can also be a source of norms. Banakar concludes with the following:

> We should bear in mind that normativity generated by social systems and the community (lifeworld) are based on different types of rationality and, following Habermas (1975 and 1984), coincide with system and socio-cultural integration, respectively (also see Banakar 2003: 291–2). One of the functions of modern law may be described in terms of its ability to mediate between the two types of normativities generated by system and lifeworld.

In the conclusions, we will get back to the 'souls of fire', and their ability to mediate between lifeworld and system, as well as being part of creating social norms.

The ambition here, using an actor's perspective, is to elaborate and clarify what has been studied regarding the role of 'souls of fire': as a link to the norm-creation processes in local organizations. These dedicated actors are, in this norm context, the important link – or even a 'putty' – between the (new) legal norms and the local norms in creation. This definition is used of the concept: a 'soul of fire' is a very dedicated, burning, key actor, who brings her or his personal engagement, beliefs and values into the professional organization and makes a difference in norm-creation processes through her or his influence.

Implementation of legal norms on sustainable development in schools

Education involves half of the population in Sweden every day. More than 30 per cent of the population is working or studying within the public education sector – and, when parents and custodians are included, half of the Swedish population is affected by education in everyday life (Lundgren, 2008). Most research into schools in Sweden is carried out from the perspective of educational science, and sometimes from sociology and political science. Sociology of law, with its emphasis on social and legal norms, has something different to offer to enable an interpretation and understanding of changes in education on different organizational levels. The author has a knowledge interest in studying implementation using a sociology of law perspective, having a professional background and experiences within different kinds of education contexts for some 40 years.

Implementation of new legal norms in environmental education (EE) and education for sustainable development (ESD) is pointed out as the most important challenge for schools by central international and national policy documents (see, for example, UNCED, 1992, Ch. 36). This challenge is also underlined by the UN (December 2002) declaring the period from 2005 to 2014 as the Decade for Education for Sustainable Development (DESD). At its 57th meeting in December 2002, the United Nations General Assembly proclaimed the UN Decade of Education for Sustainable Development, 2005–2014, 'emphasizing that education is an indispensable element for achieving sustainable development'. It designated UNESCO as the lead agency to promote and implement the Decade.[4]

The overall question is how to make these new legal norms work in practice. The Swedish curricula clearly states that 'Education *should* elucidate how the functions of society and our way of living and working can be adapted in order to create a sustainable development'.[5] A significant characteristic of ESD is the strong emphasis on the moral and ethical aspects of environmental and developmental issues (see UNCED, 1992, Ch. 36, p. 2). One outcome in UNCED was the adoption (by the 178 countries present) of the Agenda 21 action plan on sustainable development. Education was regarded as a substantial part of Agenda 21. An interesting fact is that the word 'education', alone or in combination, occurs 486 times in this UN document (Wickenberg, 1999). This means that educators are expected to implement and organize educational practices where students are given an opportunity to act in morally conscious ways on issues related to sustainable development. Ever since the concept of ESD was launched, there has been an intense policy debate about the ideological basis and the forms and content of this kind of education. The EE research field, that constitutes the source for a systematic and critical reflection on the implementation of ESD, has expanded and advanced considerably, both internationally and in Sweden, during the recent decade (see Hart and Nolan, 1999; Östman, 2003; Wickenberg, 2004; Wickenberg and Öhman, 2008; Breiting and Wickenberg, 2010; Wals and Kieft, 2010). These reviews show that there is a dominance of research directed at measuring the outcomes of environmental education, while the knowledge base regarding environmental learning processes is weak. It is particularly weak when it comes to learning processes, in which a student's moral attitudes and social norms to

4 See www.unesco.org/new/en/education/themes/leading-the-international-agenda/education-for-sustainable-development/ [Accessed 30 August 2012].

5 The objectives of education in the Swedish curricula (Lpo 94 and Lpf 94), and also really strengthened in the new curriculum for the Swedish elementary school (Lgr 2011).

issues that concern sustainable development become established. Recently, the value dimension of ESD has been addressed by Swedish researchers (see Öhman, 2008). Approaches towards studying environmental moral learning processes have been developed by Öhman (2011) and Öhman and Östman (2007). To be able to implement and apply norms for new action patterns and developing action competences (Bruun Jensen and Schnack, 1997), there is a need for support of new norms on different social levels. That is focused on in the studies at local level into how to initiate and embed new legal norms on environment and sustainable development in education (Wickenberg, 1999).

Implementation of norms on EE in Swedish schools 1993–1999

The continued work by teachers and principals in three Swedish lower secondary schools in a town of medium size was investigated, with studies of legal and policy documents, as well as repeated interviews, questionnaires and observations over six years. This research was funded by the research programme 'Utvägar'.[6] The main purpose was to follow and explore the social processes in the schools – mainly focusing on teachers and principals – during the implementation of the amendment on the new concept environment in the Education Act of 1990 (SL Chapter 1, Section 2). What was going to happen in the schools? The main part of the research during 1993–1999 into environmental education (EE) and education for sustainable development (ESD) in the schools mentioned focused on norm-supporting actors and structures. The study identified and realized that very dedicated persons – 'souls of fire' – are important as actors in transforming, mediating and supporting new norms. Those dedicated key actors were vital in starting to apply new norms on EE in the schools investigated (Wickenberg, 1999: 451). The 'souls of fire' or change agents often challenge old norms, habits and routines in their search for new pathways in establishing new norms (Leo and Wickenberg, 2012). The study also found that these key actors were bringing – in Habermas's (1986) wordings and interpretations – their values and social norms from the lifeworld into the school system.

This research was concluded by stating that the following norm-supporting actors and structures are of great importance for initiating and embedding new norms, and later followed by changes of behaviours, and the conclusions were, in short:

i) actors as leaders and the leadership in schools (principals) are vital for the support of souls of fire's or change agents' work in establishing new norms;
ii) souls of fire or change agents within schools are active in breaking the old norms, and initiating and establishing new norms;

6 'Ways Ahead – Paths to Sustainable Development', an environmental research programme based in the humanities and social sciences funded by eight Swedish research agencies during 1996–2001.

iii) creating social and professional arenas as part of the supporting infrastructure in the schools is vital for communication and participation of teachers and students for new norms to take root and to be socially reproduced;
iv) external resources and professional knowledge and experiences are to be used in these educational processes;
v) self-regulating and social instruments, such as Grön Flagg (Eco Schools), provide long-term infra-structural support for the educational processes;
vi) basic definitions of environmental knowledge are important to all actors in the development work on new norms; and
vii) legal documents and legal norms function as moral support for change agents, teachers and principals working with establishing new norms and new behaviour (Wickenberg, 1999: 501).

Implementation of norms on ESD in Swedish schools 2009–2012

Ten years later, in a joint research programme (2009–2012) involving the universities of Lund, Uppsala, Örebro and Stockholm, we were making an in-depth exploration of environmental learning processes, legal and professional norms and leadership in school and in classrooms relating to ESD. In this project, the sociology of law focus is on the role and importance of leaders and leadership in norm creation, and norm support processes in education. The aim of the research project is to focus on and problematize the implementation of ESD in three upper secondary schools in big cities in Sweden. In this research project, we have a special interest in the role of the leaders of the school and how the implementation is being led, organized and realized.[7]

The research project is about exploring norms and norm-supporting actors and structures within schools that are aiming at what ought to be done (that is, what is evident as desirable content in issues relating to sustainable development. This is done using questionnaires and repeated interviews and focus group interviews with principals and teachers, and analysis of steering documents in order to describe expectation pressure, support, hindrances and norm-supporting structures developed in the schools. Ellickson, as mentioned above, uses the term 'change agents' for those persons who are the first to mediate new norms. To bring about change in the schools for new norms to be created, the organizations are using 'souls of fire' (that is, inspiring dedicated persons or change agents who will challenge old norms and who will find new ways to create new norms). Communication of new norms and expectations is essential, as noted in the previous research project mentioned above.

---

7 We are now (September 2012) reaching the end of the final write-up of our findings and conclusions based on our empirical material from the research project. This part of this article is based on Leo and Wickenberg (2012, forthcoming) and Wickenberg and Leo (2012, forthcoming). See also the chapter by Ulf Leo in this volume.

This research project is thus confirming some of the results of the previous implementation study (1993–1999); especially in relation to creating new norms, it is clarifying the vital role of principals in being a norm-supporting actor and in building norm-supporting structures in the school (for example, creating social arenas for communication on new norms and ideas, and establishing contacts with external resources). The principals themselves can also be 'souls of fire' or change agents – or even role models – for others to identify with when new norms are being created and established (Leo and Wickenberg, 2012).

Implementation of the new Environmental Code

This creation of new norms and norm-supporting actors and structures continues the other research projects regarding implementation of new legal norms at the local level, this time in a public construction company. The 'Environmental Management in the City Tunnel' project was a three-year, sociology of law research project (1999–2003) about how the new Swedish Environmental Code (SFS 1998: 808) was applied in one of the largest infrastructure projects in Sweden: the City Tunnel construction in Malmö.[8] For further and more in-depth description of the City Tunnel project from a legal point of view, in terms of the new Environmental Code and participation via consultation, please see Hydén (2010).[9] The author followed the project from within the project company from the start in 1999, making continued interviews and observations. In addition to describing the background of the City Tunnel with its legal, economic and political history, the focus of the research from the very beginning was to closely monitor and explore how the actual building project carried out two completely different consultation processes using legal norms stipulated in the new Environmental Code. Which

8 This law came into force on 1 January 1999, so it was totally new for this great construction project in the city of Malmö in south-western Sweden near the border to Denmark (Copenhagen), divided by the narrow strait, Öresund. The City Tunnel is a 17-kilometre rail link in Malmö, Sweden, running between Malmö Central Station (Malmö C) and the Öresund Line (Öresund Bridge). The tunnel portion of the project extends for six kilometres under the city centre. The purpose of the project was mainly to increase capacity in the Skåne regional network by changing Malmö Central from a terminus to a through station. The work was projected to cost SEK 9.45 billion.

9 Regarding H. Hydén 2010 – see in Baier (2009) and in Retfaerd, 2011, 34, Nr. 2/133: 26–41. The research project also included the Sociology of Law researchers Håkan Hydén and Minna Gillberg. Two research reports were published by the project: (1) Hydén, H., Wickenberg, P. and Gillberg, M. (2000), Environmental Management in Citytunnelprojektet. MiC project, report 1: Background and consultation, Research Report in Sociology of Law 2000, 2; and (2) Wickenberg, P. (2003), The Wells in Holma. Information on concrete implementation 2000–2002 for the City tunnel in Malmö; Research Report in Sociology of Law 2003, 1.

norms and norm-supporting actors and structures were active in those processes? How to apply the new legal norms?[10]

In this research, we have seen, as above, that there was an interesting combination of both lifeworld and system-oriented perspectives and findings (Habermas, 1986 and 1987). The law (the Environmental Code), belonging to the system, and with new and bold, personal knowledge, values, and interpretations by the management of how to realize the extended consultations, could thus meet the citizens' personal demands and needs stemming from their lifeworld. In the interpretation, legality and legitimacy became two of the other key concepts in the analysis of the public consultations in the City Tunnel project. These concepts were also to have a great significance for the interpretation and understanding of what happened, and why the design of the second consultation totally changed in terms of form and content.

The need for legitimacy regarding the City Tunnel project in Malmö – with its great social pressure that the tunnel, at all costs and efforts, must be accepted (legitimacy) by the residents and citizens of Malmö – was also a driving force behind the fact that the management was using the legal means (legality), which included new opportunities.[11] This change in the City Tunnel company regarding the public consultations was thus made possible due to three factors: the need for legitimacy by the citizens for this great construction project in Malmö; an important 'soul of fire' in the management group; and a reflective and distributed leadership (see Ulf Leo's chapter in this volume), using legal norms on public participation and realizing the need for a revamp of the consultation design and communication with local and involved citizens. In this last part, the new environmental law was clearly supporting changes in a direction towards concrete public participation by citizens wanting to have a say, leading to sharing local knowledge and thus, to some extent, influencing the building project (Flyvbjerg, 2002).

The first consultation in 1999 took place in the evenings on ordinary working days, and the communication was merely a one-way communication from the project management group, with almost no dialogue or time for questions at all. Afterwards, there was quite serious external and internal criticism of this way of doing the first consultation. This was clearly validated in our research interviews with visitors to the first public consultations. After a seminar with all leaders in the project and some legal experts from the university concerning the interpretations of the new legal norms on consultations in the Environmental Code, it was decided by the leaders that the next consultation in 2001 was to be done quite differently in terms of communication with, and ways of meeting, the citizens. Various local reference groups were created, and dialogue meetings were held with the project

10 The full article on the City Tunnel in English is published in Baier (2009: 167–83), and also, updated, in *Retfaerd*, 2011, 34, No. 2/133, 42–58.

11 Aarhus Convention. This Convention was opened for signature on 25 June 1998 at a Conference of Environmental Ministers in Aarhus. The Convention came into force on 30 October 2001. Sweden ratified the Convention on 20 May 2005.

leaders involved. The second public consultation finally took place during a Saturday and Sunday in a large school building with plenty of space right in the city centre, open both days for interested and invited citizens to communicate with all the experts in the project. The project received quite a lot of new and important information, provided by citizens with local expert knowledge about water and wells in some crucial tunnel areas to be built under the city of Malmö.

As a result, this local knowledge saved a lot of time and money for the City Tunnel project (for example, in finding the unknown wells in Holma, one separate part of the city and crucial for the calculation of the water balance in the tunnel under Malmö city). Local knowledge – in a reflective and learning organization functioning like a kind of social, communicative, public educational institution – was an excellent example and a result of real public participation during the second round of the consultations, due to an open and new interpretation of the Environmental Code. That change was also dependent on the role of some key persons and leaders in the project organization itself – 'souls of fire', or change agents, norm-breakers or norm-setters – who created a new normative climate or norm culture within the organization, with social arenas for communication of new ideas stemming from a more autonomous interpretation of the Environmental Code regarding public participation.

The project leader for the consultations – a 'soul of fire' – in particular was bringing her personal values on democracy into the ways in which the public consultation was organized and based on real communication. In Habermas's words, she was bringing her knowledge from the lifeworld into the system. She communicated these norms into the project organization, and the new norms were socially reproduced, leading to changed behaviour and actions by the other professionals in the company. During this phase of the implementation process of the new legal norms on consultation, she was also the important norm-supporting actor during the application of new legal participation norms in this construction project. Thus, the law, the legal norms – in congruence with existing social norms and attitudes toward public participation inside and outside the management of the City Tunnel company – could in this case open up for broader and deeper public participation in this project through genuine communication.[12]

Implementation of legal norms in the UN Convention on the Rights of the Child

In this part of this chapter, the author's aim is, as mentor and lecturer for almost 10 years in the Advanced International Training Programme 'Child Rights, Classroom and School Management', to reflect on the empirical material and experiences from the implementation of legal norms in the UN Convention on the Rights of

12 To complete this, to some extent, success story: The City Tunnel in Malmö was open to transport in December 2010, six months earlier than originally planned, at a lower cost than forecast, and saving SEK 885 million. See Underestimating Costs in Public Works Projects, B. Flyvbjerg (2002: 279–95).

the Child (CRC) in education and schools.[13] This will be done using personal experiences from 2003–2012, especially with and in China, India and Vietnam, using the sociology of law perspective.[14]

The overarching aim is to analyse the results of the implementation of CRC-related legal norms including the experiences. Material in the Final Project Reports from the three countries mentioned above, written when the first year or cycle of the programme had been completed, will be used. Notes, observations and reflections from the Mentor Reports, written over the years when visiting the project sites and participating teams in their home countries and own educational contexts, will also be used. The overall question here is: what happened with the implementation of the new legal norms?

Here, the study uses the Report book, which was written after the first five years of the programme, by Wickenberg et al. (2009).[15] During the nine years of work in the CRC programme, with 16 batches of training sessions (number 17 in October 2012), the author has made about 30 field visits, each lasting 6–10 working days, in the three countries (see above), and participated in 15 follow-up seminars in as many countries, including local school visits. The programme as a whole currently has 160 participating teams, with three participants in each team, and thus in total about 500 participants. Most of the change projects – done by all teams as part of the training programme – in these three countries focus on the right to 'participation' related to CRC Articles 12, 13 and 14 – namely, respect for the views of the child; the child's right to freedom of expression; and the child's right to freedom of thought, conscience and religion. They are the legal norms in this context.

Points of departure in the implementation of the CRC

In the reflections, three levels of education in society – connecting to the recruiting principles for the three participants forming the country team in this training programme – have been used as the starting points: the local school and community level; the provincial/regional level; and the national/state level in society.[16] This starts as a clear 'top-down' process, starting at the national level. When starting

13 The programme has been run by Lund University since 2003 and has, so far, included 28 developing countries.

14 For further reading on this CRC programme, see https://itp.sida.se/itp/Programcatalog.nsf/0/A567E62EB2A1270BC12578F5004B1ACB?opendocument [Accessed: 30 August 2012].

15 Parts of this programme have been published in *Academia*, No. 1, 2012, 20–26. See also Wickenberg, P. et al. (2009) *Taking Child Rights Seriously*, Lund: Lund University; and *Change Projects from International Training Programme 'Child Rights, Classroom and School Management'*, 2012a, Batch 12, and later with the same title (2012b) for Batch 13.

16 These words or concepts could be very different from country to country. The organizational principles of a state or a country, experienced, realized and learned so far, is very contextual. The same applies to provincial and district levels in different countries.

to implement some new ideas, norms or policy documents at the very local level of a school or in society, it will soon be found out (as we have noticed above) that there are already existing social norms, dedicated people ('souls of fire' or change agents) and committed organizations (such as NGOs) working on the issue at stake (forming the local lifeworld when new norms are to be initiated). The question is: what is happening at each level in terms of the CRC in the education sector when the projects in this training programme have continued over the first year of the project in the training programme, and thereafter?

Establishing professional networks of change agents

Establishing professional networks of former participants is one of the most important steps in the competence- and capacity-building for supporting the new legal norms to take root. The participants are 'change agents', in the meaning as mentioned above used by Ellickson (in Hechter and Opp, 2001: 41), and that is almost the same actor here as 'souls of fire'. The network is one of the prerequisites for sustainable implementation of new norms, the second essence of the norm. The state of Kerala in the south-western part of India is a good example of autonomous networking. There are today 23 professionals within education who are former participants continuing to work on the application of new norms related to the CRC in the state's education system. They are now working in 6 of the 14 districts in the state with some 35 million people. They have established a well-functioning network which has regular meetings and workshops. They also support the state Education Department in Kerala on in-service training on the CRC for teachers, principals, teacher trainers and education officers. Furthermore, they have initiated changes in the curricula and written state policy documents and books as teaching-learning guidelines on the CRC in education for teachers and principals.

This Kerala network has some key persons or true 'souls of fire' – who are former participants in the programme – who are acting as coordinators in Kerala on further implementation of CRC-norms in schools and education. They have good contact via personal meetings, mobile phone or e-mail with all the other 23 change agents (former participants), and they meet fairly regularly in the network. The network supports its members and other professionals in applying and communicating new norms related to the CRC in education. Three of the change agents have now retired as educational leaders, but they are still committed to their continued work within applying CRC-norms in their education system in the districts in Kerala. They are also communicating the new norms to other professionals within schools and education in their nearby districts. The participants are mostly doing this continued work on implementing new norms on the CRC within their ordinary professional work positions at local, district or provincial level. They are the really burning 'souls of fire' and 'change agents' in the network, acting as supporting actors in terms of implementation of new legal norms.

The network and coordinators are very skilled in connecting to local media when they are presenting something new on norm implementation in schools and education. The change agents are bringing their values, in line with the law, into the educational system, and are socially reproducing new norms on the CRC. Similar work on establishing new legal norms on the CRC and networks of former participants can be found in Vietnam and Inner Mongolia, China (see below for further reading on these countries).

School principals as change agents and supporting actors

In the projects, it was also noted that the school principals of the local schools in Kerala – as in Vietnam – are important key persons or actors when supporting the establishment of new norms in the CRC implementation in schools. They are most often the norm-setters or norm-breakers in education arenas (see also the chapters by Ulf Leo and Lars Persson in this volume). They also create different social arenas for students, teachers and parents at meetings and in communications on new norms on the CRC within their schools. Communication is vital and important for creating and establishing the new social norms based on the legal norms. This applies to teachers, students (students' councils for active participation in decision-making processes), parents (parents and students for participation in making decisions in schools) and also including persons from the local community and local government in the communication of new legal norms (Wickenberg et al., 2009: 44).

At the same time, it is essential to take a critical look, especially at the 'souls of fire' that could act only for themselves, and not be connected to and in step with the processes in the rest of the school or organization. They could sometimes have their own agenda, based on personal needs in this process, and that could be a real problem in terms of the sustainability of the new norms (Wickenberg, 1999: 451).

Similar experiences as in Kerala regarding implementation of legal norms have been experienced in China (23 change agents in Inner Mongolia) and Vietnam (30 participants). In Inner Mongolia, an autonomous region in northern China, norms are initiated and established in three big cities, with a focus on teacher training universities (IMNU, Inner Mongolia Normal University in the Inner Mongolia capital Hohhot, and Chifeng University) and colleges (Tongliao Vocational College – see Change Projects 2012a and 2012b). Similar norm support provided by principals in schools is the experience in Vietnam, especially in Ho Chi Minh City. The network and the former participants are now forming new social arenas, students' and parents' councils, for communication and social reproduction of new norms on the CRC. They have been the driving force for change, key persons and education leaders are at a relatively high level, and they have opportunities to make changes to enlarge their space of action. The networks and the change agents are planning and producing teaching-training materials and policy documents on applying the CRC in local schools and education. They are involving other partners and testing new methods in local schools. In this way, they are also applying new norms in their local context. They are finding new ways to break old norms and introducing new norms based on the CRC (Change Projects, 2012a: 189; Change Projects, 2012b: 57 and 193).

Summing up implementing new norms on the CRC in education and schools

In the reflections on the examples from the project for change work in the different countries and teams, the following have been noted and experienced:

i) They have established norm-supporting networks of programme participants with social arenas for communication of new norms.
ii) The networks have dedicated key persons and principals – 'souls of fire' and change agents – who also are the supporting actors in organizing the continued educational and social activities on new norms on the CRC within the network.
iii) The networks and the key persons are supporting the establishment of new norms, and they understand why they are doing this and why they are acting.
iv) The dissemination and communication of CRC-norms are being done at the local level – that is, from the project school to other schools and in the local community, to parents, families, politicians, organizations and the various local media.
v) The media, local newspapers and television play an important role for the communication and social reproduction of results. This also creates support for the new norms on the CRC to be spread in schools and education.
vi) It could be seen in this empirical material that there is ongoing interplay between legal norms and social norms regarding the CRC. 'Souls of fire' or change agents are bringing in their values and beliefs from their lifeworld to the educational system.

It has become evident that implementation of CRC-norms, with dedicated 'souls of fire' or change agents and local social networks, can create new norms among children and adults, teachers and parents. All this is supporting children's rights at the local level in society, which in turn could lead to changed behaviour or action patterns. A meta-norm, 'to see the child', could in this way be created. The concept of meta-norms is also used by Lars Persson and Ulf Leo in their chapters in this volume. Meta-norms are elaborated by Robert Axelrod, a political scientist, who, among many research areas, is known for his interdisciplinary work on the complexity and evolution of cooperation: 'The existence of a meta-norm can be an effective way to get a norm started and to protect it once it is established' (Axelrod, 1986: 1102). According to Axelrod, meta-norms are general norms that can protect existing ones. Meta-norms also enable the creation of sub-norms, and this is utilized – more or less consciously – by the 'souls of fire'. An important experience is the congruence between the new legal norm and the existing social norm at the local level. These are useful findings for the development of educational practice, as well as adding new knowledge to the understanding of the function of norms in local implementation processes.

Conclusions

The following conclusions, as mentioned in the introduction, are based on three empirically based projects on implementation of new legal norms at the local level in society, in schools or in organizations. The aim of this chapter has been to focus on the significance of 'souls of fire', which was found in various research projects, and to explore the concept of 'souls of fire' and its connections to 'change agents', and the creation of norms in organizations. Secondly, the aim was to explore the need and type of support required when creating new norms.

As the main conclusion, these three different sociology of law studies have contributed new knowledge about 'souls of fire' – or change agents – as links or 'putty' between legal and social norms at the local level of implementation. They are vital for norm creation. They are also to be seen as mediators between the lifeworld and the system, in Habermas's words. The 'souls of fire' bring their personal beliefs and values from the lifeworld into the professional system, and thus create changes in the normativity in the organization. These findings connect in an interesting way to the chapter by Reza Banakar in this volume analysing relations between social norms and normativity.

Supporting actors of different kinds and at different social levels are important when implementing new legal norms and creating norms. Leaders in different organizations are vital to support 'souls of fire', change agents and other norm-setters in the implementation and communication of new norms which can lead to changes in behaviour (see Wickenberg, 1999; Leo, 2010 and 2012; Leo and Wickenberg, 2013). Key persons or dedicated actors – 'souls of fire' or principals – are those supporting actors who are trying to find ways to initiate new norms or to break old norms in their organizations or society in general. They are often seen as role models in terms of new norms for the teachers, parents, students and local community officials. They have, in most cases, built up the legitimacy as a local norm-setter. They are also the crucial actors who often bring their personal values and ideas from the lifeworld into the system, to use the concepts from Habermas (Wickenberg, 1999: 451).

Creating social and professional arenas for the communication of new norms and active participation by different actors in this process is an important supporting structure for implementing new norms in organizations. Communication or social reproduction of new norms by the supporting actors mentioned has turned out to be one of the essential factors in this process of establishing norms at the local level. Communication among actors in the organization, and clear definitions – and consequent understanding – of the concepts involved, such as 'sustainable development' or 'public participation' or 'child rights', provide important support for the implementation and realization of new norms in organizations, such as schools. The role of schools is possibly a communicative arena for the formation of new norms at local level. News media – including new social media – play an important and supportive role in the communication and social reproduction of new norms. External resources and professional knowledge provide vital support to be used in implementation processes for new norms at local level. Legal norms and legal documents with clear wording are needed as a support for change agents in establishing new norms. Another important experience and result in these implementation processes studied and explored is the matching, or congruence, between new legal norms and existing social norms at local level.

All of the items mentioned above constitute important knowledge to enable deeper understanding of the prerequisites for implementing new legal norms in organizations or in the community at local level. If the supporting actors and supporting structures are missing in the implementation processes of new norms at local level, this will, of course, constitute a clear hindrance for the creation of new norms (Hydén and Wickenberg, 2004: 39). Norm thinking is thus needed by the leaders or management when initiating changes, and a clearly formulated norm strategy is important in this context. A norm strategy should then be based on the conclusions of the role of the 'souls of fire' or change agents, and we could furthermore elaborate on the use of this concept in a broader legal situation. We know that these key actors, the 'souls of fire' or change agents, are present at the local level of implementation of new legal norms, and this fact could be taken into account by the legislator from the very beginning when formulating a new law or other regulations. These norm-supporting actors are the useful mediators in the implementation processes – and a social 'putty' – who can be counted on and empowered from the beginning within the respective regulations at stake. Furthermore, this fact should be recognized and supported beforehand by the authorized actors as well as by the law and the legislation. It is important for various legislating bodies to know about, and above all to understand, the social norm processes at the local level of application of legal norms in society. On the other hand, these 'souls of fire' – or change agents – are at the same time active in the social reproduction and communication of new norms to other parts and different actors in the local society – as we have seen clearly in Swedish schools, and in Kerala, India. This perspective of social acting and proliferation of norms is usually *not* anticipated by socio-legal researchers and legislators. It could instead be used in a conscious way in the legal processes. A third valuable finding about the role of 'souls of fire' and change agents could be to use the feedback from these local community processes and local key actors to see if, and how, the intended legal norms are able to work and fit in with the social norms at the local level of implementation. This congruence is of vital importance for the effectiveness of the new legal norm. Being aware of these norm-creating processes and the existence of 'souls of fire' and change agents, and their norm-support in society, we are moving from law towards social practice.

References

Axelrod, Robert. 1986. 'An Evolutionary Approach to Norms', *The American Political Science Review*, Vol. 80, No. 4, 1095–1111.

Baier, Matthias (ed.) 2009. *Participative aspects of law – a socio-legal perspective,* Lund Studies in Sociology of Law 31, Lund: Lund University, Sweden.

Baier, Matthias and Svensson, Måns. 2009. *Om normer*. Malmö: Liber.

Banakar, Reza. 2012. 'Can Legal Sociology Account for the Normativity of Law?' – a first draft version presented at the International Conference: 'The Normative Anatomy of Society: Relations Between Norms and Law in the 21st Century', at Lund University, Sweden, 24–5 April 2012 (and in a revised version in this volume).

Breiting, Sören and Wickenberg, Per. 2010. 'The Progressive Development of Environmental Education in Sweden and Denmark', *Environmental Education Research*, 16, 1, 9–37.

Change Projects. 2012a. Change Projects from the International Training Programme 'Child Rights, Classroom and School Management', *Final reports*, Batch 12, Lund: Lund University.

Change Projects. 2012b. Change Projects from the International Training Programme 'Child Rights, Classroom and School Management', *Final reports*, Batch 13, Lund: Lund University.

Ellickson, Robert C. 2001. 'The Evolution of Social Norms: A perspective from the legal academy', in *Social Norms*. Edited by Michael Hechter and Karl-Dieter Opp. New York: Russell Sage Foundation.

Flyvbjerg, B., Skamris Holm, B. and Buhl, S. 2002. 'Underestimating Costs in Public Works Projects. Error or lie?', *APA Journal* Vol. 68, No. 3, 279–95.

Frånberg, Gun-Marie. 1994. *Kvinnliga eldsjälar i glesbygd: lokal mobilisering, förändring och anpassning*. Östersund: Glesbygdsmyndigheten.

Frånberg, Gun-Marie. 1996. *East of Arcadia : three studies of rural women in northern Sweden and Wisconsin, USA*. Umeå: Umeå universitet.

Habermas, Jürgen. 1986 [1981]. *The Theory of Communicative Action*, Vol. 1. Cambridge: Polity Press.

Habermas, Jürgen. 1987 [1981]. *The Theory of Communicative Action*, Vol. 2. Cambridge: Polity Press.

Hallerström, Helena. 2006. *Rektorers normer i ledarskapet för skolutveckling*. Lund Studies in Sociology of Law 23. Lund: Lund University.

Hart, Paul and Nolan, Kathleen. 1999. 'A critical analysis of research in environmental education', *Studies in Science Education*, 34, 1–69.

Hechter, Michael and Opp, Karl-Dieter (eds). 2001. *Social Norms*. New York: Russell Sage Foundation.

Hydén, Håkan. 2002. *Normvetenskap*. Lund Studies in Sociology of Law. Lund: Lund University.

Hydén, Håkan. 2011. 'Looking at the World through the Lenses of Norms', in *Understanding Law in Society*. Edited by Knut Papendorf et al. Zurich: LIT Verlag.

Hydén, Håkan, Wickenberg, Per and Gillberg, Minna. 2000. *Miljöledning i Citytunnelprojektet. MiC-projektet, delrapport I: Bakgrund och samråd.* Research Report in Sociology of Law 2000, 2. Lund: Lund University.

Hydén, Håkan and Wickenberg, Per. 2004. *Utvärderingsstudie av Ven-projektet*. Sociology of Law. Lund: Lund University.

Hydén, Håkan and Svensson, Måns. 2008. 'Contributions in Sociology of Law. Remarks from a Swedish Horizon', *The Concept of Norms in Sociology of Law*. Edited by Håkan Hydén and Per Wickenberg. Lund Studies in Sociology of Law 29. Lund University. This article is also published in *Law and Society, Scandinavian Studies in Law*, Volume 53, 15–32, Stockholm University, Law Faculty 2008.

Jensen, Bjarne Bruun and Schnack, Karsten. 1997. 'The Action Competence Approach', in *Environmental Education, Environmental Education Research*, 3, 2, 163–78.

Læssøe, Jeppe. 2012. 'Professionalism, Enthusiasm, Norms, Tensions and Competences among Municipality Employed Local Agenda 21 Employees in Denmark', paper presented at the International Conference: 'The Normative Anatomy of Society: Relations Between Norms and Law in the 21st Century', at Lund University, Sweden, 24–5 April 2012.

Leo, Ulf. 2010. *Rektorer bör och rektorer gör. En rättssociologisk studie om att identifiera, analysera och förstå professionella normer*. Lund: Lund University.

Leo, Ulf and Wickenberg, Per. 2013. 'Professional Norms in School Leadership: Change Efforts in Implementation of Education for Sustainable Development'. In Journal of Educational Change.

Lundgren, Ulf P. 2008. *Utbildningsvetenskap nu och i framtiden*, Anförande vid Vetenskapsrådets Resultatdialog. Karlstad.

Markström, Urban. 2003. *Den svenska psykiatrireformen: bland brukare, eldsjälar och byråkrater*. Umeå: Umeå universitet.

Öhman, Johan. 2006. 'Pluralism and Criticism in Environmental Education and Education for Sustainable Development: A Practical Understanding', *Environmental Education Research*, 12, 2, 149–63.

Öhman, Johan. 2008. 'Environmental ethics and democratic responsibility – A pluralistic approach to ESD', in *Values in Democracy in Education for Sustainable Development: Contributions from Swedish Research: Environmental Ethics and Responsibility*, edited by Johan Öhman. Malmö: Liber, 17–32.

Öhman, Johan. 2011. 'Theme: New Swedish environmental and sustainability education research', *Tidskrift för didaktik och utbildningspolitik*, Vol. 20, No. 1, 2011, Örebro: Örebro universitet, 3–12.

Östman, Leif. 2003. *Nationell och internationell miljödidaktisk forskning. En forskningsöversikt*. Pedagogisk forskning i Uppsala, 148. Uppsala: Uppsala universitet.

Palm, Kristina. 2008. *Det riskabla engagemanget: Om regenerativ utveckling av mänskliga resurser, eldsjälar och ledarskap i radikal utveckling*. Stockholm: Kungliga Tekniska Högskolan.

Persson, Lars. 2010. *Pedagogerna och demokratin.* En rättssociologisk studie av pedagogers arbete med demokratiutveckling. Lund: Lund University.

Philips, Åke. 1988. *Eldsjälar. En studie av aktörsskap i arbetsorganisatoriskt utvecklingsarbete.* Stockholm: Handelshögskolan i Stockholm.

Rommetveit, Ragnar. 1955. *Social Norms and Roles, Explorations in the psychology of ending social pressures.* Minnesota: University of Minnesota Press.

Svensson, Måns. 2008. *Sociala normer och regelefterlevnad. Trafiksäkerhetsfrågor ur ett rättssociologiskt perspektiv.* Lund Studies in Sociology of Law 28. Lund University.

Svensson, Måns and Larsson, Stefan. 2012. 'Intellectual Property Law Compliance in Europe: Illegal File Sharing and the Role of Social Norms', *New Media Society*, (Published online 10 April 2012).

Vedung, Evert. 1991. *Utvärdering i politik och förvaltning.* Lund: Studentlitteratur.

Wals, Arjen E.J. and Kieft, Geke. 2010. *Education for Sustainable Development. Research Overview,* Sida Review 2010, 13.

Wickenberg, Per. 1999. *Normstödjande strukturer. Miljötematiken börjar slå rot i skolan.* Lund Studies in Sociology of Law 5. Lund: Lund University.

Wickenberg, Per. 2003. *Brunnarna i Holma. Samrådens konkreta genomförande 2000–2002 för Citytunnelprojektet i Malmö.* Research Report in Sociology of Law 2003, 1. Lund: Lund University.

Wickenberg, Per et al. (eds). 2004. *Learning to Change our World? Swedish Research on Education & Sustainable Development,* Lund: Studentlitteratur.

Wickenberg, Per and Öhman, Johan. 2008. *Från undervisningsområde till etablerat forskningsfält,* i Resultatdialog 2008, Forskning inom utbildningsvetenskap, Vetenskapsrådets rapportserie 12, 2008, Stockholm: Vetenskapsrådet.

Wickenberg, Per. 2009. 'The Unknown but Well-Known Wells in Holma', in *Participative aspects of law – a socio-legal perspective,* edited by Matthias Baier. Lund Studies in Sociology of Law 31, Lund University, Sweden, 167–83.

Wickenberg, Per et al. 2009. *Taking Child Rights Seriously. Reflections on Five Years of an International Training Programme.* Lund: Lund University.

Wickenberg, Per. 2010. 'The Unknown but Well-Known Wells in Holma – Public participation in the City Tunnel Project in Malmö', *Retfaerd,* 2011, 34, Nr. 2/133, 42–58.

Wickenberg, Per and Leo, Ulf. 2013. *Ett steg fram och ett tillbaka. Statens styrning av miljö och hållbar utveckling genom skollag, läroplaner och kursplaner.* Research Report in Sociology of Law 2013:1, Lund: Lund University.

Official publications and references

Miljöbalken (SFS 1998:808) (Swedish Environmental Code).

Skollagen (SFS 1985:1100) (Swedish Education Act).

Skollagen (SFS 2010:800) (Swedish Education Act).

Swedish National Agency of Education, Skolverket, Lgr 94 and Lpf 94.

Swedish National Agency of Education, Skolverket, Läroplan för grundskolan, Lgr 11.

Swedish National Agency of Education, Skolverket, Läroplan för gymnasieskolan 2011.

UN Convention on the Rights of the Child, UN General Assembly resolution 44/25, 20 November 1989, Entry into force 2 September 1990.

UNCED 1992, UN Conference on Environment and Development, Agenda 21.

PART IV
Norms and Structures

Chapter 14

Legal and Social Norms for Development: Why Legal Reform of the Informal Economy Failed to Influence Vulnerable Groups in Developing Countries

Ana Maria Vargas Falla

Introduction

The use of legal reforms in order to achieve development and poverty reduction has been historically defended by different theories and approaches (Davis, 2010; Grugel and Piper, 2009; Davis and Trebilcock, 2008; Trubek, 2006; Carothers, 2006; Trubek and Galanter, 1974; Carothers, 1998). One of the oldest schools of thought interested in connecting legal reforms with development was the 'law and development' movement that emerged in the United States during the 1960s. Scholars thought that legal institutions were necessary for developing countries to be able to compete globally and improve their economies (Trubek and Galanter, 1974).[1] Later, with a broader definition of development,[2] the United Nations have used the terms 'rights-based approach to development' during the 1990s, and 'legal empowerment' during the beginning of this century to promote development that respects basic legal rights (Golub and MacQuay, 2001; CLEP, 2008).

The school of thought known as 'law and economics' also studied the role of legal and social norms in development, and concluded that it is possible to identify the norms that are efficient for the economic system (Coase, 1960; Posner,

1 Trubek and Galanter wrote in 1974 that the 'law and development' movement failed because scholars realized that 'legal change may have little or no effect on social and economic conditions in Third World societies and, conversely, that many legal "reforms" can deepen inequality, curb participation, restrict individual freedom, and hamper efforts to increase material well-being' (1974: 1080).

2 Development was initially defined in term of economic growth, but growth was experienced in different countries and their populations were experiencing high poverty levels, diseases, and inequality problems. The term 'human development' is now used to refer to the idea proposed by the economist Amrtya Sen, which states that people and their freedoms and capabilities should be the focus of development, and not the economy (Sen, 1999).

2011). Moreover, in economic theory, New Institutional Economics (NIE) have concluded not only that individuals act on rational behaviour, but also that they are constrained by formal and informal institutions (North, 1990; Toye, 1995; Williamson, 2000; Ostrom, 2005). A common factor for all of these approaches is the special attention they give to legal norms and their arguments about the force of the law over human behaviour.

One of the areas in which legal reforms have been used to promote development is the regulation of the informal economy (Tokman, 1992; Sepulveda and Syrett, 2007; De Soto, 1989). Informality has been defined as work done without following the formalities of the law – for instance, without paying taxes, or having all the registrations and licences required by the law (Chen, 2007). For this reason, reform of labour laws and norms for business registration has been used as one of the main solutions for reducing informality in developing countries. Law and economics and NIE have been very influential in the discussions about how to reduce the informal economy in Latin America, and most countries there have engaged in ambitious reforms in order to facilitate business registrations, reducing the time and costs involved (Garcia, 2006).

However, even after many reforms and efforts to reduce the informal economy, informality continues, to a high degree, all over the world. According to a study from the International Monetary Fund (IMF), the size of the informal economy in 2000 was calculated to be about 41 per cent of the official GDP in developing countries, 35 per cent in transition countries, and 18 per cent in developed countries (Schneider, 2002).

Using the concepts of social norms and social reality used in this book, this chapter explores why legal reforms that aimed to facilitate the formalization of informal workers have largely failed to influence vulnerable groups in developing countries. It is focused on victims of war in Colombia who were displaced from rural areas and were engaged in the informal economy upon arrival in the cities, most of them as street vendors, domestic workers and small-scale entrepreneurs. For this group, society accepted informality and built a number of reasons, arguments and social norms to legitimize not following the law. Internally displaced persons were not worried by the formalities of the law and, instead, regarded the informal economy as a legitimate source of income (Vargas Falla, 2010).

Using empirical material from a qualitative study conducted in Colombia among a group of internally displaced people engaged in survival activities, as well as quantitative data from national statistical surveys, I will illustrate that there is an over-estimation of the impact of legal norms on the decision of people to work in the informal economy. In contrast to the legalistic approach supported by international organizations, such as the World Bank and the International Monetary Fund, I confirm the thesis that social norms and informal institutions play a crucial role for this type of small-scale entrepreneur. This chapter rejects a legalist-centric approach to development, and instead proposes development policies looking at the social norms that exist in society, particularly the processes by which communities construct reasons and explanations exempting certain groups from following the law.

Legal norms and development: The contributions of Sociology of Law

Sociology of law studies have insisted that legal reforms are not enough to change society, particularly where there are social norms and social practices that may contradict the law (Davis, 2010; Ellickson, 1999; Tushnet, 1998). Social norms are defined here as imperatives that tell individuals what their expected behaviour is. Society is built upon normative structures during our process of socialization; first in the family, then in the school, and later in other spaces. According to Måns Svensson (in Chapter 3 of this book), social norms have three main characteristics: they are imperatives that tell us that what we do is right or wrong; they are socially constructed; and they depend on our own understanding of what we think people around us consider as normal.

The difference between social norms and legal norms is that the former are built upon social interaction in a more spontaneous way, while legal norms are proposed and produced by the political system, such as Congress (ibid.). Additionally, social norms are not explicitly discussed and emerge from social interaction, in contrast to legal norms, which are the result of a deliberative system (Baier, 2008). Sometimes, social norms can become legal norms when they make their way into the legal system; or legal norms can become socially enforced when people reach agreements to spontaneously follow them. Social norms are part of our culture and, even though it is difficult to agree with a single definition of culture, the one given by Bourdieu may be useful from a normative perspective. Bourdieu considers that culture can be represented by a system of norms that we have internalized in the process of socialization (1987). These norms provide us with certain ways to perceive and understand the world and therefore they have the ability to influence our behaviour.

Having clarified the definition of legal and social norms, it is time to state a definition of development, since it is part of this analysis. Development in general is assumed to be the result of an action, or a process to change something for the better. It is related to economic growth, social security, gender equality, environmental protection, the prevention of certain diseases and, in general, to the well-being of the population. It is used to measure countries around the world and to compare them in terms of development standards, such as the Human Development Index or the Millennium Development Goals.[3]

3 Development as a field has been actively adopted by the United Nations (UN) and, in 2000, 189 nations at the UN's General Assembly declared their commitment to eight goals for the improvement of the world. These goals are: to eradicate extreme poverty and hunger; to achieve universal primary education; to promote gender equality and empower women; to reduce child mortality; to improve maternal health; to combat HIV/AIDS,

Social norms are important for development because, if you strive for a successful legal reform that promotes development goals, you should look closely at the normative systems operating within society. Social norms can be in conflict with legal norms that are imposed by the political system and, as Baier (2008) said, the closer the legal reform corresponds to the social norms, the more likely it is that the legal reform will work.

Looking into the social practices that are common among certain groups is essential to the study of why some legal norms are not applied or followed by society. Social practice is here understood as actions and activities based on collective attitudes (Tuomela, 2002). It is, in other words, the result of social norms in action. According to Garcia, sociologists of law in Latin America have looked into the social practice of legal compliance and found two reasons, or sets of beliefs, given by people to explain why not to comply with the law: 'strategy' and 'rebelliousness' (Garcia, 2006). Strategy means that people decide not to follow the law based on a strategic decision. In the case of informal workers, they decide to work outside the law because they can earn more money and the possibility of punishment is low. The rebellious position, on the other hand, considers that failure to comply with the law is based on an evaluation of the legitimacy of the law, creating arguments that are based in social values, culture and social norms.

The contributions made by sociologists of law in the field of social norms have been seriously discussed by scholars in the field of new institutional economics studying how social norms influence people's behaviour (Davis and North, 1971; Williamson, 1985; Schotter, 1981). While studying how cattle owners settle their disputes in Shasta County, California, Ellickson (1991) concluded that social norms emerge in close-knit communities and are more important than the law in the everyday lives of these groups. Cooter (2000) also investigated the relationship between legal and social norms and concluded that legal norms need to be aligned with social norms in order to foster cooperation in society. Susanna Johansson's contribution (in Chapter 7 of this book) insists on the importance of social norms as a means of collaboration among different organizations.

Research in both NIE and sociology of law have stressed that policy makers usually over-value legal reforms when considering social change. But legal reforms have been very popular, apart from their constant failure, particularly in the field of development.

Legal norms and the informal economy

Legal norms have been essential for defining the problem of informal work, because the term 'informal economy' or 'informal sector' usually refers to different economic activities that are undertaken without following the formalities

malaria and other diseases; to ensure environmental sustainability; and to create a global partnership for development with targets for aid, trade and debt relief.

of the law (ILO, 2002). It generally covers self-employment activities or informal businesses, and includes people working as street vendors, garbage collectors, hairdressers and cleaners, or, in rural areas, people farming or working on the land.

Since the publication of *The Other Path* by the Peruvian economist Hernando De Soto (1989), informality has been explained in relation to inefficient laws and excessive regulations. According to a study made by De Soto in Peru, people needed more than 300 days and had to invest the equivalent of 32 times the minimum monthly wage to legally set up a small business. In developed countries, like the United States, it only takes a few weeks and costs less than USD 1,000 in most states (De Soto, 2003).

This explanation is known as the legalist theory of the informal economy, and it considers that people work informally because of bad legal institutions, which impose excessive requirements on people in order to work, governed by formality (ibid.). It is similar to the 'strategic' explanation of why people fail to comply with the law.

To illustrate this theory and the reasons for considering it problematic, this chapter will use one of the most common measures of legal norms for small and medium enterprises, the 'Doing Business' Report 2012. This report gathers quantitative data from about 183 countries in the world, in order to measure and compare whether their legal systems support businesses to operate, or constrain businesses from operating, in the formal economy. The following graph illustrates the ranking (numbers on the left of the graph) of the ease of doing business under formal regulations in Latin America (the bars)[4] and the percentage of workers in the informal economy (the dots).

In this ranking system, Colombia, Peru and Mexico rank the highest in the region in terms of the time and steps that are required in order to start and operate a business under formality. However, informality at least in these three countries seems to be caused by other reasons than the legal system. Figure 14.1 shows that there is no correlation between having a good legal system (that is, one that allows for an easy business environment) and the percentage of persons working in the informal economy. Studies against the legalist theory argue that there are additional factors influencing actors' decisions to remain informal, and that legal requirements play only a marginal role (Siegel and Veiga, 2009).

In contrast to the legalist theory, the 'structuralist theory' takes a Marxist approach. Here, informal and formal economies are said to exist in relation to each other, and the informal economy has the function of providing cheap goods and cheap labour, which benefit capitalist growth (Castells and Portes, 1989; Moser, 1978). This theory claims that informality is prevalent in some groups which have been excluded from state benefits and the formal economy (Lund and

4 The 'Doing Business' Report includes a set of regulations affecting nine stages of a business's life: starting a business; dealing with construction permits; registering property; getting credit; protecting investors; paying taxes; trading across borders; enforcing contracts; and closing a business.

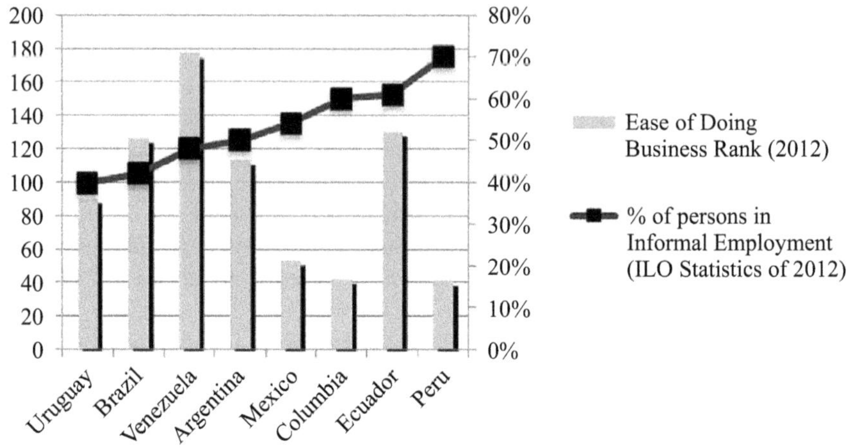

Figure 14.1 Legal Norms and the Informal Economy

Note: Graph made by the author using data from the Doing Business Report (2010) and the ILO Report of the Informal Economy (2012).

Srinivas, 2000). In a world economy where developing countries are required to have a flexible workforce in order to compete globally, people work in the informal economy because they do not have other options (Castells and Portes, 1989; Jütting and De Laiglesia, 2009; Portes, 1994).

Studies that evaluate both legalist and structuralist theories concluded that neither theory provides an accurate explanation for informality and that, instead, there are multiple factors that play a role (Williams et al., 2011). This chapter provides an alternative explanation of why legal reforms to the informal economy failed for a group of vulnerable people.

Vulnerable groups and the informal economy: The case of internally displaced persons in Colombia

In order to explain why informality is not only common but also socially accepted as a legitimate source of income for vulnerable groups, this chapter will use the case of internally displaced persons in Colombia. This group makes up about 7.8 per cent of the total population of Colombia, and consists of persons who were forced to move from their homes as a result of the internal armed conflict which has affected the country since the 1960s. They are like refugees, but inside their own country, and most of them live below the national poverty line. Internally displaced people in Colombia experience great difficulties in finding jobs, due to lack of experience in sectors other than agriculture, and also their low levels of education. According to a national survey from 2010 (Garay, 2010), about 25.5 per cent of them have less than two years of education, and the average has only the equivalent of primary school.[5]

This group was selected because about 96 per cent of them work under informal conditions, without social security benefits from their work. Furthermore, most are self-employed or work without any type of legal contract to protect their rights. It is an interesting case, because they have been part of government programs to improve their working conditions but, despite government efforts, informality continues to be the norm and not the exception.

The information presented in this chapter is based on a mixed methods design, using quantitative as well as qualitative data. The quantitative data is based on a National Survey[6] from 2010 aiming to measure the level of enjoyment of basic rights among the internally displaced people in Colombia. The qualitative data is based on the analysis of a government program aimed at supporting this group in finding employment in the formal economy, or to start up their own businesses. This part relies on 30 semi-structured interviews[7] with people who benefitted from this program, observations in their places of work, and four in-depth interviews with people working as managers and trainers on the program.

The aim of the program was to support internally displaced persons with both training and financial resources in order to help them to start working and to improve their incomes. It covered a total of 109,061 families from 2007 to 2009 (Accion Social, 2009). There were two main strategies within the program: employment, and entrepreneurship. Employment consisted of giving a cash incentive of USD 800 to employers who hired the participants for a minimum of 10 months. This strategy was not successful because of a lack of potential employers interested in participating in the program, and only 1 per cent of the participants were included under this modality.[8] The second strategy predominated inside the program, as it was easier to support people to start up their own businesses, or to support

5 Data from the third National Survey to verify the rights of internally displaced people (2010).

6 This survey was conducted by the National Commission to follow up the policies for internally displaced persons with the National University CID (Center for Development Research). 10,433 surveys represent the sample, which is considered of significance to the population studied according to general statistical theory.

7 The following are some of the questions from the interview questionnaire: What were your reasons for selecting this type of economic activity? Describe how you started your business? Describe the personal benefits of having started your own business? Describe how you benefitted from participating in the income generation program? Is your business registered with the local authorities? Do you have access to social security (health and pension)?

8 This strategy was also problematic because Colombia has suffered from endemic unemployment in recent years, and even educated people have problems finding employment opportunities. According to the National Statistics Agency (DANE), Colombia registered an annual unemployment rate of approximately 11 per cent for the years 2008/2009.

the enterprises they already had, than to help them to find formal jobs. In this strategy, participants received basic training in how to start a business, including marketing and cost analysis, but not about legal registration and other formalities. Participants had to identify their skills and use them to start small economic units. The government provided around USD 800 to fund the initial costs of machinery and raw materials. This capital was non-refundable.

One of the unintended results of the program was that more than 90 per cent of the participants entered into informal activities, such as street vendors, small manufacturers, or shop owners. From the people interviewed, three main economic activities became apparent: street vendors, vendors from home in the form of mini-supermarkets,[9] and small manufacturers. For instance, some street vendors used small carts to sell fruit or fruit juices, while others bought merchandise in retail stores and sold them in the streets. The program helped these people to buy the carts and the basic merchandise to start their sales. There was also a big group who used their homes to start mini-supermarkets to sell basic products, such as rice, sugar, milk, oil and other groceries.

Informality was the normal option for this group, and both the government and society considered that legal norms for informal work had to be flexible. It is what Garcia (2006) referred to as the negotiation of legal norms depending on the specific circumstances; people accept the law, but believe that failure to comply is allowed under certain circumstances.

Social norms and social practice in the informal economy

When a group experiences a common situation such as informality, it is important to look not only at the characteristics of this group, but also at the social structures and rules around them, in order to see whether informality is additionally explained by institutional arrangements, such as legal norms, culture, traditions or social norms. Using the framework proposed by this book for 'social norms' and 'social practice', this part will analyse the reasons and circumstances that influence the decision of internally displaced people in Colombia to work in the informal economy. First, it will present one of the social norms that help to explain why, for some groups, informality is the normal answer and society supports this kind of behaviour. It will then look into informality as a social practice, in which the legal norm that requires business registrations and other formalities is completely ignored by some groups in society and a different social activity is undertaken.

9 These are small stores where you can buy basic groceries, such as milk, bread, rice and snacks.

Social norms that explain informality

In the case of internally displaced people, informality seems to be the norm and not the exception, since about 96 per cent of them work in this sector (Garay, 2010). People in the interviews referred to a social norm that I identify as the 'norm of survival'. According to this norm, you are not expected to follow legal regulations in their entirety, provided it is a matter of survival. This is a rather universal norm, and, in the case of the informal economy, it means that people are given a social consensus to work in the 'hidden economy' or 'outside the law' in order to earn a basic income. Many justify this form of earning a basic income, because they prefer to do that than to take up criminal activities. People working in the streets of Colombia often tell you, 'I would rather work as a vendor on buses than to rob you in the street'.

This norm of survival dates from far back in history, and many different languages have popular idioms that support the norm. In English, you can say, 'necessity knows no law' to mean that, when someone is in extreme need, the law becomes unimportant. This norm exists also in highly industrialized countries. Living and studying in Sweden for four years, I have seen how many of my Swedish friends considered that it was acceptable for irregular immigrants to work in the informal economy, because this was their only means of survival. There is a kind of transnational norm exemplified in the proverb, 'in times of great hardship, even a very honest person may break the law to feed their children'.

Social practice: Making an exception to the legal norm of business registration

The social norm of 'survival' is also based in social practice. It is very common to have stronger social norms in favour of informality in economies where the informal economy is important. In Colombia, everyone who is self-employed must be registered with the national tax office and obtain an identification number known as an RUT.[10] People who work selling goods or providing services must be registered, regardless of whether or not they have to pay taxes. These are dependent on the amount of annual income, as people with low income do not have to pay certain taxes. Obtaining this tax number is free, takes only one day and it can be obtained online.[11]

From the 30 interviews I conducted, there was only one participant who had obtained her RUT. She had a small manufacture of T-shirts in her house and had two people working for her to sell the T-shirts to bigger stores. When I asked why

---

10 RUT is the National Tax Number. It was established in Article 5 of Decree 2788 of 2004. This norm was modified and complemented by Decrees 2645 and 2828 of August 2011.

11 See www.dian.gov.co.

she obtained her RUT, she said she had done so a few months ago, when one of her customers required her to have it. She said, 'in the beginning it was not necessary to obtain a RUT, because I had very low earnings, but now my business is growing'.[12] When I asked the remaining interviewees whether they had thought about registering their businesses, they showed surprise and many of them did not understand my question. One of them answered that those laws did not apply to small businesses.

Apart from the simplified tax number (RUT), people engaged in commercial activities have to register with the Chamber of Commerce in order to obtain the 'Certificate of Industry and Commerce'. Displaced people who opened mini-supermarkets in their homes are, in theory, obliged to have this certificate. However, it emerged from the 30 interviews that none of the participants had this certificate. When asked about this certificate, some stated that they had no knowledge of this obligation. The few that knew about it considered it expensive or unnecessary for small businesses. They also stated that most of the people in their neighbourhoods operated their businesses without this registration, so did not see the need to comply with this norm.[13]

The registration fee was one of the main determinants for not complying with this legal norm, and it is understandable, as the cost of the certificate is almost equivalent to the average monthly income. When people depend on this income to pay for their basic needs, their capacity to save money and comply with this regulation is unrealistic. Besides the cost of the 'Certificate of Industry and Commerce', people had to apply for other permits and certificates. They needed a certificate of land use, a certificate of copyrights, a certificate of sanitation, and a certificate of security from the fire department, among others.

Additionally, the program managers did not ask participants to comply with these certificates. The only legal requirement that participants had to follow was the need to buy their merchandise, machinery or raw materials from legally constituted enterprises which could provide them with a receipt. The lack of compliance with business registration laws was a generalized practice among this group, and the government indirectly supported informality.

Analysis: Explaining informal work

Is informal normal? According to the social norm of survival and the social practices of displaced people engaged in small businesses, informality is the normal response to their need for work and income. In a report published in 2009

12 Interview carried out on 13 January 2010.

13 According to the National Survey of Small Enterprises carried out in 2007, in Colombia 55 per cent of these businesses operated without the 'Certificate of Industry and Commerce'. Survey carried out by the National Bureau of Statistics (DANE). See www.dane.gov.co.

by the OECD,[14] informality was questioned because it seems to be the reality for many countries and it was presented as an endemic problem, criticized for the implications that it has for poverty reduction and social welfare (Jütting and De Laiglesia, 2009). But informality is normal not only for some developing countries, as this report argues, but also for some disadvantaged groups in society, such as the internally displaced in Colombia. It is highly correlated to women, youths and migrants – that is, people who, for different reasons, seek and find a source of income in the informal economy.

The social practice that allowed the internally displaced to work without following the formalities of the law is an example of what sociology of law has called a 'negotiation of the state law' (Garcia, 2006: 126). According to this approach, people in Latin America look at the legal norms and evaluate whether or not they should be constrained by them. Legal norms become a field of negotiation among citizens, who create exceptions to the law depending on the circumstances. This is the case for business registration laws, in which many groups in Colombia have created exceptions that make these norms not applicable to certain vulnerable groups.

Informality is also explained by social norms, here the norm of 'necessity knows no law'. Internally displaced people working in the informal economy considered that what they were doing was right. They have built this belief based on their traditions and customs of working in markets and squares. Thus, this social norm is not only part of their personal understanding, but also what people around them consider to be normal. In this case, even the government officials in charge of the program considered that informality was expected for this group and supported their small economic units.

In Colombia, householders could not go home to their families and tell them that they cannot provide food for them because there are no formal jobs. This would be seen as an absurdity, as most Colombians who live in desolate conditions earn their basic income in the informal economy. Informal work constitutes the prevailing expectation, and (in terms of Hydén and Svensson) it is essential to identify whether or not it is an imperative (2008).

But social norms and social practice are not the only explanation of why this group is almost entirely confined to the informal economy. In the case of displaced people, one of the main reasons requiring consideration is their low level of education. This is a structural constraint that impacts on their decision to take up informal work. According to the National Survey for internally displaced people in 2010, the level of education of this group is lower than the national average. The household head has, on average, less than five years of education, and about one quarter of all household heads are illiterate (Garay, 2010). For the group I interviewed, lack of education was also a common factor, and training

14 The acronym OECD stands for the Organization for Economic Co-operation and Development, which is formed by the richest countries in the world.

was fundamental for the ones working in small workshops for shoes, clothes and wood.

The negative relation that exists between education and informality can be explained partly by the 'structuralist' theory of the informal economy, which considers the lack of opportunities and the exclusion of certain groups from state benefits, thus explaining informality. Internally displaced people usually come from rural areas, where the education system is very weak, and therefore have almost no other choice than the informal economy.

However, the picture is not black and white, as informality among vulnerable groups is the result of multiple institutions and factors. The findings of this research show that, even in countries with legal systems that are in line with the standards of the World Bank, informality among vulnerable groups (such as the displaced) is not explained in terms of the legalist theory.

Conclusions

Trying to understand the role of legal and social norms for development, particularly in the case of informal workers, highlighted the need to transcend the classical explanations given by the 'law and development' approach, based on the idea that legal reforms can foster social change. Instead, this chapter illustrates that social norms and social practice in the informal economy are important for explaining why legal reform is often irrelevant to vulnerable groups.

Even in countries like Colombia, with legislation considered adequate for small business to operate under formality, legal norms are negotiated in the social arena in order to find exceptions and reasons not to follow the legal norms under certain circumstances. This was partly explained because there is a social norm that considers it a matter of survival for people to be exempt from the legal norms regulating business formalization. Another part of the explanation was that people consider registration fees as expensive and unnecessary for small-scale entrepreneurs who earn less than the legal minimum wage.

This chapter illustrates the social agreement that supports vulnerable people and their need to provide for their families. This is what we called the social norm of 'necessity knows no law', which applies in Colombia to the group of internally displaced people. Legal norms failed to promote the formalization of vulnerable groups. I claim that legal reforms with development goals, such as poverty reduction and social inclusion, should take into account the arguments proposed by socio-legal analysis and New Institutional Economics, particularly the study of social norms.

In Latin America, as well as many other developing countries, formalization has failed to foster development and welfare for vulnerable groups. Excessive focus on legal reforms, expressed in indicators like the 'Doing Business' Report, show no correlation at all with the high levels of informal work experienced in the world. International organizations need to consider the context in which legal reforms are proposed. Cultural values and social norms can influence people's lives to a much greater extent than formal institutions. This does not mean that we should abandon any kind of legal reforms; there are necessary norms, which can improve the lives of people in poverty. However, before looking into legal reforms as the solution to the problems of every society, we should look into the reasons why people act in the way they do.

References

Accion Social. 2009. Programa de Atencion Inicial en Generacion de Ingresos PAI-GI. Bogotá.

Baier, M. 2008. 'Norms and rules governing the preparedness for oil catastrophes at sea', in Hydén, H.K. and Wickenberg, P. (eds) *Contributions in Sociology of Law: Remarks from a Swedish Horizon.* Lund: Lund University.

Bourdieu, P. 1987. 'The force of law: towards a sociology of the juridical field', *Hastings Law Journal* 38, 814–53.

Carothers, T. 1998. 'The Rule of Law Revival', *Foreign Affairs* 95.

Carothers, T. (ed.). 2006. *Promoting the Rule of Law Abroad: In Search of Knowledge*. Washington DC.

Castells, M. and Portes, A. 1989. 'World Underneath: The Origins, Dynamics and Effects of the Informal Economy', in Portes, A., Castells, M. and Benton, L.A. (eds) *The Informal Economy: Studies in Advanced and Less Developed Countries.* Baltimore: John Hopkins University Press.

Chen, M. 2007. 'Rethinking the Informal Economy: Linkages with the Formal Economy and the Formal Regulatory Environment', *DESA Working Paper* No. 46.

CLEP. 2008. *Making the Law Work for Everyone*. New York: UN Commission on Legal Empowerment of the Poor.

Coase, R.H. 1960. 'The Problem of Social Cost', *Journal of Law and Economics*, 3.

Cooter, R.D. 2000. *Do Good Laws Make Good Citizens? An Economic Analysis of Internalized Norms*, available at: http://works.bepress.com/robert_cooter/10.

Davis, K. 2010. 'Legal Universalism: Persistent Objections', *University of Toronto Law Journal*.

Davis, K. and Trebilcock, M. 2008. 'The Relationship Between Law and Development: Optimists versus Skeptics', *American Journal of Comparative Law*.

Davis, L. and North, D. 1971. *Institutional Change and American Economic Growth*. New York: Cambridge University Press.

De Soto, H. 1989. *The other path: the invisible revolution in the Third World.* Hernando de Soto, in collaboration with the Instituto Libertad y Democracia; foreword by Mario Vargas Llosa; translated by June Abbott. London: Tauris.

De Soto, H. 2003. *The mystery of capital: why capitalism triumphs in the West and fails everywhere else*. Basic Books.

Doing Business. 2012. *Doing Business 2012: Doing Business in a More Transparent World*. Washington: The World Bank.

Ellickson, R. 1991. *Order without law : how neighbors settle disputes*. Harvard University Press.

Ellickson, R.C. 1999. *The Evolution of Social Norms: A Perspective from the Legal Academy*. Yale Law School.

Garay, L.J. 2010. *Resultados de la III Encuesta Nacional de Verificación de los Derechos de la Poblacón Desplazda.*

Garcia, M. 2006. 'No Sólo de Mercado Vive la Democracia', *Economía Institucional*, 8.

Golub, S. and MacQuay, K. 2001. 'Legal Empowerment: Advancing Good Governance and Poverty Reduction. Overview Report', *Law and Policy Reforms at the Asian Development Bank.* Manila: Asian Development Bank.

Grugel, J. and Piper, N. 2009. 'Do Rights Promote Development?' *Global Social Policy*, 9, 79–98.

Hydén, H. and Svensson, M. 2008. 'The Concept of Norms in Sociology of Law', *Scandinavian Studies in Law*, 53.

ILO. 2002. *Resolution concerning decent work and the informal economy*. The General Council of the International Labour Organization.

ILO. 2012. *Women and Men in the Informal Economy: Data Base*, available at www.ilo.org/global/statistics-and-databases/WCMS_179795/lang--en/index.htm.

Johansson, S. 2012. 'Institutions and norms in collaboration: Toward a framework for analysing law and normativity in inter-organizational collaboration', in Baier, M. and Åstrom, K. (eds) *Social and Legal Norms.* Ashgate.

Jütting, J. and De Laiglesia, J.R. 2009. *Is informal normal?: towards more and better jobs in developing countries*, edited by Johannes P. Jütting and Juan R. De Laiglesia, Paris, Development Centre of the Organisation for Economic Co-operation and Development.

Lund, F. and Srinivas, S. 2000. *Learning from Experience: A Gendered Approach to Social Protection for Workers in the Informal Economy,* Geneva, International Labour Organization.

Moser, C.N. 1978. 'Informal sector or petty commodity production: Dualism or independence in urban development', *World Development*, 6.

North, D.C. 1990. *Institutions, Institutional Change, and Economic Performance*. Cambridge University Press.

Ostrom, E. 2005. 'Doing Institutional Analysis: Digging Deeper than Markets and Hierarchies', in Ménard, C. & Shirley, M. (eds) *Handbook of New Institutional Economics.*

Portes, A. 1994. The Informal Economy and Its Paradoxes', in Smelser, N. and Swedberg, R. (eds) *Handbook of Economic Sociology.* London: Sage.

Posner, R.A. 2011. *Economic Analysis of Law*. Aspen Publishers.

Schneider, F. 2002. *Size and Measurement of the Informal Economy in 110 Countries around the World*. Canberra: Australian National University, Australian National Tax Centre.

Schotter, A. 1981. *The Economic Theory of Social Institutions*. New York: Cambridge University Press.

Sen, A. 1999. *Development as freedom*. New York: Knopf.

Sepulveda, L. and Syrett, S. 2007. 'Out of the shadows? Formalisation approaches to informal economic activity', *Policy & Politics*, 35, 87–104.

Siegel, S. and Veiga, M.M. 2009. 'Artisanal and small-scale mining as an extralegal economy: De Soto and the redefinition of "formalization"', *Resources Policy*, 34, 51–6.

Tokman, V.E. (ed.). 1992. *Beyond Regulation: The Informal Economy in Latin America,* Boulder, CO: Lynne Rienner Publishers.

Toye, J. 1995. 'The New Institutional Economics and its Implications for Development Theory', in Harriss, J., Hunter, J. and Lewis, C.M. (eds) *The New Institutional Economics and Third World Development*. London: Routledge.

Trubek, D. 2006. 'The Rule of Law in Development Assistance: Past, Present, and Future' in Trubek, D.M. and Santos, A. (eds) *The New Law and Economic Development.* Cambridge University Press.

Trubek, D.M. and Galanter, M. 1974. 'Scholars in Self-Estrangement: Some Reflections on the Crisis in Law and Development', *Wisconsin Law Review*, 1062–1101.

Tuomela, R. 2002. *The Philosophy of Social Practices*. Cambridge, UK: Cambridge University Press.

Tushnet, M. 1998. 'Everything Old is New Again: Early Reflections on the New Chicago School', *Wisconsin Law Review*, 579.

Vargas Falla, A.M. 2010. *Legal Empowerment in Development Programs: The Case of Internally Displaced Persons in Colombia.* Master in Development Studies, Lund University.

Williams, C.C., Round, J. and Rodgers, P. 2011. 'Explaining the Normality of Informal Employment in Ukraine: A Product of Exit or Exclusion?', *American Journal of Economics and Sociology*, 70, 729–55.

Williamson, O.E. 1985. *The Economic Institutions of Capitalism*. New York: Free Press.

Williamson, O.E. 2000. 'The New Institutional Economics: Taking Stock, Looking Ahead', *Journal of Economic Literature*, 38, 595–613.

Chapter 15
Norms and Normality – Framing Normality: An Eye-Catcher on the Swedish Labour Court[1]

Eva Schömer

One of the central questions of sociology of law is how human behaviour and law in books affect the evolution and status of living law (Hertogh, 2009). Ehrlich defines the concept of 'living law' as 'the law that dominates life itself, even though it has not been printed in legal propositions', but I find that this definition lacks substance and is merely a negative expression of what is not contained in the contents of 'living law' (Ehrlich, 1936: 493). While social sciences speak of taken-for-granted ideas about images of people and phenomena created (or re-created) by society, law rarely describes such phenomena. I will make the distinction here between questions that involve relationships about law, as is the case for research in the sociology of law, and questions that involve relationships in law, as is the case for traditional legal research. My chapter proceeds from an intersectional sociology of law perspective by attempting to explain what happens when societal norms in the labour market ('common sense') encounter law in books in the labour market, and vice versa.

Sweden is frequently described both as one of the most advanced Western countries when it comes to social and economic equality, and as one of the most segregated with respect to gender and ethnicity (Nyberg, 2008). This kind of ambiguity leads to problems when discussing ways of bringing immigrants into the Swedish labour market. In order to explore the interaction between everyday life (event) and law in books, this chapter examines some of the issues that such a situation raises when looking at multiple discrimination from the perspective of sociology of law. An investigation of this type can proceed from an intersectional perspective to analyse how judicial bodies assess everyday life. Intersectionality is an analytical tool for explaining the ways in which domination and subordination are constructed and maintained in various social contexts. The concept is based on the assumption that the experiences people have or are ascribed, in terms of access to power and societal resources, are shaped by structural power relationships and social identities (Grabham, 2009).

---

1 A similar article was published in *Retfæerd*. The publisher has agreed to the publication of this article.

This chapter begins by briefly describing the ethnicization of the Swedish labour market, including a presentation of a few central concepts. In conclusion, it proceeds (from the perspective of intersectionality and sociology of law) to analyse some Swedish Labour Court rulings that focus on multiple discrimination. Although intersectionality has been discussed since the end of 1990s, there is still a lot of discussion about how it could be used as an analytical tool. McCall writes of 'the complexity that arises when the subject of analysis expands to include multiple dimensions of social life and categories of analysis' (2005: 1773). I will use an intersectional analysis of Swedish Labour Court findings as a reflection of the interplay between everyday life (the testimony of one party) and law in books. This is how everyday life may be said to interact with law (the legal system), but it also works the other way around. Studying courtroom testimonies and the findings of judges reveals ways in which law could be used as a tool to effect social change.

A comprehensive law against discrimination

Almost half a century after the protracted integration process, and five years after the major overhaul of the Swedish concept of gender equality and integration policy, a comprehensive Discrimination Act (Swedish Code of Statutes 2008: 567, Government Bill 2007/08:95) was passed for essentially the entire public sphere: the labour market, education, labour market policy measures, starting or running a business, authorization to practise a profession, membership of certain organizations, trading in goods and services, housing, health care, social services, the social insurance system, military and civilian service, and other equivalent military training in the armed forces. The main purpose of a comprehensive law was to disentangle Sweden's anti-discrimination legislation and to incorporate the remaining EC directives in the area (Government Bill 2007/08:95 at 79–86). The law has also been described as a response to the intersectional critique of previous legislation (ibid.). The argument is often made that legislation alone cannot alter the attitudes, behaviour and social viewpoints of individuals. But some laws target social change, such as the Discrimination Act of 1 January 2009, which includes both affirmative action and prohibitions. The media and the Government have described the Act as a legislative turning point: the various anti-discrimination laws that were previously on the statute books were combined into one (Government Bill 2007/08:95). Does this mean that legislators have understood the importance of an intersectional perspective that considers gender, class, ethnicity and race? It is my ambition to illustrate how the legal system (legislator and courts) has understood the intersectional perspective in the Discrimination Act through analyses of some cases from the Swedish Labour Court.

Normalization processes: Ethnicization of the labour force

Although the concepts of multiple discrimination and intersectionality are closely related, they are by no means synonymous. The frequent confusion of the terms creates both perplexity and lack of comprehension when it comes to interpreting current phenomena from a legal point of view. Multiple discrimination involves unequal treatment based on various socially constructed categories, such as gender, transgender identity or expression, ethnicity, religion, creed, disability status and sexual orientation (Crenshaw, 1989; Williams, 1991). An intersectional perspective may also be understood as an acknowledgement that 'those who have experienced discrimination speak with a special voice to which we should listen' (Matsuda, 1987: 324). Matsuda suggests that intersectionality works by enabling scholars to 'ask the other question':

> The way I try to understand the interconnection of all forms of subordination is through a method I call "ask the other question". When I see something that looks racist, I ask "where is the patriarchy in this?" When I see something that looks sexist, I ask, "Where is the heterosexism in this?" When I see something that looks homophobic, I ask, "Where are the class interests in this?" (Matsuda, 1990: 1189)

However, the concept of multiple discrimination says nothing about how the various categories interact. Intersectionality, the effect of multiple discrimination, is an analytical tool that is used to address this issue. The concept has attracted a great deal of attention in Sweden and the other Nordic countries over the past few years as a means of identifying concurrent forms of discrimination (gender, class, race, and so on) in hierarchical social structures (Molina, 2004; de los Reyes, Molina and Mulinari, 2002) or, as Johanna Kantola and Kevät Nousiainen summarize Leslie McCall and Laurel Weldon (McCall, 2005), 'the conjuncture of social structures and not identities ... The pre-given identity categories that human rights discourse, anti-discrimination act, equality policies and institutions presume are thus rendered problematic' (Kantola and Nousiainen, 2009a).

The concept of intersectionality originated in the American anti-discrimination discourse, within which black women challenged a fairly homogeneous feminist movement by questioning the assumptions that guided privileged white women. An article by Kimberlé Crenshaw used the case of *DeGraffenreid v General Motors* to illustrate the way that black women fell outside the purview of anti-discrimination legislation (Crenshaw, 1989). The plaintiff claimed that the company had discriminated against black women. The Court ruled that women could not have been discriminated against, on the basis of either race or gender, given that nearly all the factory workers were black men and all the office workers were white women. The article had an enormous impact, particularly in British and American literature and law (Harris, 1989). It was followed by a slew of other articles demonstrating that white women were given priority, both in the anti-discrimination discourse as such and by the way in which leading white feminists ignored the interests and perspectives of black women (Frankenberg, 1993).

An intersectional perspective focuses on how vectors of gender, class, race and sexuality have pervaded the writing of black feminist scholars (Davis, 2001; Smith, 2000; Speleman, 1990; Collins, 2000). Scandinavian feminists have long turned a blind eye to black feminism on the grounds that their societies have no history of slavery or colonialism. Their focus on gender equality has neglected differences among women and/or men as such. In my view, this situation is a result of the discourse about equality that pervades Swedish and other Nordic societies. Sweden has long boasted of its high ranking when it comes to social equality. But these statements say more about formal regulations than actual conditions. Criticism of Western ethnocentric feminism has been stronger in non-Nordic countries (Mohanty, 2006; de los Reyes, 2011). From my point of view, it would be quite fruitful to apply an intersectional perspective to rulings of the Swedish Labour Court, as there is almost no critical discussion of law or its implications in a Swedish context. I will try to adapt the method that Crenshaw applied to an American case from 1977, even though the legal systems are not equivalent (the Anglo-Saxon legal system focuses on case studies). However, both systems are based on the idea that it is possible to make sense of the court's reasoning.

Sweden's first Anti-Discrimination Act took effect on 1 July 1980. Although the measure had long been called for, its ethnocentric perspective offered few benefits for immigrant women. In 1986, Woukko Knocke demonstrated that Swedish history was replete with racism and ethnocentrism (Knocke, 1986). Her article criticizes the regulation of the labour market, which is permeated by both open and covert racialization (Miles, 1993; Ålund and Schierup, 1991). Structural discrimination divided up society between the 'we' who belong and 'the others' who remain outside (deviate from) societal norms. This process is commonly characterized as 'otherization' (SOU 2006:30). For example, a group is defined on the basis of ethnic affiliation as 'other,' as opposed to the normal 'we' (SOU 2005:41). Such ideas originate in post-colonialism, which assumes a feminist perspective to examine gender against the backdrop of an historical context in which colonialism involved both economic exploitation and political domination, leading to norms that view Western ideals as true and universal, thereby calling into question any knowledge that arises elsewhere (Ahmed and de los Reyes, 2011).

The racialized labour market emerged through the interplay of societal norms and legal regulations. Various aliens' laws explicitly sought to preserve the 'uniform and unpolluted Swedish race' and its 'purity'. For instance, the 1927 law reflected racism against citizens of both southern European countries and Finland, who were regarded as undesirables in Sweden. Due to labour shortages after World War II, foreign workers were welcomed as a means of stimulating industrial growth and development. But they were subject to segregation, based on both ancestry and country of origin, which led to structural processes of domination/subordination, marginalizing mechanisms and consignment to the lowest income brackets. That set the stage for ethnicization of the labour force. Research into the 1960s and 1970s has shown that progressive voices existed but that culturalization and racialization were constantly present in perceptions of 'the others' (SOU 2005: 41; SOU 2006: 30). When non-Europeans began to arrive in Sweden in the 1980s and 1990s, and the Act on Measures against Ethnic Discrimination in Working Life was passed, racialization took new forms, while structural discrimination became more subtle and insidious. The discriminatory practices of employers and the Public Employment Service, which had previously been transparent and unapologetic, were now more devious and indirect. Knocke argues that the way structural discrimination manifested itself, both before and after legislation against ethnic and religious discrimination was passed, caused employers to resort to more sophisticated methods in order to avoid litigation and accusations of racism. For instance, alluding to Swedish social codes was a relatively simple way of excluding immigrants (SOU 2006: 60).

In the following section, I will use an intersectional method to try to understand the arguments of the Swedish Labour Court in cases with intersectional complexity, which Ferguson (2005) describes as subject positions that are fundamentally constituted by the interplay of race, gender, sexuality, class, and so on. The Swedish legal system belongs to the German-Roman legal tradition, in which law is studied in a strictly formal way, starting with the particular paragraph of law and going backwards to the Government Bills and Official Reports to give sense to the judicial decision. This means that there is almost no room for criticism of decisions; the aim of this legal tradition is to stabilize the legal system (that is, to create consensus in law). So, to shed light on intersectional complexity, I will compare the court's arguments through an intersectional analysis of cases that have intersectional complexity with arguments in a case where the complexity is based on an older Swedish woman's experience of working life. Although it could be argued, as Peter Kwan (1996) does, that intersectionality should focus on marginalized subjects, there is still intersectional complexity in this case, as it illuminates the problematic situation of the exposed position of elderly women (Zach, 2005).

Equality and gender equality

The concepts of equality and gender equality are often mixed up, but they are no more interchangeable than the concepts of multiple discrimination and intersectionality. Despite their close connection, using them synonymously creates both confusion and lack of comprehension when it comes to phenomena that require explanation and clarity.

Equality may be defined as an umbrella concept which comprises a number of different aspects of ideal human relations (Government Bill 1987/88: 105). Equality reflects the belief that all people are of equal value, regardless of gender, ethnicity, religion, social class, sexual orientation, and so on. The Swedish concept of gender equality reflects the belief that women and men should enjoy the same rights, obligations and equal opportunity to:

- hold a job that provides financial security;
- take care of a home and children; and
- participate in political, trade unions and other community activities. (Swedish Government Official Reports 1990: 41, p. 219)

While equality is a value-laden term that stresses people's similarities, gender equality is a relational concept that compares women and men as groups. The comparison proceeds from the fact that women and men are not identical, but they are different both biologically and physically. The concept of gender equality captures the highly relevant issue of whether biological differences translate into differences from a social and psychological point of view as well. Feminist research has devoted a great deal of attention to these issues. The point of distinguishing between the Swedish terms for equality and gender equality was to avoid the English and French conflict between equal and special treatment (Williams, W., 1993). Equality feminists, who advocate equal treatment of women and men, argue that women have a subordinate position in the labour market (for example, lower salaries and poorer career prospects) due to the belief that women cannot 'perform' as well as men because they are physically weaker and bear children. Thus, emphasizing the physical gender differences reinforces gender segregation and discrimination. Difference feminists, on the other hand, advocate special treatment, arguing that the differences between women and men should be the starting point. The fact that women bear children necessitates the adoption of special rules that make it easier for them to perform their particular role, such as the opportunity to take maternity leave and use the nurturing qualities that are ascribed to them by virtue of their gender. Difference feminists argue that failure to improve women's ability to stay at home and care for children shores up gender discrimination.

Although the equality principle which pervaded public debate had good intentions, the emphasis on rights – that all people are of equal value and should be treated the same – overlooked the injustices that arise when resources and opportunities vary. Having a cultural, educational or linguistic background that differs from the societal norm blocks access to influence and power, or the ability to enter the labour market.

My view is that the Swedish concept of gender equality should be seen as a response to criticism of the equality principle in view of the above considerations. Nevertheless, the concept of gender equality gave rise to other problems, because it was used primarily as a means of comparing women and men on the basis of a normality perspective, the chief aim of which was to ensure equal rights between ethnic Swedish women and all men (Schömer, 2011). One consequence has been the growing exclusion of women who are not ethnic Swedes. This has also widened the gulf between 'we Swedish women' and the 'other foreign women', further solidifying otherization (Swedish Government Official Reports 2005: 41).

One problem in the jurisprudential area is that the law *de facto* supports otherization – for example, by hiding those who are not normally part of the mainstream through setting up separate discrimination categories (that is, speaking of discrimination in terms of gender, ethnicity, disability, and so on). I would argue that this process helps to ethnically code the Swedish concept of gender equality (Lundström, 2007); women of non-Swedish ethnic origin are overlooked in the Swedish concept of gender equality debate (Schömer, 2009).

The concept of gender equality debate has focused on establishing conditions whereby women and men can enjoy the same rights, obligations and opportunity to hold a job that provides financial security, take care of a home and children, and participate in political, trade unions and other community activities. The basic perspective has always been 'Swedish'; the idea that there is a universal, 'normal' brand of justice. But the downside of the concept of normality is that it denies the validity of that which is 'different' or 'deviant'. The ideal of normality thereby proceeds from an absolute standard of hegemonic feminism (Ahmed and de los Reyes, 2011).

Prohibitions against discrimination – an intersectional analysis

From a legal perspective, studying findings is the most common way of clarifying the content of law (Bernitz, 2010). The idea of this analysis is not to present a complete general overview, but rather to illustrate the legal system and how the Swedish Labour Court rules in cases with at least two grounds of discrimination. From the perspective of sociology of law, a discussion of how law interacts with society, and the other way around, is of particular interest. In this context, law is also examined as an instrument of social change (Hydén, 2002; Mathiesen, 2005). Although I illustrate the use of law with only a few cases, I would argue that the relationship between law, justice and society could be understood through rulings in which intersectional complexity is present. As defined above, intersectionality could be seen as a tool for analysing discrimination of subordinate groups (Nash, 2008).

Subtle racism

A revealing Labour Court case, in which intersectionality was not discussed but nevertheless played an undeniable role, concerned a woman of Czech origin who was not granted an interview for a job at a car rental service (AD 2009:11). The company argued that she 'did not fit in'; she turned up 'unannounced' to ask about a job advertisement she had read. She was told that it was not the right time to talk about the job, because a car was in the process of being rented out. However, the woman ignored the remark. According to the company, she was thereby being 'disrespectful and disagreeable'. Moreover, she had not put her address and age on the application form. The plaintiff objected that she had left her business card instead. The findings of the Court stated that the information requested on the form was relevant to assessing the qualifications of applicants, and that the plaintiff's failure to provide all such information 'suggested that she was either careless or intentionally ignored the company's wishes'. Furthermore, the plaintiff claimed that she had once been a CEO, which the Court did not regard as a qualification for the job. While somewhat subtle, the intersectional aspects of the case become fairly apparent when scrutinizing the accusations of 'not fitting in' and being 'disrespectful'. From a typical Swedish point of view, it might be obvious that a remark to the effect that 'it is not the right time to discuss a job' should be respected. However, that is far from a universal principle; it is rooted in a particular cultural context. In another context, it is just 'natural' for a woman to stand her ground and show that she is genuinely interested in the job. In my view, she was stigmatized both as a foreigner who could not conduct herself 'properly' and as a rude woman who was unable to control herself and who failed to understand that she should not try to blow her own trumpet, but should be willing to cooperate. The arguments that the Labour Court accepted – that the woman 'didn't fit in' and that she had filled out the job application incorrectly – bear a strong resemblance to Knocke's definition of 'subtle racism'. Fiona Essed has pointed out the cumulative effect of racism in everyday life (1991).

Processes that normalize harassment and everyday racism

Two additional cases illustrate the Labour Court's lack of understanding or concern about the intersectional critique that people may find themselves simultaneously inside and outside mainstream society by virtue of having a job, but still being excluded because they are not ethnic Swedes. Both cases were heard under the old legislation, but are still relevant. In the first case, the employer for a large exercise association had discriminated against two hourly employed substitutes who wore hijabs, by harassing them because of their gender and religion (AD 2010: 21). The employer's representative had said that fasting was a stupid thing to do. He had gone into their dressing room several times when they were changing, even when one of them had taken off her hijab. As a result, she decided to change at home instead. He had joked about 'halal pigs', claimed that Arabic men kill unfaithful wives, and asked one of them if she thought it was right to stone adulteresses. The Court ruled that the latter incident had not been confirmed and could not be held against the employer. In reference to the preparatory work for the law, the Court conceded that harassing someone is equivalent to insulting their dignity. However, it found that petty acts, attitudes and jokes that are not directed at a particular person are not covered. In my view, the Court helped to normalize everyday racism by adopting such a stance.

The Court ruled that the women had felt discriminated against on the grounds of gender and religion, but that they had not clearly stated that the man's remarks insulted their dignity. While a joke about 'halal pigs' could be interpreted as ridicule, the fact that it was not repeated, and that the women did not object sufficiently, suggested that it was not an insult in the legal sense. The Court found that the man had demonstrably talked about fasting and the punishment of unfaithful wives. But it ruled that the law did not regard such comments as harassment.

In the manner presented above, this case can be interpreted and discussed from an intersectional point of view which examines whether it is possible to object sufficiently without crossing the line and becoming rude. Standing outside secularized Swedish society and knocking on the door to the labour market requires thorough knowledge of social codes. Sweden has a wider employment gap between natives and immigrants than any other OECD country (Riksdag and Departement, 2011). Because the women were working on a temporary basis, they were dependent on their employer and had to tiptoe about, so as not give offence. Is it reasonable to demand that a person who is subjected to insulting treatment has the courage to object so strenuously before being taken seriously? Jokes about 'halal pigs' are assuredly not funny, and especially not if one happens to be a Muslim. Under the Work Environment Act, an employer is responsible for maintaining a safe and healthy workplace. Thus, the employer should certainly see to it that employees are not the targets of jokes with racist overtones.

In the second case (AD 2011: 13), a male supervisor had made various statements and drawn a picture that discriminated against two women employees, one from the former Soviet Union and the other from Bosnia, by means of gender, ethnic and sexual harassment, as well as in retaliation. The women had criticized the supervisor several years earlier for the lack of a preventive anti-violence effort and for not ensuring that the alarm system at the assisted living facility where they worked functioned properly. The conflict escalated. The women felt that the supervisor had retaliated against them for having criticized the way he did his job. He nicknamed them the 'Eastern girls'. When one of the women was attacked by a client, the supervisor did not report it to the police or take any other action, because he 'wanted to see how long the shock would last. Women from the East can put up with a lot'. According to the woman, she asked him to address her by name but he ignored her request. With that in mind, the Labour Court ruled that the woman had been harassed due to her ethnicity, but not her gender, given the lack of evidence that the remark was an allusion to trafficking or prostitution, as the Equality Ombudsman had alleged. Nor could the Ombudsman prove that the supervisor had continued to call them the 'Eastern girls' after they objected. During the 2007 Christmas season, a picture with sexual content was put up. The picture showed a man with an erect penis. Dressed in leather and a knitted cap, he had a whip and two Christmas tree balls in his hand. The caption was, 'Are there any naughty children here?' Even though the Government's official report argued that the perspective of the abused should be considered and not the other way around (SOU 1990: 41), the Court argued that there must 'be latitude for putting up pictures of a sexual nature that are not directed at anyone in particular, even if a member of the group finds them disagreeable'. This statement is in direct opposition to the Swedish regulation on working life. According to the court, it had not been established that the picture was intended to insult either of the employees. The same picture was e-mailed to the women and others the following year. At that point, the man was acting director of the company's social psychology unit, and the women had already made it clear to him that they were offended by the picture. The Court found that the man had sexually harassed them by sending the e-mail, but that the company had not violated the prohibition against retaliation, given that e-mailing was not in itself a 'typical' retaliatory measure.

Normalization of social codes

In my view, the Court would have arrived at the same conclusion if the issues were to be considered today, while the various categories on which discrimination is based are now covered by a single law, the way in which they interact and accumulate (compounds) has not been taken into consideration. For instance, the total experience of being discriminated against as both a woman and a Muslim is more than the sum of its parts.

The case against the exercise association and the one involving the woman of Czech origin are typical of the way that incomprehension of social codes leads to exclusion, which produces the compound effect. As I see it, the Court lacks both the basis and ability to draw any other conclusions. Because the law does not mention the concept of compound effect, the Court must limit itself to the criteria that the rules specify. The Court's inability to draw any other conclusion is also evident in the case of the two women who had been offended by the expression 'Eastern girls', which they viewed as a condescending invective triggered by their previous criticism of the way the supervisor did his job. Once again, the Court is incapable of appreciating the situation in which disadvantaged members of society find themselves, even though that is one of its primary responsibilities.

Age and ethnicity

In 2010, the Labour Court drew the opposite conclusion, and ruled that an employer had discriminated against a 60-year-old ethnic Swedish woman in favour of two younger men (AD 2010:91). Although the woman was exceedingly capable and easily met the qualifications for a position as a job coach, she was not even granted an interview. There was no doubt that she was the most skilled and qualified applicant. The employer admittedly interviewed more women than men, as well as people of different ages. Because the woman was far more qualified than the younger men, however, the employer could not refute the charge that it had discriminated against her on the basis of gender and age. While the ruling was based on the new law, the reasoning itself is not very different from what might have been expected earlier. Since the case involved an ethnic Swedish woman who was considerably more qualified than the male applicants, enforcement of the first law would have produced the same outcome. Although age had not earlier been one of the categories of discrimination, it is important to keep in mind that the new Discrimination Act does not entail any significant changes without regard to protection of disadvantaged individuals. The Court stated:

> The defendant violated the prohibition against discrimination as stipulated by the law both by not interviewing the plaintiff and by not offering her employment. In determining compensation, the Court does not believe that it is either possible or meaningful to assess the two violations separately. Nor are there any grounds for giving special consideration to the fact that one violation was associated with both gender and age and the other violation with age only. (AD 2010: 91)

The statement may be interpreted as indicating that discrimination categories should not be separated unless there are special grounds for doing so, and that multiple categories should not be regarded as compound. The fact that the woman was an ethnic Swede is highly relevant (Ahmed, 2011). The Court never mentions that the woman was of Swedish origin, which suggests that her ethnicity is the normal state of affairs. I will elaborate on the complexity inherent in the various assessments of this case, as well as the case involving the woman of Czech origin, in the section below entitled 'Normalization of discrimination'.

The new law was accompanied by the adoption of discrimination compensation. The Equality Ombudsman had requested compensation of EUR 34,066.52 (SEK 300,000), but the Court awarded the plaintiff only EUR 8,516.63 (SEK 75,000). The Court stated that treating the violations separately was neither possible nor meaningful, but that they were of the same type as those that an employer may commit in connection with the right of priority to re-employment. However, the statement has no basis in either the preparatory work or the Discrimination Act (the codes). The preparatory work stresses that the measure should enable compensation to the plaintiff for having been discriminated against, and that the amount should be high enough to discourage offenders from continuing to violate the prohibitions against discrimination and retaliation, as well as encourage them to investigate and take corrective action to prevent sexual or other types of harassment. The only logical conclusion appears to be that the Court lacks the ability to assess multiple violations and compensate the plaintiff for them.

Normalization of discrimination

An intersectional perspective sheds light on the compound effect of discrimination. A woman who wears a hijab is already disadvantaged by virtue of her gender. In addition, she is at risk of being discriminated against on the basis of her ethnic background (de los Reyes and Mulinari, 2005). However, the compound effect is more than the sum of the individual parts (Ahmed and de los Reyes, 2011). The cases discussed above illustrate exclusion from the Swedish labour market due to lack of knowledge about social codes and norms.

The assumption that ethnic discrimination refers only to outward characteristics, such as wearing a hijab, promotes 'otherization' of immigrant women. This becomes obvious when comparing the case of the woman of Czech origin with that of the older ethnic Swedish woman. Arguments central to one case were accorded no significance in the other. The case of the woman of Czech origin fell outside the purview of the law on the basis that she 'did not fit in'. She had suggested that the rental car company had no choice but to hire her. Her 'non-Swedish behaviour' was equated with being 'rude'. A woman who argues and makes demands in this manner places herself in a marginal position and is not protected by the Swedish Discrimination Act (AD 1996: 41; Schömer, 1999). But the opposite reasoning was applied in the case of the two women who worked for an exercise association: they had failed to express their preferences with sufficient clarity; they should have protested sufficiently so that there was no doubt that they were offended by jokes about 'halal pigs'. Thus, social norms concerning right and wrong are essentially impossible to comprehend. As a result, exclusion becomes even stronger, since the Court appears to be clutching at straws.

In determining whether the ethnic Swedish woman had been discriminated against on the basis of age and gender, the Court ruled that there were no grounds for separating the two categories, given that she was the most qualified applicant – for instance, she had managed a business area previously. On the other hand, the Court stressed that the woman of Czech origin was not qualified merely because she had been a CEO (AD 2009: 11). While such criteria clearly vary from job to job, it is extremely difficult to navigate the Swedish labour market without contacts and knowledge of social codes; exclusion grows, and opportunities for integration into mainstream society diminish even more. Conflicting assertions that advanced qualifications are either important or irrelevant contribute to a lack of comprehension and construct walls of social norms between those who are capable of understanding the subtleties and everyone else.

The new Discrimination Act goes beyond indirect and direct discrimination to include sexual and other harassment, as well as instructions to discriminate. Furthermore, it adds age and transgender identity or expression to the possible categories on which discrimination may be based. While an important step forward, the law hardly promotes the integration of immigrants into the labour market, given that an anti-discrimination plan is not required to consider any category other than gender. Preventive efforts to break down existing norms are central to encouraging inclusion, rather than exclusion, from the labour market. Although the new law highlights the categories of gender, class, ethnicity and race, it rates them according to a descending scale. Gender is given priority, followed by ethnicity. Employees with transgender identity or expression, disabilities, sexual orientations that deviate from the norm, or who are of a certain age, are essentially shut out from the active anti-discrimination efforts (McCall, 2005).

Considering that both McCall (2005) and Sandra Fredman (2002 and 2008) argue that affirmative action is the most effective means of preventing multiple discrimination, it appears rather obvious to me that the purpose of the new law was not to change labour market conditions (Fredman, 2008). The objective was rather to comply with EU regulations and harmonize Swedish legislation with them. Fredman writes:

> Intersectionality becomes more visible through positive duties to promote equality than under a complaints led approach, since those responsible for instituting change are required to identify group inequalities and to craft solutions, rather than reacting to self-identified complaints. (Fredman, 2008)

The effect of the new Discrimination Act is that various groups of employees are juxtaposed and ranked; rather than bridging gaps and differences, it treats individuals as members of groups. Crenshaw distinguishes between structural and political intersectionality (Crenshaw, 1991). Structural intersectionality refers to the experience of discrimination, whereas political intersectionality refers to political strategies and policy documents. Affirmative action to prevent discrimination and change labour market norms is certainly not the only solution, but it represents a commitment by the Government and/or other judicial bodies to prioritize such objectives. As Kantola and Nousiainen put it, 'political institutions and structures are theorized as governing and reproducing inequalities. They can be used to remedy existing problems but also have the power to ignore and silence others' (Kantola and Nousiainen, 2009a).

An intersectional perspective on discrimination and preventive measures requires an analysis of all power relationships, both between and within groups (de los Reyes et al., 2005). In the cases discussed above, the Court did not examine the issue of power at all, even though each of them involved the relationship between an employee and her supervisor. The law's assumption that all individuals have the same opportunity to make their voices heard both marginalizes and excludes disadvantaged women. While the liberal credo that all people are equal is praiseworthy, enforcement of the law is of limited value unless actual social conditions are considered. Bhabha argues that the liberal credo and the complexity of the multicultural predicament are extremely critical:

> With a zealousness not unlike the colonial civilizing mission, the "liberal" agenda is articulated without a shadow of self-doubt, except perhaps an acknowledgement of its contingent failings in the practice of everyday life. If the failures of liberalism are always practical then what kind of perfectibility does the principle claim for itself? Such a campaigning stance obscures indigenous traditions of reform and resistance, ignores "local" leavenings of liberty, flies in the face of feminist campaigns within nationalist and anticolonial struggles, leaves out well established debates by minority intellectuals and activists concerned with the difficult "translation" of gender and sexual politics in the world of migration and resettlement. (Bhabha, 1999: 83)

A useful complement to the discourse could be to take the subordinate position of disadvantaged groups into account as a compensatory mechanism.

Gender slices through all categories, and women are still discriminated against *vis-à-vis* men in most areas (SOU 2005: 66). Nevertheless, neither women, men, people with transgender identity or expression – nor particular ethnic backgrounds, disabilities, sexual orientations or ages – are homogeneous. However, all groups have a clear need to be protected against discrimination. Prioritizing gender *vis-à-vis* ethnic minorities in deference to normalization, when carrying out preventive anti-discrimination efforts aimed at changing views of 'the others' (social norms), will generate problems if the aim is to create an inclusive labour market. In the first place, the category of gender does not comprise women or men only. In the second place, the category also includes individuals of differing ethnic backgrounds and religions and/or creeds. Moreover, women (and men) vary with respect to age and sexual orientation. Others have disabilities. Treating the categories as equivalent, while disregarding the possibility of actively preventing discrimination, widens the gaps between women, men, ethnic minorities, people with disabilities, the elderly and younger employees, and/or people with a non-heterosexual orientation. This ambiguous treatment of the various categories creates the impression that some of them have a higher priority, as a result of which they are juxtaposed and compared with each other. In line with the EU and American concept, however, Swedish courts have ignored the issue of class. Presumably, they feel that that parameter is much more difficult to define than race, religion or disability. Disadvantaged groups (subordinate classes) are among those that most deserve protection, given that they start off in an inferior position. Johanna Kantola and Kevät Nousiainen write:

> We have already hinted that anti-discrimination may not be the most suitable tool of political intersectionality. At least, it should not be the only one. If the mismatch between intersectionality and Discrimination Act is too profound, should the umbilical cord between them be cut in favour of a wider consideration of different types of policies and legal measures? (Kantola and Nousiainen, 2009b: 19)

Sweden's self-image of being a gender-equal pioneer encourages attempts to export an ideology based on the triumph of reason, secularism and enlightenment as the building blocks of the ideal of modernity (Ahmed and de los Reyes, 2011). Exporting the ideology of the concept of gender equality, however, translates the notion of women and men who are 'different' into an opposition between the 'we' who belong to the enlightened world and the 'others' who still have a long way to go. Such ideas emerge, both in interviews about the concept of gender equality with representatives of various business sectors, and in rulings of the Labour Court when it comes to employment discrimination cases. Similarly, images of the 'other (different)' women are constructed by means of markers in Labour Court rulings, such as pointing out that women who had been verbally attacked through allusions to their religion had not objected strenuously enough, whereas a woman who had not managed to fill out a form correctly was seen as 'giving the impression of either being careless or ignoring the company's preferences and information' (AD 2009: 11).

I would argue that the new Swedish Discrimination Act is the kind of mismatch that Kantola and Nousiainen (2009b) describe, and that the opportunity to create legislation that promotes equality between people of various categories in addition to gender has been squandered (Schömer, 2009). If the intent of the law had been to create genuine change, the basic perspective would not have been to juxtapose various subordinate groups as separate categories, as though they had nothing to do with each other (Scott, 1989). Instead, their inferior positions would have served as a foundation for a type of compensatory (commutative) global justice. Such an approach would pay greater attention to the compound effect of multiple discrimination. It might also justify an increase in compensatory discrimination compensation (that is, without any connection to the compensation to which an applicant is entitled after being bypassed for re-employment). Given the extensive criticism of the way in which subordinate groups are excluded from Swedish society that is evident in the preparatory work for the new law, the Court would be making a useful gesture if it assumed its responsibilities and took advantage of the options it already has for stressing that disadvantaged people must not be discriminated against. The idea was that high fines would help prevent disadvantaged people from falling victim to discrimination. Such an approach would also have improved the chances of ending social exclusion and combating the norms with which it is associated.

The Discrimination Act has clearly achieved its purpose of integrating previous legislation, but it will fail to change conditions, either in terms of active gender equality efforts (given that its fundamental assumptions are the same as in the first law from 1980 – based, again, on a hegemonic Swedish concept) or in terms of preventing or deterring discrimination, because it proceeds from the same discourse and excludes arguments that depart from the traditional Swedish view of women and men. Instead of enabling change, the law has permitted the idea that women and men are 'comparable', in order to hide differences by refusing to consider departures from the norm. This has eliminated any prospect of preventing discrimination, because it is always possible to refer to conditions outside normality, such as being too pushy and making excessively strident demands, on the one hand, and being too cautious and not forcefully objecting to attacks that allude to religion and appearance, on the other hand.

The fact that equality is a value-laden term, which stresses similarities between people, throws a smokescreen over that which is different. Thus, fear or conscious choice, when it comes to not seeing 'the others', becomes a kind of covert racism, which flourishes because nobody makes an effort to reject it (Ahmed and de los Reyes, 2011: 33). The relational term 'gender equality', which was intended to be a way out of the difficult debate about similarity, turns into a cover for discrimination of those who choose not to live in accordance with Swedish norms.

Even though Sweden is regarded as having abandoned assimilation politics, notions of difference and deviation have survived in day-to-day working life, leading to the hegemonic discourse that gender equality is a matter for ethnic Swedish women who are denied the ability to pursue a career because of men. The 'other' women gum up the works – they are seen as standing in the way of a successful gender equality effort by abstaining from the good secular life. This effort becomes fragmented, because it must also concentrate on normalizing 'deviant' women who want to wear hijabs, for instance.

One way of altering the discourse about gender equality and fairness would be to follow Chandra Talpade Mohanty's approach, and proceed from the most 'powerless groups of women in the world' in order to understand what a just and democratic society would be like. Proceeding from the most privileged groups excludes and ignores those who do not live like 'us'. 'Privilege nurtures blindness to those without the same privileges' (Mohanty, 2006: 257). Changing the starting point would thereby permit another perspective about 'the other' – perhaps a greater understanding of why people are marginalized, which might make the mechanisms of power more visible and thereby transform its use and abuse. To the extent that the gap between formal and real gender equality narrows, faith in society as democratic and inclusive will increase. Adopting such a point of departure may not be the only solution to the problems, but it reflects a genuine desire to create change for subordinate groups; allowing room in the discussion for more perspectives may alter views about similarity and fairness as well.

References

AD 1996: 41. Judgment from the Swedish Labour Court.

AD 2009: 11. Judgment from the Swedish Labour Court.

AD 2010: 21. Judgment from the Swedish Labour Court.

AD 2010: 91. Judgment from the Swedish Labour Court.

AD 2011: 13. Judgment from the Swedish Labour Court.

Ahmed, S. 2011. *Vithetens hegemoni*. Hägersten: Tankekraft.

Ahmed, S. and de los Reyes, P. 2011. *Postkolonial feminism.* Stockholm: Tankekraft.

Ålund, A. and Schierup, C.-U. 1991. *Paradoxes of multiculturalism: essays on Swedish society*. Aldershot: Avebury.

Bernitz, U. (ed.) 2010. *Finna rätt: juristens källmaterial och arbetsmetoder*. 11. uppl. Stockholm: Norstedts juridik.

Bhabha, H.K. 1999. 'Liberalism's Sacred Cow', in S. Moller Okin *Is multiculturalism bad for women?* Princeton, N.J.: Princeton University Press.

Collins, P. Hill. 2000. *Black feminist thought: knowledge, consciousness, and the politics of empowerment*. Rev. 10th anniversary edition. New York: Routledge.

Crenshaw, K. 1989. 'Demarginalizing the Intersection of Race and Sex: A Black Feminist Theory and Antiracist Politics', *The University of Chicago Legal*

Forum. Edited by the University of Chicago Law Review and Legal Forum. 139–67.

Crenshaw, K. 1991. 'Demarginalizing the Intersection of Race and Sex: A Black Feminist Critique of Antidiscrimination Doctrine, Feminist Theory and Antiracist Politics', in *Feminist Legal Theory: Readings in Law and Gender*, edited by K. Bartlett and R. Kennedy. San Francisco, CA: Westview Press, 57–80.

Davis, A. 2001 [1981]. *Women, Race and Class*. London: The Women's Press Ltd.

de los Reyes, P., Molina, I. and Mulinari, D. (eds) 2002. *Maktens (o)lika förklädnader: kön, klass & etnicitet i det postkoloniala Sverige: en festskrift till Wuokko Knocke.* Stockholm: Atlas.

de los Reyes, P. and Mulinari, D. 2005. *Intersektionalitet: kritiska reflektioner över (o)jämlikhetens landskap.* 1 uppl. Malmö: Liber.

DeGraffenreid v GM. 558 F.2d. 480 (8th Cir. 1977).

Ehrlich, Eugen and Moll, Walter Lewis (1936). *Fundamental principles of the sociology of law*. Cambridge, Mass.: Harvard University Press.

Essed, P. 1991. *Understanding everyday racism: an interdisciplinary theory*. Newbury Park: Sage.

Ferguson, A. 1998. 'Resisting the veil of privilege: building bridge identities as an ethico-politics of global feminisms', in *Hypatia* 13 (1998), 3, 95–113.

Frankenberg, R. 1993. *White women, race matters: the social construction of whiteness*. London: Routledge.

Fredman, S. 2002. 'Positive Rights and Positive Duties: Addressing Intersectionality', in *European Non-Discrimination Law: Comparative Perspectives in Multidimensional Equality Law*, edited by D. Schiek and V. Chege. London: Routledge, 73–89.

Fredman, S. 2008. *Human rights transformed: positive rights and positive duties*. Oxford: Oxford University Press.

Government Bill 2007/08:95. *Ett starkare skydd mot diskriminering*. Regeringen: Stockholm.

Grabham, E. (ed.). 2009. *Intersectionality and beyond: law, power and the politics of location.* Abingdon: Routledge-Cavendish.

Harris, A. 1989. 'Race and Essentialism in Feminist Legal Theory', *Stanford Law Review*, Vol. 42, 581–616.

Hertogh, M.L.M. (ed.). 2009. *Living law: reconsidering Eugen Ehrlich*. Oxford: Hart.

Hydén, H. 2002. *Normvetenskap*. Lund: Sociologiska institutionen, Lund University.

Kantola, J. and Nousiainen, K. 2009a. 'Institutionalizing Intersectionality in Europe', *International Feminist Journal of Politics*, 11(4). London: Routledge, 459–77.

Kantola, J. and Nousiainen, K. 2009b. *Institutionalizing Intersectionality in Europe: Legal and Political Analyses*. Paper presented at the First European

Conference on Politics and Gender, Queen's University Belfast, 21–3 January 2009.

Knocke, W. 1986. *Invandrade kvinnor i lönearbete och fack: en studie om kvinnor från fyra länder inom Kommunal- och Fabriksarbetareförbundets avtalsområde*. Stockholm: Arbetslivscentrum.

Kwan, P. 1996. 'Jeffry Dahmer and the cosynthesis of categories', *Hastings Law Journal*, Vol. 48, 1257–92.

Mathiesen, T. 2005. *Rätten i samhället: en introduktion till rättssociologin*. Lund: Studentlitteratur.

Matsuda, M. 1987. 'Looking to the bottom: critical legal studies and reparations', *Harvard Civil Rights – Civil Liberties Law Review*, Vol. 22, 323–99.

Matsuda, M. 1990. 'Beside my sister, facing the enemy: legal theory out of coalition', *Stanford Law Review*, Vol. 14, 297–300.

McCall, L. 2005. 'Intersektionalitetens komplexitet', *Kvinnovetenskaplig tidskrift*. 2005(26), 2/3, 31–56.

Miles, R. 1993. *Racism after 'race relations'*. London: Routledge.

Mohanty, C.T. 2006. *Feminism utan gränser: avkoloniserad teori, praktiserad solidaritet*. Stockholm: Tankekraft.

Molina, I. 2004. 'Intersubjektivitet och intersektionalitet för en subversiv antirasistisk feminism', *Sociologisk forskning*. 2004, 3, 19–24.

Nash, J.C. 2008. 'Re-thinking intersectionality', *Feminist Review* (Print). 2008, 89, 1–15.

Nyberg, A. 2008. *Könssegregering – Jämställt och könssegregerat*. Stockholm: Bokförlaget Premiss.

Riksdag och Departement. 2011. 19 May 2011.

Schömer, E. 1999. *Konstruktion av genus i rätten och samhället: en tvärvetenskaplig studie av svenska kvinnors rätt till jämställdhet i ett formellt jämlikt rättssystem*. Diss. Lund: Lund University.

Schömer, E. 2009. 'Genusvetenskapliga perspektiv på rätten', in *En bok om genus: nyfikenhet, nytänkande, nytta*, edited by C. Angelfors and E. Schömer. Växjö: Växjö University Press, 207–34.

Schömer, E. 2011. 'Rätten att säga det man tänker – mänskliga rättigheter i ett intersektionellt perspektiv', in *Mänskliga rättigheter i svensk belysning*, edited by A. Staaf and L. Zanderin. Malmö: Liber, 107–25.

Schömer, E. 2012. 'Multiple discrimination. A smokescreen over differences', in *Retfærd*, 2012 (35) No. 3, 29–50.

Scott, J. W. 1989. 'Deconstructing equality-versus-difference: or, the uses of post-structuralist theory for feminism', in *Applications of feminist legal theory to women's lives: sex, violence, work, and reproduction*, edited by D. Kelly Weisberg. Philadelphia: Temple University Press, 611–23.

Smith, B. 2000 (ed.). *Home girls: a Black feminist anthology*. [New ed.] New Brunswick, N.J.: Rutgers University Press.

SOU 2005: 41. 'Utredningen om makt, integration och strukturell diskriminering', de los Reyes, Paulina and Kamali, Masoud (2005), *Bortom vi och dom:*

teoretiska refl ektioner om makt, integration och strukturell diskriminering, rapport.

SOU 2006: 30. 'Utredningen om makt, integration och strukturell diskriminering (2006), *Är rätt visan rätt vis? Tio perspektiv på diskriminering av etniska och religiösa minoriteter inom rätt ssystemet.*

SOU 2006: 60. Utredningen om makt, integration och strukturell diskriminering (2006), *På tröskeln till lönearbete: diskriminering, exkludering och underordning av personer med utländsk bakgrund*, rapport.

Spelman, E.V. 1990. *Inessential woman: problems of exclusion in feminist thought.* London: The Women's Press Ltd.

Weisberg, D. Kelly (eds). 1993. *Feminist legal theory: foundations*. Philadelphia: Temple University Press.

Weldon, L.S. 2008. 'Difference and Social Structure: Iris Young's Legacy of Critical Social Theory of Gender', *Politics & Gender*, Vol. 4, 311–17.

Williams, P.J. 1991. *The alchemy of race and rights*. Cambridge, Mass.: Harvard University Press.

Williams, W.W. 1993. 'Equality's Riddle: Pregnancy and the Equal Treatment/ Special Treatment Debate', in *Feminist Legal Theory: Foundations*, edited by I. Weisberg and D. Kelly. Philadelphia: Temple University Press.

Zack, N. 2005. *Inclusive feminism: a third wave theory of women's commonality*. Lanham, MD: Rowman & Littlefield Publishers, Inc.

Chapter 16
Corruption in a Culture of Money: Understanding Social Norms in Post-Soviet Uzbekistan

Rustamjon Urinboyev and Måns Svensson

Introduction

There was a widespread euphoria in the 1990s, in Uzbekistan and the outside world, that the introduction of Western-style political institutions and legal system would promote democratic governance in post-Soviet Uzbekistan. However, many commentators now argue that Uzbekistan has made little progress in promoting the rule of law and good governance, and that many formal institutions of government have achieved merely a showcase quality. One of the main problems in this regard is corruption. According to the 2011 Corruption Perceptions Index, released annually by Transparency International, Uzbekistan is among the 10 most corrupt countries in the world (TI, 2011). Also, the control of corruption indicator of the World Bank Governance Studies shows an extremely high level of corruption in Uzbekistan and other Central Asian countries (Libman, 2008).

Understandably, post-Soviet Uzbekistan has been the subject of a great surge in academic research and writing on corruption. Much of the literature tends to concentrate on macro-level topics and state-centred approaches, focusing on kleptocratic elites in the upper echelons of the state organization, malfunctioning public administration structures, administratively commanded economic policies, inefficient post-Soviet agricultural reforms, corrupt law-enforcement agencies, and inadequate ways of dealing with corruption on the part of state authorities (Ergashev et al., 2006; Wegerich, 2006; Trevisani, 2007; Markowitz, 2008; Kandiyoti, 2007; Luong, 2004). The bulk of these authors argue that the struggles among these various state actors to gain control over scarce resources have resulted in contradictory state policies, thereby making corruption and bribery a survival strategy among ordinary citizens (including low-level officials, such as police officers). At the same time, these studies also claim that corruption and bribery may be practised by state elites themselves for more predatory reasons, which have nothing to do with survival strategies. Another portrait gleaned from scholarly works suggests that it is the penetration of clans and regional patronage networks into official structures that deplete the state's organizational powers and cause corruption and inefficiencies in the public administration system (Kubicek,

1998; Pashkun, 2003; Ilkhamov, 2007; Collins, 2006; Luong, 2002). There is also a tendency to explain the ubiquity of corruption in Uzbekistan as an outcome of its communist past (Gleason, 1995; Staples, 1993; Ergashev et al., 2006).

The conclusion of previous research seems clear: Uzbekistan is regarded by Western academics and policy makers as an authoritarian state with a strong central government that is capable of penetrating deeply into the fabric of society and controlling and moulding even the intimate aspects of social life. However, the strong focus on the state and its policies has a tendency to aggrandize the role of the state into being the prime mover of widespread corruption, as if it alone shapes the basic patterns of economic life and determines the parameters of daily social relations. With few exceptions (Abramson, 2000; Rasanayagam, 2011), scholarly literature has paid little heed to the local perceptions of moral codes and values of informal transactions in Uzbekistan, where the nitty-gritty of social relations are established and maintained through informal exchange and reciprocation of money, material goods and services.

In this study, we accept and use the working definition of 'corruption' presented by Transparency International: 'corruption is the abuse of entrusted power for private gain' (hereinafter we refer to this basic understanding of corruption as a pure Western perspective). However, when applying this concept we emphasize the need to take into consideration the critique by scholars such as Tanzi (1998: 8–10), who notes that the meaning of the word 'abuse' varies according to local legal and cultural standards (see also Werner, 2000; Gupta, 1995; Polese, 2008; Humphrey, 2002). It is also necessary to acknowledge the fact that corruption has different meanings and logic among different levels of society; and that there is a difference between large numbers of low-level officials, on the one hand, and the smaller group of state elites, on the other. It is not that corruption at higher levels of governance merely mirrors understandings of reciprocity and exchange at the grass-roots of society. However, state officials on lower levels are as dependent on informal coping strategies in order to survive as the ordinary citizens. Kandiyoti (1998 and 2007) has demonstrated that both ordinary citizens and public officials in Uzbekistan are becoming heavily reliant on informal coping strategies, due to economic stagnation and shrinkage of the welfare state in the post-Soviet period. From this perspective, there is a connection between informal transactions of everyday life and the corruption of the state.

Research aim

In this study, we focus on socio-economic structures, such as networks of reciprocity and exchange in Uzbekistan, and use ethnographic data on wedding ceremonies to show the local moral codes and values of informal transactions and how these could undermine a pure Western perspective on corruption. A theoretically founded hypothesis is that informal transactions in Uzbek society are surrounded by a different cultural meaning than in most of the Western world. If this is true, there may be reasons to re-evaluate the concept of corruption in order to reflect the morality of exchange in Uzbekistan. The intention is not to establish a causal relationship between informal transactions in weddings and corruption within the public organizations. Instead, by using ethnographic methods we aim to explore the social meaning and ordinary activities surrounding informal transactions, in order to better understand the social context forming the premises and informing the meaning of transactions in Uzbekistan. The bulk of informal transactions in everyday life are simply manifestations of deeply embedded social norms and customs in Uzbekistan. It could be described as a culture of money, characterized by networks of reciprocity and exchange.

Previous research

Corruption was studied before the fall of the Soviet Union (Zemtsov, 1991; Staples, 1993; Critchlow, 1988; Srubar, 1991; Simis, 1978), but much of that literature was entirely state-centred. Since the collapse of the Soviet Union, there has been a shift in perspectives. There is an extensive literature on corruption in post-Soviet states that focuses on the problems of using a purely Western perspective (Werner, 2000, Humphrey, 2002, Polese, 2008, Patico, 2003; Ledeneva, 1998; Wanner, 2005; Rasanayagam, 2011; Sneath, 2006; Abramson, 2000). This literature is based upon a theoretical understanding of money, gifts and the morality of exchange (Mauss, 1990; Parry and Bloch, 1989) and empirical studies concerned with different kind of transactions between citizens and state officials. At first glance, many of these transactions may come across as bribes; however, the research shows that, taking the cultural context into consideration, these transactions may very well be considered to be morally acceptable gifts. For example, Abel Polese (2008) empirically studied the context and morality of transactions between citizens and university teachers, doctors and road traffic officers in Ukraine, and concluded that corruption needs to be redefined, at least when dealing with cases in which the alleged corrupt transactions help people to survive. Caroline Humphrey (2002) describes the multi-faceted morality of different illegal transactions when giving numerous examples of custom and police officers involved in dubious transactions. It leads her to argue towards rethinking bribery in some spheres in Russia. The similarities between Russian and other post-socialist societies make it possible to generalize Humphrey's results from one country to the other. Cynthia Werner's (1997 and 2000) anthropological work on understanding and problematizing the blurred boundary between gifts and bribes in Kazakhstan has been influential in this field. Her work points to the necessity of considering whether the anti-corruption legislation promoted by powerful global organizations is appropriate for a local setting where gift exchange is an integral part of the culture. Johan Rasanayagam (2011), through an empirical case study of a local teacher, shows how this line of argumentation is also true for Uzbekistan. He even claims that the informal economy is so influential that, in a sense, it is all that there is.

In our study, we depart from the scholarly context described above. However, we are not focusing on the exchange between citizens and official representatives, but rather on the exchanges between ordinary citizens in general in their everyday life. The reason for this focus is that we want to get a deeper understanding of the social structures that underlie the blurred boundary between gifts and bribes.

There is another scientific field of importance to our study that has to do with the specific choice of weddings as the social arena that we focus on in our empirical studies. Weddings are considered to be extremely geared towards money and gift exchange, and therefore of great interest when understanding different aspects of socio-economic structures (Agadjanian and Makarova, 2003; White, 1994; Kandiyoti and Azimova, 2004; Kandiyoti, 1998; Peters, 1990; Bates, 1974; Mundy, 1995; Yalçin-Heckmann, 2001; Annaklychev, 1984; Borozna, 1984). We will elaborate on this literature in the analysis section.

Theoretical framework – contextualizing informal transactions

Although scholars studying the developing world have significantly moved away from extreme state-centred theories (Boone, 1994; Kohli, 1994; Migdal, 1994 and 1988; Shue, 1994; van Klinken and Barker, 2009), the state-centred (macro) perspective still seems to pervade academic and policy debates in the context of post-Soviet Central Asia. Much of this literature argues that the state consists of multiple actors operating at the central, regional, local, and rural or village level, and that the struggles among those actors are likely to be more crucial in determining the shape and outcomes of state policies than the struggles between the state and social forces (Ilkhamov, 2004; Adams, 2004; Kamp, 2004; McMann, 2004; Ergashev et al., 2006; Trevisani, 2007; Markowitz, 2008; Luong, 2004). However, as we will demonstrate later, there might be reasons to focus on the micro-level when studying corruption in the context of Uzbekistan, where society is mostly based on informal economy and kinship networks, and the state fails to secure the basic needs of their citizens. Therefore, in this study, to put informal transactions in a socio-legal context, we draw on Joel S. Migdal's (1994, 2001 and 1988; Migdal et al., 1994) the state-in-society approach and the concept of norms. The norm concept utilized in this chapter is consistent with the definition used by Måns Svensson (in Chapter 3 of this volume). Accordingly, norms are (a) normative statements that (b) are socially reproduced and (c) represent the individual's perception of the expectations surrounding their behaviour. Ultimately, these norm attributes form the definition of all norms (formal and informal) constituting the culture of money.

A central idea of the state-in-society approach is that the state and society are not separate entities; rather, they are intertwined entities that engage in mutually transforming interactions. According to Midgal, Kohli and Shue (1994: 2), 'states are parts of societies. States may help mould, but they are also continually moulded by, the societies within which they are embedded. Societies affect states as much as, or possibly more than, states affect societies'. From this perspective, the state is just a sprawling organization within society, and not very different from other informal or formal social organizations (such as family, clans and tribes), and coexists symbiotically with those other social organizations. States face enormous resistance from social forces in implementing their policies, since their laws and regulations must compete with the norms of other social structures that promote different versions of how people should behave. When Migdal talks about social forces, he includes both the structural dimension (for instance, clan or mosque) and the meaning (normative elements) that those structures provide to individuals. Therefore, he sees structures beneath the social forces, such as social norms and traditions, as part of the state-in-society.

There is strong support for Migdal's perspective in the field of law and economics, where Robert C. Ellickson was one of the first scholars to fully recognize the importance of socially enforced norms. Ellickson (1998: 540) states that 'much of the glue of a society comes not from law enforcement, as the classicists would have it, but rather from the informal enforcement of social mores by acquaintances, bystanders, trading partners, and others'; and he continues 'informal systems of external social control are far more important than law in many contexts, especially ones where interacting parties have a continuing relationship and little at stake' (ibid.). Social norms guide people's actions and social interaction to a greater degree than law does (Drobak, 2006). In organization theory and economics, in particular, it has been possible to demonstrate the importance of the informal norms in human behaviour. Also, Anthony Giddens' (1984) theory of structuration, and his descriptions of the relationship between micro- and macro-levels, are comparable to the ideas of Migdal and Ellickson. As Giddens claims, the micro- and macro-levels should not be treated as fundamentally parted from each other – in fact, they are interconnected and moulding one another. One of the main propositions of structuration theory is that the rules and resources drawn upon in the production and reproduction of social action are at the same time the means of system reproduction (the duality of structure) (Giddens, 1984: 19).

Armed with the state-in-society approach and the concept of norms, it could be inferred that public administration practices are not fundamentally separated from the norms of other informal structures of society. It is important to emphasize, however, that we do not attempt to show any causal relation between micro and macro structures. Rather, we want to show the importance of taking the micro-level into consideration when trying to understand corruption in non-Western societies like Uzbekistan, where society is mostly based on informal economy and kinship networks. Furthermore, we aim to enhance the understanding of such structures in Uzbekistan through our empirical example of weddings. When doing this, it is of great importance to remember the distinction between low-level officials and more predatory state elites. The arguments presented as a result of this research have stronger relevance when talking about the state-in-society than when analysing state elites. It could be stated that there is a need to distinguish between functional redistributive informal transactions and more predatory transactions where resources go from weak to strong. This is, of course, true; but, in our case it is more important to show how there are informal standards in everyday life regulating transactions of resources between citizens. If this can be shown, it is a strong indicator that there are similar informal standards regulating transactions between citizens and low-level officials that will be regarded as bribery or corruption by a pure Western perspective. These transactions are, however, accepted within society and culture as legitimate coping strategies – regardless of whether they are functional or not. It is therefore more a question of a culture of money than of corruption.

Methodology

This study is based on two periods of field research in the Oltiariq district of the Fergana region, Uzbekistan. The first field research was conducted during April–May 2009, and the second lasted for three months, during June–August 2010. The fieldsite was chosen based on contacts and available social networks. The methods employed for data collection were participant observation, informal interviews and semi-structured interview. The first author, being native Uzbek, had the advantage of knowing the language, and possessed the pre-understanding of local conditions and situation, whereas the second author, from Sweden (non-native), added to the study an external perspective. Both authors went to Uzbekistan for the first period in 2009 and stayed in the fieldsite together. The first author was alone during the second field study in 2010.

We used ethnographic methods and the case of wedding ceremonies in order to illustrate social meaning and ordinary activities surrounding informal transactions on a micro-level in Uzbekistan. During the first period, we both observed three wedding ceremonies that were hosted and attended by different social groups, ranging from local elites to ordinary farm workers. The first author observed the next three weddings during the second field period. Our observations frequently took the shape of opportunistic chats, questions that arose on the spur of the moment. The weddings took place in Oltiariq district in the Fergana region of Uzbekistan, during April 2009–August 2010. The choice of using wedding ceremonies for collecting empirical data is based on three main arguments. First, the wedding ceremonies embody authentic features of Uzbek culture: traditions, values, collectivism, age and gender hierarchies, social networks and kinship relations, central role of *mahalla* (a residential neighbourhood institution), and power and status-based relations. After independence, weddings became central occasions where the return to authentic Uzbek forms was clearly in evidence (Kandiyoti and Azimova, 2004). Second, the arrangement of a marriage in Uzbekistan is both a lengthy and a costly process, involving a complex traditional exchange of gifts and money between the in-laws. Money and gifts have a conspicuous presence during both marriage negotiations and the wedding ceremony. Hence, weddings display multivocality in the meaning of money and gift exchanges, and thereby exhibit a culture of money. Third, the wedding ceremony is the concern of the whole community, as it is arranged with the support of and resources from local society, and thereby reflects the status and social position of the families that are to be united. In this regard, the wedding institution involves both formal and informal aspects of the local community when gathering the necessary resources.

Apart from observing weddings, during the second period of fieldwork in 2010 the first author conducted five individual semi-structured interviews with the following key informants: *oqsoqol* (informal leader of *mahalla*); *rais* (formal leader of *mahalla* committee); *dasturhonchi* (women ritual specialist in *mahalla*); *ustalar* (wedding logistics coordinators in *mahalla*); and *imam* (worship leader of a mosque). Key informants were selected on the basis of their role in the community, knowledge, willingness, and communicability. The interviews were more free-flowing and focused on such questions as the role of *mahalla* and the mosque in everyday life, the importance of monetary and gift exchanges in social interactions, local traditions, rituals and norms, the arrangement of life-cycle rituals, public perceptions of social hierarchies, kinship relations and status contestations within *mahalla*, and the perceived role of the state in everyday life. We used the questions mainly as a guide, adapting questions to the pace of interview. For instance, *rais* was asked a slightly different set of questions from *dasturhonchi*. The interviews lasted for between 45 minutes and 2 hours, depending on the informant's status, location and available time. The interview with *rais* took place in his office, while the other four interviews were conducted in *choyhona* (teahouse) or in private places. To protect the anonymity of our informants, we have not mentioned their names in the text.

Empirical findings – the case of weddings in rural Fergana

Amongst numerous life-cycle rituals, *nikoh toi* (wedding ceremony) is the most central ceremony in rural Fergana, and one in which Uzbeks invest a great deal of their time, energy, resources, dreams, reputations and socio-economic status. *Nikoh toi* is often held inside the host family's home in rural Fergana. All *mahalla* residents, relatives, classmates, colleagues and friends are invited to the wedding ceremony. To turn down an invitation to a wedding is considered impolite. *Nikoh toi* is attended by, on average, approximately 200–500 guests. Men and women sit separately at different guest tables during *nikoh toi*. *Mahalla* is responsible for the organization and preparation of such life-cycle rituals.

Nikoh toi also fulfils a redistributive and a risk-reducing function in rural Fergana: it is the social norm that directs each wedding guest to contribute to the wedding with money, gifts or labour. By arranging or attending a *nikoh toi*, a household broadens its social networks and engages in reciprocal transactions, since the wedding involves a great deal of exchange and reciprocation of money and material goods within networks of kin and friendship. Consequently, such large amounts of transactions during weddings enact the ties of obligations and expectations within networks of kinship and friendship, blending the moral aspects of social relations with their material aspects.

The morality of marriage transactions in rural Fergana

The establishment of marriage relationships in rural Fergana is a lengthy and costly process. Marriage is not just a formal relationship between two young persons, but it is also an alliance between wife-takers and wife-givers that involves a life-cycle relationship. Usually the bride leaves her parents' house forever for the house of her groom. By tradition, a boy's parents should go first to the girl's family to ask for her hand in marriage. Before visiting the girl's home, the boy's family usually conducts a thorough investigation of the girl's personality and her family background by asking neighbours, *mahalla* elders, school teachers, and friends who may know the girl or her family. Since respect towards elderly people and gender hierarchies is a social norm in Uzbek society, the bride is expected to submit to the orders and wishes of her mother-in-law and groom without any objections. Therefore, the boy's family usually investigates the girl's behaviour (is she going to be a good submissive bride?), cooking skills, educational background and who is the dominant parent in the girl's family (her father or mother), and also the ancestors of the girl going back seven generations. If the girl and her family meet all these criteria, the boy's family pays a visit to the girl's family to ask for her hand in marriage. After receiving a marriage proposal from the boy's family, the girl's side investigates the boy in a similar fashion. If the girl's parents agree, the boy's family presents a white dress to the new bride's family. This pre-engagement ritual is called *oq kiydi* (white dressing). Parents often try to find a rich husband or wife for their children in order to elevate their socio-economic status in the *mahalla*. When we interviewed *oqsoqol* and *dasturhonchi*, they said that social norms regarding girls' submissive behaviour and personal qualities do not matter much in relation to girls who come from rich families. Lured by expectations of expensive *sep-sarpo* (dowry and clothing gifts), the groom's family conducts very little or no investigation into the girl's behaviour, personal qualities and family history.

After this ritual, the groom's family sends a minimum of 80 kg of refined cotton to the bride's family, and the bride's family prepares bedspreads and sitting mattresses using this cotton. A *fotiha toi* (engagement ceremony) is the next stage. Prior to the wedding, *qudalar* (wife-takers and wife-givers) agree to organize a *fotiha toi* at the wife-givers' house. On the scheduled day, respected elders, neighbours and relatives come to the wife-givers' house, and *qudalar* perform a *non sindirish* (breaking of bread), a ritual that publicly declares the engagement of the new couple. *Qudalar* also exchange gifts with each other and set the exact date of a *nikoh toi*. The *qudalar* also discuss the most controversial issue – *sep-sarpo* – during *fotiha toi*. By tradition, prior to *nikoh toi*, the bride's family sends 40 trays loaded with a variety of fruits, confectionery, nuts and cooked and baked foods to the wife-takers' family.

Since a wedding includes numerous pre- and post-wedding ceremonies, enormous financial and labour resources are expended on wedding ceremonies. Uzbek parents usually save money for wedding feast expenses, and expensive *sep-sarpo*, almost all their life. According to social norms, parents should arrange their children's weddings and provide them with a house and household goods. The groom's family provides the married couple with separate rooms in the family house or a separate house to live in. In addition, before the wedding ceremony, the groom sends the *yuk* (bride-price) to the bride's family. A *yuk* often consists of two sheep, vegetables and rice for the wedding pilaf, 100 kg of flour, 10 kg of cotton, oil and traditional clothes for the bride. In return, the bride's family should fully furnish the groom's house and provide all necessary supplies that the young couple might need during the initial years of married life. Since the failure to comply with local norms might result in indirect sanctions, such as gossip and censure in the *mahalla*, both the bride's and the groom's family often take out interest-free loans from friends and relatives to preserve their reputation and social status in the *mahalla*. In most cases, the bride's family fails to comply with local norms, due to high *sep-sarpo* costs, and in turn faces *mahalla* sanctions.

As each wedding ceremony is subject to intense public discussion and gossip in the *mahalla*, weddings are transformed into a display of a family's wealth and social status. The local norms for gift exchange and *sep-sarpo* are maintained and reproduced through heavy social interactions in the *mahalla*. Since information networks in the *mahalla* are quick and comprehensive, a person can simply elevate his or her socio-economic status in *mahalla* by expending more on wedding feasts and gift-giving than others. The bride's *sep-sarpo* plays a crucial role in this process. By tradition, several women in the *mahalla* visit the groom's house to see and assess the bride's *sep-sarpo*, and hence, they conduct the bulk of *mahalla* information exchange regarding the *sep-sarpo*. The *sep-sarpo* also has a moral dimension: by looking at the quality and size of the *sep-sarpo*, *mahalla* women judge whether or not the bride's family holds the groom in respect. As the *sep-sarpo* has both a financial and moral dimension, it also determines the nature of power relations between a bride and her mother-in-law. Usually, brides with a high-quality *sep-sarpo* are decently treated by their mother-in-law, and brides with modest *sep-sarpo* are gossiped about by their mothers-in-law and women in the *mahalla*. When talking informally, we noticed that most households, despite their limited financial resources, were committed to expend a great deal of money on *sep-sarpo* in order to keep their honour and buy decent treatment for their daughters in the groom's family and the *mahalla*.

Preliminary analysis I

Our fieldwork in rural Fergana shows that the practice of giving and taking of gifts and money has turned into institutionalized practice, in which economic and social life are permeated by large amounts of informal transactions. Networks of kinship and friendship are increasingly mobilized and tied to one another through the exchange and reciprocation of money, material goods and services. Kandiyoti and Azimova (2004) noted that weddings are occasions when alliances are cemented through the exchange of gifts, mutual help and participation in crucial phases of marriage negotiations. The concern for monetary and gift exchanges is evident in all marriage negotiations and preparations. Wedding rituals are extremely geared towards money and gift exchanges. Such aspects of weddings have been widely discussed in the anthropological, theoretical and ethnographic literature in relation to, for example, Africa, the Middle East and Caucasus (Peters, 1990; Bates, 1974; Mundy, 1995; Yalçin-Heckmann, 2001), but also by Soviet and Western ethnographers in relation to Central Asian societies (Werner, 1997; Annaklychev, 1984; Borozna, 1984; Kandiyoti and Azimova, 2004).

The specificity of wedding transactions can be seen if they are examined within the framework of gift exchange proposed by Marcel Mauss (1990). To Mauss, a distinctive aspect of a gift exchange is that it engages the person in social relations of obligation and reciprocity, and therefore there is no pure gift. In this respect, the nature of wedding transactions in rural Fergana is consistent with Mauss's argument that the wedding transactions are not a pure gift exchange, since the spontaneity of the gift seems lacking. It is closer to a social norm, in the sense that the wedding host expects some gift or cash gift from each wedding guest. As we attended several weddings in rural Fergana, we have realized that money and gift exchanges are an inalienable part of social interactions. Even though weddings involve honourable practices, such as appreciative gift-giving and fulfilling moral obligations to help family and friends, it seems that the moral aspects of social relations are blended with their material aspects. Consequently, the socialization of individuals in rural Fergana mainly takes place in an extremely monetized social environment, where individuals are bound to one another through the amount and type of (cash) gifts they exchange. This observation comes closer to Werner's (1997) description of wedding ceremonies in post-Soviet Kazakhstan. As Werner shows, despite post-Soviet economic collapse, many Kazakhs continue to expend a large amount of financial and labour resources on life-cycle rituals, since they provide a means for social networking and redistributive activities.

The quality and size of *sep-sarpo* plays a crucial role in determining one's social status in *mahalla* in relation to others. Due to the existence of strong social norms that support gift exchanges and networks of reciprocity, weddings have largely become sites of demonstrative and competitive exchanges of wealth between families and the community. This observation supports Sneath's (2006) argument that the exchange of gifts, goods and assistance can be better viewed as materializations of various types of social relations. In her study of the political economy of Azeri weddings, Yalçin-Heckmann (2001) also demonstrated that wife-takers and wife-givers used the payments and the wedding arrangements for redefining their mutual status positions.

Financial and property transactions are the glue of marriage negotiations. Even though weddings involve enormous transactions, the nature of transactions is non-commercial; instead, they are increasingly geared to displaying one's social status and power. Such features of wedding transactions represent what Gibson-Graham (1996) describes as non-capitalist economic forms. This observation may provide a starting point for us to reconsider the nature and context of other informal transactions in Uzbekistan, viewing transactions not so much as corruption and more as providing insight into the manifestations of social norms, status contestations and social hierarchies. This situation is comparable to the Russian case that Humphrey (2002: 146) describes as 'the bribe is not in essence just a payment for a commodity or service but it is also recognition of a person's socio-political, nonmarket status'.

Festivities and rituals during the wedding day

The *nikoh toi* starts at five o'clock in the morning, with a male-only event *nahor oshi* (morning *pilaf* feast) at the groom's house. An identical *nahor oshi* is also arranged at the bride's house. Joyful sounds of *karnay* and *surnay* (traditional Uzbek musical instruments) reach far from the house and signal to the whole *mahalla* that the wedding ceremony has begun. According to the social norms, each invited guest should give *toyana* (gifts, such as carpets, or cash gifts) while shaking hands with the head of the family. The value of the *toyana* depends on the type and nature of the relationship between the guest and the host household. Luxurious and cosy tables are often reserved for the people of influence, such as local government officials, police, highly educated people, successful businessmen and wealthy relatives and friends. The presence of people of influence in the wedding sends an important signal to *mahalla* that the wedding host is well-connected. Guests with lower socio-economic status and reputation are offered more modest tables. Guests leave the tables as soon as they have finished eating their *pilaf*, and the guest tables are hurriedly cleaned up to welcome new arrivals.

After the *nahor oshi*, the groom brings the bride from her house to the central mosque for a religious ritual. By tradition, during this ceremony the bride does not initially give her consent to the marriage, and the groom then gives some money to the bride's side to get her consent. Money does not fulfil an economic purpose in this case, but it is a ritual payment for the bride's consent.

The bride's arrival at the groom's house is the high point of the wedding party, as she is welcomed with joyful traditional Uzbek song and showered with sweets. The main wedding party begins with a *kelin salom* (bride's greeting) ceremony to welcome the bride to the groom's family. In this ceremony, the bride bows to greet everyone, ranging from the groom's parents to neighbours. There is a special Uzbek song for this ceremony, and the singer tells the names and types of people to whom the bride should bow a greeting. By tradition, the people who are greeted by the bride are expected to come up in person to the front and give money to the bride; in this way, the bride receives money every time she greets a guest or her husband's relatives and friends. Since brides cannot afford to buy new wedding gowns in rural Fergana, they usually rent one from local shops. The money generated from the *kelin salom* ceremony is used to pay for such rental expenses.

The visibility of the money during the wedding dance is striking; everybody, ranging from children to the elderly, dances with money in their hands. This tradition is called *pul qistirish* (giving money). The amount of money that guests give depends on the age, social status and occupation of the dancing person. By giving money, a person can pay his or her respect and express loyalty to the person who is dancing. If the dancing person is the groom's father or a local government employee or a wealthy man, a large number of guests come up to him and give money. In such cases, it is possible to see a crowd of people lined up to give money to a dancing person. This is the most central aspect of the wedding where it can be seen how social status and reputation are translated into hard cash. After observing this, it is very easy to compare one person's social status and reputation with that of others. All the money generated during the dancing is given to the singer and musicians that are playing, as payment for their efforts.

The wedding ends with a women-only ceremony called *yuz ochdi* (unveiling of the bride). During this ceremony, the bride usually wears a white handkerchief to cover her face, and the groom's nephew unveils her face afterwards. Women sing traditional songs, and the groom's side and neighbours give gifts to the bride. Shortly after this ceremony, the bride is taken by *yanga* (female relative of the bride) to the room intended for the young couple where the bride gets ready to meet the groom. A few hours later, the groom accompanied by his best man appears at the threshold of the room where the bride is waiting for the groom. To gain access to the bride's room, the groom symbolically buys the bride from the *yanga* by means of a bargain; and then the *yanga* leaves the young couple alone for the night.

Preliminary analysis II

One remarkable aspect of *nikoh toy* is that it articulates key orientations and features of various social structures towards kinship, gender roles, social inequalities and hierarchies, and the redistributive activities. In this respect, *nikoh toy* provides numerous ritual symbols through which individuals and groups can display their social status and power, and shape their relations with one another. The public acceptance of social hierarchies, status contestations and gender divisions becomes clearly articulated in *nikoh toy*. Men and women sit separated at different guest tables during the wedding. Status contestations and social hierarchies are even reflected in the placement of guests: people of influence are seated at the best tables and served more quickly than others. If people of influence dance during the wedding party, one can observe that the crowd of people hurriedly line up to give money to a dancing person. However, if the dancing person does not belong to the category of people of influence, very few people approach the dancing person with money. This is the most central aspect of the wedding that shows the importance of money as a means to display one's social status and prestige. This observation reinforces Kandiyoti and Azimova's (2004) argument that the custom and ritual in Uzbekistan became the terrain upon which changing social stratification and widening disparities in wealth and status were played out through the medium of new patterns of consumption. Although it is always risky to draw parallels between different social contexts, social hierarchies that are omnipresent in Uzbek weddings could be comparable to North West American potlatch[1] culture, where gifts are distributed according to the rank of the receiver. During the potlatch, the donor (gift-giver), by giving the gift selectively, gives expression to the esteem in which he holds each recipient with respect to every other recipient (Barnett, 1938). Thus, the selective character of the gift is indicative of esteem, and reflects a judgement of comparative social worth from the particular donor's point of view (ibid.).

Another noteworthy feature of *nikoh toy* is the high visibility of *toyana* exchanges. Each guest is expected to give carpets or cash gifts to the wedding host. Since weddings are very expensive to hold, the *toyana* considerably lessens the burden of weddings on families, particularly in impoverished rural areas. As Kandiyoti (1998) noted, such a system of social obligations was already established during the Soviet period as an important strategy for social survival. White (1994) has described a similar situation in Turkey, where weddings were sites of redistributive activity and debt exchanges.

The major item on display during the *kelin salom* and wedding dance was – money. Payments made to the bride's side during the religious ritual reveal that the meaning of a monetary transaction is deeply embedded in the cultural practices. The conspicuous presence of money during the wedding dance fulfils more ritual role and serves to enhance the reputation of both money-giver and dancing person. Such an enormous visibility of the money during the wedding dance shows the deep embeddedness of money in local culture and traditions. From this perspective, the use of money and morality of exchanges that we have observed during weddings is consistent with Parry and Bloch (1989), who argued that the meaning of goods and money is significantly determined by local culture, political use and context.

As the example of *nikoh toy* shows, money is not only the matter of business or economic activity, but it also plays a very important cultural role in Uzbekistan: it acts as a glue in social interactions and solidarity, as a means of performing traditions, as a part of a traditional dance, as a way of paying respect, and many more. Since people dance holding money, since the *kelin salom* generates money, since hands are shaken with money, since respect is translated into hard cash, the money has turned into a social phenomenon, simply a culture of money. Looking at such a central role of money and gifts in the fulfilment of rituals, it is safe to say that there are informal structures which assign ceremonial and cultural meaning to informal transactions.

1 The potlatch is a gift-giving ceremony and informal economic activity practised by indigenous peoples of the Pacific Northwest Coast of Canada and the United States.

Concluding remarks

The aim of this study is to explore the social meaning and ordinary activities surrounding informal transactions in order to better understand the social context forming the premises and informing the meaning of corruption (especially among low-level officials) in Uzbekistan. We have argued that the informal transactions are mainly manifestations of social norms, a culture of money, characterized by networks of reciprocity and exchange. We have focused on socio-economic structures and their normative elements, drawing on the state-in-society perspective and the concept of social norms as a theoretical framework. The ethnographic data on wedding ceremonies was analysed in order to describe and understand the local perceptions of moral codes and values of informal transactions.

One could argue that the connection, painted in this chapter, between social practices in weddings and corruption is too tenuous. The reader might wish that we had done some observation of actual corruption in order to note the parallels, in structure and meaning, of exchanges at weddings and corruption in public transactions; hence, demonstrating the relation, rather than surmising it. However, it is important to underline that we did not set out to prove any causal relation between (a) social norms and practices in weddings and (b) corruption. Rather, our aim was to show the underlying social norms, moral codes and local perceptions in order to describe a society where corruption occurs. In a metaphorical sense, we are more interested in examining the soil than the actual wheat.

Our results can be summarized in three points: (a) informal transactions are deeply embedded in cultural practices; (b) not all informal transactions are corrupt; and (c) (when talking about, or measuring, corruption), social norms, moral codes and local perceptions should be considered. If these are not taken into consideration, informal transactions that are not corrupt run the risk of being labelled as illicit. 'Corruption' is an overly general term, which often simply masks competing sets of rules with those of the state. Similar points have been made before by scholars such as Werner (2000), Humphrey (2002) and Polese (2008). In that sense, our research could be said to empirically support findings of previous research, calling for a more nuanced view, at grass-roots level, of informal transactions in developing countries. Our research differs in one aspect from previous research, by focusing on interactions and exchange between ordinary citizens (and not on those between citizens and state officials). By adding this perspective, we underline the importance of understanding the very culture of the society in which corruption is being discussed and/or measured.

Even though the state in Uzbekistan might look omnipotent, due to its infrastructural and coercive capacity, our fieldwork suggests that it has limited meaning in the everyday life at local level. The decline of the Soviet-type welfare state spurred the monetization of society in Uzbekistan, since the people in rural Fergana have become increasingly dependent on informal coping strategies for meeting their livelihood needs. The unrelenting increase in informal transactions during, for example, weddings (such as *toyana* and *pul qistirish*) is one illustration of a general monetization of society that gained momentum following the post-Soviet economic decline.

In the introduction of this chapter we state that we accept the definition of 'corruption' as Transparency International describes it: 'corruption is the abuse of entrusted power for private gain'. However, we also stress the need to focus on the key word 'abuse' from a sociological understanding of the specific cultural context in which corruption is viewed. It is obvious that many of the activities that are considered to be corruption, from a pure Western perspective, have little to do with abuse. Rather, informal coping strategies are incorporated into Uzbek culture as a rational way of getting things done. Hence, anti-corruption measures are not simply a matter of getting people to obey the law. It is, more importantly, about promoting socio-economic change.

References

Abramson, D.M. 2000. *Constructing Corruption: Foreign Aid, Bureaucratization, and Uzbek Social Networks*. Paper presented at Harvard University. Available at: http://turkmeny.h1.ru/cas/abramson.html [Accessed: 25 April 2011].

Adams, L. 2004. 'Cultural Elites in Uzbekistan: Ideological Production and the State', in *The Transformation of Central Asia. States and Societies from Soviet Rule to Independence*, edited by P.J. Luong. Ithaca, NY: Cornell University Press, 93–119.

Agadjanian, V. and Makarova, E. 2003. 'From Soviet Modernization to Post-Soviet Transformation: Understanding Marriage and Fertility Dynamics in Uzbekistan', *Development and Change*, 34(3), 447–73.

Annaklychev, S. 1984. 'The wedding ceremonies of Turkmen workers', in *Kinship and Marriage in the Soviet Union. Field Studies*, edited by T. Dragadze. London and Boston: Routledge and Kegan Paul, 15–39.

Barnett, H.G. 1938. 'The nature of the potlatch', *American Anthropologist*, 40(3), 349–58.

Bates, D.G. 1974. 'Normative and Alternative Systems of Marriage among the Yörük of Southeastern Turkey', *Anthropological Quarterly*, 47(3), 270–87.

Boone, C. 1994. 'States and ruling classes in postcolonial Africa: the enduring contradictions of power', in *State Power and Social Forces: Domination and Transformation in the Third World*, edited by J.S. Migdal et al. New York: Cambridge University Press, 108–40.

Borozna, N.G. 1984. 'Some features of the traditional wedding ceremony of the Uzbek-Durmen of the southern raions of Tadzhikistan and Uzbekistan', in *Kinship and Marriage in the Soviet Union. Field Studies*, edited by T. Dragadze. London and Boston: Routledge and Kegan Paul, 60–73.

Collins, K. 2006. *Clan politics and regime transition in Central Asia.* Cambridge: Cambridge University Press.

Critchlow, J. 1988. 'Corruption, Nationalism, and the Native Elites in Central Asia', *The Journal of Communist Studies*, 4(2), 142–61.
Drobak, J.N. (ed.) 2006. *Norms and the Law.* New York: Cambridge University Press.
Ellickson, R.C. 1998. 'Law and Economics Discovers Social Norms', *The Journal of Legal Studies*, 27, 537–52.
Ergashev, B., et al. 2006. 'Public Administration Reform in Uzbekistan', *Problems of Economic Transition*, 48(12), 32–82.
Gibson-Graham, J.K. 1996. *The End of Capitalism (as we knew it): A Feminist Critique of Political Economy.* Cambridge, MA: Blackwell.
Giddens, A. 1984. *The Constitution of Society.* Cambridge: Polity Press.
Gleason, G. 1995. 'Corruption, decolonization and development in Central Asia', *European Journal on Criminal Policy and Research*, 3(2), 38–47.
Gupta, A. 1995. 'Blurred boundaries: the discourse of corruption, the culture of politics, and the imagined state', *American Ethnologist*, 22(2), 375–402.
Humphrey, C. 2002. *The Unmaking of Soviet Life: Everyday Economies after Socialism.* Ithaca, NY: Cornell University Press.
Ilkhamov, A. 2004. 'The limits of centralization: regional challenges in Uzbekistan', in *The Transformation of Central Asia. States and Societies from Soviet Rule to Independence*, edited by P.J. Luong. Ithaca, NY: Cornell University Press, 159–81.
Ilkhamov, A. 2007. 'Neopatrimonialism, interest groups and patronage networks: the impasses of the governance system in Uzbekistan', *Central Asian Survey*, 26(1), 65–84.
Kamp, M. 2004. 'Between Women and the State: Mahalla Committees and Social Welfare in Uzbekistan', in *The Transformation of Central Asia: States and Societies from Soviet Rule to Independence*, edited by P.J. Luong. Ithaca: Cornell University Press, 29–58.
Kandiyoti, D. 1998. 'Rural livelihoods and social networks in Uzbekistan: Perspectives from Andijan', *Central Asian Survey*, 17(4), 561–78.
Kandiyoti, D. 2007. 'Post-Soviet institutional design and the paradoxes of the Uzbek path', *Central Asian Survey*, 26(1), 31–48.
Kandiyoti, D. and Azimova, N. 2004. 'The Communal and the Sacred: Women's World of Ritual in Uzbekistan', *Royal Anthropological Institute*, 10, 327–49.
Kohli, A. 1994. 'Centralization and powerlessness: India's democracy in a comparative perspective', in *State Power and Social Forces: Domination and Transformation in the Third World*, edited by J.S. Migdal, A. Kohli, and V. Shue. New York: Cambridge University Press, 89–107.
Kubicek, P. 1998. 'Authoritarianism in Central Asia: curse or cure?', *Third World Quarterly*, 19(1), 29–43.
Ledeneva, A. 1998. *Russia's Economy of Favors: 'Blat', Networking and Informal Exchange.* Cambridge: Cambridge University Press.
Libman, A. 2008. *The Economic Role of Public Administration in Central Asia: Decentralization and Hybrid Political Regime*: MPRA Paper No. 10940.

Available at: http://mpra.ub.uni-muenchen.de/10940/1/MPRA_paper_10940.pdf [Accessed: 15 May 2011].
Luong, P.J. 2002. *Institutional change and political continuity in post-Soviet Central Asia.* Cambridge: Cambridge University Press.
Luong, P.J. (ed.). 2004. *The Transformation of Central Asia. States and Societies from Soviet Rule to Independence.* Ithaca, NY: Cornell University Press.
Markowitz, L.P. 2008. 'Local elites, prokurators and extraction in rural Uzbekistan', *Central Asian Survey*, 27(1), 1–14.
Mauss, M. 1990 [1924]. *The Gift: Forms and Functions of Exchange in Archaic Societies.* London: Routledge.
McMann, K.M. 2004. 'The Civic Realm in Kyrgyzstan: Soviet Economic Legacies and Activists' Expectations in *The Transformation of Central Asia. States and Societies from Soviet Rule to Independence*, edited by P.J. Luong. Ithaca, NY: Cornell University Press, 213–45.
Migdal, J.S. 1988. *Strong Societies and Weak States: State-Society Relations and State Capabilities in the Third World.* Princeton, N.J.: Princeton University Press.
Migdal, J.S. 1994. 'The state in society: an approach to struggles for domination', in *State Power and Social Forces: Domination and Transformation in the Third World*, edited by J.S. Migdal et al. Cambridge and New York: Cambridge University Press, 7–36.
Migdal, J.S. 2001. *State in Society: Studying How States and Societies Transform and Constitute One Another.* Cambridge: Cambridge University Press.
Migdal, J.S., Kohli, A. and Shue, V. (eds). 1994. *State Power and Social Forces: Domination and Transformation in the Third World.* Cambridge and New York: Cambridge University Press.
Mundy, M. 1995. *Domestic Government. Kinship, Community and Polity in North Yemen.* London and New York: I.B. Tauris.
Parry, J. and Bloch, M. (eds). 1989. *Money and the Morality of Exchange.* Cambridge: Cambridge University Press.
Pashkun, D. 2003. *Structure and practice of the state administration in Uzbekistan: Discussion Paper No. 27.* Budapest: Open Society Institute.
Patico, J. 2003. 'Consuming the West but Becoming Third World: Food Import and the Experience of Russianness', *Anthropology of Eastern Europe Review*, 21(1).
Peters, E.L. 1990. *The Bedouin of Cyrenaica. Studies in Personal and Corporate Power*, edited by Jack Goody and Marx Emmanuel. New York: Cambridge University Press.
Polese, A. 2008. '"If I receive it, it is a gift; if I demand it, then it is a bribe": On the Local Meaning of Economic Transactions in Post-Soviet Ukraine', *Anthropology in Action*, 15(3), 47–60.
Rasanayagam, J. 2011. 'Informal economy, informal state: The case of Uzbekistan', *International Journal of Sociology and Social Policy*, 31(11/12), 681–96.

Shue, V. 1994. 'State power and social organization in China', in *State Power and Social Forces: Domination and Transformation in the Third World*, edited by J.S. Migdal et al., New York: Cambridge University Press, 65–88.

Simis, K. 1978. 'The machinery of corruption in the Soviet Union', *Survey*, 23(4), 35–55.

Sneath, D. 2006. 'Transacting and enacting: Corruption, obligation and the use of monies in Mongolia', *Ethnos*, 71(1), 89–112.

Srubar, I. 1991. 'War der Reale Sozialismus modern? Versuch einer strukturellen Bestimmung', *Kölner Zeitschrift für Soziologie und Sozialpsychologie*, 43(3), 415–32.

Staples, J. 1993. 'Soviet Use of Corruption Purges as a Control Mechanism: The Uzbekistan Case', *Past Imperfect*, 2, 29–48.

Tanzi, V. 1998. 'Corruption Around the World: Causes, Consequences, Scopes and Cures' *IMF Working Paper* (Washington DC: International Monetary Fund).

TI. 2011. *Corruption Perceptions Index 2011* [online]. Transparency International. Available at: http://cpi.transparency.org/cpi2011/ [Accessed: 23 January 2012].

Trevisani, T. 2007. 'After the Kolkhoz: rural elites in competition', *Central Asian Survey*, 26(1), 85–104.

van Klinken, G., and Barker, J. 2009. *State of Authority: State in Society in Indonesia.* Ithaca, NY: Cornell Southeast Asia Program.

Wanner, C. 2005. 'Money, morality and new forms of exchange in post-socialist Ukraine', *Ethnos*, 70(4), 515–37.

Wegerich, K. 2006. '"A little help from my friend?" Analysis of network links on the meso level in Uzbekistan', *Central Asian Survey*, 25(1–2), 115–28.

Werner, C.A. 1997. 'Women and the Art of Household Networking in Rural Kazakstan', *The Islamic Quarterly*, XLI(1), 52–68.

Werner, C.A. 2000. 'Gifts, Bribes, and Development in Post-Soviet Kazakstan', *Human Organization*, 59(1), 11–22.

White, J.B. 1994. *Money makes us relatives: Women's labor in urban Turkey.* Austin: University of Texas Press.

Yalçin-Heckmann, L. 2001. 'The political economy of an Azeri wedding', *Max Planck Institute for Social Anthropology Working Papers*.

Zemtsov, I. 1991. *Encyclopedia of Soviet life.* New Brunswick and London: Transaction Publishers.

Chapter 17
On Legal Complexity: Between Law in Books and Planning in Practice

Stefan Larsson

Introduction – law and planning

This chapter addresses the difference between the intentions of the law and its application, using mobile telephony infrastructure development in Sweden as a case study. Three possible pitfalls for policy management in general are concluded and analysed. The first pitfall deals with legal complexity, which may be a result of piecemeal changes to the governing legal bodies over a longer time and is here argued to be of relevance for issues of public participation and access to justice. Another problematic pitfall concerns when law is internally contradictory, without any clear hierarchy, which is exemplified below. The third possible pitfall, which is often a point of focus in sociology of law, concerns when extra-legal factors interfere in the legal decision-making, without this being pronounced or acknowledged. This means that economy and politics can affect the application of law, to the extent that legal security and predictability are jeopardized. These three possible pitfalls in policy represent issues of general character in the legal government of land use and spatial planning, and are here analysed from a socio-legal perspective.

The first step towards a socio-legal perspective on law follows with the quite laconic statement, 'Law is not action'. This means that not even the most succinct and clear law by necessity equals a good application, in line with the motives and purpose of the law. An environmental impact assessment (EIA), for instance, as a tool for influencing decision-making processes, is often legally regulated. The use of this tool is put down in the 'law in books', but it is the application of the legal provisions (that is, the 'law in action') that bears the true implications of environmental and other concerns that were the aim of the assessment.[1] Hence, when there is a problem with EIA, the problem is not always the EIA itself but the decision-making process which it is part of. Although one could consider the same normative duality in types of norms other than legal, which of course has been done in a number of socio-legal studies (for example, Ellickson, 1991; Svensson, 2008; or, in a digital environment, Larsson and Svensson, 2010; Larsson et al.,

---

1 The terminology is often credited to the American legal realist Roscoe Pound (cf Pound, 1910).

2012 and 2013; Svensson et al., 2014), this study's main focus lies in the internal intricacies of law, particularly in their relation to its practice.

The purpose of the chapter is to display possible pitfalls in policy management, particularly related to spatial planning, and with special attention to legal challenges that are found in its practice – that is, in the relation between law's intentions and its outcome. The example of the Swedish 3G infrastructure development and planning is used as a case study in order to pursue this purpose by investigating the policy management in this particular case. The Swedish 3G infrastructure development entailed a national infrastructure development following from a European policy and a strongly optimistic agenda at a national level which, at the same time, depended on spatial planning and handling of 3G mast-building permits by the local municipalities (Larsson, 2008a; Larsson and Emmelin, 2007). In short, and what is of relevance for a socio-legal analysis of the events, is that the four licence winning operators (out of 10 contestants) were set to develop the infrastructure from 2001 to 2003 to cover 99.98 per cent of the populated areas (PTA report of 10 March 2004). However, when the deadline was reached, the reported coverage was, at most, between 65 and 75 per cent. The responsible governing authority, the Post and Telecommunications Agency (PTA), had the mandate, through legal and other means, to impose sanctions on the operators (for example, through fines). Nevertheless, despite the fact that the coverage was not reached until 2007, no fines were imposed on the operators for failing to comply with the promises they had made in order to receive the licences. In addition, two main legislative bodies governed this infrastructure development. These events display some of the difficulties that may appear when different regulations have different backgrounds and purposes, even though they have partly overlapping addressees. Under the given purpose, the following research questions can be posed:

1. To what extent is complexity an issue in the case of relevant legislation for 3G development in Sweden?
2. To what extent does the policy that regulates the development suffer from internal contradictions?
3. To what extent can extra-legal interference explain some of the outcomes of the PTA/operators' relationship?

Before I further address the particular case of developing infrastructure for third generation mobile telephony in Sweden, the socio-legal approach needs to be outlined in a little more detail.

Theory: Socio-legal perspectives on law

Let us settle for a simplistic definition of law, stating that it is a formalized normative structure often vindicated in an authoritarian order. It can be set up to assure that proper tools are used in order to ensure that certain values, such as environmental concerns, are taken into account in a large project or undertaking of some kind, such as a national development of mobile telephony infrastructure. Law is, then, the predetermined order of ensuring the enforcement of values that otherwise might not be taken into account. Legal structures naturally vary throughout the world, but the key expectations that follow from most legal structures are predictability, non-discrimination and a non-ad hoc nature, meaning that they should apply in the same way to every new case arising from the same circumstances. Predictability, as described by the legal scholar Peczenik, is 'one of the basic values in democracy and a state governed by law', and many legal theorists hold that the norm of 'jurisdiction and the actions of public authorities in a democratic state should be predictable' (Peczenik, 1995: 89–90; see also Larsson, 2008c, 2011a and 2011c). The Norwegian sociologist of law, Vilhelm Aubert, speaks of law as something that serves to safeguard expectations, as one of five main tasks of law (1989: 62) and, as Niklas Luhmann has argued, its most important one (1972: 31 onwards; see also Larsson, 2011b).

Trubek calls for an agenda of critical social inquiry on law. By this, he calls for an analysis of the tension between 'ideals and reality' in the legal order (Trubek, 1977: 566) which, to some extent, is a similar call to the one made by Roscoe Pound much earlier regarding the difference between law in books and law in action (Pound, 1910) and one that inquires into the relations between law and society. Such a socio-legal approach reminds us here to bear in mind the difference between law and its application. A law can seem predictable and non-discriminatory in 'the books', but an empirical investigation can reveal that it is not in its application. The predictability, or lack thereof, can be related to the law's interface towards the public and, for example, citizen participation (Arnstein, 1969) and 'access to justice' (Baier, 2010; Larsson, 2013). Pound was influenced by the European socio-legal scholar, Eugene Ehrlich, who focused on the social side of law by expanding far beyond the dogmatic legal boundaries, not least in the concept of 'living law' (Ehrlich, 1913/1936). In Pound's concept of law, the idea is that there are two sides to law: one dogmatic, often written down; and one empirical, which you can only find outside the dogma – for it is the application of law, the consequence. This can be seen in relation to a theoretical viewpoint of sociology of law, where law can be found on one side and its application or consequence on the other, sometimes described in terms of an 'ought' side and an 'is' side (Svensson, 2008; Svensson and Larsson, 2009 and 2012; see also the introduction to this volume, as well as Svensson's contribution), even though the identity of sociology of law has been debated (Banakar, 2001; Dahlberg-Larsen, 2000; Mathiesen, 1998; Hydén, 1999). This relation, and the interaction of the two, goes beyond a strict, legal, dogmatic study of existing law. With this follows a critical view that takes its origin in social science, which needs to be additionally outlined, in order to make a further analysis of the Swedish case study of 3G development reliable and possible.

In other fields of socio-legal research, the American sociologist Robert Merton's functionalist theories (1938 and 1968) have been used in order to analyse consequences of legal implementation. Of particular interest here would be when law is concluded to not function well in its social context – for example, when the legal norms are ill-fitted to the social norms and the societal context that they try to regulate. For example, Larsson and Svensson (2010) have, in the field of online copyright enforcement, displayed consequences that are of direct dysfunctional character for the law. Instead of compliance, the addressees for the specific legislation use complicated technology in order to avoid enforcement. Larsson and Svensson see the explanation in a gap that is too wide between the legal and the social norms in society (see also Larsson et al., 2013). Thereby, Larsson and Svensson connect to a scholarly tradition emanating from Merton's 'theory on functions and dysfunctions of law', with significant focus on the unintended consequences of legal implementation (see, for example, Aubert, 1954; Mathiesen, 2005; Sunstein, 1994). In the governance and control over the spatial environment, the legal framework plays a significant role. How the legal provisions are manifested in the factual sense, showing the empirical side of law, is one of the important fields of study in sociology of law, not least in the field of environmental and sustainable development (Baier, 2002; Hydén, 1997 and 2004; Wickenberg et al., 2004; Larsson, 2008a).

A clear challenge for law is that its complexity may become overwhelming. In order to address this field and to break it down into understandable pieces, Peter Schuck divides legal complexity into four subcategories of density, technicality, differentiation, and indeterminacy of uncertainty (Schuck, 1992: 3). In Schuck's view, law's complexity is an 'ancient concern' that has continued to 'obsess lawyers, policymakers, social critics, editorial writers, and men and women in the street, who almost invariably condemn legal complexity in the most caustic terms' (1992: 2–3). Legal complexity is of key importance in terms of how participation works in a legal context (Baier, 2009). As mentioned, the purpose of this chapter is to focus not only on formal and instrumental challenges and pitfalls concerning environmental policy, but also on the informal consequences that have to be looked for in empirical investigations. Citizen participation partly refers to what has been described as 'access to justice', a movement that (according to Baier) has traditionally had a focus more on the formal side than the informal:

> Hitherto, participation from a socio-legal viewpoint has indeed mostly been treated with a focus on instrumental action. Whether or not a citizen has the formal possibilities to act, or has the actual possibilities to act, is still a matter of analysing citizen participation from an instrumental point of view. (Baier, 2009: 21)

The socio-legal perspective of this chapter complements the instrumental view in the sense that formal participation does not necessarily mean inclusion in practice. Where the legal dogmatic perspective gives a very clear picture of which knowledge and which factors should influence legal decision-making, the socio-legal perspective often means an examination of legal decision-making empirically in order to see if there may have been other factors, generally not voiced, that have influenced the legal decision-making (Hydén and Wickenberg, 2008; see also Larsson, 2011a). If one wants to apply this perspective to the subject of environmental impact assessment (EIA), Sager (2001) compares five large-scale Nordic projects and the role of the EIA in them. He finds that the EIA was 'neglected in the decision making process' (a tunnel project, studied by Päivö and Wallentinus, 2001), that '[i]t is unclear whether the performance of the EIA procedure influenced decision-making' (a rail-link studied by Kjellerup, 2001), and that 'regarding decisions concerning the design and implementation of the project, there is little evidence that the EIA had a significant role' (the Gardermoen project, studied by Stenstadvold, 2001). This tells us that, even though a legally regulated instrument was at hand, there were unspoken reasons for not applying it in the actual process. As a result, this chapter focuses on legally controlled decision-making in a large-scale infrastructure development, such as the one for third generation mobile telephony in Sweden. Although no EIA had to be made, the case is of interest as an example of the power struggles embedded in large-scale projects – power struggles that move below the surface of law and what is formally expressed, but still affecting the decisions taken within the project.

Background on Swedish 3G development

The development of the third generation of mobile telephony in Europe has been criticized for being subject to overbidding and for neglecting the health risks. A critical review of the development of 3G mobile telecommunications in Europe concludes that the number of firms that have introduced 3G services is much smaller than the number of firms that actually received a licence, and also that overbidding was common (Gruber, 2007). A number of telecommunication companies collapsed due, in part, to the debts that they had accumulated while acquiring the licences (Whalley and Curwen, 2006: 622). Whalley and Curwen (2006) show how rare it was for entrants to the mobile infrastructure development, new to 3G, to actually remain active in the European mobile telecommunications market. The possible health effects have been debated and protested (Drake, 2006 and 2010; Larsson, 2009 and 2013; Stilgoe, 2007), and a Danish study concludes that the majority of the population has little concern for mobile phone radiation, while a small minority is very concerned (Kristiansen et al., 2009).

The Swedish infrastructure roll out for 3G formally started in December 2000, with the PTA, the responsible governing agency, deciding on which applicants should receive licences. It essentially continued until 2007. At the time for the decision on the licence terms for the development of the 3G infrastructure, the goal of the Swedish government was to maintain Sweden's position as one of the leading nations in IT and telecommunications (SOU 1999: 85, p. 29 onwards). However, the years following the initial decision were filled with protests from people fearing radiation and from land owners that wanted to be left alone (Larsson,

2008a). Many felt they had been disregarded by the central decision to roll out an infrastructure when it was uncertain whether it would be beneficial (Emmelin and Söderblom, 2002: 35–7; Emmelin and Lerman, 2004: 85–7; Larsson, 2008: 142–3).

The agreement: The licence allocation and conditions

The reason for considering the licence allocation process here is that it offers some preconditions for understanding what part of the agreement the operators later breached and why. On 12 May 2000, the PTA invited operators to apply for a licence. The number of licences was decided in April 2000 by the board of the PTA, after Parliament had decided upon the framework of the licence process (PTSFS 2000: 5). While various other countries had an auction concerning the licences, the Swedish licences were offered in a 'beauty contest' to those who promised the highest coverage reached within the shortest time-span. The PTA regulations stated 'at the most, four licences for a national coverage according to the UMTS/IMT-2000-standard will be available' (PTSFS 2000: 5, §6). The intention seemed to be to reach the highest number of licensees, with regard to the 3G services that could then be offered from a consumer perspective, and not least with reference to achieving competition between the operators (Larsson, 2008b). Four licences were issued, valid until 31 December 2015. The selection process was divided into two steps, in which the contestants were reviewed using certain criteria. The initial evaluation of the contestants was formulated to review whether or not they had fulfilled the preconditions for the establishment of a UMTS network. This included financial capacity, technical as well as commercial feasibility, and appropriate expertise and experience (PTA, 12 May 2000: 8–9; Andersson, Hulthén and Valiente, 2005: 583). Five of the ten contestants failed to prove this.

At the second stage of the beauty contest, the operators were awarded points according to the extent and speed at which they offered coverage by the end of 2003, 2006 and 2009. Coverage was defined on the basis of three factors: proportion of population; territorial coverage; and distribution throughout Sweden. The importance of good access throughout the country regarding broadband and UMTS was stated at an early point (PTA report, 27 June 2001: 9). At the same time, the PTA did not want to put in a clause requiring too high a coverage in the licences, fearing it would discourage operators from taking part in the development of the 3G system, which was the case in the earlier application process regarding the GSM licences in the 1800 MHz spectrum (PTA report, 27 June 2001: 9). This was the reason for application criteria that required the applicant to promise such coverage, and the promise of higher coverage trumped the promise of lower.

The PTA decided that Europolitan (later Vodafone, now Telenor), Hi3G (now 3), Orange and Tele2 should each get a licence. All four undertook to cover at least 8,860,000 people by the end of 2003. These licences apply up to and including 31 December 2015 and the licence conditions applied to 31 March 2006 (PTA decision, 22 March 2001: 8). Telia became a part of the infrastructure development via collaboration with Tele2 (which obtained a licence). The three operators – Hi3G, Telenor (Europolitan at the time) and Orange – signed a deal regarding collaboration on the coverage requirements of the licence conditions. The licence conditions stated that each operator had to have 30 per cent of its own infrastructure and a maximum of 70 per cent shared coverage (PTA decision, 22 March 2001: 3.1). An estimation conducted for the PTA stated that a reasonable area coverage would be around 170,000 km², about 41 per cent of the total Swedish surface area (Björkdahl and Bohlin, 2003). Parts of the licence conditions, such as the maximum of 70 per cent shared infrastructure, followed from set values that were decided prior to the 'beauty contest', and some conditions emanated from the contest itself, such as the degree of coverage and the speed of the roll-out.

The most important licence condition declares that the licence holders, at the latest by 1 March 2004, should have verified that 8,860,000 persons in Sweden were covered by 31 December 2003 (PTA decision, 22 March 2001: 1.1.2 and 1.3.1). Regarding the starting point of a functional network, the licence holders were to make net capacity available by 1 January 2002 (PTA decision, 22 March 2001: 2). Another important aspect is that the licence conditions were in force until 31 March 2006. After this date, they could be reviewed, which also later was the case.

Findings

The findings have been categorized according to the three research questions. This means that it is the empirical work that has shaped this categorization in iteration with theory. The approach is therefore neither solely deductive nor inductive but, rather, abductive (Baier and Svensson, 2004; Svensson 2008). The following sections look at some examples, and, although the Planning and Building Act (1987: 10) ('the PBA') has been revised since the 3G infrastructure development (2010: 900), much remains the same, and the division in terms of culture and history between the PBA and the Environmental Act (1998: 808) is still valid, so the relevance of the following examples is by no means diminished.

A first possible pitfall for law: Complexity

Environmental management and planning in the Swedish 3G case is upheld by a legal system that is complex (Emmelin and Lerman, 2004). The assessment is done at different administrative levels, under several legislations tied to differently structured court hierarchies and facing different governmental and municipal authorities. The Swedish 3G infrastructure development depended on a mast-by-mast assessment tied to the building permit system at the local municipal level (Larsson, 2008a). Although this legislation is not that complex in itself, a single 3G mast site can, in addition to the trial under the municipal authority regarding a building permit under the PBA, require the trial under two regional authorities, with one being the County Administration performing an assessment under chapter 12, section 6 of the Environmental Code, and the other being the national Land Surveying Agency (LSA) performing an assessment of the site for utility easement under the Utility Easement Act. The LSA decision can be appealed to the Land Court by either the land owner or the operator; the municipal decision can be appealed to the County Administration by any concerned party for whom the decision has been negative; and the chapter 12, section 6 consultation decision can be appealed to the Environmental Court by the operators, if the site is prohibited, or by land owners if they can be found to be concerned parties.

Three different legal institutes, handled at two administrative levels, by three authorities – all with its own court hierarchy for appeal – create a complex assessment system. With the processes being run in parallel, it is hard for the entrepreneur, as well as any concerned party, to gain an overview of, and essentially comprehend, the legal system. In addition to this, it could also be considered bad resource usage of the authorities handling the case, as well as resulting overall in uncertainty in the outcome of a process, thus affecting all involved actors. The complexity of the assessment system is shown in the implementation of the 3G roll out. The solution offered by policymakers and politicians, to reduce complexity, is often the 'one-stop shop', representing an authority that would collect and coordinate all processes.

A second possible pitfall for law: Internal contradictions

Within any complex legal structure, there is a risk that internal contradictions will appear. The complexity of the spatial planning structures, and the problem of overlapping legislation based on slightly different purposes, can be illustrated by the issue of electromagnetic radiation in the Swedish 3G development and how it was handled under the Planning and Building Act (PBA), on the one side, and the Environmental Code, on the other. The PBA application of electromagnetic radiation and the fear of radiation can be illustrated by the County Administrative decision in the Aspö case of Karlskrona, in which the County Administration concluded that 'significant impact' in legal practice is regarded to mean that there must be concrete circumstances that suggest the existence of a risk of disturbance.[2] The court continued, 'the circumstance that the mobile telephony mast causes discomfort or concern for disturbances cannot be considered to be of such significant impact that is intended in chapter 3, section 2 of the PBA' (CA decision of 4 May 2006, p. 2, author's translation).

The status of the Environmental Code, when it comes to the activity of running a base station (mobile telephony mast), has been the subject of much dispute. Many building permit appeals under the PBA have been appealed with reference to the precautionary principle expressed in the Environmental Code, a demand that

2 '... betydande olägenheter ...'.

is always denied in a permit process (Larsson, 2007a, 2008b, 2009 and 2013). The municipalities can most likely apply the Environmental Code in accordance with its environmental supervision responsibility for activities in the municipalities, although not specifically in the building permit process. The case regarding this supervision was the one of the Environmental Court of Appeal, where the mast activities were up for trial in the municipality of Landskrona. The municipal environmental committee required the operators to provide a map of the location of the base stations, in line with its supervision responsibility. In order to gain the right to such a map, however, it needed to be stated that the base station activity fell under the scope of the law by being an 'environmentally hazardous activity'. The Environmental Court of Appeal also found it to be such an activity, based on the fact that it is sufficient that there is a risk of the radiation being hazardous (for instance, if a person is in close proximity to the base station antenna). Furthermore, the court stated that the fear itself, expressed as psychological or mental anxiety, was included in the Environmental Code definition of 'damage or detriment to human health' (chapter 9, sections 1 and 3 of the Environmental Code; Environmental Court of Appeal, Case no. M 7485-04, 12 October 2005).[3]

If we compare the result of the decision of the Environmental Court of Appeal (leaving aside the mental anxiety aspect), and focus on the fact that it is sufficient that the activity risks being hazardous, and so the condition in chapter 9, section 1 of the Environmental Code is fulfilled, the internal contradiction between the two legislative bodies is further emphasized. When comparing the section in the Environmental Code – defining the activities that shall be found as environmentally hazardous – and the preparatory work of the PBA – commenting on the activities that are targeted by chapter 3, section 2 of the PBA (the one with 'significant impact', today found in chapter 2, section 9 of the PBA (2010: 900)) – one sees that the formulations are similar.[4] The requirement may be lower in the Environmental Code – the impact does not have to be 'significant' – but it is still a fact that, legally, the radiation activity is found to be detrimental or hazardous under one piece of legislation (the Environmental Code) but never detrimental or hazardous under the other (the PBA). Or, to put it differently, how the radiation issue has been handled, or not handled, gives the counter-intuitive result that an environmentally hazardous activity is not found to have a significant impact on

3 '... kan medföra olägenhet ...'.

4 The formulations are not exact, but similar. The 'inconveniences' (author's translation) that can mean a 'significant impact' in the PBA are the same as the activities in chapter 9, section 1 of the Environmental Code that the Environmental Court of Appeal found the 3G mast activities to be included in. Although the latter definition also explicitly includes non-ionizing radiation, the stating of 'similar impacts' and 'similar disturbances' indicates that the activities should not be interpreted exclusively; it is the activities of this type that are hazardous.

the environment. This is a result of complex and uncoordinated legislation that is central to the Swedish spatial planning.[5]

A third possible pitfall for law: The extra-legal interference

This third example addresses the bigger picture of large-scale projects, where the problem can be that the size of the project creates a game that is 'bigger than law', letting non-legally identified values (such as national development politics and economy) affect the decision-making in – from a legal point of view – an unpredictable manner. The story of the actions between the governing authority, the PTA, and the developers of the infrastructure, the operators, is examined here in more detail in order to show the intricate game that was played to avoid the sanctions that the PTA should have imposed on the operators, if they had followed the legal provisions strictly and predictably (see also Larsson, 2008c).

The law: The Electronic Communications Act

The Electronic Communications Act covers all electronic communication networks and electronic communication services, which includes the role of the PTA's relation towards the operators, and the legal grounds for the agency actions that affect the operators.[6] The PTA may, for example, issue 'such orders and prohibitions as are necessary for a rectification to take place' when it comes to operators not fulfilling the conditions bound to the 3G licence.[7] Section 4 of the Act gives the operators a respite to correct what they have not fulfilled, on notification from the PTA. The minimum period for rectification is one month and, while the maximum time is not prescribed, the time is tied to the wording 'within a reasonable time' of section 4.[8] Such orders may, 'when there is a need for it', be combined with a fine (Government Bill 2002/03:110, s. 299). For such an order, specific legislation regarding fines is applicable (Viteslagen 1985: 206).

5 '9 kap. 1 § MB: Med miljöfarlig verksamhet avses … 3. användning av mark, byggnader eller anläggningar på ett sätt som kan medföra olägenhet för omgivningen genom buller, skakningar, ljus, joniserande eller icke-joniserande strålning eller annat liknande.' PBL prop 1985/86:1, s 484, angående 3 kap. 2 §: 'Olägenheterna kan bestå av luftföroreningar, buller, skakningar, ljus eller andra liknande störningar som inte är helt tillfälliga'.

6 The Electronic Communications Act (2003:389) came into force on 25 July 2003 (prop 2002/03:110). The act replaced the Telecommunications Act (1993:597) and the Radio Communications Act (1993:599). The Telecommunications Act was, in other words, the main legislation controlling the introduction of the 3G development in Sweden.

7 According to chapter 7 section 5 of the Electronic Communications Act.

8 'Inom skälig tid', PTA translation.

The parties: The PTA and the operators

The licence conditions in themselves did not include any sanctions for the operators if they failed to fulfil the requirements. Instead, the sanctions have a more general description in the legal provisions of the Electronic Communications Act controlling the PTA, mentioned above. When the operators started to apply for an extended time limit, the PTA turned down the requests. Orange was first to apply for an extended deadline and less coverage in August 2002, followed by Vodafone (which was the name of Europolitan, by now) in September 2002, Hi3G in November 2002, and Svenska UMTS-Licens AB (Tele2/Telia) in April 2003. The operators' requests were all denied (PTA decisions of 30 September 2002, 25 November 2002 and 14 May 2003). As a reason for the delay, the operators all pointed out that the municipal permit handling process had been slower than expected, which has been shown to be, to a large extent, a false argument (Larsson, 2008a: 125–7).

When the operators, in April 2004, were addressed with the fact that they had failed to reach the coverage condition by the deadline of 31 December 2003, the reported coverage had been at the most between 65 and 75 per cent, when it was supposed to be 99.98 per cent of the populated areas (PTA report, 10 March 2004). The operators were given 'a reasonable time' to 'voluntarily' (as expressed in the PTA decision of 17 May 2004) rectify the lack of coverage, with a referral to the preparatory works of the Electronic Communications Act (Government Bill 2002/03: 110, p. 398). The time limit for reaching the full coverage, according to the licence conditions, was extended to 1 December 2004 (that is, 11 months later than the original time limit). The PTA justified this extension of the time limit by acknowledging the operators' position that the operators' prerequisites for the construction had been changed, after the initial licence agreement, by factors outside the control of the operators. These factors were said to be a slow municipal permit process, and the fact that the assessment (from a flight hindrance and telecommunications conflict perspective) performed by the Armed Forces had, in different respects, delayed the processes (PTA decision of 17 May 2004). The PTA concluded:

> In some respects, the conditions for the company have been changed in a way that could not have been foreseen at the time for the application, and that have been outside the control of Hi3G. (PTA decision of 17 May 2004, p. 3)[9]

The same wording has been used in the decision to all four operators. The wording is interesting, especially in reference to the time acquired for the permit processes. In what way had the conditions changed? And in what way could these 'changes' not have been foreseen? Is this a legitimate reason for the coverage delay at all?

---

9 'I vissa avseenden har emellertid förutsättningarna för bolaget ändrats på sätt som inte kunnat förutses vid ansökningstillfället och som legat utanför Hi3G:s kontroll'.

To be able to answer these questions, we have to take a look at the actual roll-out, from an empirical side, which is done below.

In the time following the decision, in 28 June 2004, all operators except Orange – that is, Hi3G, Vodafone and SULAB (Tele2 and TeliaSonera) – applied for a change in the licence conditions, which mainly concerned a delay in the coverage conditions to be fulfilled by 31 December 2007 and a reduced pilot signal in the sparsely populated areas. The operators' main arguments regarding the delayed coverage were that the permit processes had taken considerably longer than expected (due to the public debate on the effects on the environment, cultural and nature values) and the concern about electromagnetic radiation (PTA decision, 7 December 2004, p. 4). Parts of the arguments from the recent postponement decision of the PTA were re-used, but with a bigger jackpot at stake (that is, more than three extra years to reach the full coverage). The PTA found that the reasons to change the licence conditions regarding the delayed coverage were not strong enough to change them.

This was partly based on a Communication from the European Commission (2002) stating the importance of predictability and stability in the regulatory environment:

> When balancing the benefits and drawbacks of a rigid application of the conditions determined by the issued 3G licences, the Commission is of the opinion that, in principle, the **licensing conditions should not be changed,** because the sector is best served by a predictable environment. Predictability allows business cases to be established in a reliable manner and to be credibly defended when accessing investment funds. (Underlining and bold letters are as in the text at European Commission (2002: 3.1) and PTA decision of 7 December 2004, p. 8)

And the Communication continues by stating that 'changes to licence conditions should be envisaged only when circumstances have changed unpredictably and, in these cases, any modification should be proportional, transparent and non-discriminatory' (European Commission (2002: 3.1) and PTA decision of 7 December 2004, p. 8). The reasons that led to a delay of six months from the PTA notice to the operators until 1 December 2004 (and 11 months from the promised reach of full coverage, according to the licence conditions) were not considered strong enough to change the licence conditions. The operators were just given a respite. The reported coverage by 1 December 2004 was, for Hi3G, 84 per cent, for Telia and Tele2, 86 per cent, and for Vodafone, 84 per cent (PTA report, 27 January 2005). The fact that the operators were given a respite nevertheless means that the PTA gave their arguments some credibility. On what empirical grounds is, however, unclear.

Hi3G and SULAB did, in late December 2004, appeal the decision (in addition to the reduced pilot signal, they had applied the decision of not extending the deadline) to the County Administrative Court (Länsrätten) on the basis that more areas of Sweden should be included in the reduced pilot signal requirements, beyond the extended time limit. The processes forced the PTA to accept a reduced pilot signal in some further areas, which was to the benefit of the operators, and the appeal was withdrawn. By January 2005, the PTA stated that, since the licence conditions had been changed (reduced requirement in the way of measuring coverage in the sparsely populated areas), the operators should have a new respite to rectify the lack of coverage. This time, the respite period was set at a month; and, by 28 February 2005, the operators should have reached the coverage of the licence conditions, or the PTA 'may issue an order', according to chapter 7, section 5 of the Electronic Communications Act, that could be combined with a fine (PTA report, 22 February 2005).

What is interesting here is that the changes of the obligations connected to the pilot signal in the rural areas of Sweden constituted a beneficial way to measure the coverage for the operators. It was this beneficial change (namely, fewer base stations required for the same degree of coverage) that gave the operators another respite, due to the 'changes of the licence conditions'. The logic here is not obvious. It is possible that the radio planning connected to these conditions demanded some extra planning time, a relocation of resources which, on the other hand, could be balanced against the fact that the operators saved up to 25 per cent (according to the PTA press release of 24 October 2005) of the infrastructure cost of the remaining parts, after the PTA decision of 7 December 2004 (when the coverage was somewhere around 80–85 per cent of the coverage requirements). The pilot signal was allowed to be decreased even more in the so-called buffer zone in October 2005 (PTA report of 22 February 2006, p. 20).[10]

So, on the one hand, when it comes to the coverage percentage, the PTA stresses the importance of predictability and no change of the coverage requirements from the original licence conditions; and, on the other hand, when it comes to, perhaps, the slightly less easily understood pilot signal issue, the PTA changes the licence conditions in favour of the operators. Instead of changing the coverage conditions, the definition of coverage is changed. What happened when the operators by 1 March 2005 reported that the lack of coverage was not rectified? In fact, SULAB had not raised the level of coverage at all between 1 December 2004 and 1 March 2005. The story told on this issue in the PTA report of 22 February 2006 stops here. Nothing is said about the order that 'may be issued' or the sanctions that could follow (see PTA report of 22 February 2006, pp. 12–13).[11]

---

10 This buffer zone consists of the area that reaches three kilometres from the boundaries of the population centres for places with more than 1,000 inhabitants, according to the Statistics Sweden, SCB, of the 31 December 2000.

11 When Hi3G and Vodafone, in June 2005, applied for the PTA to allow some of the 3G activity to be performed through an alternative 3G technology, the so called CDMA2000 in the 450 MHz band, the PTA decided to ask all operators if they could ensure the continued infrastructure development with this new technology. At the same time, the PTA decided to await these results before issuing an order combined with a sanction for the operators to rectify the lack of coverage. But why did the PTA not act during the

When the first licence condition period was due by 1 July 2006, the coverage was between 93 and 94 per cent of 8,860,000 persons. The new licence conditions were favourable for the operators. The pilot signal in the outskirts of the urban areas was lowered, rendering a higher coverage. With the lowered demands for the pilot signal, the area (considered to be) covered increased to 98 per cent. This was without any new base stations being constructed. On 9 August 2006, the PTA notified the operators when the full coverage should be reached, and the new dates were based on the operators' own estimates of when they would be ready. This means that the operators had managed to reach the end of the first licence period without completing the promised amount of coverage and without having expensive fines imposed on them by the PTA. After 1 July 2006, the coverage requirements were lowered and dependent on the operators' own estimates. The PTA had avoided heavy critique as well as being sued by other applicants that did not receive a licence. On 1 December 2006, about three years after the initial deadline for reach of coverage, the first operator (Tele2/TeliaSonera) reported to the PTA that they had reached the coverage of 8,860,000 inhabitants of Sweden, followed by the remaining two operators, Hi3G and Telenor, seven months later (PTS fact sheet of 1 June 2007: 6).

Analysis – between fixation and flexibility

The strategies behind legal construction can differ. It is not necessarily only an advantage that legal concepts remain unchanged throughout the different sections of law in a national legislation – a fact which can be illustrated by the Bürgerliches Gesetzbuch (BGB), the classic twentieth-century German civil code. When it was created, it was a reflection of the society of Bismarck's empire. The preparatory time was extensive, beginning in 1874 and finishing in 1896, with the code in force in 1900 (Tamm, 1996: 321). The BGB became famous for its systemic construction of general rules. The foundation was based on certain terms that were used consistently throughout the whole BGB. The concepts used by draftsmen – 'Verfügung', 'Vollmacht', 'Einwilligung', 'Unverzüglich' and many others – are always used in exactly the same sense. The language is complex but exact, and has been described as 'the calculating machine par excellence' (Schwarz, 1950). The BGB is not addressed to the citizen at all, but rather to the professional lawyer (Zweigert and Kötz, 1987: 149 onwards). The BGB was considered such a high standard that, for instance, the Japanese civil law was based on the German model

three months following from the reported lack of coverage by 1 March? PTA concluded, regarding NMT450 and 3G (UMTS), that there was no way to bridge the technologies without lowered quality for the consumers. For instance, there were no handsets on the market covering both technologies. The PTA turned down the request, and through this, the operators had again gained some time in the continuing reach for an adequate coverage. The decision came on 24 October 2005.

(Zweigert and Kötz, 1987: 160, 324). On the other hand – getting back to the point – the BGB has been criticized for being a too rigorous and inflexible legislation, unable to adapt to the complexities of a changing society. This critique has its base in the legal phrases of the law that had to mean the same thing in the different fields comprised by the law. The rigid and precise terms of the BGB did not easily meet with social change (Zweigert and Kötz, 1987: 158).

This example shows two things. First, it shows the rather obvious fact that legislation can be of variable quality, to better or worse handle conflicts of the regulated field. Secondly, and more importantly, it shows the dilemma of a grand unified legislative body incorporating a vast field that, on the one side, can be both predictable and lead to a more legally secure application and, on the other side, can stifle legal development, rendering it unable to adapt to the complexities of social change, which has been addressed in terms of 'path dependency' (Larsson, 2011a and 2011c). This means that one downside of fragmented legislation is that it runs the risk of being too unpredictable, even impossible to overview for ordinary individuals not educated in the legal method. The same legal phrases may come to mean different things in different legislative areas, leading to confusion for people facing the law. How the legal solution to the problem is designed has implications for the outcome of law and the legal decision-making process. In the context of the layman facing the legislation, the law can become unreachable and less understandable. This is problematic, not least from a socio-legal perspective.

RQ1: Complexity in law

Complexity in regulations may work as a threshold for public participation in its practice. Legal complexity is, as noted above by law professor Peter Schuck, of great interest to several sectors in society, and by many seen as a very problematic issue (Schuck, 1992: 2–3). Peter Schuck divides legal complexity into four subcategories: density; technicality; differentiation; and indeterminacy of uncertainty (Schuck, 1992: 3). Systems that are too fragmented and complex are difficult to overview and understand; they exclude people by their own intricacy. Swedish spatial planning is upheld by a legal system that is complex, to which the 3G case bears witness. The assessment is done at different administrative levels under several pieces of legislation tied to differently structured court hierarchies and facing different governmental and municipal authorities.

RQ2: Internal contradiction

Schuck's subcategory of 'differentiation' is closely connected to – in its worst consequences – the example of internal contradictions. These can, for example, insert unpredictability in the legal ruling. From a participative point of view, both the complexity as well as internal contradictions, shown above, of the regulations controlling the environmental management and planning are problematic, both for the public and the operators, as well as for the authorities involved. The assessments are parallel and not linked to each other formally, although the matters, from a reasonable perspective, could just as well be. Not only does the authority to contact differ, but so do both the court hierarchy and who is a concerned party.

The examples mentioned above, regarding how electromagnetic radiation should be handled, may be an example of technical rules requiring 'special sophistication or expertise on the part of those who wish to understand and apply them' (Schuck, 1992: 3). The different modes of appeal in the different types of judicial categories described regarding 3G antennas represent Schuck's subcategory of being institutionally differentiated. It can be said to contain a number of decision structures that draw upon 'different sources of legitimacy, possess different kinds of organizational intelligence, and deploy different decision processes for creating, elaborating and applying the rules' (Schuck, 1992: 3). This most certainly affects the public's participation, from a practical point of view. Even though participation is instrumentally regulated (Baier, 2009), it may, in practice, be difficult for concerned parties to actually perform these rights.

RQ3: Extra-legal interference

The third example may address the bigger picture of large-scale projects, where the problem can be that the size of the project creates a game that is 'bigger than law', letting non-legally identified values, such as national development politics and economy, affect the decision-making in a – from a legal point of view – unpredictable manner. This is a common critique in socio-legal research, alongside a realist approach, dating back to Roscoe Pound, that any legal analysis must include the 'law in action' perspective. Schuck's fourth subcategory – indeterminacy – of legal complexity relates to the third research question concerning extra-legal interference. Indeterminate rules are usually 'open-textured', flexible, multi-factored and fluid (Schuck, 1992: 4). The indeterminacy of the policies governing the responsible authority in this case has allowed for extra-legal interference to occur without repercussions. When turning to the third example (that is, the PTA and the operators' relationship), this shows the generally relevant 'bigger picture' of external values trickling into the decision-making that is presented as legally controlled and being in the vertical perspective (see also Larsson, 2008c).

When having strict and clear conditions attached to the allocated 3G licences, and a governmental authority to enforce these conditions armed with legal tools for making it possible to order substantial fines, one would think that the alternatives would be clear: either the conditions are fulfilled, or they are not fulfilled and sanctions are imposed. Although the picture is not all that simple, there are legally legitimate ways to stall the deadline as well – a certain space for actions. And some PTA actions can be explained in a more legally dogmatic perspective (for instance, giving the operators a chance to correct the lack of coverage within a 'reasonable time'), but not all of their actions. Some of the delay of the PTA enforcement seems to be without explanation in the stricter legal dogmatic perspective, and any explanation must reasonably, to a greater or lesser extent, be related to the massive changes in the market, from an IT boom in the late 1990s to the bursting of the 'IT bubble'. A strict PTA enforcement of the licence conditions would likely have risked collapsing the operators due to debts, which was the case for several operators around this time (Whalley and Curwen, 2006: 622).

The PTA is, here, the 'applier' of the legal order that describes and sets the stage for the legitimate PTA actions towards the operators. The PTA role is mainly regulated by the Electronic Communications Act (the 'ECA'). As an applier, the PTA has to follow the legal order and, if it deviates from this in some sense, it will most likely still formulate and legitimize this deviance in the manners of the legal order. The ECA sets the framework for the PTA, meaning that the PTA can have different strategies for how strictly it will control the operators, all within this framework. This is where it is reasonable to assume that both political values (advanced IT nation, development) as well as causes (such as an IT sector in a period of decline) will affect the PTA application within the legal framework. The PTA has, in other words, some strategic freedom within the legal framework, the application will be ad hoc (there is only one 3G development in Sweden) and will include non-legal aspects to a decision-making process that will be defended by legal rhetoric. This means that the actions are affected by values that are never voiced. It is in this sense that the PTA can accept both a delay in reaching coverage, while at the same time claiming that the licence conditions have not changed and blame the operators for stalling the infrastructure development by referring to the legal order. Such an analysis of the PTA/operator relationship suggests a PTA handling of the operators' responsibilities, in consensus with the operators, as two participants in a game teaming up in a way that the rules of the game do not intend them to do. The problem is that this flexibility leads to a system that is neither transparent nor predictable. If what is stated in the licence conditions is not what will later be fulfilled, the conditions are not transparent in the terms of the aforementioned Peczenik, who states that predictability is 'one of the basic values in democracy and a state governed by law' (Peczenik, 1995: 89 onwards). The licence conditions of the 3G development can also be judged in the light of the most basic principle of civil law, described by the Latin phrase '*pacta sunt servanda*' – 'agreements must be respected'.

There were three basic alternatives for the PTA to handle the operators' breach in fulfilling the licence conditions. One was the 'the hard way', meaning issuing heavy sanctions on the operators in order to make them comply with the licence conditions. Another was 'the honest way', meaning that the PTA would have confessed that the results of the so-called 'beauty contest' were not reasonable in light of the changed market conditions of 2001 and 2002, and hence allowing changes in the conditions, running the risk of being sued by other applicants as well as being criticized for not sustaining a predictable environment and transparent and non-discriminatory handling. But the PTA chose a third alternative, a middle path, the balancing act of not formally changing the licence conditions which (formally) sustain the above stated, and not imposing sanctions on the operators for their breaches which, from several aspects, informally leads to an application that is unpredictable, non-transparent and discriminatory (Larsson, 2008a). The reason that the PTA has not been more heavily criticized probably lies in the fact that the 3G development became such a costly endeavour. The disappointment, that applicants who did not receive a licence at first experienced, may somewhere along the line have been turned into relief.

Conclusions

Norms are often said to reduce complexity; but, in some cases that are displayed in this chapter, the complexity may increase, as the legal normative system presents dual or multiple legal norms that are not consistent with each other. Of course, to state the fact of norm-pluralism is common ground in sociology of law. This does, however, by no means diminish the importance of addressing legal challenges, for example, in terms of a difference between the formal statutes and the outcome of their practice. From a public participation point of view, it can be problematic for individuals to interact with a legal system that is too complex, not only in relation to spatial planning and environmental concerns. The case of mobile telephony infrastructure development in Sweden has been analysed in terms of legal complexity, internal contradictions and extra-legal interference, which all are policy-related pitfalls adding to legal uncertainty and unpredictability. An analysis of possible pitfalls in planning relevant policy holds important lessons for lawmakers, citizens and scholars, and is of relevance from a norm perspective in sociology of law. The extra-legal interference may be of the most obvious relevance when it comes to adding understanding to the relationship between legal norms as they are 'in the books' compared to their practice and outcome 'in action'. The process of enforcing law may distort the initially formulated imperative into an outcome that can be not only different but also dysfunctional in relation to the purpose of the law or policy. In the case of 3G development in Sweden, and the relationship between the operators and the governing authority, this chapter shows that the outcome can only be understood when taking into account other, for example, economic or politically influencing factors than just those of policy and the designated actions. As has been suggested in this chapter, a more systematic view of the constraints of legal steering may bring useful knowledge to a policymaking process.

References

Andersson, P., Hulthén, S. and Valiente, P. 2005. *Beauty contest licensing lessons from the 3G process in Sweden.* Telecommunications Policy 29, 577–93.

Arnstein, S.R. 1969. 'A ladder of citizen participation', *Journal of the American Planning Association* 35(4), 216–24.

Aubert, V. 1989. *Continuity and Development in Law and Society*. Oslo: Norwegian University Press.

Aubert, V. 1954. *Om straffens sosiale funksjon.* Oslo: Akad. forl.

Baier, M. 2010. 'Citizen participation in legal decision-making', in Lemann Kristiansen and Storgaard (eds) *Nordisk retssociologi. Status – aktuelle udfordringer – visioner*. Aarhus, Denmark: Jurist- og Økonomforbundets Forlag.

Baier, M. 2003. *Norm och rättsregel. En undersökning av tunnelbygget genom Hallandsåsen.* Lund: Sociologiska institutionen.

Baier, M. (ed.) 2008. *Participative aspects on law – a socio-legal perspective.* Lund University: Lund Studies in Sociology of Law.

Baier, M. and Svensson, M. 2004. 'Normforskning som abduktion', in Rejmer (ed.) *Normvetenskapliga reflektioner.* Research Report in Sociology of Law 2004, 5.

Banakar, R. 2001. 'The identity crisis of a "stepchild". Reflections on the paradigmatic deficiencies of Sociology of Law', *Retfærd* 81, No. 2.

Björkdahl, J. and Bohlin, E. 2003. *3G Network Investments in Sweden.* PTS-ER-2003:9, by IMIT & Chalmers, conducted for the PTS.

Dahlberg-Larsen, J. 2000. 'How to improve the doctrinal analysis of legal pluralism: a comparison of the legal doctrine about custom and local law in Zimbabwe and Norway', *Retfærd* 89, No. 2.

Doornbos, M. 2003. '"Good governance": The metamorphosis of a policy metaphor', *Journal of International Affairs*, 57(1), 2–17.

Drake, F. 2006. 'Mobile phone masts: protesting the scientific evidence', *Public Understanding of Science* 15, 387–410.

Drake, F. 2010. 'Protesting Mobile Phone Masts: Risk, Neoliberalism, and Governmentality', *Science Technology & Human Values* 36(4), 522–48.

Ebbesson, J. 2003. *Miljörätt.* Uppsala: Iustus Förlag AB.

Ehrlich, E. 1913/1936. *Fundamental Principles of the Sociology of Law.* Cambridge, Mass.: Harvard University Press.

Ellickson, R.C. 1991. *Order without law: how neighbours settle disputes.* Cambridge, Mass.: Harvard University Press.

Emmelin, L. and Lerman, P. 2004. *Miljöregler – Hinder för utveckling och god miljö?* Research Report 2004:9. Blekinge Institute of Technology.

Emmelin, L. and Söderblom, I. *Spelet om 3G – en förstudie av mastfrågan.* Research report no 2002:07. Karlskrona: Blekinge Institute of Technology.

European Commission. 2002. COM(2002) 0301. *Towards the Full Roll-Out of Third Generation Mobile Communications.* Communication to the Council, the European Parliament, the Economic and Social Committee and the Committee of the Regions (June 2002).

Government Bill 2002/03: 110 *Lag om elektronisk kommunikation, m.m.*

Graham J., Amos, B. and Plumptre, T. 2003. *Principles for good governance in the 21st century. Policy brief 15.* Ontario: Institute on Governance.

Gruber, H. 2007. '3G mobile telecommunications licenses in Europe: a critical review', *Info* 9(6), 35–44.

Hultkrantz, L. and Nilsson, J.-E. 2001. *Nya bud – En ESO-rapport om auktioner och upphandling*. Ds 2001: 40.
Hydén, H. 1999. 'Even a stepchild eventually grows up: On the identity of Sociology of Law', *Retfærd* 85, No. 2.
Hydén, H. 1997. 'Miljö och vetenskap – miljövetenskap?', in Hilding-Rydevik, T. (ed.) *Samspelet mark – vatten – miljö. Fysisk planering för att nå samhälleliga mål*. FRN Rapport 97: 1.
Hydén, H. 2004. 'Normativa tendenser på miljöområdet', in Wickenberg, P., Nilsson, A. and Steneroth Sillén, M. (eds) *Miljö och hållbar utveckling – samhällsvetenskapliga perspektiv från en lundahorisont*. Lund: Studentlitteratur.
Hydén, H. 2002. *Rättssociologi som rättsvetenskap*. Lund: Studentlitteratur.
Kjellerup, U. 2001. 'Horsens-Skanderborg rail-link', in Hilding-Rydevik, T. (ed.) *EIA, large development projects and decision-making in the Nordic countries*. Stockholm, Nordregio report 2001: 6.
Kristiansen, I.S., Elstein, A.S., Gyrd-Hansen, D.H., Kildemoes, W. and Nielsen, J.B. 2009. 'Radiation From Mobile Phone Systems: Is it Perceived as a Threat to People's Health?', *Bioelectromagnetics* 30, 393–401.
Larsson, S. 2006. '3G of Sweden – Technological growth and sustainability issues' in Emmelin, L. (ed.) *Effective Environmental Assessment Tools – critical reflections on concepts and practice*. Blekinge Institute of Technology Research Report 2006: 3.
Larsson, S. 2008a. *Between daring and deliberating – 3G as a sustainability issue in Swedish spatial planning*. Blekinge Institute of Technology, Licentiate Dissertation Series No. 2008: 02, School of Technoculture, Humanities and Planning.
Larsson, S. 2011a. 'Den stigberoende upphovsrätten. Om konsekvenserna av rättslig inlåsning i en digital tid', *Retfærd, Nordic Journal of Law and Justice*, 4(135): 122–46.
Larsson, S. 2008b. 'Law as a gate keeper for participation. The case of 3G infrastructure development in Sweden', in Baier, M. (ed.) *Participative aspects on law – a socio-legal perspective*. Lund Studies in Sociology of Law.
Larsson, S. 2011b. *Metaphors and Norms. Understanding Copyright Law in a Digital Society*. PhD Thesis, Lund Studies in Sociology of Law, Lund University.
Larsson, S. 2008c. 'Non-legal aspects of legally controlled decision-making – The failure of predictability in governing the 3G infrastructure development in Sweden', in Hydén, H. and Wickenberg, P. (eds) *Contributions in Sociology of Law. Remarks from a Swedish Horizon*. Lund Studies of Sociology of Law.
Larsson, S. 2009. *Problematisering av vindkraftens regelverk. En pilotstudie*, Forskningsrapport Nr. 2009:04, Rapport nr 7 från MiSt-programmet, Blekinge Tekniska Högskola.
Larsson, S. 2011c. 'The Path Dependence of European Copyright', *SCRIPT:ed. A Journal of Law, Technology & Society* 8: 8–31.

Larsson, S. 2013. 'What type of knowledge rules where? Legally regulated participation in a large-scale mobile infrastructure planning in Sweden', *Environment & Planning C: Government & Policy* advance online publication. doi:10.1068/c11305

Larsson, S. and Emmelin, L. 2007. *Sustainable development in practice: infrastructure for the third generation mobile telephone system in Sweden.* Published in the conference proceedings of IAIA07 in Seoul, Korea, 4–9 June 2007.

Larsson, S. and Svensson, M. 2010. 'Compliance or Obscurity? Online Anonymity as a Consequence of Fighting Unauthorised File-sharing', *Policy & Internet,* 2(4): 77–105.

Larsson, S., Svensson, M., de Kaminski, M., Rönkkö, K. and Alkan Olsson, J. 2012. 'Law, norms, piracy and online anonymity – Practices of de-identification in the global file sharing community', *Journal of Research in Interactive Marketing* 6(4): 260–80

Larsson, S., Svensson, M. and de Kaminski, M. 2013. 'Online piracy, Anonymity and Social Change – Innovation through Deviance', *Convergence: The International Journal of Research into New Media Technologies* 19(1): 95–114.

Larsson, S. and Åström, K. 2007. 'Spatial Planning and Sociology of Law: Sustainable development issues in constructing infrastructure for the third generation mobile telephone system in Sweden'. Paper for the Berlin 2007 International Conference: *Law and Society in the 21st Century*. Sociology of Law, Lund University.

Law, A. and McNeish, W. 2007. 'Contesting the New Irrational Actor Model: A Case Study of Mobile Phone Mast Protest', *Sociology* 41(3), 439–56.

Luhmann, N. 1972. *Rechtssoziologie.* Reinbek bei Hamburg: Rowohlt.

Mathiesen, T. 1998. 'Is it all that bad to be a stepchild? Comments on the state of Sociology of Law', *Retfærd* 83, No. 4.

Mathiesen, T. 2005. *Rätten i samhället.* Lund: Studentlitteratur.

Merton, R.K. 1938. 'Social Structure and Anomie', *American Sociological Review* 3, 672–82.

Merton, R.K. 1968. *Social Theory and Social Structure.* Enlarged ed. New York: The Free Press.

Päivö, J. and Wallentinus, H.-G. 2001. 'The Hallandsås railway tunnel project', in Hilding-Rydevik, T. (ed.) *EIA, large development projects and decision-making in the Nordic countries.* Stockholm, Nordregio report 2001: 6.

Peczenik, A. 1995. *Vad är rätt? Om demokrati, rättssäkerhet, etik och juridisk* argumentation. Fritzes: Stockholm.

Pound, R. 1910. 'Law in Books and Law in Action', *American Law Review*, 12–36.

PTA. 12 May 2000. *Inbjudan till ansökan om tillstånd att tillhandahålla nätkapacitet för mobila teletjänster enligt UMTS/IMT-2000 standard samt GSM standard i Sverige.*

PTA decision of 16 December 2000.

PTA decision of 22 March 2001.
PTA report of 27 June 2001. *Tillståndsgivningen för UMTS i Sverige.*
PTA decision of 30 September 2002.
PTA decisions of 30 September 2002, 25 November 2002 and 14 May 2003.
PTA report of 10 March 2004. *Population coverage by 31 December 2003.*
PTA decision of 17 May 2004.
PTA decision of 26 May 2004.
PTA decision of 7 December 2004.
PTA report of 27 January 2005.
PTA report of 22 February 2005.
PTA press release of 24 October 2005.
PTA report of 22 February 2006.
PTA fact sheet of 1 June 2007, PTS-F-2005: 5.
PTSFS 2000: 5, *Post- och Telestyrelsens föreskrifter om tillstånd att tillhandahålla nätkapacitet för mobila teletjänster enligt UMTS/IMT-2000-standard respektive GSM-standard* (PTSFS 2000: 5), 14 April 2000.
Sager, T. 2001. 'A planning theory perspective on the EIA', in Hilding-Rydevik, T. (ed.) *EIA, large development projects and decision-making in the Nordic countries*. Stockholm, Nordregio report 2001: 6.
Schuck, P. 1992. 'Legal complexity: Some causes, consequences, and cures', *Duke Law Journal* 41(1): 1–52.
Schwarz, A.B. 1950. *Das schweizerische Zivilgesetzbuch in der ausländischen Rechtsentwicklung*. Zürich: Schulthess.
Stenstadvold, M. 2001. 'The case of the Gardermoen project', in Hilding-Rydevik, T. (ed.) *EIA, large development projects and decision-making in the Nordic countries*. Stockholm, Nordregio report 2001:6.
Stilgoe J. 2007. 'The (co-)production of public uncertainty: UK scientific advice on mobile phone health risks', *The Public Understanding of Science* 16, 45–61.
Sunstein, C.R. 1994. 'Political Equality and Unintended Consequences', *Columbia Law Review* 94(4), 1390–414.
Svensson, M. 2008. *Sociala normer och regelefterlevnad. Trafiksäkerhetsfrågor ur ett rättssociologiskt perspektiv* [Social Norms and the Observance of Law]. Lund University, Lund Studies in Sociology of Law 28.
Svensson, M. and Larsson, S. 2012. 'Intellectual Property Law Compliance in Europe: Illegal File sharing and the Role of Social Norms', *New Media & Society*.
Svensson, M. and Larsson, S. 2009. *Social Norms and Intellectual Property. Online norms and the European legal development*. Research Report in Sociology of Law, Lund University.
Svensson, M., Larsson, S. and de Kaminski, M. 2014. 'The research bay – studying the global file sharing community', in Gallagher, W. and Halbert, D. (eds) *Intellectual Property in Context: Law and Society Perspectives on IP*. Cambridge: Cambridge University Press.

Tamm, D. 1996. *Romersk rätt och europeisk rättsutveckling*. Translated to Swedish by Claes Peterson. Stockholm: Nerenius & Santérius Förlag.

Trubek, D.M. 1977. 'Complexity and Contradiction in the Legal Order – Balbus and the Challenge of Critical Social Thought about Law', *Law & Society Review*, 11(3), 529–69.

Whalley, J. and Curwen, P. 2006. 'Third generation new entrants in the European mobile telecommunications industry', *Telecommunications Policy* 30, 622–32.

Wickenberg, P., Nilsson, A. and Steneroth Sillén, M., (eds) 2004. *Miljö och hållbar utveckling – samhällsvetenskapliga perspektiv från en lundahorisont.* Lund: Studentlitteratur.

Zweigert, K. and Kötz, H. 1987. *Introduction to comparative law*. Oxford: Clarendon Press.

Chapter 18
Studying Norms and Social Change in a Digital Age: Identifying and Understanding a Multidimensional Gap Problem

Marcin de Kaminski, Måns Svensson, Stefan Larsson, Johanna Alkan Olsson and Kari Rönkkö

Introduction

The fact that the debate concerning copyright in a digital society has been both intense and filled with polemic conflicts ever since the late 1990s makes it clear that it is a most complicated issue to solve, or even grasp. Basically, both the legal and societal discussion and development are explicitly dependent on a greater understanding of the on-going processes surrounding copyright. This presents a well-suited point of departure for research such as the one conducted within the Cybernorms research group – both in terms of providing valuable insights into the field of sociology of law when it comes to understanding how to relate to the framework provided by digitalization in general and the Internet in particular, and in terms of providing more accurate knowledge and toolsets to legislators in related fields.

Several perspectives on the issue of online copyright have been covered, such as the incompatible relationship between online behaviour and copyright regulation (Lessig, 2006 and 2008; Litman, 2006 and 2010; Morris, 2009; Vaidhyanathan, 2003), law and social norms (Altschuller and Benbunan-Fich, 2009; Feldman and Nadler, 2006; Jensen, 2003; Larsson, 2011b; Moohr, 2003; Schultz, 2006b and 2006a; Strahilevitz, 2003a and 2003b; Svensson and Larsson, 2009 and 2012; Tehranian, 2007; Wingrove, Korpas and Weisz, 2010) and the digitized era of networks, which several scholars have verified (for instance, Boyle, 2010; Jensen, 2003; Larsson, 2010; Lessig, 2008; Litman, 2006; Vaidhyanathan, 2003; Netanel, 2008). By tracking and analysing changes in legal and social norms in online environments, sociology of law can be properly equipped to face a digitalized world. This is of relevance for issues of legal enforcement in an online environment (Larsson and Svensson, 2010) that are particularly related to identification, methods of encryption and other anonymity practices (Larsson, Svensson and Kaminski, 2012; Larsson et al., 2012). The clearly observable conflicts between copyright legislation and its enforcement, on the one hand, and a seemingly non-compliant online community, on the other, will not decrease in the near future. Therefore, it is imperative to scrutinize the inter-normative relations and conflicts in order to find a working model for understanding historical, current and future developments. It is within this context that this chapter presents a practical application of a four-dimensional socio-legal model to explain one of the major contemporary fields of conflict.

This chapter collects results from five different studies, all conducted by scholars active within Cybernorms. Cybernorms is a research group founded by sociologists of law with a specific focus on exploring social and legal norm structures that appear in the wake of technological and social change. The emphasis within the group is on the gap that currently runs the risk of emerging between traditional society's rules and the social norms that are generated in connection with young net cultures. Based on the underlying understanding that the digitalization of society is producing a growing divide between legal and social norms, the Cybernorms research aims to identify and analyse norm-related conflicts between law and common online practices. The issue of file-sharing is clearly an ever-present case to illustrate these conflicts.

Therefore, the overall research question asks how a deepened and thorough understanding of the norm-related conflicts surrounding copyright and its enforcement, as well as of unauthorized file-sharing, may be used to provide a useful set of tools for dealing with the growing gap problem between legal and social norms in a digitized world.

Previous research

The literature regarding the effects of the enforcement of intellectual property, and the punishment for unauthorized file-sharing related to actual online behaviour and strategies, is contradictory. In scenario-based survey studies, Kwong and Lee (2002) suggest that laws related to unauthorized file-sharing have some impact on the downloading of CDs, which is also supported by Levin et al. (2007). On the one hand, this suggests that 'the use of severe threats seems to be an effective way to diminish downloading'. On the other hand, Hsu and Shiue (2008), in scenario-based studies, found no increased willingness to pay for software due to a high or raised risk of prosecution. Nevertheless, when carrying out statistical and quantitative research, Lysonski and Durvasula (2008) point out that lawsuits do not seem to slow down the rate of unauthorized file-sharing or solve the issue. Combined studies, covering enforcement and prosecution of intellectual property infringement, show that severe punishment seems to have an impact. However, the current level of lawsuits is not perceived as being sufficient to dissuade Internet users from engaging in the sharing of unauthorized digital material. A survey study by Karaganis, Grassmuck and Renkema (2012), in which Internet users were asked about appropriate penalties for unauthorized file-sharing, shows that there is broader support for minor fines or warnings than for jail time or disconnection from the Internet.

The Swedish context has been thoroughly described in the annual demographic study 'Svenskarna och Internet' (Findahl, 2012). Findahl reports that 25 per cent of the Swedish population engaged in file-sharing activities in 2011, which is a notable increase from previous years during which the same study was performed: in 2004, 8 per cent said they file-shared; in 2007, 15.3 per cent; in 2008, 19.1 per cent; in 2009, 17.6 per cent; and, in 2010, 20 per cent (Findahl, 2011). Youths and young adults are more active when it comes to file-sharing: 53.5 per cent claim to file-share at least once per week (Findahl, 2012). This is somewhat in accordance with the studies performed by Svensson and Larsson in 2009 (Svensson and Larsson, 2009 and 2012) and Svensson, de Kaminski and Larsson in 2012 (Svensson, Larsson and de Kaminski, 2013 (forthcoming)), as presented below in this chapter.

Theoretical framework

The on-going research within the Cybernorms research group draws much of its theoretical understanding from the norm perspective within sociology of law. Hence, its focus lies mainly on understanding the interrelationships between social and legal norms. The core of this perspective is presented in Chapter 3 of this volume. According to this perspective, there is no ontological difference between law and other norms (Ehrlich, 2001). All norms, regardless of category, share the same basic essential attributes: they are (a) normative statements that (b) are socially reproduced and (c) represent the individual's perception of the expectations surrounding their own behaviour.

This set of common ontological attributes admits analytical comparisons between social control emanating from law, on the one hand, and social control emanating from society, on the other (see, for example, Ellickson, 1991). Furthermore, both social and legal norms can be viewed from their normative and/or factual dimension. This gives us the four categories or, rather, the four-dimensional socio-legal model (the FDSL-model) (Svensson, 2013) that forms the basic structure of the research presented here: (1) the normative dimension of social norms; (2) the factual dimension of social norms; (3) the normative dimension of legal norms; and (4) the factual dimension of legal norms. These four dimensions constitute the framework for the choices of scientific method. The normative dimension of social norms is preferably studied through qualitative methods; and, in order to describe the factual dimension of social norms, quantitative methods are superior. The normative dimension of legal norms requires text analysis of some sort, either purely jurisprudential or socio-legal. In this study, we apply a socio-legal metaphor analysis to understand some of the cognitive content of law. We also theorize about 'path dependency' in order to analyse and understand the legal development in this field and its lock-in effects over time. In addition, an understanding of the factual dimension of legal norms requires empirical studies of how the law is actually executed within society. This four-dimensional approach to socio-legal research allows for a complex instrument for analysing interrelationships between social and legal norms. In the research presented in this chapter, this instrument is used primarily to understand different aspects of what has been described as the gap problem in sociology of law – in this case, in relation to the emerging digital net cultures that form new challenges for the rule of law.

The gap problem has classically been viewed from two distinct perspectives (Tamanaha, 2008) within socio-legal studies. The first perspective was originally described by Roscoe Pound (1910) as a gap between law in books and law in action. In the FDSL-model (see Chapter 3 in this volume), this gap can be described as a disparity between the normative and the factual dimensions of law (or legal norms). On the one hand, there is law as it is declared via the legal rules; and, on the other hand, there is law as it is conducted by its officials (such as judges and the police). The second classic view of the gap problem deals with the gap between law in books and living law – the rules of conduct adhered to in society (see, for example, Ehrlich, 2001). One reason for this gap is that rules of social behaviour constantly evolve, while the law remains more conservative, path-dependent and slower to change. In the FDSL-model, this classic viewpoint is best illustrated through the disparity between the normative dimension of legal and social norms. In addition to the two distinct angles of the gap problem identified by classical sociology of law, the FDSL-model indicates that the gap problem is actually much more complex than that. Theoretically, disparity can occur between the four dimensions (shown above) in six different ways. Hence, there are six theoretically possible variants of the gap problem:

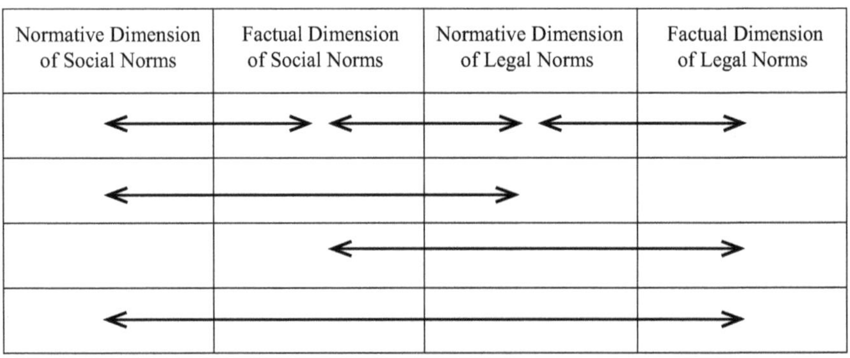

Figure 18.1 The Four Dimensional Socio-Legal Model (FDSL-model) – illustrating a multidimensional understanding of the gap problem in sociology of law

This added complexity to the classic gap problem provides a set of tools for socio-legal analysis to utilize in order to better understand the phenomenon of law in a digital context. In the following, we account for data collected to describe all four dimensions of the FDSL-model and then analyse the results in order to discuss the six theoretically possible variants of the gap problem.

Methodology

In this chapter, the case of illegal file-sharing on the Internet (and the imminent challenges to IP law) is utilized to illustrate and examine different aspects of socio-legal consequences due to digitalization of society. The various studies conducted within the Cybernorms research group are all related to the model presented above, by which legal and social norms are analysed from both a normative and a factual dimension. By using such a well-arranged model, it becomes possible to place the findings from the different studies into a relevant context within the norm studies field of research.

Study 1 – The global file-sharing community

The Research Bay is an immense quantitative study that aims to provide an inside look into one of the world's most active file-sharing communities. To establish a descriptive overview of the field of file-sharing, a strategic cooperation was set up with the global file-sharing community, The Pirate Bay. In April 2011, the logo of the site was complemented with a picture of a magnifying glass, and the site's name was changed to The Research Bay. Visitors who clicked on the altered logo were transferred to an online survey and, during the 72 hours that the study ran, 75,000 file-sharers filled out a questionnaire. This makes it the largest survey ever conducted within a file-sharing community. The survey was conducted in English and contained both multiple choice and open questions. The aim of the online study was to descriptively examine the demographics in the global file-sharing community, to describe a file-sharing community from within, and, to some extent, to shed light on the question of why illegal file-sharing persists, despite it being illegal. By using methods that allow us to learn a little more about the people conducting file-sharing, their opinions and norms – social norms that clearly differ from the ones stipulated in law – we may examine the underlying demographics and social structures of a phenomenon that has emerged as one of the greatest challenges to IP law ever (Svensson, Larsson and de Kaminski, 2013b; Larsson, Svensson and de Kaminski, 2012). This was accomplished by asking questions related to file-sharing habits and practices related to the use of The Pirate Bay and to other file-sharing techniques, as well as possible counter-strategies to the activities of law enforcement and copyright holder organizations.

Study 2 – Interviewing young Swedes

To more deeply explore the living Internet culture of today's youth, a number of focus group interviews among ninth-graders were conducted. The interviews, to be repeated on a yearly basis, aimed to identify the on-going movements and emerging trends within what has been defined as young net cultures and, furthermore, to be a qualitative addition to the more quantitative survey studies. The focus group interviews, ten in all, were conducted at five public schools in Linköping County, a medium-sized county in the south of Sweden (Svensson, Larsson, and de Kaminski, 2013b).

The interviews were conducted in accordance with a semi-structured model, using an interview template with open questions. Due to the flexible form of the focus group interview, the essence of the interviews shifted, depending on what each group collaboratively chose to focus on. The study attempted to establish four main themes: 'social life online', 'file-sharing', 'publication of images' and 'news consumption'. The questions focused on solution aspects, and were intentionally kept very open to try to maximize the synergy effects of the focus groups. Discussions between respondents were encouraged as much as possible. Regarding the overall structure of the interview, questions were presented to the respondents and discussion was stimulated. Quite often, letting each and every one of the respondents answer the same question, and then allowing them to comment on the answers given, opened up the discussions. One example of opening questions regarding file-sharing was, 'when did you last watch a movie?', which encouraged the respondents to reflect on and compare the answers within the group.

Study 3 – Measuring social norms

The norm study is a series of three studies, so far, that aim to measure, among other things, Social Norm Strength (SNS). In these studies, this is closely linked to the theory of planned behaviour (TPB) developed by Icek Ajzen (2005) and Martin Fishbein and Icek Ajzen (Fishbein and Ajzen, 2009). This theory explains how subjective norms play a crucial role when people form intentions. In the following, we show how the model for calculating subjective norms developed by Fishbein and Ajzen can be used, together with the socio-legal definition of norms (described above), to calculate the strength of social norms. The socio-legal method used in this study, inspired by Fishbein and Ajzen, has been employed in numerous studies (for a more thorough description, see Svensson, 2008; Svensson and Larsson, 2009 and 2012; Larsson, 2011b). We conducted three surveys of approximately 1,000 Swedish Internet users between 15 and 25 years of age (Larsson and Svensson, 2010; Larsson, Svensson and de Kaminski, 2012). The first survey was conducted in January and February 2009. After the implementation of IPRED (Directive 2004/48/EC) in Sweden on 1 April 2009, it was followed up with the repeat study in October 2009; and, most recently, the third, long-term follow-up study in January 2012.

Study 4 – Studying law

Legal norms are often studied using what is commonly described as traditional legal method. It is frequently described as a deductive method used by lawyers and jurists, which means that the methodological approach of this profession is to analyse, debate, discuss and theorize law as doctrine – norms, rules, principles, concepts – and analyse the modes of their interpretation and validation (Cotterrell, 1998). The aim of much legal scholarship is to clarify and influence legal reasoning within a self-referential system, rather than to further public understanding of law, legal institutions or processes (Hillyard, 2007). Many of the studies conducted by the Cybernorms research group have examined copyright law in Sweden and Europe. Some studies have explicitly dealt with the legal setting and its development (Larsson, 2011a and 2011c). Others have dealt with its relation to social norms (Svensson and Larsson, 2009 and 2012), enforcement issues and online anonymity (Larsson and Svensson, 2010; Larsson, Svensson and de Kaminski, 2012; Larsson et al., 2012) or societal change (Larsson, 2012a; Larsson and Hydén, 2010). In addition, the Cybernorms research group has also studied some of the central, underlying conceptions at the heart of copyright regulation (Larsson, 2011b) and its specific terminology by applying conceptual metaphor theory (Larsson, 2011c and 2011b). Of the legal sources studied for this chapter, the most important have been IPRED, the EU Data Retention Directive and the court cases against ePhone, TeliaSonera and The Pirate Bay.

Study 5 – Studying the legal practice

In an effort to analyse the factual dimension of the legal norms in terms of copyright enforcement, several judicial cases or processes have been thoroughly studied and analysed. One of the most vital components of such an analysis would be the official evaluation of the Swedish implementation of the IPRED law (SOU 2012:51). This evaluation was presented as a public report in mid-August 2012 and constitutes a detailed presentation of how the implementation of IPRED has affected different parts of Swedish legislation, along with fluctuations in file-sharing practices, but also includes comments from different stakeholders directly or indirectly affected by the legal developments.

Besides the official evaluation, the few court cases regarding IPRED-related indictments have been identified and analysed (Larsson, 2011c). In particular, two cases (those against the Internet service providers TeliaSonera and ePhone) have been closely studied. This is because not only were these the first IPRED-related cases to be tried in Swedish courts, but also they were both appealed through the Swedish court system. The ePhone case is still being processed in the European Court of Justice, to establish how well the IPRED law corresponds to the EU Data Retention Directive. As one of the most high-profile file-sharing court cases in Sweden, and possibly globally, it is also essential to review and relate this to the case against the operators of The Pirate Bay.

Law in action is not only about the factual implementation of the legal rules, but also how the legal practitioners interpret the implementation. During the last couple of years, the Swedish Prosecution Authority has explained its intention to intensify efforts in identifying and prosecuting alleged file-sharers (Larsson,

Svensson and de Kaminski, 2012). Currently, there have been 28 cases, all of which have generated lawsuits and verdicts, but also some appeals and other legal documents that are of great interest. Representatives for the Swedish Prosecution Authority have stated that there are several cases coming up, making this field more active than ever when it comes to court cases.

Findings

Study 1

The study made on the file-sharing site The Pirate Bay (TPB) rendered a huge respondent database. In the 2011 study, a total of 75,901 file-sharers answered the survey, which gives us a good demographical base to proceed from. Surprisingly, of the 75,616 file-sharers that answered the question of gender, 93.8 per cent are male (70,938) and only 6.2 per cent (4,678) are female. This overrepresentation of men is consistent throughout all age groups. Furthermore, file-sharers tend to be young. Almost half of the respondents (32,301) are between 18 and 24, and about 5 per cent of them are over 46 years old (Svensson, Larsson and de Kaminski, 2013b and 2013a); see table 18.1.

When it comes to geographical location of the file-sharers, Europe is clearly predominant with 54.7 per cent of all respondents, and North America with almost 27.7 per cent of all respondents. Of the remaining 17.8 per cent, Asia has the most respondents with 7.3 per cent, followed by Oceania (4.8), Central and South America (4.1) and Africa (1.6).

It is clear that BitTorrent is not the only technique used for sharing files. For example, so-called 'one click' hosting sites, where you can share a folder or upload files for others to download via a specific link, are used by almost half of the respondents (47.6 per cent); see table 18.2. Note that more than half of the respondents (53.3 per cent) claim to use offline sharing (for example, USB sticks, mobile phones and CDs); see table 18.2. This is likely a sign that other social networks are important too, which we return to below.

Table 18.1 Age of respondents to The Pirate Bay survey

	up to 17	18–24	25–29	30–36	37–45	46–52	53–65	66 and over	No response	Total
Count	11,345	32,301	13,934	8,671	4,566	1,663	1,409	571	1,441	74,460
Per cent	15.2	43.4	18.7	11.7	6.1	2.2	1.9	0.8		100

Table 18.2 Other file-sharing techniques that are used (besides TPB)

	Count	Per cent
Other/Private BitTorrent Trackers	39,395	57.1
Other peer to peer networks	17,824	25.8
'One click' hosting sites (such as Dropbox, Rapidshare, Megafile)	32,850	47.6
FTP servers	11,367	16.5
Instant messaging (such as MSN, Skype; Gtalk)	17,546	25.4
E-mail	16,120	23.4
Offline file-sharing (USB sticks, mobile phones, CDs/DVDs)	36,823	53.3
Other	8,495	12.3
None	7,724	11.2
No response	6,859	
Total	69,042	

One particular area that is important to highlight is the frequency of usage of anonymity services. This is especially interesting, due to this being the nature of a typical counter-measure against different forms of increased enforcement (Larsson and Svensson, 2010; Larsson, Svensson and de Kaminski, 2012; Larsson et al., 2012). In the study carried out at The Pirate Bay, the respondents were asked if they 'use a VPN or similar product to protect their anonymity', with a range of given alternative responses. A number of results stand out; for example, when it comes to uploading new material to the file-sharing community, the users that upload more frequently are also more inclined to use some kind of anonymity service. Among those that upload every day, or almost every day, 31 per cent use either a free or paid version of anonymity services, which can be compared to the average of 17.8 per cent (see Larsson, Svensson and de Kaminski, 2012).

Study 2

The focus group interviews conducted with ninth-graders give us a good picture of the position that file-sharing holds in young net cultures, as it is clearly a very common practice and most of the respondents can handle the technologies that are available (Svensson, Larsson and de Kaminski, 2013b). Most common, without doubt, is the BitTorrent technology, which is the technology used by file-sharing sites such as The Pirate Bay and others. Aside from The Pirate Bay, all respondents are familiar with other similar sites. At each interview, they collectively presented three or four other sites that offer illegal downloads using BitTorrent technology. Two frequent sources are tankafett.com (no longer using BitTorrent) and tankafetast.com, which both have names encouraging downloads, as well as either focusing exclusively on Swedish or subtitled material. In some cases, respondents used technologies and services such as Direct Connect and Mega Upload (no longer using cyberlocker).

A number of respondents also use USB sticks to pass on downloaded movies when planning to see something together with friends, so-called 'sneakernet' solutions or offline file-sharing. Bluetooth file-sharing is considered to be an old and outdated technology. It turns out that this is because many people own iPhones that do not allow bluetooth sharing of all sorts of files (for instance, music files). Those who use smartphones with the Android operating system, however, still have ample possibilities to download straight to their mobile phones and share with friends, since the phones have applications for these specific tasks.

Nonetheless, there is concern among interview participants regarding the legislation. Some respondents are aware of the fact that BitTorrent clients automatically and simultaneously, by default, also share the files that are being downloaded. Still, file-sharing generally tends to be a hit-and-run activity, in which users download what they want and then, as a precautionary measure, turn off file uploading completely. It is basically the only safety measure mentioned in the interviews. A few respondents mention anonymization, which several expressed interest in using; but, out of the entire group, only one respondent claimed to use VPN services to de-identify their IP address, thereby making browsing and file-sharing more anonymous. The respondents who lack the skills to handle such technologies, or are too anxious to dare to share files from home, usually arrange for someone else to conduct the file-sharing in their place. This user is often a technologically skilled or less than cautious acquaintance or relative, or – since many of those who lack the interest to share files are girls – a boyfriend.

This concern does not appear to be based on more than hearsay, it seems. None of the respondents know anyone who has been prosecuted for copyright violations or file-sharing. The case most often referred to concerns the allegations levelled against the administrators of The Pirate Bay, which does not really involve direct file-sharing – but, rather, the administration of a file-sharing service. Nevertheless, concerns lie at the back of the minds of many respondents. It is noteworthy that this concern seems to have a large enough impact for some of the respondents to actually refrain from illegal file-sharing. Interview participants commonly mention that they no longer download as much as before, but nobody seems to have completely given up the practice.

File-sharing is a very significant part of the respondents' media consumption. With some important exceptions, it is clear that the media should preferably be free or, at least, very cheap. The exceptions are cinema visits and mobile music; that is, the respondents value the social aspect of watching movies outside the home in the company of friends, and the freedom and mobility that music on mobile phone offers – to the extent that it seems worth paying for (see Svensson and Larsson, 2009). Participants in the focus groups do not adhere to any particular ideological or theoretical reasoning as regards their file-sharing. At some point, the question arises as to who actually earns money on the purchased music, but it is not an issue that seems crucial to legitimizing illegal downloading. Instead, it is, above all, the price for purchased media that keeps the respondents from legally buying music and movies. Since there is an urge to listen to music at all times and to watch movies, if not daily then at least several times a week, it would be impossible to maintain such habits if actually paying for everything. A reasonable argument raised is that the unit price of single songs via any of the available digital services is so high that it becomes absurdly costly to put together a good collection or, for instance, fill a phone of normal storage capacity with music (see Larsson, 2011c).

Ready accessibility to legitimate services comes into play here. Legitimate streaming services, such as Voddler and other video-on-demand services, do not have interesting enough catalogues to be a serious alternative, at this time. The respondents agree that the movies offered within the lower price ranges are too outdated to even be considered. This, together with the overall pricing, constitutes an important listed reason for downloading movies illegally.

Overall, however, the issue of legal versus illegal file-sharing seems be a non-issue. The direct question of whether the illegality of file-sharing matters was posed to all focus groups. The general response was that it does not matter at all. The legality is not a factor that is taken into consideration when searching for media or other types of content. Although there is a clear concern for being caught file-sharing, the fact that file-sharing is both illegal and, for the moment, a high-profile crime is not enough to discourage the respondents from their file-sharing habits.

Study 3

The surveys of 1,000 Swedish respondents are of particular interest because they were conducted before and after implementation of IPRED in 2009, and in early 2012 (Larsson and Svensson, 2010; Svensson and Larsson, 2009 and 2012). Table 18.3 shows the respondents' reports on how often they file-share – both in the survey conducted before the implementation of IPRED and the two conducted afterwards. The data in this table can therefore be regarded as a self-reported effect study. The changes are statistically significant.

Before the implementation of IPRED, 21.6 per cent of the respondents reported that they never file-shared and, six months after IPRED, this figure was almost 38.9 per cent. Two and a half years after IPRED, 38.7 per cent of the respondents reported that they never file-share, which is at the same level as six months after IPRED. At the same time, the percentage of respondents who claimed to file-share on a daily basis decreased from 10.6 per cent to 6.4 per cent, and then increased slightly again to 7.4 per cent. Both the increased number of those who never file-share, and the changes in the group who reported file-sharing on a daily basis, are statistically significant. In conclusion, Table 18.3 suggests that IPRED had an effect on file-sharing around the time it was implemented.

In the following section, we show the Social Norm Strength (SNS) data collected before, and then twice after, the implementation of IPRED. First, the respondents' perceptions of important referents are presented in terms of the strength of

Table 18.3 Frequency of illegally downloading copyright-protected material

	Study 1 (before IPRED)	Study 2 (6 months after IPRED)	Study 3 (2.5 years after IPRED)
Never	21.6% (217 persons)	38.9% (383 persons)	38.7% (392 persons)
Once a month at a maximum	24.0% (242 persons)	26.1% (258 persons)	25.0% (253 persons)
Once a week at a maximum	22.0% (222 persons)	16.1% (158 persons)	16.0% (162 persons)
More than once a week	21.6% (218 persons)	12.5% (124 persons)	13.0% (132 persons)
Daily	10.6% (107 persons)	6.4% (63 persons)	7.4% (75 persons)
Chi-Square Tests: Asymp. Sig. (2-sided) .000.			

normative belief (n) and the motivation to comply (m). Then, the SNS is calculated, which represents the capacity of a social norm to influence behaviour towards legal compliance. All SNS data are presented on a scale from 1 to 7. SNS values below 1 indicate that there is no significant Social Norm Strength. Table 18.4 shows the SNS data for all the respondents before and after IPRED.

Table 18.4 shows, in general, that there are only very weak social norms promoting compliance with the law in the case of file-sharing. In fact, the respondents feel no substantial social pressure from any of the important referents, and furthermore, the respondents claim that they only care slightly about the opinion of any of the important referents, with regard to file-sharing. Moreover, it is significant that there is no major change in Social Norm Strength between Study 1 prior to IPRED, Study 2 after IPRED, and Study 3 after IPRED. When analysing the results, we can see that neither of the two extremes (that is, file-sharing daily and never file-sharing) experience that their decision on whether or not to file-share is influenced by any social control. Even those who never file-share report a minimal Social Norm Strength of 1.04 on a scale of 1–7; furthermore, there is no statistically significant increase after the implementation of IPRED. The respondents are all young people, between 15 and 25 years old, and there are no indications in the data that society is applying any social pressure on them to comply with the law. Those who choose to never file-share obviously do so for reasons other than social norms. With regard to whether the respondents believe that copyright enforcement laws would stop them or others from file-sharing illegally, 28.5 per cent thought they would, while 71.5 per cent thought they would not, in the first pre-IPRED study (Svensson and Larsson, 2009). This can be compared to the slightly increased figure of 38.1 per cent who responded affirmatively and, hence, the slightly decreased figure of 61.9 per cent who stated no, respectively, in the second post-IPRED study (Svensson and Larsson, 2012).

Table 18.4 Social Norm Strength before and after implementation of IPRED

Important referents	Study 1 (before IPRED)		Study 2 (6 months after IPRED)		Study 3 (2.5 years after IPRED)	
	Strength of normative belief (n)	Motivation to comply (m)	Strength of normative belief (n)	Motivation to comply (m)	Strength of normative belief (n)	Motivation to comply (m)
a) Mother	2.42	2.97	2.95	3.22	3.17	3.27
b) Father	2.28	2.96	2.82	3.20	2.88	3.25
c) Other close relatives	2.06	2.23	2.26	2.42	2.42	2.49
d) Partner	1.57	3.29	1.97	3.46	2.03	3.19
e) Friends	1.53	2.96	1.86	3.03	1.81	2.91
f)Internet acquaintances	1.44	1.88	1.75	2.04	1.74	1.99
g) Teacher/bosses	2.62	2.11	2.98	2.24	3.16	2.29
h) Neighbours	1.72	1.50	1.98	1.74	2.03	1.75
i) Casual acquaintances	1.64	1.55	1.86	1.72	1.91	1.70
Mean	1.92	2.39	2.27	2.56	2.36	2.54
Statistically significant change (2-tailed)			No ($p = 0.135$)	No ($p = 0.580$)		
Social Norm Strength	<1		<1		<1	

In the third study, the numbers have returned, if only slightly, towards the starting point: 29.8 per cent think copyright enforcement laws will stop them or others from file-sharing, while 70.2 per cent do not (Svensson, de Kaminski and Larsson, forthcoming).

Concerning whether the respondents think that it is wrong to file-share merely because it is illegal, 24 per cent answered 'yes' and 76 per cent 'no', in the first study. In the second study, 30.1 per cent answered 'yes' to that question and 69.9 per cent 'no'. In the third study, 32.2 per cent answered 'yes' and 67.8 per cent 'no'. These changes in beliefs and opinions are statistically significant ($p < 5$ per cent) and could be an indication that norms may gain acceptance over time if legal pressure is continuously applied.

The most interesting data from the repeat study demonstrate both that the correlation between high-frequency file-sharing is still very strong, and that the biggest increase in use of anonymity services is seen among the groups that file-share less frequently. For example, from survey 2 (October 2009) to the repeat study (January 2012), the increase in use of anonymity services is significant for the combined group of those who 'never' file-share and those who file-share 'once a month at the most' (Larsson, Svensson and de Kaminski, 2012).

The proportions of those who file-share the most frequently, in categories 4, 5 and 6, are continuously high, and the share is between 24.3 per cent and 29.7 per cent. It is also interesting to note that the increase in use of anonymity services for the entire group of respondents, from survey 2 to survey 3, is statistically significant.

Study 4

The main analyses of copyright regulation conducted by the Cybernorms research group regard either its development over time in the last 10 to 15 years (Larsson, 2011a and 2011c) or its conceptual expansion and transition in the digital environment. The development of copyright is directly connected to contemporary technological development. Copyright is a component of what is called intellectual property, which also includes, for instance, patents and trademarks. Copyright is the right that authors, composers, artists and other originators have to their literary or artistic work. This right needs no registration, unlike innovations that require patents. This is a key idea of the Berne Convention for the Protection for Literary and Artistic Works.[1] The economic rights are the rights of reproduction, broadcasting, public performance, adaptation, distribution and so on, and the moral rights – *droit moral* – include the author's right to object to any distortion, mutilation or other modification of his work that might be harmful to his honour

1 Berne Convention for the Protection for Literary and Artistic Works, last amended at Paris on September 28, 1979. Sweden signed the Convention on the 1 August 1904 and has adopted all the amendments of the Convention since then. Agreement on Trade-Related Aspects of Intellectual Property Rights signed in Marrakech, Morocco on 15 April 1994.

or reputation. The national copyright regulations are connected to international treaties and, in the Swedish case, also to EU law.

Depending on how copyright is conceptualized, debates and arguments follow naturally in its wake (Larsson, 2011b, 2012a and 2012b; Yar, 2008). Potential legislative amendments will always be hopelessly trapped within the logical walls inherent in prevailing ideological structures. It is in this sense that the concept of 'copy' in copyright is renegotiated within a digital context to also include digital copies, which are conceptualized in a similar way to physical copies. This negotiation is rhetorically supported by other concepts, mainly relating to physical property, in order to make this renegotiation seem just and for the ensuing means of enforcement to seem meaningful.

During the last decade, the trend in Europe with regard to copyright has been concluded as 'path dependent', in that it follows a set of key concepts of creativity, property and incentives that are also applied to a digital context (Larsson, 2011a and 2011c). This comes with some rather repressive consequences, in terms of adding centrally located control of data, in order to make individuals and their online actions more traceable (Larsson, 2011c). In a global perspective, the European Union has played a leading role in creating stronger copyright protection. Key regulatory initiatives in this area within the European Union are INFOSOC (Directive 2001/29/EC) and IPRED (Directive 2004/48/EC). However, other legislation also affects the enforcement of copyright, such as the Data Retention Directive (Directive 2006/24/EC).

A vital point of focus is to understand the continuation of the particular development that copyright law has had in this context, even under the extreme challenge of non-compliance by, what is often perceived as, the majority of the younger generations. Larsson uses the concept of 'path dependence' in order to explain at least part of the lock-in effects that the legal development suffers from (2011a and 2011c). Larsson concludes with a number of findings in a path dependence analysis of European copyright development; and one of them, the legitimacy issue, 'deals with the fundamental conflict between social and legal norms, making the path dependence analysis important in the first place' (Larsson, 2011c: 24). The issue of how copyright 'colonizes' other paths of law is interesting, not least in terms of privacy and integrity in relation to increased governmental tracking of traffic data and online surveillance, sometimes for copyright enforcement purposes. This connects to aspects of online anonymity, outlined above, as well as the ongoing debate on the extent to which Internet service providers should be liable for the data that they traffic.

Study 5

The governmental IPRED evaluation is interesting from a variety of aspects (SOU 2012:51). It acknowledges the fact that the number of file-sharing-related court cases has grown during 2011. During 2011, a total of 125 copyright-related indictments were reported, of which approximately half related to file-sharing. Out of 21 cases, which went as far as to legal action and prosecution, 15 were file-sharing related. The majority of the indictments were initiated by copyright holders and their legal representatives. The number of specific IPRED-related cases has been very low. In the proceedings prior to the implementation of the directive in Swedish law, the Swedish Prosecution Authority prepared to handle at least 400–800 cases per year; but, by June 2012, only 11 cases had been registered at Swedish courts, of which only four have actually been tried in court. A general understanding is that the copyright holders are waiting to see clear results from previous cases before filing more reports. Since the courts have had a hard time handling the current cases, this has caused a significant, practical bottleneck problem. One of the major issues has been the integrity factors surrounding the personal information of Internet users – and, in these cases, alleged file-sharers. There have been legal discussions concerning whether the Data Retention Directive puts restraints on how user data is to be handled, and whether that might be counter-productive when it comes to the IPRED legislation. The Swedish implementation of the Data Retention Directive contains strong limitations concerning when user data can be retrieved from Internet service providers. It has only been possible when suspicions of criminality have been related to crimes that could generate more than two years in prison, which has excluded file-sharing-related cases. In early 2012, this issue was included in the new Electronic Communications Act, which stipulates that even minor offences can be enough to force Internet service providers to release user data upon request. However, the providers are still not obliged to actually save user data – at least, not for any particular IPRED-related reason – which continues to present some obstacles to the realization of the legislation.

Data from the studies conducted by the Cybernorms research group are present throughout the report evaluating IPRED. In particular, the studies related to social norms, presented as Study 3 in this chapter, have been relevant in understanding whether the current enforcement strategy is functional.

Conclusions

Central to this chapter is the gap between the social and legal norms within the field of copyright-related behaviour in an online context. Many of the studies mentioned in this chapter have pointed out this gap and displayed the lack of social norms that correspond to those parts of copyright that deal with control over reproduction and distribution (see, for example, Svensson and Larsson, 2012). The overall and long-lasting consequences of the gap between social norms and copyright law are hard to predict but, by using the FDSL-model, they may be both highlighted and analysed in a meaningful way. By addressing the gaps between the different dimensions of socio-legal norms that are presented in the model, a greater understanding of the on-going gap-related processes could be achieved.

A multidimensional gap problem

The gap between the normative and the factual dimensions of social norms relates to the difference in societal norms concerning file-sharing and the actual inter-group norms within groups involved in file-sharing. While the factual dimensions are measurable through the use of quantitative studies, the normative dimension of social norms needs to be penetrated and explored with a more qualitative approach. The social norms related to file-sharing are somewhat consistent; the findings in Study 2 (interviews with young Swedes) confirm that social pressure and norms measured in Study 3 are not strong enough to dissuade young people from illegal file-sharing activities. However, the findings in Study 2 suggest that this is mainly due to an internalized pattern of behaviour, where file-sharing tends to be handled as unproblematic. The legal status of file-sharing of copyright-protected material overall is a non-issue to the respondents of the focus group interviews of Study 2. This suggests that the findings in Study 3 related to Social Norm Strength have a real impact on young file-sharers; but also, that this lack of norm pressure concerning these issues means that it is generally of little interest to even relate to the legal grounds of file-sharing.

This may also be understood by the findings in both Study 2, as well as the descriptive Study 1 (global file-sharing community), regarding the different methods of acquiring file-shared material. This suggests that the file-sharing methods are not a key factor, but rather a sign of an on-going professionalization or specialization, including different roles in the 'eco system' of sharing files, further supported by Svensson, Larsson and de Kaminski (2013b and 2013a) and Larsson et al. (2012). This means that those informants we have found via The Pirate Bay website may represent a link in a bigger chain, as a technologically competent and vital link for a bigger eco system of file-sharing. This professionalization hints at a larger, structured organization within the file-sharing community, of which BitTorrent plays an important, but not all-encompassing, role. It is not a result of a planned form of organization; nonetheless, it constitutes a structure for content dissemination, where gender plays a significant role (Svensson, Larsson and de Kaminski, 2013a and 2013b). This is supported in the focus group interviews in Study 2, where respondents not feeling competent enough to handle technical file-sharing solutions often fall back on 'sneakernet' methods, such as USB sticks or offline social gatherings, to gain access to file-shared media.

In a more cognitive theoretical terminology (see Larsson's contribution in Chapter 8 of this volume), the gaps may be described as portraying the changing conceptions of right – and wrong – (Larsson 2011b), along with the means for achieving accepted goals, visible in the case of file-sharing norms (Larsson, 2011b; Larsson, Svensson and de Kaminski, 2012) and the ways that file-sharers justify their behaviour (Andersson and Larsson, 2013). The latter is confirmed in Study 2, in which the respondents in general do not consider file-sharing to be an actual crime. Differentiated from the legal formulations described in Study 5, file-sharing is – at least, in young age groups – not regarded as a criminal act. Rather, it is a normal way of consuming media, where accessibility is more important than legal status. Several of the respondents claim to use different streaming solutions that are still legal for the receiving party within this technical solution, pointing to the fact that simplicity – not legality – is a major issue in contemporary media consumption. Still, a fundamental reason why social norms are relevant to study in this field is the fact that the corresponding legal regulation is completely locked to a number of key conceptions that will not easily change in the globally homogeneous copyright regime. On the contrary, as Study 4 shows, legal development has proven to further emphasize more control over a longer time and harsher enforcement strategies.

The respondents of Study 2 are, in broad terms, aware of the legal situation as presented in Study 4. They have kept themselves informed of legal reinforcements during recent years, but the discussions tend to return to the fact that the number of cases, as referred to in Study 5, remains very low and that no-one personally seems to know anyone who has been charged with anything related to file-sharing. In Studies 1 and 3, we clearly see an increased awareness of encryption technologies and services to ensure that the user is less identifiable online (Larsson and Svensson, 2010; Larsson, Svensson and de Kaminski, 2012; Larsson et al., 2012; Svensson and Larsson, 2012). This is an issue that is also mentioned in Study 5, in which the legal rapporteurs write about the problematic increase of anonymity services. However, the respondents in Study 2 do not see this as a major issue, since they generally do not reflect in those terms at all. They do not feel the same legal pressure as the respondents in the other studies.

Therefore, this relates to the conceptions of reality in terms of legality, distribution and reproduction of media content, which create a collision between social and legal norms of copyright, analysed in Larsson (2011b). These conceptions of reality are likely to form a basis for how file-sharers justify their behaviour and relate both to its illegality and to what the digitalization of society entails (Larsson, 2012a; Andersson and Larsson, 2013). Such cross-model conflicts and relationships generate unbalanced gap problems, where the distance between different norm-sets is seemingly uneven. The four fields of the FDSL-model suggest six possible relations between different parts of the model. As shown, the relations are often multi-party processes, making both the understanding, as well as the solutions to potential problems, difficult. The outcome of a process in which new norms emerge can only be understood if all parts of the model are taken into consideration, thus showing the relation between the different parallel processes.

References

Ajzen, I. 2005. *Attitudes, Personality and Behavior.* 2nd ed. Maidenhead: Open University Press.

Altschuller, S. and Benbunan-Fich, R. 2009. 'Is Music Downloading the New Prohibition? What Students Reveal Through an Ethical Dilemma', *Ethics and Information Technology* 11(1) (17 January), 49–56.

Andersson, J. and Larsson, S. 2013. 'On the justifications of piracy: Differences in conceptualization and argumentation between active uploaders and other file-sharers', in Arvanitakis, J. and Fredriksson, M. (eds), *Piracy: Leakages from Modernity*. Los Angeles, CA: Litwin Books.

Boyle, J. 2010. *The Public Domain: Enclosing the Commons of the Mind.* Yale University Press.

Cotterrell, R. 1998. 'Why Must Legal Ideas Be Interpreted Sociologically?', *Journal of Law and Society* 25 (2), 171–92.

Directive 2001/29/EC. Directive of the European Parliament and of the Council of 22 May 2001 on the Harmonisation of Certain Aspects of Copyright and Related Rights in the Information Society, OJ L 167, 22.6.2001, 10–19.

Directive 2004/48/EC. Directive of the European Parliament and of the Council of 29 April 2004 on the Enforcement of Intellectual Property Rights. OJ L 157, 30.4.2004, 45–86 (known as 'IPRED').

Directive 2006/24/EC. Directive of the European Parliament and of the Council of 15 March 2006 on the Retention of Data Generated or Processed in Connection with the Provision of Publicly Available Electronic Communications Services or of Public Communications Networks, and Amending Directive 2002/58/EC. OJ L 105, 13.4.2006, 54–63 (known as the 'Data Retention Directive').

Ehrlich, E. 2001. *Fundamental Principles of the Sociology of Law*. London: Transaction Publishers.

Ellickson, R.C. 1991. *Order Without Law : How Neighbors Settle Disputes*. Cambridge, Mass; London: Harvard University Press.

Feldman, Y, and Nadler, J. 2006. 'The Law and Norms of File Sharing', *The San Diego Law Review* 43 (3), 577–618.

Findahl, O. 2011. *Svenskarna och Internet 2010*. Ödeshög: .SE.

Findahl, O. 2012. *Svenskarna och Internet 2011*. Ödeshög: .SE.

Fishbein, M. and Ajzen, I. 2009. *Predicting and Changing Behavior: The Reasoned Action Approach*. New York; Hove: Psychology Press.

Hillyard, P. 2007. 'Law's Empire: Socio-legal Empirical Research in the Twenty-first Century', *Journal of Law and Society* 34 (2), 266–79.

Hsu, J.L. and Shiue, C.W. 2008. 'Consumers' Willingness to Pay for Non-Pirated Software', *Journal of Business Ethics* 81 (4), 715–32.

Jensen, C. 2003. 'The More Things Change, the More They Stay the Same: Copyright, Digital Technology, and Social Norms', *Stanford Law Review* 56 (2), 531–70.

Karaganis, J., Grassmuck, V. and Renkema, L. 2012. *Copy Culture in the US and Germany*. Columbia University: The American Assembly.

Kwong, T.C.H. and Lee, M.K.O. 2002. 'Behavioral Intention Model for the Exchange Mode Internet Music Piracy', in *Proceedings of the 35th Annual Hawaii International Conference on System Sciences, 2002. HICSS*, 2481–90.

Larsson, S. 2010. '459 miljarder kronor – om metaforer, flöden & exemplar', in *Efter The Pirate Bay*, edited by J. Andersson and P. Snickars. Stockholm: Mediehistoriskt arkiv, Kungliga biblioteket.

Larsson, S. 2011a. 'Den Stigberoende Upphovsrätten. Om Konsekvenserna Av Rättslig Inlåsning i En Digital Tid', *Retfærd, Nordic Journal of Law and Justice* (4).

Larsson, S. 2011b. *Metaphors and Norms: Understanding Copyright Law in a Digital Society*. Vol. 36. Lund Studies in Sociology of Law. Lund: Media-Tryck.

Larsson, S. 2011c. 'The Path Dependence of European Copyright', *SCRIPT:ed. A Journal of Law, Technology & Society* 8, 1.

Larsson, S. 2012a. 'Conceptions in the Code: What "The Copyright Wars" Tell Us About Creativity, Social Change and Normative Conflicts in the Digital Society', *Societal Studies* 4(3), 1009–30.

Larsson, S. 2012b. 'Metaforerna och rätten', *Retfærd. Nordic Journal of Law and Justice.*

Larsson, S. and Hydén, H. 2010. 'Law, Deviation and Paradigmatic Change: Copyright and Its Metaphors', in *Technology for Facilitating Humanity and Combating Social Deviations: Interdisciplinary Perspectives*, ed. Miguel Vargas Martin, Miguel A. Garcia-Ruiz, and Arthur Edwards. Hershey: IGI Global.

Larsson, S. and Svensson, M. 2010. 'Compliance or Obscurity? Online Anonymity as a Consequence of Fighting Unauthorised File-sharing', *Policy & Internet* 2(4).

Larsson, S., Svensson, M. and de Kaminski, M. 2012. 'Online Piracy, Anonymity and Social Change: Innovation Through Deviance', *Convergence: The International Journal of Research into New Media Technologies* (20 September).

Larsson, S., Svensson, M., de Kaminski, M., Rönkkö, K. and Alkan Olsson, J. 2012. 'Law, Norms, Piracy and Online Anonymity – Practices of De-identification in the Global File Sharing Community', *Journal of Research in Interactive Marketing* 6(4), 4.

Lessig, L. 2006. *Code and Other Laws of Cyberspace*. 2nd ed. New York: Basic Books.

Lessig, L. 2008. *Remix: Making Art and Commerce Thrive in the Hybrid Economy*. New York; London: Penguin Press.

Levin, A.M., Conway Dato-on, M. and Manolis, C. 2007. 'Deterring Illegal Downloading: The Effects of Threat Appeals, Past Behavior, Subjective Norms, and Attributions of Harm', *Journal of Consumer Behaviour* 6 (2–3), 111–22.

Litman, J. 2006. *Digital Copyright*. Prometheus Books.

Litman, J. 2010. 'Real Copyright Reform', *Iowa Law Review* 96 (1), 1–55.

Lysonski, S. and Durvasula, S. 2008. 'Digital Piracy of MP3s: Consumer and Ethical Predispositions', *Journal of Consumer Marketing* 25(3), 167–78.

Moohr, G.S. 2003. 'The Crime of Copyright Infringement: An Inquiry Based on Morality, Harm, and Criminal Theory', *Boston University Law Review*, Vol. 83, No. 4.

Morris, P.S. 2009. 'Pirates of the Internet, At Intellectual Property's End With Torrents and Challenges for Choice of Law', *International Journal of Law and Information Technology* 17(3), 282–303.

Netanel, N.W. 2008. *Copyright's Paradox*. Oxford University Press.

Pound, R. 1910. 'Law in Books and Law in Action', *American Law Review*, 12–36.

Schultz, M.F. 2006a. 'Fear and Norms and Rock & Roll: What Jambands Can Teach Us About Persuading People to Obey Copyright Law', *Berkeley Technology Law Journal*.

Schultz, M.F. 2006b. 'Copynorms: Copyright and Social Norms', *SSRN eLibrary* (27 September).

SOU 2012:51. *Utvärdering Av Ipredlagen* (Evaluation of the IPRED law).

Strahilevitz, L.J. 2003a. 'Social Norms from Close-Knit Groups to Loose-Knit Groups', *The University of Chicago Law Review* 70 (1), 359–72.

Strahilevitz, L.J. 2003b. 'Charismatic Code, Social Norms, and the Emergence of Cooperation on the File-Swapping Networks', *Virginia Law Review* 89 (3), 505–95.

Svensson, M. 2008. *Sociala Normer Och Regelefterlevnad*. Vol. 28. Lund Studies in Sociology of Law. Lund: Media-Tryck.

Svensson, M. and Larsson, S. 2009. *Social Norms and Intellectual Property. Online Norms and the European Legal Development*. SSRN.

Svensson, M. and Larsson, S. 2012. 'Intellectual Property Law Compliance in Europe: Illegal File Sharing and the Role of Social Norms', *New Media & Society* (10 April).

Svensson M., Larsson, S. and de Kaminski, M. 2013a. 'Professionalization, Gender and Anonymity in the Global File Sharing Community' / 'Professionalizzazione, Genere e Anonimato Nella Comunità Globale File Sharing', in *Piracy Effect*, ed. R. Braga and G. Caruso.

Svensson, M., Larsson, S. and de Kaminski, M. 2013b. 'The Research Bay – Studying the Global File Sharing Community', in *IP in Context: Law and Society Perspectives on Intellectual Property*, ed. Bill Gallagher and Debora Halbert. Forthcoming in Cambridge Studies in Law and Society. Cambridge: Cambridge University Press.

Tamanaha, B.Z. 2008. 'Understanding Legal Pluralism: Past to Present, Local to Global', *Sydney Law Review* 30, 375.

Tehranian, J. 2007. 'Infringement Nation: Copyright Reform and the Law/Norm Gap', *Utah Law Review* 2007 (3).

Vaidhyanathan, S. 2003. *Copyrights and Copywrongs: The Rise of Intellectual Property and How It Threatens Creativity*. NYU Press.

Wingrove, T., Korpas, A.L. and Weisz, V. 2010. 'Why Were Millions of People Not Obeying the Law? Motivational Influences on Non-compliance with the Law in the Case of Music Piracy', *Psychology, Crime & Law* 17(3), 261–76.

Yar, M. 2008. 'The Rhetorics and Myths of Anti-piracy Campaigns: Criminalization, Moral Pedagogy and Capitalist Property Relations in the Classroom', *New Media & Society* 10(4), 605–23.

PART V
Socio-legal Normativity

Chapter 19
Towards a Socio-legal Understanding of Normativity

Matthias Baier

Dealing with normativity

This book approaches the question of how normativity comes about. In that respect, it does not provide an answer to this question; rather, it introduces a perspective from which it is possible to understand the question. This question is posed from a socio-legal perspective, and the book concentrates on the relations between social and legal norms. But what is meant by the concept of normativity? The issue of normativity is very complex and can be approached in different ways. It is important to state that it extends beyond legal theory, sociology of law and sociology. It is, of course, a crucial issue in philosophy and the social sciences in general. As with the concept of norms, it is common to several sciences. Due to the normative character of parts of philosophy and legal theory, normativity seems to be of special interest in those fields.

In an overview, Korsgaard (1992) identifies four major categories of answers to the question of what makes morality normative. One answer is to explain normativity with reference to the legitimate authority that we voluntarily place in a sovereign lawmaker, divine or not. Another line of answers places normativity in the quality of the moral claims, such as they are; a moral claim can be intrinsically true and thus normative. A third category of answers assumes that morality is grounded in human nature; instead of arguing that a moral claim is true, proponents of this theory try to answer why we use moral concepts and why we feel ourselves bound by them. The last answer concerns individual autonomy; the source of normativity is found in the agent's own free will. The capacity to freely reflect on our own actions is an authority over ourselves that also renders normativity to moral claims.

As noted by Reza Banakar in Chapter 2, the debate about the nature of normativity is as vigorous as ever, especially regarding law's normativity. Many participants in this debate, however, seek to account for law's normativity by taking law as general phenomena and thus reducing law to those features that are common to all legal systems. This entails an ambition to find the one normativity of law, a normativity that applies to law in a universal sense. But this ambition does not go along well with the socio-legal ambition adopted here. The position in this book is that, other than for analytical reasons, it is problematic to regard law as such a united system of norms. Instead, as noted by, for example, Kaarlo Tuori (2000), law needs to accommodate the different legal paradigms emanating from different historical eras (Habermas, 1996). Law, as the system of norms that supplies models for how to come to an agreement or to issue an obligation, is not the same law that is used to compensate social differences or to regulate modern techno-ethical issues, such as sustainable development, the human body or integrity. Law operates quite differently when operating in the formal mode, the substantial mode or the reflexive mode (Teubner, 1983). Globalisation leads to an increase of legal norms at the international and supranational levels. Today, we also talk about hybrid law, complicating the situation even more (Åkerstrøm, Andersen and Sand, 2012). We know that the observance of law differs greatly between different legal fields and between many other factors. Law might thus be very much present in daily life for some and completely absent for others (Genn, 1999). For some groups, law is not just absent in terms of inaccessibility, but also contrary to their needs. Taking these aspects into consideration, it becomes evident that we need to abandon the idea of law as one united system of norms and, rather, treat law in a more differentiated way. From this point of view, it seems problematic to talk about one normativity of law.

Partly in line with this position is Sylvie Delacroix's (2006) treatment of law's normativity. As the title of her book indicates, she argues that, when understanding the normativity of law, law must be looked upon in an historical perspective. Following Delacroix's methodological course of line, Hans Kelsen might then have arrived at a different understanding of law today and subsequently come to a different conclusion regarding law's normativity. Law's normativity must always be understood in relation to the times in which law is situated. Contrary to positions in analytical jurisprudence, Delacroix (2006) argues that legal normativity is brought about every day through the many cases in courts, public debates and other procedures invoking law. This significance of historical, contingent facts will inspire the following argumentation when approaching a socio-legal understanding of normativity. The argumentation will proceed in two steps. First, I will argue that the normativity is an outcome of the normative interdependence and co-production between the four aspects of norms that were presented at the beginning of this book: law, social norms, legal practice and social practice. This argumentation follows primarily from the cases in this book. Secondly, I will argue that this normativity is also dependent on other structures in society. As put by Banakar in Chapter 2, norms produce normativity, but normativity also produces norms. That norms produce normativity follows from the perspective of norms being exogenous; that normativity produces norms follows from the perspective of the emergence of norms. This argumentation takes its starting point in one rich example, but will also include other examples.

Norms produce normativity

It was argued in Chapter 4 that norms are composed of both the normative expression of a symbol, or an utterance, and the actual practice that is the effect of the normative expression. This is true for all norms, both social and legal. The actual normative effect we encounter in different situations is thus a combination of social and legal norms operating, and the combination of normative expressions and the actual practice. It is true that the matrix in Chapter 4 illustrating these aspects of normativity allows for examples of simply law, or simply social norms, and so on. But, as many of the cases in this book show and which follow from general socio-legal experience, these refined examples are exceptions. Even a purely legal, dogmatic enterprise that analyses, for example, the normative status of legal norms still includes a social aspect. The person performing this operation is socialised into this position and eventually has to communicate the result to other persons. But without these social aspects, the operation is mere neurobiology.

Instead, we should expect that actual, socio-legal normativity follows from the combined effects of the four aspects. Law, as well as social norms, must not just be produced but also reproduced. The obligation to follow norms results from the fact that normative expressions are confirmed by actions. It is not possible, however, to put this interdependence into a simple formula. Rather, there is a normative negotiation going on that includes these four aspects. This means that the result of these negotiations can, in some cases, be highly contested and even result in a disorderly situation. On the other hand, in many other cases, these negotiations can be very consistent and result in very strong normativity leading to stability, inertia, path dependencies and similar states.

Several of the contributions point to the fact that law's normative content is not necessarily unambiguous or possible to understand. Law might not receive its normative content until it is implemented (see Åström in Chapter 5), or it might seemingly be unable to produce an unambiguous normative content at all (see Larsson in Chapter 17). Sometimes, the situation might produce an inherent institutional tension between different legal logics (see Johansson in Chapter 7) or different social logics (see Friis in Chapter 10). As Åström puts it, 'there is no law in books' (see Chapter 5). In these cases, different actors have to negotiate or mediate between different normative positions in order to overcome the normative ambiguity. Normativity might thus be dependent on different actors negotiating the normative positions and probably be dependent on a certain time frame before this negotiating has arrived at a result. Eva Schömer (see Chapter 15), however, provides an example where law and social norms ('common sense') within the labour market arrive at a quite unambiguous normative situation that, unfortunately, has the result of excluding some groups of people.

Other strategies to overcome normative ambiguity are shown by Leo (see Chapter 12) and Persson (see Chapter 11) concerning the regulation of schools. They both come to the conclusion that the normative complexity inherent in the field has to be solved by the construction of meta-norms that reduce this complexity.

The very important 'soul of fire' described by Wickenberg (see Chapter 13) further demonstrates the need for the negotiation of the normative content, especially when the normative landscape is changing. Presumably, social and legal practice will gradually replace this catalyst in forming a robust normative situation.

The example provided by Vargas (see Chapter 14) shows the importance of social practice when normativity is negotiated. Conditions of poverty or survival allow for another way of life than the one that is formally imposed. The meta-norm of survival solves what might be labelled an asymmetrical normative situation for the group of displaced persons in Colombia. The result is that a kind of informal normality arises. Of importance in this case are the structural constraints that economic conditions entail for this group. Another example of the importance of social structures comes from Urinboyev and Svensson (see Chapter 16). The deeply rooted and widespread wedding institution in Uzbekistan actually constitutes a normative situation that would make it more or less problematic to cope with corruption, as defined by international agencies. The practices of file-sharing on the Internet constitute a similar, very strong, social structure, and de Kaminski et al. (see Chapter 18) provide a very insightful understanding of the negotiations between one traditional social and legal structure and another new social structure in society that we are witnessing at this very moment. Here, we can talk about a path dependence structure that is challenged by quite new social norms which have taken hold in the new technology. This is a good case of a very uncertain normativity subject to negotiation. Copyright law seems quite established and unambiguous, but legal practice has almost no chance of reproducing this law when it comes to file-sharing. The very strong social practice among large groups in Swedish society seems to challenge and even change social norms on this issue. One clear example of that is the establishment of the Pirate Party acting to get into the Swedish Parliament.

Normativity produces norms

I shall begin this part by providing a rich example (Baier, 2003). During the autumn and winter of 1997, an environmental scandal dominated public discussion and the mass media in Sweden, originating from the construction of two 8.5 kilometre railway tunnels through a ridge in southern Sweden. The ridge was seen as an obstacle to a fast and efficient railway line connecting Oslo and Gothenburg with primarily Malmö and Copenhagen and, ultimately, mainland Europe. The project commenced in 1992 but proceeded quite badly and suffered from a number of problems. The controversy arose as problems culminated in 1997 when a toxic sealing compound was pumped out in a creek, subsequently killing fish and cattle that drank from it. This event again drew attention to the way in which the project was being managed and brought it to a standstill. It then became the object of public scrutiny from several different perspectives. Reports were written focusing on economy, management, communication, technology, chemistry and geology, to mention some aspects. As expected, legal reports established that the law was ineffective in protecting the natural environment and the work environment. From a socio-legal point of view, it was important to go beyond the simple explanation that the law failed in protecting the environment and, rather, to understand what role the law actually played and, most importantly, what forces drive a project such as this (Baier, 2003). In terms of societal norms, what kind of normative structure emerges in a project like this, and when is this structure strong enough to affect the project's outcome? In answering these questions, the issue of the law's role is easier to understand.

After a timeout and subsequent discussions about accountability, cost benefit analyses, political responsibility and technical solutions, the project restarted in 2003 with a new contractor. The government was still responsible for the project and for being the acting developer. The project was due to be completed by 2015. The budget today totals approximately EUR 1.2 billion, ten times more than was initially allotted. Several governments have been politically responsible for the project over the years. The tunnels are still part of the overall railway infrastructure in Sweden, the Nordic countries and, finally, mainland Europe.

The 2003 investigation assumed that law is a subcategory of societal norms. Another point of departure was the assumption that subsystems, such as economy and politics, can have normative effects and therefore must be included in the understanding of the normative structure of the project. The investigation proceeded by describing the course of events, the legal dimension and finally the normative dimension. This last part was reconstructed with a heuristic model. Methodologically, four action-oriented systems were considered in the reconstruction: the socio-cultural system, the political-administrative system, the economic system, and the natural system. As a result, a normative structure that guided the actions in the project was constructed. Having done this, the role of law could be understood and analysed in relation to this normative structure. In this sense, a reversed design was used when starting in norms and norms in action.

The investigation concluded that an unambiguous normative structure emerged within the project and that the law was part of this structure. One important aspect of this structure was the strong consensus concerning the values in which the project was (and still is) deeply rooted. The strong vision of a high-speed railway connecting the south of Sweden to the continent was anchored in a set of modern values, such as economic and social development, future, technology, but also the environment. The formation of value consensus motivated the project. But an infrastructure project cannot be accomplished by motivation alone. It needs cooperation from other subsystems. Thus, when economic resources were allocated to the project, it could literally take off. Management was set up, public procurement processes initiated, technical solutions were discussed and legal-administrative measures were taken. In retrospect, it is clear that many of the decisions made were bad and based on poor preparation. Solutions to several challenges were postponed, and the management quite optimistically relied on them being solvable. Technology (especially combined with economy) assumes that problems can be solved. Over time, the project revealed a dynamic that confirmed the normative structure. On several occasions, postponed problems resurfaced and then had to be solved. More money had to be allocated, additional decisions had to be made, and administrative measures had to be taken. It was clear that it proceeded due to the very strong normativity that it had acquired. In socio-technical literature, this might be described in terms of momentum (Callon, 1991). The conclusion was that the momentum was based in a strong alliance between values, politics, economic conditions and technical systems. Law could relate to this strong alliance and did, in fact, facilitate and support it. Put simply, the project was first decided and then tried legally. This reversed order put much pressure on the legal-administrative system, and the value consensus was continuously referred to in legal-administrative decisions. The same applied to its finances. Every day that the project was delayed had cost implications. Legal-administrative decisions corroborated, to a large extent, decisions that had already been taken. In this capacity, it also safeguarded the project from legal intervention by those who actually opposed it. The function of law, in this project, was clearly to facilitate and support it. In the case of legal conflicts, courts very often granted interim decisions and, in fact, contributed to the momentum of the project which, in turn, put more pressure on actors and decision-makers.

Translated into the language used in this book, the case illustrated that legal and social norms, together with legal and social practice, make up a normative structure. The tunnel project is still running and, since 1992 until now, many persons have entered and left the project at different levels. The project is not dependent on any particular person or official, but is running on its own. This means that there is a set of legal and social norms that is reproduced not only within the project but also elsewhere. Having described and analysed this part of the project, the next part traced the history of the project in order to reconstruct its roots in a normative sense. It became obvious that anchoring the project in a value structure, connecting it to economic structures and socio-technical structures, also meant anchoring the project in another level of normativity. The project was not an isolated project, but part of the bigger infrastructure. This means that the entire infrastructure related to the project. The project was resistant to political changes at both party level and government level. Therefore, an overall idea of the infrastructure did relate to the project. The financial budget for the project was repeatedly exceeded, due to political ambitions but also due to effects similar to sunk costs effects (Arkes and Ayrton, 1999). This means that the general understanding was that previous investments burdened future decisions of the project, and the only perceived rational decision was to continue the project. It was further testified that failure would also affect the reputation of Swedish engineering science in general and, for this reason, the project must continue. It was thus obvious that the manifest normative structure of the project was deeply anchored in structures that exert indirect normativity.

The case thus illustrates the point that norms are not solely independent, isolated facts, but that they are also rooted, or anchored, in social structures. To be effective, however, norms must be simple and therefore must rely on normative mechanisms that we can accept, despite not having the full picture of the reasons behind them. The reconstruction of the roots might not be a simple task. To reconstruct why we should obey, for instance, norms of reciprocity might even entail philosophical discussions. Having hopefully made this point, I will give more examples illustrating that normativity can be understood as, and traced to, structures exogenous of norms.

Susanna Johansson (see Chapter 7) argues that normativity must be located within, for example, organisational fields, which her example of collaboration shows. The normativity of such a field might even be viewed as hybrid normativity. Whatever term we use, Johansson convincingly argues that an institution carries normativity. The nature of this normativity, however, is not all that clear. Anderson (2000) argues that the commitments of different collective agencies (different 'we's, as she puts it) constitute normativity of social norms. We can thus expect a similar kind of reason for normativity in the school described by Leo and Persson (see Chapters 12 and 11 respectively). Teaching different core subjects is part of a curriculum that is firmly connected to democratic values today. Both Eva Schömer (see Chapter 15) and Ana Maria Vargas-Falla (see Chapter 16) provide us with insights into the structures of a labour market that exerts normativity in combination with social and legal norms, albeit in different ways. In the latter case, the legal norms do not obtain sufficient normative power and so, through the application of the norm of survival, people do not feel obligated to follow the law.

Lucas Konzen argues (in Chapter 9) that space matters for norms. Despite the universality of law, people invoke place and space as factors that influence the normative negotiation between social and legal norms. Place can suspend the obligation to follow the law. The importance of artefacts is brought out by, for example, Bruno Latour and the Actor Network Theory, and applied by Mariana Valverde when analysing how social and legal norms are negotiated in a local legal-administrative setting (Valverde, 2008). When it comes to technology, Apel (2003) argues well for how technology is considered as improving life and thus being ethically justified. This technological imperative, to choose a new technique, establishes duties within the legal system through various innovation institutes, such as patents. The normativity of this part of law can thus be traced back to a society and technology nexus. A similar nexus, but in the field of science and technology governance, is described by Alfons Bora (2010). The observation is that law and science (expert knowledge) build a techno-scientific normativity that excludes political discourse.

In some areas, it seems to be more obvious that a structure exerts normativity. That economy or technology has this kind of property is perhaps easy to understand. The same goes for the social system that, for instance, exerts normativity concerning gender or sexuality (Jackson, 2006). The more intriguing normativity described by Bora is less evident and might be an example of hybrid law having hybrid normativity. These examples, however, are used to draw attention to the fact that law's normativity must also be traced beyond law itself. Håkan Hydén uses the term 'independent imperatives' (2011: 135) when arguing that different subsystems in society are structured in certain ways and, in turn, structure society in certain ways. He traces this structuration to the notion of structural causality developed by the French structuralist school (2011: 123). The notion of independent imperatives is thus developed further here. The main point is that the manifest normativity is expressed through social and legal norms, together with the normative practices of social and legal norms. Social and legal norms do, however, rely on normativity on another level, as the examples suggest. What we also have to assume is that there is interdependence between norms producing normativity and normativity producing norms.

Describing socio-legal normativity in this way has consequences. The very concept of normativity, especially law's normativity, is broadened, differentiated and dependent on structures beyond the level of social and legal norms. This makes it almost impossible to answer the question of normativity in a simple way or a single way. The answer becomes contingent on the fact that there might be several normativities. What is suggested here is more specifically the kind of aspects that might be included when approaching the issue, but not at all a complete set of answers. As mentioned in Chapter 4, the normative setup between social and legal norms will most certainly look different in different legal fields. Is it likely that law remains the same when enabling citizens to conclude an agreement, compared to when sentencing someone to prison, or when used as a tool for post-modern governance? Is it then likely that law's normativity is the same in these different areas when also connected to social structures? I believe not.

References

Åkerstrøm Andersen, N. and Sand, I.-J. (eds) 2012. *Hybrid forms of governance: self-suspension of power*. Basingstoke: Palgrave Macmillan.

Anderson, E. 2000. 'Beyond Homo Economicus: New Developments in Theories of Social Norms', *Philosophy & Public Affairs*, 29(2) 170–200.

Apel, A. 2003. 'The Virtue of Innovation and the Technological Imperative', www.butterfliesandwheels.org/2003/the-virtue-of-innovation-and-the-technological-imperative [Accessed 28 October 2012].

Arkes, H.R. and Ayton, P. 1999. 'The sunk cost and Concorde effects: Are humans less rational than lower animals?' *Psychological Bulletin*, 125, 591–600.

Bora, A. 2010. 'Technoscientific Normativity and the "Iron Cage" of Law', *Science, technology and human values*, 35(1), 3–28.

Callon, M. 1991. 'Techno-economic networks and irreversibility', John Law (ed.) *A sociology of monsters: essays on power, technology and domination*. London: Routledge, 132–65.

Delacroix, S. 2006. *Legal norms and normativity: an essay in genealogy*. Oxford: Hart.

Frommel, M. (ed.). 1996. *Normenerosion*. Baden-Baden: Nomos-Verl.-Ges.

Genn, H. 1999. *Paths to justice*. Oxford: Hart.

Habermas, J. 1996. *Between facts and norms*. London: Polity.

Hyden, H. 2011. 'Looking at the world through the lenses of norms', in Papendorf, K., MacHura, S., Andenaes, K. (eds), *Understanding Law in Society, Developments in Socio-legal Studies*. LIT Verlag GmbH & Co: Hamburg, 120–59.

Jackson, S. 2006. 'Gender, sexuality and heterosexuality. The complex (and limits) of heternormativity', *Feminist theory* 7(1) 105–21.

Korsgaard, C.M. 1992. *The sources of normativity*. Tanner Lectures on Human Values 12, 19–112.

Teubner, G. 1983. 'Substantive and reflexive elements in modern law', *Law and Society Review*, 17(2), 239–85.

Tuori, K. 2002. *Critical legal positivism*. Aldershot: Ashgate.

Valverde, M. 2008. 'The Ethic of Diversity: Local Law and the Negotiation of Urban Norms', *Law & Social Inquiry*, 33(4), 895–923.

Index

For Product Safety Concerns and Information please contact our EU
representative GPSR@taylorandfrancis.com
Taylor & Francis Verlag GmbH, Kaufingerstraße 24, 80331 München, Germany

www.ingramcontent.com/pod-product-compliance
Ingram Content Group UK Ltd.
Pitfield, Milton Keynes, MK11 3LW, UK
UKHW020021200926
475702UK00014B/2002
9780367601225